PARTNERING WITH CHINESE FIRMS

Partnering with Chinese Firms

Lessons for international managers

YADONG LUO
University of Hawaii

Routledge
Taylor & Francis Group
LONDON AND NEW YORK

First published 2000 by Ashgate Publishing

Reissued 2019 by Routledge
2 Park Square, Milton Park, Abingdon, Oxon, OXl 4 4RN
52 Vanderbilt Avenue, New York, NY 10017

Routledge is an imprint of the Taylor & Francis Group, an informa business

A Library of Congress record exists under LC control number:

ISBN 13: 978-1-138-71118-1 (hbk)
ISBN 13: 978-1-138-71114-3 (pbk)
ISBN 13: 978-1-315-20049-1 (ebk)

Contents

List of Figures

List of Tables

Preface

In an attempt to achieve sustained competitive advantages in global marketplaces, multinational enterprises (MNEs) have turned increasingly to the use of international cooperative ventures. This is particularly evident when MNEs expand into the People's Republic of China, the world's largest emerging market and fastest growing economy in recent years. It has been recognized, however, that making these ventures profitable in China, like elsewhere, is by no means easy. Partner selection significantly determines the success of these cross-border, interorganizational ventures.

This book is mainly written for international managers or business students who are interested in emerging markets, particularly China. It provides conceptual backgrounds, analytical frameworks, managerial insights, business guidance, and practical evidence concerning partner selection for both foreign and Chinese investors. It addresses how foreign companies should select ideal Chinese firms as well as what Chinese firms are looking for from foreign investors.

This book is divided into three parts. The first part (Chapters 1-2) presents an overview of MNEs in China and outlines the economic environment facing these firms. The second part (Chapters 3-4) delineates how to select appropriate partner firms from both foreign and Chinese parent's perspectives. The third part includes ten case studies showing how leading MNEs in the world adopt entry and cooperative strategies (including partner selection) that align properly with internal capabilities, external environment, and organizational needs. Based on a variety of archival and internet sources, these case studies are prepared by the author for the purposes of discussion.

In the course of writing this book, I have benefited from a research grant provided by the Center for International Business Education and Research at the University of Hawaii. I am very thankful to David Brice, a doctoral candidate at UH, for his professional and impressive assistance in formatting, typesetting, and indexing the manuscript. As always, this book is dedicated to my family in recognition of their patience and understanding throughout this project.

Yadong Luo, Ph.D.
University of Hawaii

PART I
PARTNERING WITH CHINESE FIRMS: OVERVIEW

1 Multinational Corporations in China: An Overview

Chapter Purpose

This chapter describes the background on foreign direct investment and multinational corporations in China. The discussion is divided into four sections. The first section provides an overview of foreign direct investment in the world. This is followed by an introduction to some of the characteristics of foreign direct investment in Asia. The third section is a historical review of such investment over the past two decades (1979-1998). The last section illuminates what is occurring now, especially with respect to recently emerging policy changes, and speculates on the future of foreign investment in China.

1.1 MNCs and Worldwide Investment

The 1990s have been an era of globalization, in which rapid growth of international trade, financial flows, and foreign direct investment (FDI) have affected more and more economies in deeper and deeper ways. The benefits of financial globalization, in particular, have been many, but the world economy has also been periodically buffeted by international financial shocks. The latest of these has been the most severe, beginning with the collapse of the Thai baht on 2 July 1997, then spreading to other Asian economies. It has since touched countries on every continent.

Global FDI flow on a balance of payments basis reached record levels in 1997. Both outward and inward investment broke through the US$400 billion mark for the first time, with outward investment up 27.0 percent on 1996 to US$423.7 billion, and inward investment up 18.6 percent to US$400.5 billion. Outward FDI, despite annual decline in 1996, picked up in 1997 due to greater investment by developed nations. Growth in FDI in 1997 was driven mainly by the U.S. and U.K., with the U.S. contributing 12.2 and 4.7 points and the U.K. contributing 7.9 and 3.6 points to growth in outflow and inflow, respectively. Much of the increase in outward FDI by the U.S. was directed at Dutch and British holding companies. U.S. investment in the Netherlands was targeted ultimately at investment in Asia via this country.

According to U.S. statistics, in recent years reinvestment of profits by overseas subsidiaries has accounted for nearly 50 percent of U.S. FDI, as a large proportion of the equity capital comprising new investments takes the form of mergers and acquisitions. Stock-for-stock transactions, developed in the U.S. as a means of acquiring companies, have become widely used for cross-border mergers and acquisitions.

FDI received by developing countries in 1997 rose 14.7 percent over the previous year. FDI inflow to Latin America rose sharply thanks to strong growth in investment in Brazil and Mexico. In Brazil, foreign firms were attracted by large-scale privatization of the electricity and telecom sectors. This was a result of the Brazilian government policy of attracting foreign capital to improve its infrastructure; more than 80 percent of inward FDI was in Brazil's non-manufacturing sector in 1997. Within East Asia, investment grew in China, the Republic of Korea (R.O.K.), Singapore, Taiwan, and Thailand, but fell in Indonesia and the Philippines. FDI inflow to the four members of the Association of Southeast Asian Nations (ASEAN) continued downward, but this accounted for only a small proportion of global FDI. The United Nations Conference on Trade and Development (UNCTAD) estimated that global FDI outflow in 1998 would reach US$430-US$440 billion, even higher than that of 1997.

International production by multinational corporations (MNCs) has been continuously growing in recent years. As shown in Table 1.1, all major indicators related to MNC activities demonstrated high rates of growth over the past several years. Specifically, worldwide FDI stock, which constitutes the capital base for MNC corporations, rose by over 10 percent annually over the past decade. It is held by a minimum of 53,000 MNCs, large and small (*World Investment Report*, 1998). The regional distribution of outward FDI stock is heavily skewed towards developed countries, indicating that, in the past, most FDI originated and stayed in developed countries. There are some noticeable recent increases in the stock of developing countries, however. The share of South, East, and South-East Asia in world inward FDI nearly doubled during the past decade. Table 1.2 lists the world's largest host and home economy FDI flows. It shows that China is the second largest FDI inflow country in the world, surpassed only by the United States.

There are at least 448,000 foreign affiliates worldwide (*World Investment Report*, 1998). The role that they play in host countries has become more and more important. Total assets held by all foreign affiliates in 1997 were 3.5 times as large as FDI stocks. Assets imply the level of ability of foreign affiliates to produce goods and services. The average assets owned by foreign affiliates worldwide in the mid-1990s were about $28

Table 1.1 Major Indicators of FDI during 1986-1997

Item	Annual Growth Rate (%)			
	1986-1990	1991-1995	1996	1997
FDI inflows	23.6	20.1	1.9	18.6
FDI outflows	27.1	15.1	-0.5	27.1
FDI inward stock	18.2	9.7	12.2	12.7
FDI outward stock	21.0	10.3	11.5	13.7
Cross-border M&A	21.0	30.2	15.5	45.2
Foreign affiliates sales	16.3	13.4	6.0	7.3
Foreign affiliates assets	18.3	24.4	12.0	13.0

Source: Adapted from UNCTAD: *World Investment Report* 1998, p.2

Table 1.2 The World's Top Host and Home Nations for FDI, 1996

	FDI Inflows ($bil)		FDI Outflows ($bil)	
Rank	Economy	Value	Economy	Value
1	United States	76.5	United States	74.8
2	China	40.8	UK	34.1
3	United Kingdom	26.0	France	30.4
4	France	22.0	Germany	29.5
5	Belgium & Lux.	14.1	HK, China	26.4
6	Brazil	11.1	Japan	23.4
7	Singapore	9.4	Netherlands	23.1
8	Mexico	8.2	Switzerland	11.6
9	Netherlands	7.8	Canada	8.5
10	Spain	6.5	Belgium & Lux.	8.4

Source: Adapted from UNCTAD: *World Investment Report* 1998, p.11

million. Sales of goods and services by foreign affiliates were about $9.5 trillion in 1997, which grew faster than worldwide exports to ($6.4 trillion in the same year). This suggests that MNCs use FDI more than they use exports - by a factor of 1.5 - to service foreign markets. Foreign affiliates worldwide also generated more than $2 trillion in value added in 1997. They accounted for an increasing share in world GDP: close to 7 percent in 1997, as compared to 5 percent in the mid-1980s. Moreover, MNC affiliates have accounted for some one-third of world exports in 1995, compared to about one-quarter during the latter half of the 1980s. Since the mid-1980s, the export propensity of MNE affiliates (i.e., the ratio of exports to total sales) has remained close to one-quarter. Since 1980, the ratio of FDI stock to GDP for the world as a whole has increased steadily and at a much faster path than the ratio of world trade to GDP, suggesting that global integration seems to have proceeded faster through FDI than through trade.

As a function of the extent to which firm activities are located abroad, the transnationality of MNCs has remained high in recent years. The value of this index, measured by a composite of foreign assets/total assets, foreign sales/total sales, and foreign employment/total employment, for the top 100 MNCs was 55 percent in 1996, an increase of 4 percentage points over 1995. Growing internationalization of assets has contributed most to this increase in the transnationality index. The index ranged from 97 percent for Seagram, a Canadian beverages company with interests increasingly geared to the entertainment and publishing industries, to 16 percent for GTE in 1996; this was quite similar to 1990, when the range was from 97 percent for Nestle to 15 percent for General Electric. Table 1.3 shows that the ten MNCs with the highest transnationality have values of between 85 and 97 percent.

Table 1.3 Top Ten MNCs in Terms of Transnationality in 1996

Rank	MNCs	Country	Industry	Transnationality
1	Seagram Co.	Canada	Beverages	97.3
2	Asea Brown Boveri	Switzerland	Electrical equipment	96.1
3	Nestle SA	Switzerland	Food	95.3
4	Thomson Corp.	Canada	Printing/publishing	94.9
5	Solvay SA	Belgium	Chemicals/pharmaceuticals	92.2
6	Holderbank	Switzerland	Construction	89.8
7	Electrolux AB	Sweden	Electrical appliances	88.7
8	Unilever	Netherlands	Food	87.1
9	Roche Holding AG	Switzerland	Pharmaceutical	87.0
10	Michelin	France	Rubber/plastic	84.9

Source: Adapted from UNCTAD: *World Investment Report* 1998, p.45

As seen above, the firms with the highest transnationality index, such as ABB, Nestle, Solvay, Electrolux, Unilever, and Roche, come from small industrial countries. Over the 1990-1996 period, the average transnationality of the top ten firms from small countries increased from an already high 77 percent to an even higher 79 percent. During the same period, the average transnationality for the top ten firms located in larger countries remained around 50 percent. Food and beverages, chemicals and pharmaceuticals, electronics and electrical equipment, oil and petroleum, and telecommunications are among the industries leading in terms of average transnationality index.

Cross-border mergers and acquisitions have fundamentally increased recently, accounting for about one-quarter of all mergers and acquisitions worldwide. These transactions amounted to $342 billion in 1997. Their value in relation to total FDI inflow rose from 49 percent in 1996 to 58 percent in 1997, the highest share attained in the 1990s.

Repeated episodes of financial turmoil have focused international attention on the problem of volatility of private foreign capital flows and the extent to which the volatility creates an unstable environment detrimental to economic development, particularly in developing and transitional economies. In most cases, while foreign portfolio investments show high volatility, FDI does not. For instance, when portfolio investments fell sharply in Mexico in 1994-1995 during the peso crisis, FDI was very much sustained. MNCs are normally more interested in longer-term profits from the production of goods and services, whereas portfolio investors are normally more interested in quick financial returns. Thus FDI is less prone to reversals in response to short-term adverse situations. Moreover, divestment and reversibility are more difficult for FDI than for portfolio investments, which can be sold off easily in financial markets. Portfolio investor strategies, combined with the problems of asymmetrical information and the inherent volatility of emerging markets, are more prone to herd behavior and affected by short-term fluctuations in financial markets that influence investors' expectations of capital gains.

1.2 MNCs and FDI Flows to Asia

Despite the financial crisis that erupted in July 1997 and continues to affect a number of Asian economies, FDI in Asia rose by about 8 percent to about $87 billion in 1997. The region accounted for 57 percent of flow into all developing countries and over half of the FDI stock in China. An overwhelming proportion of the region's inward FDI went to East and Southeast Asia in the 1990s. China, Taiwan, and Singapore are the leading FDI destinations in these subregions. Even in the five Asian economies most affected by the crisis (Indonesia, South Korea, Malaysia, Philippines, and Thailand), overall inflow remained at a level similar to that a year before the crisis began. This suggests that foreign direct investment in Asia has not been significantly affected by the financial crisis. FDI has proven much less variable than portfolio capital flow and commercial lending, both of which declined sharply as a result of the crisis. The share of FDI in total resource flows to East and Southeast Asia has increased remarkably, from 10 percent in 1990 to 53 percent in 1997. Indeed, FDI has become the single most important source of private development financing for the region; it is likely to be particularly important for the economies most affected by the crisis.

China is the front runner, with a record inflow of $45 billion in 1997, accounting for over half of the total flow to Asia and 11 percent of the world total. The country continues to maintain its position as the second largest FDI recipient in the world and the largest of the developing countries. China's FDI boom has now lasted for six consecutive years.

The four mini-dragons (Hong Kong, Singapore, South Korea, and Taiwan) achieved a modest combined FDI growth of 6 percent in 1997. Total flow into these economies reached a record $17 billion in 1997, twice as much as FDI flow to the entire African continent. Singapore remained the single largest recipient among the four economies, ranking at the top of Asian countries in terms of the ratio of FDI stock to GDP.

Total flow to the ASEAN5 countries (Indonesia, Malaysia, the Philippines, Thailand, and Vietnam) remained at a level similar to that in 1996 despite the crisis. FDI flow to South Asia rose to another record level of about $4.4 billion in 1997, as compared with $3.3 billion in 1996 (mostly reflecting an increase of about 37 percent flow to India). FDI into the eight Central Asian economies also increased for a fifth consecutive year, reaching $2.4 million in 1997. Finally, flow to West Asia increased by a multiple of six, from a level of some $300 million in 1996 to 1.9 billion in 1997. Table 1.4 indicates FDI inflow in selected Asian countries, especially those affected by the financial crisis.

Receipt of FDI in 1997 by the R.O.K. and ASEAN5, according to each country's own statistics, showed no sign of being affected by the currency and economic crises. With the exception of Malaysia, all rates of FDI rose, although growth rates varied from country to country. In 1998, however, receipt of FDI fell across the board. This was due to: 1) a decline in investor confidence caused by serious slumps in domestic production and the wider economic malaise caused by the crisis; and 2) sudden drops in investment

Table 1.4 FDI Inflow into Selected Asian Countries ($bil)

Country	1990	1991	1992	1993	1994	1995	1996	1997
China	3.5	4.4	11.2	27.5	33.8	35.8	40.8	45.3
Indonesia	1.1	1.5	1.8	2.0	2.1	4.3	6.2	5.4
S. Korea	0.8	1.2	0.7	0.6	0.8	1.8	2.3	2.3
Malaysia	2.3	4.0	5.2	5.0	4.3	4.1	4.7	3.8
Philippines	0.5	0.5	0.2	1.2	1.6	1.5	1.5	1.3
Thailand	7.2	9.2	10.0	10.6	10.2	13.7	16.9	16.4

Source: Adapted from UNCTAD: *World Investment Report* 1998, p.201

from Japan due to its prolonged economic recession. Other factors related to the currency and economic crises played major roles, such as the tendency of firms to hold back on new investments in Indonesia because of political unrest. Both Vietnam and Myanmar, meanwhile, suffered heavy falls in investment in 1997 and the first six months of 1998 due to declining investment from other ASEAN countries.

In Southwest Asia, the currency and economic crises had relatively little impact on the real economy. Investment in India in 1997 was up 150 percent over the previous year due mainly to growth in investment in the electricity industry. Bangladesh saw FDI rise five-fold in fiscal 1997 (July 1997 to June 1998) due mainly to investment in social infrastructure and utilities. In Australia, investment was up 2.3 percent in fiscal 1996-97 (July 1996 to June 1997) as a result of greater investment in manufacturing, but in New Zealand there was a 24.1 percent drop as sell-offs of state-owned enterprises to foreign firms came to a halt.

The financial crisis led to a sharp decrease in private capital flow to some developing Asian countries. Net private foreign bank lending and portfolio equity investment turned negative in 1997 for the group of countries most affected by the crisis. However, while large amounts of short-term capital left these countries, FDI inflow remained positive and continued to add to the existing FDI stock. The behavior of these two types of investment flows to Asian economies most influenced by the crisis is reminiscent of the behavior during the crisis that struck Mexico from 1994 to 1995. Total portfolio investment to Mexico fell by nearly 40 percent, from $12 billion to $7.5 billion, with portfolio equity investment falling by almost 90 percent, from $4.5 billion to $0.5 billion. FDI flow, in contrast, which had more than doubled in 1994, fell by only 13 percent in 1995.

Even though FDI is more stable than portfolio investment, it is not insensitive to crises, especially changes in the determinants of investment induced by a crisis. Some MNCs may consider increasing FDI in the short or medium term because of the decrease in the costs of establishing and expanding production facilities in crisis-affected countries. The cost decrease is the result of exchange rate depreciation, lower property prices, and more company assets being offered for sale, because of the heavy indebtedness of domestic firms and their reduced access to liquidity. Export-oriented FDI may also benefit from currency devaluation, even though inflation can eventually eliminate this advantage. The impact of the crisis could therefore be mitigated somewhat for the affected Asian economies because international integration at the level of production allows MNCs to compensate for declining local sales through increased exports spurred by devaluation. The downturn in domestic demand in Asia, however, has adverse consequences for host-market-oriented FDI. Reduced demand and slower growth lead to some cancellations, scaling down, or postponement of FDI.

The financial crisis also affects FDI regulations. Some countries have further liberalized FDI policies. In addition to unilateral measures and measures implemented in pursuit of multilateral commitments, liberalization has occurred in the context of adjustment programs linked to financial support packages from the IMF. Recent moves by crisis-affected countries include opening industries like banking and other financial services to FDI and relaxing rules with respect to ownership, mode of entry, and finance. While these new policies create more favorable conditions for FDI, they could lead to market distortions and intensify incentives competition in the region.

Overall, easing control over foreign capital is accelerating. Recognizing that the introduction of foreign capital is essential to economic recovery, Thailand, Malaysia, Indonesia, the Philippines, and the R.O.K. have all rushed to loosen controls over foreign investment. As of December 1997, the BOI allows 100percent foreign equity ownership of those currently approved enterprises in Thailand eligible for investment incentives. In May 1998, 100percent foreign ownership became allowed for non-approved enterprises in industries where investment is encouraged. In August, cabinet approval was given for the abolition of ceilings on foreign equity ownership in 30 of the 68 sectors covered by the Foreign Enterprise Control Act, such as the retail sector. Meanwhile, in August 1998, Malaysia announced the abolition of controls over foreign equity ownership in most areas of manufacturing until the end of 2000. In July 1998, Indonesia too amended its 'negative list' of sectors subject to control to allow 100 percent foreign capital participation, under certain conditions, in the wholesale and retail sectors. In October 1998, the Philippines amended its negative list to allow 100 percent foreign capital participation in the construction industry. In the R.O.K., the Foreign Direct Investment and Foreign Capital Inducement Act was revised, and renamed as the Foreign Investment Promotion Act, in November 1998, allowing investment in 21 sectors such as the securities exchange business.

The crisis has several policy implications. First, given that sudden, massive short-term capital flow brought about the currency and economic crises in Asia, international rules need to be established for monitoring short-term capital movement to prevent a reoccurrence of such crises. Second, the Asian economic crises have prompted developing countries to reaffirm the importance of FDI inflow. The resulting relaxation and abolition of regulations on FDI is improving the investment environments in these countries. In the future, industrial bases must also be improved. This includes not only infrastructure, such as roads, ports and electricity, but also the development of financial systems and human resources and the stabilization of labor-management relations. Doing so will require the technical and financial support of developed nations, including official development assistance. Third, local authorities seeking to attract foreign investment must provide more detailed, wider ranging information. So far, information has concerned mainly industrial estates and the level of development of local infrastructures. In the future, greater emphasis will have to be placed on information of specific interest to foreign firms, such as residential environments and growth prospects of local economies, industries, and markets.

1.3 FDI in China: 1979-1998

China officially opened its doors to foreign investment in 1979 with the promulgation of a joint venture law. Since then, through the end of 1998, Chinese authorities have approved the establishment of over 300,000 foreign invested enterprises (FIEs) involving $522.4 billion in foreign capital. Of these, over 150,000 FIEs representing $221.04 billion investment commenced operations by the end of 1997 (Table 1.5).

FDI has undergone three phases in China. Phase 1 (1979-1985) was the initial stage of foreign investment in China, starting with the promulgation of the Joint Venture Law by the Chinese government in 1979 and the establishment of four Special Economic Zones (SEZs) in Guangdong and

Table 1.5 Actual Value of FDI in China: 1979-1997 (US$100 mil)

Year	Total Foreign Investment	Foreign Direct Investment	Other Foreign Investment*
1979-1983	26.83	18.02	8.81
1984	14.19	12.58	1.61
1985	19.59	16.61	2.98
1986	22.44	18.74	3.70
1987	26.47	23.14	3.33
1988	37.39	31.94	5.45
1989	37.73	33.92	3.81
1990	37.55	34.87	2.68
1991	46.66	43.66	3.00
1992	112.91	110.07	2.84
1993	277.71	275.15	2.56
1994	339.46	337.67	1.79
1995	378.06	375.21	2.85
1996	421.35	417.26	4.09
1997	456.50	452.60	3.90
1979-1997	2254.84	2201.44	53.40

* Other foreign investments include 1) international leasing; 2) compensation trade; and 3) processing and assembling.

Sources: (1) Data of 1979-1996: *China Statistical Yearbook*, 1997, p.605; (2) Data of 1997: *World Investment Report*, 1998, p.204

Fujian provinces. In 1984, fourteen coastal cities were opened to foreign investment, resulting in a spread of DFI from the SEZs to other coastal regions and the first boom of DFI in 1984-1985. However, the initial boom ended in later 1985 due to high inflation and lack of legal clarity about DFI. During this stage, foreign investments were concentrated in small-scale assembling and processing export projects.

At the beginning of Phase 2 (1986-1989), in response to a decline in DFI, the Chinese government published the 'Provisions for the Encouragement of Foreign Investment'. This was followed by a set of central implementation regulations and a flurry of provincial and municipal-level regulations clarifying the legal environment for DFI. They also provided solutions to some major problems facing foreign-invested enterprises such as foreign exchange imbalances. To encourage foreign investment in highly technological industries, all open coastal cities set up

Economic and Technical Development Zones where extra tax breaks and other incentives were offered. The improved investment environment promoted a quick recovery of DFI after 1986. In contrast to the prior-1986 structure, over 70 per cent of DFI projects were involved in manufacturing industries in this period. The new investment boom ended in mid-1989 due to worsening economic and political conditions.

Phase 3 (1990-1997) was triggered by a recognition of negative reactions on the part of foreign investors to a worsening investment climate. The Chinese government issued Amendments to the Joint Venture Law in April 1990 which codified several rules designed to encourage investment. In 1991, the Income Tax Law for Enterprises with Foreign Capital and Foreign Enterprises was passed, standardizing income tax rates for different forms of FIE. Since 1992, the Chinese government has adopted a socialist market economy strategy, speeding up market-oriented reforms. A set of commercial laws and regulations were passed to improve the legal framework and policy settings in which foreign businesses operate. As a result, foreign investment surged after 1992. Since 1994, foreign investment in China has entered a new stage of adjustment and consolidation, presenting some new features. The average capital size of foreign investment projects has increased, with the main focus shifting to large infrastructure and manufacturing projects. The growth rate of DFI is back to a sustainable level from an unusually high level.

FIEs have played a major role in the modernization of the Chinese economy. As shown in Table 1.6, the share of total industrial output in China made by FIEs reached 18.6 percent in 1997. The share of total national export volume made by FIEs climbed to 41 percent in the same year. The tax contribution as a share of the nation's total was 13.2 percent. FDI already accounted for 17 percent of total gross domestic investment in 1996. 17.5 million Chinese were employed in FIEs in 1997, 12.7 million more than six years earlier.

FDI can affect a local economy at both macro and micro levels. At the micro level, FDI may influence the technological and managerial efficiency of joint ventures and local firms through technological transfer, labor training, and spill-over effects. At the macro level, FDI may affect both 'real' macroeconomic variables (e.g., domestic investment, economic growth, employment, export, and import) and 'financial' variables (e.g., interest rates, exchange rates, inflation). The macroeconomic impact of FDI in China is primarily reflected in its effects on real economic variables as financial variables are controlled by the government.

Table 1.6 Contribution of FDI to China's Economy: 1991-1997

Item	91	92	93	94	95	96	97
FDI inflow ($bil)	4.4	11.2	27.5	33.8	35.8	40.8	45.3
Average amount per project ($mil)	0.9	1.2	1.3	1.8	2.5	na	na
FDI/gross domestic investment (%)	3.9	7.4	12.7	17.3	15.1	17.0	14.8
FDI stock/GDP (%)	5.6	7.1	10.2	17.6	18.8	24.7	na
FIE export ($bil)	12.0	17.4	25.2	34.7	46.9	61.5	75.0
FIE export/national export (%)	17.0	20.4	27.5	28.7	31.3	41.0	41.0
FIE output/national output (%)	5.0	6.0	9.0	11.0	13.0	na	18.6
Number of employees (mil)	4.8	6.0	10.0	14.0	16.0	17.0	17.5
Tax contribution as share of total	na	4.1	na	na	10.0	na	13.2

Source: Adapted from UNCTAD: *World Investment Report*, 1996, p. 198; 1998, p. 204

Several recent studies find that FDI significantly promoted the economic growth of China during the 1979-1996 period by contributing to domestic capital formation, increasing export, and creating new employment. Moreover, FDI improves the productive and resource allocation efficiencies of Chinese domestic sectors by transferring technology and facilitating inter-regional and inter-sector flows of labor and capital. While realizing these benefits, some side effects must be acknowledged as well. These include worsening environment pollution as a result of shifting polluting industries to China, and resultant income loss for the host state and firms as a result of MNCs transferring pricing between foreign affiliates.

FIEs come from diverse foreign sources. Table 1.7 lists the top 10 countries or regions of origin for FDI in China in 1995 and 1996. The top ten sources together constituted 92.61 percent of China's total FDI in 1996. Of these, Hong Kong and Macau made the most direct investment in the mainland, contributing $21.46 billion, or 51.43 percent of the national total. They were followed by Japan (8.85 percent), Taiwan (8.34 percent), the United States (8.25 percent), Singapore (5.39 percent), South Korea (3.60 percent), and the United Kingdom (3.12 percent).

Interestingly, of the top 10 foreign countries of origin, 5 are developing Asian countries that collectively undertook about 70 percent of the total actual FDI in China. Japan, the U.S., the U.K., and Germany accounted for only 21.46 percent. The accumulated amount of FDI by the end of 1996 also suggests that FDI in China, launched by businesses from developing countries, has been more than three times more than that made by those from developed countries over the last 17 years.

Although Hong Kong and Taiwan are the top two countries of investment origin, most businesses from these areas are simply moving labor-intensive activities into China in an attempt to escape rising labor costs and space constraints at home. Moreover, the average size of investment from each firm is relatively small. For instance, the average equity pledged by US investors is nearly twice as high as that put forth by FDI from Hong Kong businesses and about 50 percent higher than the average FDI project from Taiwan and Southeast Asian countries.

While Hong Kong and Taiwan investors emphasize labor-intensive and simple industrial processing for light industrial and textile goods aimed at the international market, U.S. and European firms tend to place their emphasis on capital- or technology-intensive manufacturing sectors in an effort to gain access to the growing Chinese domestic market. Japanese investors, while also interested in China's domestic market, have tended to become more involved in various forms of property development than in manufacturing.

Table 1.7 Foreign Direct Investment in China from Top 10 Countries or Regions in 1995 and 1996 (in US$ million)

Rank	Country/Region	1995	1996	% of Total
1	Hong Kong/Macao	20,625	21,458	51.43
2	Japan	3,212	3,692	8.85
3	Taiwan	3,165	3,482	8.34
4	United States	3,084	3,444	8.25
5	Singapore	1,861	2,247	5.39
6	Republic of Korea	1,047	1,504	3.60
7	United Kingdom	915	1,302	3.12
8	Virgin Islands	304	539	1.29
9	Germany	391	519	1.24
10	Malaysia	259	460	1.10

Source: *China Statistical Yearbook,* 1997, p.606-607

FDI in China has gone into a variety of industries. Table 1.8 presents the industrial patterns of foreign direct investment in China in 1996, when the industrial sector accounted for 68.90 percent of total FDI, leading all other sectors in influencing the economy. The real estate and utility sectors follow, involving $12.85 billion in investments or 17.54 percent of the total. Commercial and food services, construction, transportation and telecommunications services, and agriculture are also important sectors, ranking from third to sixth, respectively.

Different sectors have idiosyncratic patterns of FDI growth. FDI in agriculture, industry, transportation and telecommunications, and health care and social welfare services boomed between 1993 and 1995, growing from 12 percent to 75 percent. FDI in other sectors, especially real estate and construction, has slowed down. For instance, foreign investment in hotel and construction sectors decreased by 55.35 percent and 102 percent, respectively, during the same period. This reflects structural changes in Chinese FDI policies over the past few years.

Table 1.8 Approved FDI in China by Sector

Sector	# of Projects	Value ($mil)
Agriculture	812	1,139
Industry	18,280	50,486
Construction	387	2,001
Transport & telecom	196	1,599
Commerce & food service	1,655	2,347
Real estate & utilities	1,961	12,851
(Tourist hotels)	(81)	(291)
Health care & sports	128	354
Education, culture & arts	63	171
Scientific research	124	175
Others	950	2,154
Total	24,556	73,277

Source: *China Statistical Yearbook*, 1997, p.611.

FDI in China is located throughout the country. Table 1.9 shows that FDI was made in every province in recent years (except Tibet). However, the obviously uneven geographical distribution of FDI within various regions is a critical issue. For example, in 1996, the total value of FDI in 18 Central and Western provinces or autonomous regions was $4.8 billion, only 11.40 percent of nationwide FDI. The number of registered FIEs in all Central and Western provinces as of 1995 was 44,875, or just 23.78 percent of those in Eastern regions. Meanwhile, the portion of registered foreign capital in

Table 1.9 Realized FDI in China by Locations (US$mil)

Rank	Region	1994	1995	1996
1	Guandong	9,463	10,260	11,754
2	Jiangsu	3,763	5,191	5,210
3	Fujian	3,713	4,044	4,085
4	Shanghai	2,473	2,893	3,941
5	Shandong	2,552	2,689	2,634
6	Tianjin	1,015	1,521	2,153
7	Liaoning	1,440	1,425	1,738
8	Beijing	1,372	1,080	1,553
9	Zhejiang	1,150	1,258	1,521
10	Hebei	523	547	830
11	Hainan	918	1,062	789
12	Hunan	331	508	745
13	Hubei	602	625	681
14	Guangxi	838	673	663
15	Heilongjiang	348	517	567
16	Henan	387	479	524
17	Anhui	370	483	507
18	Jilin	242	408	452
19	Sichuan	922	542	441
20	Shaanxi	239	324	326
21	Jiangxi	262	289	301
24	Shanxi	32	64	138
23	Gansu	88	64	90
24	Inner Mongolia	40	58	72
25	Yunnan	65	98	65
26	Xinjiang	48	55	64
27	Guizhou	64	57	31
28	Ningxia	7	4	6
29	Qinghai	2	2	1
30	Tibet	0	0	0
	Total	33,269	37,220	41,882

Source: *China Statistical Yearbook*, 1997, p.608

Central and Western regions by the end of 1995 were $40,249 million, constituting only 15.67 percent of the nation's total. The distribution of FDI in China has not shown a marked change in recent years. By the end of 1994, the number of FIEs in Central and Western provinces regions represented about 18 percent of the total number of FIEs. This pattern has remained unchanged since 1994.

Foreign investors are generally free to choose their mode of entry into the deregulated Chinese industries. Table 1.10 depicts the recent pattern of foreign investment, including both FDI and foreign loans. FDI represented about 90 percent of the nation's total of foreign capital inflow. In 1996, equity joint ventures accounted for 43.5 percent of FDI, while wholly foreign-owned enterprise represented 36.59 percent, and contractual joint ventures 19.51 percent. Longitudinally, the ratio of wholly foreign-owned ventures has been growing (only 7 percent prior to 1990). Nevertheless, the equity joint venture remains the primary entry mode used by MNCs to expand to the Chinese market.

Table 1.10 Approved Foreign Investment in China by Entry Mode
(US$mil)

Entry Mode	1995	1996
Foreign Direct Investment Total	91,282	73,276
Equity JVs	39,741	31,876
Contract JVs	17,825	14,297
Wholly foreign-owned	33,658	26,810
Joint exploration	57	293
Other Foreign Investment Total	635	371
International lease	42	33
Compensation trade	404	129
Processing & assembling	189	209
Foreign Loans Total	11,288	7,962
Government loans	4,754	4,203
Loans from intl. organizations	3,680	1,682
Commercial loans	2,854	2,077
Total	103,205	81,610

Sources: *China Statistical Yearbook*, 1997, p.605

1.4 Present Situation and Future Outlook

China has experienced an unprecedented boom in FDI inflow over the past six years, reaching $45 billion in 1997. The boom has been fueled by various factors, including the country's large and continuously growing domestic market, its export-oriented strategy and successful penetration of world markets, the liberalization of its inward-industrial upgrading of neighboring economies (the so-called 'flying-geese' pattern), and the low level of FDI stock relative to the size of the economy until recently. However, the rate of growth of FDI inflow has slowed in recent years, from an average of 165 percent in 1992-1993 to 17 percent in 1994-1995; in 1997, it declined further to 11 percent. This slowdown raises the question of whether the FDI boom in China is nearing an end. The relevance of this question is twofold. First, considering the position of FDI in both gross fixed capital formation and GDP in China (amongst the highest in the world), a major change in FDI inflow could have wide-ranging consequences for the Chinese economy. Second, FDI developments in China will have a sizable impact on FDI trends throughout Asia and the developing world generally, since China has become the single largest FDI recipient of all developing countries.

FDI Approval: If FDI approvals are a good indication, they suggest that actual flow may decline in the coming years since approvals have been dropping, from $111 billion in 1993 to $52 billion in 1997. Experience suggests that increased approvals precede future implementation. If the reverse is true, the decline in approvals by 20 percent in 1996 and 30 percent in 1997 could be followed by a decline in actual inflow in the short-to-medium term.

Slowdown of economic growth: FDI tends to be positively correlated with GDP growth. Reduced economic growth in China can be expected to have a negative impact on FDI inflow. Although GDP growth has remained high in China (at 8.8 percent in 1997), it is below the double-digit growth of earlier years. More importantly, GDP projections point to a further slowdown of about 7 percent for 1998 and 1999. Market-seeking FDI, in particular, would be depressed by weaker demand in China.

Excess capacity: FDI in China's industrial sector will be the first to be affected by worsening demand. It may turn out that the massive foreign and domestic investment of the recent past has resulted in excess capacity in a number of industries, such as in some consumer electrical and electronics products, textiles and clothing, and other light industrial products. The capacity of such industries to absorb further FDI inflow may thus be limited over the next few years. This is true especially of industries in the coastal area where FDI has concentrated. Competition in the coastal area for sales in the domestic market is becoming more intense. In addition to foreign enterprises, a few domestic firms are emerging as strong competitors. This suggests that the 'gold rush' by investors into certain manufacturing industries in China may be coming to an end. The pressure on profit rates stemming from excess capacity and increased competition could reduce the incentive for latecomers MNCs to undertake new FDI. At the same time, established MNCs are likely to postpone sequential FDI unless a reasonable balance between demand and supply is restored.

Declining locational advantages: When China emerged as a major host country for FDI, most investment went into labor-intensive export processing operations. Several factors have played a role in creating a new set of conditions. First, wage increases, particularly in China's coastal areas, are eroding incentives for MNCs to establish labor-intensive export processing operations. Second, despite special efforts by the government, relocation of investment from the coastal regions to the interior has not been significant. MNCs have preferred to move to other low-income countries instead, where transportation costs are lower and infrastructure more advanced than in China's interior provinces. Third, certain labor-intensive products, even though they are internationally competitive, are constrained from being exported from China by trade barriers in major export markets (import quotas, anti-dumping provisions, etc.). In addition, the demand for labor-intensive products in these markets is likely to decline if the predicted slowdown of the world economy occurs. The recession in Japan is of particular relevance here. Finally, China's international price competitiveness has decreased compared to a number of Southeast Asian countries that recently devalued their currencies. This could break the flying-geese pattern of industrialization in Asia from which labor-intensive industries in China have benefited in the past.

These problems could not only discourage efficiency-seeking FDI in China but also affect its impressive export performance. In the short run, export growth is indeed likely to slow down, especially export to Southeast Asian countries currently affected by the financial crisis.

As noted earlier, FDI in China has mainly come from within the Asian region. Another problem is reduced outward FDI from China's Asian neighbors. It is questionable, however, to what extent the 1996-1997 FDI approvals will be realized, given constraints on outward investment facing some of these countries.

To sum up, FDI in China will probably decline over the short run. Although the financial crisis in Asia has not directly affected China, indirect repercussions are as yet unclear. If they are serious, and if the country's economic growth slows down considerably, various structural weaknesses may surface, eroding investors' confidence for the short and medium term. It should be noted, however, that FDI flow is incremental. It represents additions to a stock of assets for production and cannot be expected to grow forever at the same rate, even if a host country continues to have a relatively high rate of economic growth. As long as flows fluctuate around a relatively high level, they contribute, other things being equal, to an increase in stock and therefore play an important role in the host economies.

The Chinese central government has recently introduced measures to prevent speculative investment (e.g., in real estate), and has forced some 'phantom' foreign affiliates to terminate operations. It has also strengthened monitoring activities by setting up administrative procedures for appraising foreign invested property. These appraisals aim at preventing speculative investments or the use of inferior capital equipment. China has also become more selective in screening FDI projects to ensure compliance with economic development objectives. This is reflected in the government's newly adopted FDI guidelines that are in line with the national development plan and industrial policies. Moreover, the nation is targeting large MNE investments. This is reflected in incentives aimed at attracting large MNEs to technologically-advanced or capital-intensive projects.

China is making a national effort to level the playing field for domestic and foreign firms and facilitate its own entry into the World Trade Organization (WTO). Policy measures since 1994 are meant to eliminate preferences for foreign investors that have distorted markets and led to a bias against domestic firms. Such measures include a unified tax system and eliminating import duty exemptions previously granted to FIEs.

To be more specific, in the 1994 tax reform, the turnover tax and individual income tax were unified. As a result, both domestic and foreign firms are now governed by the same set of rules concerning value-added, consumption, business, and individual income taxation. A notable exception, however, is the corporate income tax, under which foreign investors still enjoy preferential treatment.

In April 1996, China substantially reduced the average general tariff level from 35.9 percent to 23 percent, covering nearly 5000 tariff lines with an average reduction margin of 36 percent. At the 1996 APEC meeting, China again announced that it would reduce the average general tariff level to 15 percent by the year 2000. China is phasing out non-tariff measures and has submitted a timetable for the gradual elimination of the remaining non-tariff measures applied to around 400 tariff lines. FIEs have faced the same duties and import-related taxes as domestic firms on all imported equipment, materials, and all other items since April 1996. Although overall tariff rates had already been lowered considerably at the beginning of 1996, the abolition of preferential import duties awarded to FIEs is important, given that nearly 70 percent of China's FDI is in the form of imported capital equipment or raw materials.

In 1996, China incorporated FIEs into the system of buying and selling foreign exchange through banks and realized the convertibility of the Renminbi (RMB) under current account on December 1 of the same year. At the same time, China maintains a foreign exchange swap center as a source of procurement and settlement of foreign exchange. Nevertheless, more and more FIEs are likely to choose designated banks to buy or sell foreign exchanges because the new scheme offers much greater benefits. RMB convertibility under current account will help improve the investment and operating environments for foreigners. It provides a more adequate institutional guarantee of the legitimate revenues of foreign investors, minimizes the risks involved in the remittance of profits, and gives a stronger sense of security to foreign investors. Meanwhile, the removal of restrictions on payment and transfer of foreign exchanges helps streamline the procedures for examination and approval, which will in turn increase the turnover rate of capital, thus improving business performance.

China is now experimenting with Sino-foreign joint venture trading companies in Pudong, Shanghai. A pilot registration system for granting trading rights to production enterprises in five Special Economic Zones (SEZs) has been introduced. Foreign banks have begun to do local currency business in Pudong on a trial basis.

Although investments implemented in China in 1997 rose 8.5 percent to reach a record $45.26 billion, the value of contracts fell 30.4 percent from 1996 to $51.04 billion. This decline appears to have been the result of the emergence of problems surrounding policies on foreign capital (such as the problem of value-added tax on exports and the scrapping of tax exemptions for imported equipment) and the shift of foreign capital from starting new ventures to the operation and maintenance of existing affiliates.

The value of investments implemented posted a slight decline of 0.6 percent in the first nine months of 1998, but the value of contracts bounced back with a year-on-year increase of 2.4 percent. While the value of investment from Asia generally stagnated in terms of both investments implemented and investment contracts, the active role played by Western firms helped push investment up overall. Japanese investment registered negative year-on-year growth of 18.5 percent in terms of contract value, and minus 25.4 percent in implementation.

The combination of the Asian financial crisis and China's restrictive investment environment has continued to hamper foreign direct investment (FDI) in 1998. Contracted FDI was up only 2.5 percent through the third quarter over the same period last year, to 53.58 billion. Utilized investment for the period was down 0.6 percent to $31.4 billion. The composition of FDI in China is also changing. Though Asian investment still constitutes the majority of FDI, its share is slipping. In the first three-quarters of 1998, it accounted for 74 percent of projects (down 3 percent from 1997), 53 percent of contracted investment (down 9 percent), and 70 percent of utilized investment (down 4 percent). Despite a 36 percent increase in Singaporean investment over the period, utilized investment from Asia dropped over 10 percent. Investment from Hong Kong, which constituted 43 percent of utilized FDI, fell almost 11 percent. As capital flows from other parts of Asia slow, the shares of FDI coming from the United States and Europe are growing. Utilized investments from the United States and Europe were up 45 and 20 percent respectively over the same period in 1997. The most dramatic increase in FDI came from the Virgin Islands, which rose 198 percent.

Foreign companies continue to prefer strong managerial control. They have taken advantage of China's 1996 move to allow greater flexibility in establishing wholly foreign-owned enterprises (WFOEs). WFOEs have become the favored investment vehicle for FDI, making up 50 percent of all projects through the first nine months. While 7,395 WFOEs were approved, up almost 9 percent from 1997, only 5,841 equity joint ventures were approved, down almost 11 percent. Most contracted FDI went into WFOEs, which accounted for roughly 43 percent of total FDI, compared to 34 percent for EJVs. Nevertheless, EJVs still make up the lion's share of utilized investment, perhaps reflecting past commitments. Only about a third of utilized investment went into WFOEs.

The decline in foreign investment appears to have attracted the Chinese government's attention. Recent moves, including the reinstatement of certain capital equipment duty exemptions, accelerated approval procedures, and attempts to abolish illicit fees, are aimed at increasing FDI. The government is now planning to open China's service industries to foreign investment, promoting investment in central and western China, and increasing investment incentives for multinational corporations. Problems for foreign investors persist, however. New administrative procedures for obtaining foreign exchange are complicating bilateral trade and causing costly delays or restricting current-account transactions. Reevaluation of both locally approved retail ventures and the so-called 'Chinese-Chinese-Foreign' telecom investment structure, as well as the ban on direct selling, calls into question the security of investments in China. Though overall investment flow in 1998 is likely to approximate 1997's total of $45 billion, it could drop in 1999 unless China takes concrete measures to improve the deteriorating investment environment.

Recent policy changes are expected to have certain impacts on FDI over the next few years. The movement towards national treatment discourages 'round-tripping' (that is, capital outflows that are repatriated back to China disguised as FDI, taking advantage of tax and regulatory incentives to FIEs) and 'phantom' foreign ventures. Tighter screening and monitoring of FDI projects may significantly reduce the overvaluation of FDI that takes place through incorrect invoicing of imported equipment. In addition, strict monetary policies, likely to be pursued by the government in the near future to curb inflation and cool the overheated economy, will have a bearing on FDI. This is because FDI projects usually have to be coupled with domestic capital (an entry requirement for FDI in some industries). More expensive domestic capital discourages domestic investment and hence diminishes the ability of foreign investors to find joint venture partners.

China's attractiveness to foreign investors remains bright, however. First, China's growth performance is outstanding. With an average annual GDP growth of 12 percent in 1991-1996, China is one of the fastest growing economies in the world. This trend is expected to continue. Second, the liberalization of FDI policies is still under way. Some industries that have been off limits to foreign investors (air transport, general aviation, retail trade, foreign trade, banking, insurance, accounting, auditing, legal services, the mining and smelting of precious metals, and the prospecting, extracting and processing of diamonds and other precious non-metal minerals) are gradually being opened. Third, there is a significant potential for FDI participation in the infrastructure. Several build-operate-transfer (BOT) schemes have already been concluded. Foreign investors are now allowed to acquire state-owned firms. Fourth, to the extent that the Chinese currency becomes convertible, profit repatriation will be easier, making it more attractive to invest in China. Lastly, according to the Ministry of Foreign Trade and Economic Cooperation (MOFTEC), China, the following tax policies will guide FDI in the future: (1) General preferential rate: For manufacturing businesses, a preferential income tax rate of 33 percent will apply; (2) Reduced tax rate extended to special areas: For FIEs located in the SEZs or manufacturing businesses in the economic and technological development zones (ETDZs), a 15 percent income tax will apply. The income tax rate of 24 percent will apply for foreign-invested manufacturing enterprises located in the old towns of cities located in the coastal economic open areas, SEZs, or ETDZs; (3) Reduced tax rate extended to special sectors: For Sino-foreign joint ventures which meet certain qualifications and engage in energy, transportation, port or pier construction, a 15 percent income tax rate will apply; (4) Preferential rate extended to special businesses: The flow of FDI to high-tech businesses or export-oriented businesses will continuously be encouraged. Once confirmed as one of these two types, businesses will be granted special tax incentives; (5) Manufacturing FIEs with a term of operation over 10 years will be continuously granted tax exemption for two years starting from the profit-making year and given a half rate for three years afterwards; (6) If foreign investors make additional investments using profits from the FIEs, they shall get a refund of 40 percent of the income tax they have already paid.

As a result of the above, the already great importance of FDI to China's economy is likely to grow. Thus, while FDI inflow to China might fall below $30 billion in the next few years, there is reason to believe that this will be a temporary adjustment rather than a response to a change in general economic factors. One strong piece of evidence supporting this speculation is that the top 12 MNEs from the United States with the biggest stakes in China are maintaining their commitments through ongoing construction and investment. In short, China will remain one of the top FDI destinations in the world.

References

Beamish, P.W. (1993), 'The Characteristics of Joint Ventures in the People's Republic of China', *Journal of International Marketing*, vol. 1, pp. 29-48.

Casson, M. and Zheng, R. (1991), 'Western Joint Ventures in China', *Journal of International Development*, vol. 3, pp. 293-323.

Davidson, W.H. (1987), 'Creating and Managing Joint Ventures in China', *California Management Review*, vol. 29, pp. 77-94.

Editorial Board of the Almanac of China's Foreign Economic Relations and Trade (1997), *Almanac of China's Foreign Economic Relations and Trade (1996/1997)*, Hong Kong: China Resources Advertising Co., Ltd.

Luo, Y. (1996), 'Evaluating Strategic Alliance Performance in China', *Long Range Planning*, vol. 29, pp. 532-540.

Luo, Y. (1998), *International Investment Strategies in the People's Republic of China*, Aldershot, UK: Ashgate.

National Council (1991), National Council for US-China Trade, *Special Report on US Investment in China*, Washington, D.C.: Department of Commerce.

Osland, G.E. and Cavusgil, S.T. (1996), 'Performance Issues in US-China Joint Ventures', *California Management Review*, vol. 38, pp. 106-130.

State Statistical Bureau of China (1997), *China Statistical Yearbook*, Beijing.

Sun, H. (1998), 'Macroeconomic Impact of Direct Foreign Investment in China: 1979-1996', *The World Economy*, vol. 21, pp. 675-694.

United Nations Conference on Trade and Development (UNCTAD) (1998), *World Investment Report 1998*, New York: United Nations.

World Bank (1998), *China 2020: China Engaged*, Washington, D.C.: The World Bank.

World Bank (1999), *Global Economic Prospects and the Developing Countries*, Washington, D.C.: The World Bank.

2 The Economic Environment at the Turn of the Century

Chapter Purpose

China's rapid growth over the past two decades is set to continue well into the next century, as reform momentum continues in the post-Deng era. Markets now allocate most of the resources in China, while state planning plays a shrinking role. However, China is now entering the most difficult phase of reform, developing the legal, administrative, and regulatory framework that supports a modern economy. Until this is complete, China will be a challenging and sometimes difficult environment for MNCs. This chapter reviews China's economic environment at the turn of the century, presents recent economic policies that may affect MNC operations, and elaborates on managerial implications for foreign companies that are active in the Chinese market today.

2.1 Overview of the Chinese Economy

China is a huge economic success story. The past two decades have brought big increases in every imaginable indicator of economic performance. China is now in the throes of two kinds of transitions, first from a command economy to a market-based one, and second from a rural, agricultural society to an urban, industrial one. So far both transitions have been spectacularly successful. China is the fastest growing economy in the world, with per capita income more than quadrupling since 1978. Economic reforms have advanced China's integration with the world economy, maintained a strong external payments position, privatized farming, liberalized markets for many goods and services, intensified industrial competition, and introduced modern macroeconomic management. In two generations China has achieved what took other countries centuries. For a country whose population exceeds that of Sub-Saharan Africa and Latin America combined, this has been a most remarkable development. By the year 2000, China's consumer market will be larger than the United States or Western Europe.

China's growth has been outstanding during the second half of this century (see Table 2.1). Record growth began in 1978 when it officially opened the door to the outside world. Between 1978 and 1995, annual per capita real GDP growth in China averaged 8 percent, compared to only 1.5 percent in the United States. This makes China the fastest growing economy in the world for the past two decades. Starting from a position of near-autarky, China has been catching up rapidly with other developing countries in integrating with the global economy. Increased integration and openness have paid rich dividends in the way of faster growth, despite much room for progress. Remarkably, these improvements were achieved entirely by improving total factor productivity growth, by between 3.6 and 4.1 percentage points. Market-based transactions now dominate the Chinese economy, with over 90 percent of retail prices and 80 percent of production and agricultural prices determined by the market. Tables 2.2-2.5 exhibit major economic indicators of economic growth, consumer price inflation, foreign reserves, origins and outlays of GDP, and import-export patterns.

Table 2.1 Major Indicators of the Chinese Economy: 1966-1998

	1966-73 China/World	1974-90 China/World	1991-97 China/World	1997 China/World	1998 China/World
Real GDP growth	9.0 5.1	9.0 2.8	11.8 2.3	9.1 3.2	7.2 1.8
GDP/capita growth	6.2 2.9	7.5 1.1	10.6 0.8	8.1 1.8	6.2 0.3
Inflation	-1.7 5.4	3.8 7.8	11.2 4.4	2.3 2.8	1.7 2.9
Cur. acc. balance (% of GDP)	-0.4 -0.1	0.1 -0.4	1.0 -0.1	2.1 0.2	2.6 0.0

Source: World Bank, *Global Economic Prospects 1998/99*, p.194-197

Table 2.2 Geographic and Economic Indicators: 1993-1997

Economic Indicators	**1993**	**1994**	**1995**	**1996**	**1997**
GDP at current market prices (Rmb bn)	3,450.1	4,711.1	5,940.5	6,936.6	7,607.7
Real GDP growth (%)	13.5	12.6	10.5	9.7	8.8
Consumer price inflation (av; %)	14.7	24.1	17.1	8.3	2.8
Population (m)	1,178	1,192	1,205	1,218	1,230
Merchandise exports fob ($ bn)	75.7	102.6	128.1	151.1	182.7
Merchandise imports fob ($ bn)	86.3	95.3	110.1	131.5	136.4
Current-account balance ($ bn)	-11.6	6.9	1.6	7.2	29.7
Total debt (includes undisbursed) ($ bn)	86.3	103.7	130.2	141.5	150.9
Reserves excl gold (year-end; $ bn)	22.4	52.9	75.4	107.0	142.8
Exchange rate (av; Rmb:$)	5.8	8.6	8.4	8.3	8.3

Source: *EIU Country Report* (1998), p.6

Table 2.3 Origin and Components of GDP in 1997

Origins of GDP 1997	% of total	Components of GDP 1997	% of total
Primary industry	18.7	Private consumption	47.5
Secondary industry	49.2	Government consumption	11.4
Tertiary industry	32.1	Gross fixed investment	33.8
Total	**100.0**	Exports of goods & services	24.5
		Imports of goods & services	-20.9
		Total incl others	**100.0**

Source: *EIU Country Report* (1998), p.6

Table 2.4 Imports and Exports in 1997

Principal exports 1997	$ bn	Principal Imports 1997	$ bn
Textiles & clothing	45.6	Machinery & electrical equipment	46.7
Machinery & electrical equipment	38.3	Textiles & textile articles	17.2
Garments & clothing accessories	31.8	Chemicals & chemical products	10.3
Textiles yarn & fabrics	13.8	Mineral fuels	10.3
Foodstuffs, beverages & tobacco	12.1	Iron & steel	6.7
Footwear, headgear & umbrellas	10.2		
Chemicals & chemical products	9.4		
Mineral fuels & electricity	7.0		

Source: *EIU Country Report* (1998), p.6

Table 2.5 Regional Pattern of Imports and Exports in 1997

Main destinations of exports	% of total	Main origins of imports	% of total
Hong Kong	24.0	Japan	20.4
US	17.9	Taiwan	11.5
Japan	17.4	US	11.4
South Korea	5.0	South Korea	10.5
Germany	3.6	Hong Kong	4.9
Netherlands	2.4	Germany	4.4
Singapore	2.4	Singapore	3.2
Taiwan	1.9	Russia	2.9

Source: *EIU Country Report* (1998), p.6

China's effort to engineer industrial growth has included measures designed to gradually introduce market competition, encourage mergers and acquisitions, and foster the expansion of collective enterprises. As a result of industrial reform, firms have had increasing autonomy over determining how and with whom they will conduct business. From methods of production to decisions about hiring and firing workers, Chinese business organizations are becoming less and less dependent on centralized authority. Managers have more responsibility for finding productive inputs, determining appropriate production and inventory levels, and locating markets for their products. Bankruptcy and unemployment, unheard of in the past, have also increased in recent years, demonstrating that poor firm performance may result in failure for the firm and unemployment of the firm's managers.

Three features of China's rapid growth since 1978 are especially noteworthy. First, the benefits of growth have been widely shared among China's large provincial economies. Although the coastal provinces grew faster than average, at 9.7 percent a year, the other provinces also fared well. In fact, if China's thirty provinces were counted as individual economies, the twenty fastest-growing economies in the world would be Chinese. Second, Chinese economic development has been coupled with a cyclical pattern of economic growth. The growth cycles have been accompanied by similar fluctuations in the rate of inflation, revealing fault lines in macroeconomic management stemming from partially completed reforms in the fiscal, enterprise, and banking systems. Third, China's growth has been less dependent on volume increase in inputs of capital and labor but more on productivity growth, relative to other emerging economies. This suggests that factors other than capital accumulation have been important determinants of China's GDP growth.

China's remarkably rapid growth since 1978 has been driven by several factors. The first is a high savings rate which has supported vigorous rates of investment and capital accumulation. China's savings rate averaged 37 percent of GDP between 1978 and 1995, in sharp contrast to the collapse of savings in the transitional economies of Eastern Europe and the former Soviet Union. Contributing half of total savings, household savings exploded from about 1 percent as a share of income before reform to 21 percent since then. Second, structural change has been both a cause and an effect of growth. This change has given a significant boost to China's growth over the past two decades. Since a large portion of the agricultural labor force was underemployed, productivity leaped as workers moved from low-productivity agriculture to more productive employment in industry and services. This process contributes about 1 percentage point a year to GDP growth. The changing pattern of ownership also accounts for about 0.5 percent of growth, as employment has shifted to the collective and private sectors where productivity is higher. Third, pragmatic reforms were well suited to China's unusual circumstances and enjoyed broad support. China's economic reform in 1978 was triggered by neither an economic crisis nor an ideological epiphany. Reform measures were introduced incrementally and involved decentralizing authority over capital spending. A favored approach was for the central authorities to experiment with new policies in selected provinces, prefectures, countries, and even firms. If the experiments worked, they were quickly replicated. This approach, called 'crossing the river by groping for stepping-stones', has been a systematic component of Chinese reform. Pragmatism and incrementalism were also behind the government's evolving objectives (see Table 2.6). Lastly, the economic conditions in 1978 were especially receptive to reform. Contrary to popular perception, planning was less entrenched in China than in other transitional economies. China's economy could be described as a dry prairie, parched by years of planning, awaiting the first sprinklings of market reform.

Table 2.6 The Evolving Objectives of Economic Reform

Period	*Objectives*
1978-79	A planned economy that is the basis for market exchange value
1979-84	A planned economy supplemented by market regulation
1984-87	A planned commodity economy
1987-89	An economy in which the state regulates the market and the market regulates enterprises
1989-91	An economy with organic integration of a planned economy and market regulation
1993-present	A socialist market economy with Chinese characteristics

Source: World Bank, China 2020, 1997, p.9

Interactive reform is the basic mechanism of China's transition. The profit motive appears everywhere. Even large state-owned enterprises (SOEs) are pushed to adopt the culture of the market. Despite the continuation of various forms of subsidy, agents throughout China's economy are increasingly forced to live with market-generated financial outcomes. Domestic industries, formerly insulated from international market trends, find themselves buffeted by global as well as domestic market forces. Institutional arrangements bend in the face of external pressures. These developments continue to reshape individual attitudes, expectations, and behavior at every level of Chinese society.

Early reform was partial and tentative. The current objective of creating a 'socialist market economy' is an outcome of reform processes that emerged only in the 1990s. Until recently, reform policies have consistently focused on measures that enable (profit sharing and market opening) rather than force (privatization and bankruptcy) change. Despite their limited scope, these enabling measures erode entry barriers, intensify competition, reduce profit rates, and undermine the growth of public revenue, especially at the central level. The resulting financial pressures continue to push enterprises and policy-makers in the direction of innovation, cost reduction, and shifting toward a market economy.

In China, reform has not simply been a sequence of events in which the state makes decisions to which businesses and individuals react. Reform has unfolded as an extended process including interaction and feedback between government administrations, enterprises, workers, and consumers. Erosion of governmental power is both an unintended consequence and a powerful engine of China's reform. The most difficult reform task is to force state enterprises and their employees out of comfortably protected niches into the hurly-burly of market competition. The declining revenue share of the state and the emergence of fierce economic competition among China's provinces and localities have been essential in motivating this change.

Semi-market systems can generate growth spurts. As critics rail about insecure property rights, the absence of commercial law, internal trade barriers, corruption, and many other difficulties, China's crude semi-market system continues to deliver massive gains. Achievement of a full market system is not a prerequisite of accelerated economic growth, structural change, and technological development. Economic reforms are built on large numbers of complex and intricately connected institutions. Western-style economic policies may turn out to be the best long-run option for China, although not necessarily the best currently.

The Chinese economy is still only about half way between a centrally planned economy and a market-driven economy. Difficult reforms are ongoing. Developing a legal, administrative, and regulatory framework that supports a modern economy is crucial. As reform rolls ahead, a seemingly endless array of gaps, obstacles, shortcomings, and problems are surfacing. Swift growth and structural change, while resolving many problems, have created new challenges, such as employment insecurity, inequality, poverty, environmental pressures, and periods of macroeconomic instability stemming from incomplete reform. Unmet, these challenges could undermine the sustainability of China's growth.

Lack of progress in reforming SOEs is a major bottleneck hampering reform in China. The delay in SOE reform is largely responsible for delays in fiscal, financial, and trade reforms. A bankruptcy law introduced in the late 1980s has had minimal effect since until recently it has hardly been used because of fear of social consequences. State banks cannot refuse loans to profitless SOEs if the authorities request it. Liberalization of bank interest rates and trade protection has slowed because of fear of the consequences to cash strapped SOEs. Wage pressures sometimes divert earnings away from much needed long-term investment. Government supervisory agencies continue to interfere with the management of shareholding firms. It is still too early for shareholders to gauge firm performance through the two stock markets, which have had their share of insider trading and stock manipulation. Moreover, most SOEs will be restructured, at least in the medium term, into limited liability companies rather than limited liability stock companies. Bank credit rather than issuing shares, will be the dominant source of finance for most SOEs.

The most daunting challenge that has yet to be solved is how to manage state assets efficiently and who should be responsible for doing so. Currently, the State Asset Management Commissions at various levels of government are the major authorities managing state assets. It is well recognized that asset management by these commissions is ineffective due to lack of professional knowledge, organizational responsibility, and managerial incentive. It is easy to change SOE ownership structure, but difficult, if not impossible, to manage state assets effectively and maximize their value when the government still controls the ownership of these assets. As loss-making SOEs continue to demand soft loans, the success of banking, taxation, and social welfare reforms are all affected by the pace and pattern of SOE reforms in productive sectors.

2.2 Current Situation and Future Direction

The Asian crisis has plunged several of the fastest growing economies in the world into a severe recession and slowed the growth of world output and trade. Individual countries in crisis are facing steep social costs that may be long lasting. Recovering from depressed economic conditions will be difficult. The crisis showed that one of the most competitive markets in the world, the international market in financial assets, could fail in a major way.

Economic growth in China slowed in 1997, but was still almost 9 percent as the country continued its soft-landing strategy of reducing inflation without delivering a major shock to economic growth. The lessening of growth in consumption, combined with a slow restructuring pace in the State sector, exacerbated losses incurred by SOEs as inventories of unsold goods rose. Losses by SOEs reached about 10 percent of GDP in 1997. SOEs continued to lag behind the non-State industrial sector output in growth rates, exemplifying a trend that has been maintained since the mid-1980s. Growth also decelerated in the non-State sector recently owing to slowing demand and, probably, a need for small and medium-sized collective and private businesses to upgrade their managerial and technological skills.

Weakening domestic demand was counterbalanced by strong external demand. Exports grew almost 21 percent in 1997, rebounding from the slowdown of 1996, while imports increased by only 2.5 percent. Moderate inflation continued as a result of slower growth in domestic demand, aided by the effect of good harvests on prices. Consequently, the rate of inflation in 1997 was only 2.3 percent, the lowest since 1985. In order to strengthen the national economy, the government has relaxed its monetary policy further by cutting interest rates and lowering the required reserve ratio, while increasing public spending in support of infrastructure development. Because the fallout from the Asian financial crisis slowed down China's export growth, the impetus for growth is largely reliant on the domestic sphere, bolstered by the more expansionary macroeconomic policies.

The Chinese yuan largely escaped the contagion of the Asian financial crisis, thanks to a sizable foreign exchange reserve (over $140 billion at the end of 1997) and control over the capital account. The Asian crisis nevertheless highlighted the urgency of economic reform, in particular regarding the development of the financial and enterprise sectors and market institutions in China. Over the next three years (1998-2000), enterprises operating at a loss will be closed down or merged with profitable ones. Firms that are deemed inherently viable but are sinking under an unsupportable debt burden may receive a measure of debt relief. The coverage of the experiment in converting SOEs into joint stock companies broadened since 1991 as both the number of firms and cities under the scheme have doubled. China is now also reforming the civil service by merging 40 government ministries into 29 new ones and by reducing its 8 million person staff by half.

Financial sector reform has progressed as well, with measures boosting the independence of the central bank and developing a market-oriented commercial banking sector. These measures include the administrative streamlining of regional centers of the central bank to reduce the political influence of local governments on the operations of bank branches. Top-down credit quota allocation was replaced with guidelines for capital-to-loan ratios and regulations governing prudential supervision of commercial banks. These measures are intended to increase operational autonomy in the banking sector while strengthening bank supervision.

The implementation of a public, in lieu of a firm-based, social welfare system is necessary to mitigate the impact of unemployment resulting from large-scale SOE restructuring. China is gradually expanding city-based experimentation in public pension funds and health and unemployment insurance schemes. Although these welfare reforms lessen the financial burden on enterprises, which used to provide such benefits, they do require support from the government budget, which may call for tax increases. In addition, accelerated housing reform is envisioned by the government as a means of stimulating domestic demand in the near term. Although commercialization of housing has been carried out on an experimental basis in some cities, housing subsidies for employees are still a major responsibility of SOEs and government agencies. The elimination of such subsidies and the commercialization of residential housing will free up public resources, thus lessening the financial burdens of SOEs and the pressure on the public budget. Conversion to private ownership of housing will also stimulate investment in renovation and expenditures on household appliances. Nevertheless, the concurrent implementation of these major reforms and the initiation of new ones launched by Premier Zhu Rongqi will be more challenging as economic growth decelerates, the social environment destabilizes, and/or the political climate becomes conservative.

The government has been seeking to boost growth during 1998. The marked slowdown in the first half of this year, when both domestic and external demand were constrained, caused serious concern. The government, worried that GDP growth would fall below the official target of 8 percent, embarked on a program of accelerated spending. It has also ordered the resumption of active lending by the state banks to the sectors which the state wants supported - selected large SOEs, small and medium-sized enterprises (SMEs), and exporters.

Interest rates have been lowered on several occasions over the past year. Further reductions will only be made if the government believes such cuts will not undermine public confidence in the ability of the government to maintain the exchange rate at Rmb8.3:$1. The looser monetary policy has therefore also encouraged a greater volume of lending by the state-owned banks.

At the same time there has been a large increase in governmental spending directed mainly at infrastructure projects in particular central and western areas that have experienced slower growth during the 1990s. Spending was also stimulated by a massive resource-deployment effort in response to the flood emergency in mid-1998. In the first nine months, government expenditure rose by 17.5 percent, compared with a budgeted target of 10.3 percent for the year as a whole, while revenue rose by 10.4 percent compared with a budgeted rise of 12.1 percent.

The additional spending and the resulting increased budget deficit are being financed by additional debt, mainly domestic debt owing to the difficulty of raising funds abroad. By mid-October, Rmb220bn ($26.5bn) had been issued in state bonds, over and above the Rmb100bn bonds issued to finance infrastructure spending. The state is also monetising its broader deficit by expanding the money supply in order for state banks to support state-owned industries.

Pressure to boost export competitiveness, lost as a result of the large-scale devaluation of currencies in many other emerging markets, has been exerted by some industry sectors but resisted by the government. The official calculus still reckons that the gains would outweigh the costs of devaluation - political loss of face, more expensive imports, the risk of higher inflation at a time of economic stimulus, more expensive debt-service costs for some shaky Chinese borrowers, and a generally heightened sense of instability as a result of the government's reversal of policy on an issue on which it has previously been adamant. The gains would include an enhanced ability to compete on price without denting margins or being accused of dumping as well as deterring cheap imports. But many export markets, especially in Asia, are regarded as being too severely depressed to respond to a devaluation of the Renminbi on any scale that has occurred previously.

Meanwhile China is acting to deter imports by administrative means, including what may be a rather liberal interpretation of the concept of smuggling. Exports are being supported by increased tax rebates on VAT and increased export credits. Western trade partners regard current Chinese moves as lessening the country's eligibility for WTO membership. It must be concluded that the Chinese government has decided that WTO membership is not at the top of its policy agenda, at least not while the current weakness and instability of the world economy persists. The overriding goal of its economic policy is now the maintenance of domestic stability. The government believes this means that growth must accelerate. However, the longer-term problems of industrial and financial-sector reforms and the urgent need to raise the productivity of agriculture and combat environmental degradation have not disappeared. These problems will need to be tackled sooner rather than later.

Although a certain amount of restructuring of the SOE sector has continued this year, the process of enterprise reform is not proceeding at the pace envisaged by Mr. Zhu at the beginning of 1998. The recapitalisation of the state-owned banks, in particular, has been set back by their deployment, once more, as channels of working capital to allow SOEs to continue to produce during the current economic downturn. There is virtually complete agreement within China that state enterprise reform is of the highest priority. State enterprises absorb a disproportionately large share of the country's resources and have become a drag on growth and employment creation.

The government's enterprise reform program operates at two levels: improving economic performance through stricter market discipline and developing better governance within firms to improve productivity. State-owned enterprises are being disciplined by the market through tough competition created by trade liberalization and the proliferation of non-state enterprises. At the same time, financial support for state enterprises is being cut back. The combination of these two pressures is encouraging enterprise restructuring, especially at provincial and municipal levels. To focus its efforts, the central government recently selected 1,000 large state enterprises as priority for reform and development. The other state enterprises will undergo a variety of approaches to reform, mostly experiments at the provincial and municipal levels.

Looking ahead, the task of improving the efficiency and competitiveness of China's state enterprises is expected to be complex and difficult. The following areas are future directions the Chinese government may consider in advancing SOE reform: (1) Implement programs to improve internal governance, diversify ownership, and lower budgetary and financial subsidies. A first priority would be to implement the new accounting system, set clear commercial objectives, streamline asset management bureaus, clarify representation of the government on boards of directors, and transfer autonomous management rights to enterprises; (2) Accelerate the transfer of pension, health, and educational obligations from state-owned enterprises to governmental authorities. It would be difficult to liquidate, sell, merge, or restructure enterprises if they were still required to meet these social expenditures. Pilot programs to transfer such expenditures to municipal authorities need to be accelerated. At an appropriate point, these could be merged with the national pension and health program; (3) Further promote competition to encourage greater efficiency in state enterprises. Reduce interprovincial and international trade and investment barriers. Lower foreign trade and investment barriers would have the added advantage of strengthening China's case for joining the World Trade Organization (WTO).

In implementing these policies, the government will need to consider the specific needs and circumstances of different groups of state enterprises. First, it should use competition and governance policies, not subsidies, to foster efficient development of the prioritized large state enterprises that are expected to eventually form the core of China's modern enterprise system. An appropriate way to improve their efficiency would be to provide them greater management autonomy and better governance structures, expose them gradually to domestic and international competition, diversify their sources of finance, and apply better regulations. In cases where the government feels compelled to provide subsidies, these should be limited, time-bound, and channeled through the budget rather than the financial system. Second, improve the efficiency of the other 14,000 large and medium-sized industrial enterprises by diversifying ownership, reconfiguring operations, restructuring debt, encouraging mergers and consolidations, and, where necessary, liquidating them. Shedding labor, investing in new equipment, and reengineering finances could restructure marginal loss-making firms that are inherently viable financially. Debt restructuring should occur only when a corporate strategy is agreed between the bank, the (local) government, and enterprise management, and on the strict understanding of no future bailouts. Heavy losers with little future would need to be closed down, while highly profitable enterprises could be corporatized. Third, systematically develop and implement a program to transfer the remaining 90,000 small industrial state enterprises to the non-state sector through sales, leases, or mergers. The government's proposed policy for such enterprises is to loosen controls on leasing, mergers, sales, restructuring, and bankruptcies. A first phase could include the transfer of 10,000-20,000 state enterprises to the non-state sector in the eighteen reform cities over the next two years.

Over the past twenty-five years China's GDP growth has averaged 10 percent a year and its share of world trade has tripled to about 3 percent. The strength of the Chinese economy over the past two decades, however, does not guarantee that China will continue to grow rapidly in the future. Nevertheless, China has some real advantages that can bolster its economy. Its high saving rate, large domestic market, and record of progressive reform bode well for future growth. China's Five-Year Plan for 1996-2000 targets GDP growth of 8 percent a year. To achieve this, it will need to grow by an average of 7.6 percent a year over the next two years. From the standards of recent years, such growth does not seem unduly ambitious.

Even so, the future will be increasingly challenging. Rapid economic growth is not the government's sole objective nor should it be. It is very likely that the pace of reform will slow down if social instability intensifies as a result of income disparity, bureaucratic corruption, and hyper-underemployment. Hurdles to future growth also include an incomplete foundation for reform. China is midstream in its transition to a market economy. The government's role in laying the institutional, social, physical, and legal foundations for market development will be crucial in completing the transition. Although China is now restructuring and downsizing its government at various levels, it remains to be seen to what extent, and for how long, it can fulfill its goal of establishing an efficient, clean governmental system.

The bracing effects of competition are being accompanied by increased risk, especially to employment and income. As China grows richer, it will require policies and institutions that ensure a caring yet competitive system to help manage these risks and promote human potential in all dimensions. This will require the creation of entirely new social structures for the next century. Changing employment patterns and shifts in the age structure of China's population call for a fresh look at policies and institutions affecting labor markets, the welfare of the poor, the financial security of the elderly, and equal access for all to jobs, health care, and education.

Whether or not China can meet these challenges and sustain rapid growth depends largely on continuing reform. First, the spread of market forces must be encouraged, especially through reforms of state enterprises, the financial system, grain and labor markets, and pricing of natural resources. Second, the government must begin serving markets by building the legal, social, physical, and institutional infrastructure needed for rapid growth. Finally, integration with the world economy must be deepened by lowering import barriers, increasing the transparency and predictability of the trade regime, and gradually integrating with international financial markets.

In balance, China's role in the world economy in the next century should increase, although its pace of economic growth is expected to slow to more sustainable levels. According to the World Bank forecast (1997), China's share in world trade will more than triple by 2020 (to about 10 percent) and it is expected to become the second largest trading nation, only after the United States. China will account for some 40 percent of the increase in all developing country imports between 1992 and 2020 and serve as an engine of growth for world trade.

2.3 Implications for MNCs

Despite uncertainties, the spectacular growth of China's consumer market is drawing MNCs from all over the globe. MNCs that entered China in the mid-1980s have the benefit of perspective, which is serving them well in the current climate of stiff competition and retreating tax benefits. Facing China's economic environment as described above, most foreign companies choose to make a further commitment to this market, although many firms have adopted a more cautious approach than during their first entry, tempered by the realization that the market itself is in flux.

Despite the fact that not all of the original ventures have been success stories, many firms that entered the market in the early days achieved profitability within a reasonable time frame. The question for newcomers now is not 'Is it worth it to be in China?' but rather 'How can we make it worth while to be in China?' In an effort to create payoffs, investments in China require commitment, patience, and planning. For instance, Johnson & Johnson has boosted its presence from one equity joint venture (EJV) to 3 EJVs, 2 wholly-owned subsidiaries, and a representative office. Eastman Kodak, which initially transferred technology for color film and paper, has seen its presence grow to one cooperative joint venture, which manufactures optical lenses, 2 EJVs in document management, 2 wholly-owned (one for electric flash units and the other to manufacture mini-labs) and 10 representative offices nationwide. In March 1998, Kodak announced it would invest more than $1 billion in the next several years to produce Kodak brand world class products in China. Ingersoll-Rand has also increased its total number of EJVs from one to five. The company now has ventures manufacturing rock drills and accessories, bearings, pneumatic tools, compressors, and road machinery. It also set up a holding company in 1996 in Shanghai.

Among all factors that contribute to MNC success in China, partner selection is the most important. MNCs with appropriate partners tend to be superior in terms of profitability, competitive position, joint venture stability, and operational efficiency. A foreign firm that makes an investment and is 10,000 miles away will not find the Chinese legal system well equipped to provide much assistance. If disputes arise, even those who are ultimately successful in pursuing claims have to deal with a totally foreign legal process, time-consuming and costly proceedings, and remedies that may or may not provide adequate compensation. Thus, a good partner can help with many of the steps necessary to making a joint venture successful, from getting approvals as painlessly as possible and supervising and smoothing project construction to running the operation profitably and managing it properly. A bad partner, on the other hand, can ruin the operation by constantly disagreeing with the foreign partner, usurping company funds for its own benefit, or even getting the foreign partner into trouble. In general, careful partner selection leads to reduced political risks, greater political advantages, and access to production factors such as labor force, capital, and land. Most importantly, joint ventures will help the foreign investor gain easy access to the Chinese market, share costs and other risks, and provide it with country-specific knowledge.

Kentucky Fried Chicken, for instance, allied itself with the Chinese arm of CP Pokphand, which supplies chickens, and the local New Asia Group, a sleeping partner as far as production is concerned. Its role is to secure, through guanxi, prime sites for KFC and ensure that permits arrive promptly and without trouble. The Sino Infrastructure Partnership, a Shanghai-based joint-venture engineering and construction company, combines the engineering company Sir Alexander Gibb, building materials supplier Rugby Group, and builder Taylor Woodrow International. Its Chinese partners are the Shanghai Municipal Engineering Design Institute and Beijing Municipal Engineering Design and Research Institute. The local partners take charge of the processing of permits, enabling the Sino Infrastructure Partnership to offer Shanghai's only all-in-one design-construction approvals service.

While partner selection criteria vary depending on a foreign investor's objectives, a synergy of interests and mutual dedication to achieving similar goals facilitates a venture's progress. Some foreign investors choose to link up with partners that manufacture complementary products or components. Others form ventures with manufacturers of similar products, both to take advantage of their existing product knowledge as well as to preempt future competition. MNCs with strong partners tend to want to sustain their partnerships rather than buy out their counterparts. For instance, Xerox Shanghai, a joint venture between Xerox and the Shanghai Moving Photo Industry Corp., started to produce copiers only a year after the venture was formed in 1987. Within another year, Xerox Shanghai turned in a profit. Now the company has more than 700 employees, produces six different models, and has been one of the most profitable MNCs in China for more than 10 consecutive years.

References

Chow, G. and Kwan, Y. (1996), 'Estimating Economic Effects of the Political Movements in China', *Journal of Comparative Economics*, vol. 23, pp. 192-208.

Kelley, L. and Luo, Y. (1998), *China 2000: Emerging Business Issues*, Thousand Oaks, CA: Sage.

Lin, J.Y. (1992), 'Rural Reforms and Agricultural Growth in China', *American Economic Review*, vol. 82, pp. 34-51.

Naughton, B. (1995), *Growing Out of the Plan: Chinese Economic Reform*, 1978-1993, New York: Cambridge University Press.

Perkins, F. and Raiser, M. (1996), 'Productivity Performance and Priorities for the Reform of China's State Owned Enterprises', *Journal of Development Studies*, vol. 32, pp. 414-444.

Raswki, T. G. (1999), 'Reforming China's Economy: What Have We Learned?', *The China Journal*, vol. 41, pp. 139-156.

Shaw, S. M. and Meier, J. (1993), 'Second Generation MNCs in China', *The McKinsey Quarterly*, vol. 4, pp. 3-16.

World Bank (1995), *China: Reform of State-Owned Enterprises*, Washington, D.C.: China and Mongolia Department, World Bank.

World Bank (1996), *The Chinese Economy: Fighting Inflation, Deepening Reforms*, Washington, D.C.: The World Bank.

World Bank (1997), *China 2020*, Washington, D.C.: The World Bank.

Yusuf, S. (1994), 'China's Macroeconomic Performance and Management During Transition', *Journal of Economic Perspectives*, vol. 8, pp. 71-92.

PART II
PARTNERING WITH CHINESE FIRMS: FOREIGN vs. CHINESE PERSPECTIVE

3 Partner Selection: A Foreign Parent Perspective

Chapter Purpose

This chapter delineates how to select appropriate Chinese partners for foreign companies. It focuses on what partner attributes or selection criteria must be considered in the selection process. For this purpose, this chapter illustrates three categories of criteria: strategic, organizational, and financial. A partner with superior strategic traits but lacking strong organizational and financial characteristics may result in an unstable joint venture. The possession of desirable organizational attributes without corresponding strategic and financial competence may leave the joint venture unprofitable. A partner with superior financial strengths without strategic and organizational competencies can lead to an unsustainable venture. After discussing these criteria, this chapter presents some empirical results about the importance of such criteria obtained from the recent survey conducted in China. Mini-cases are provided at the end.

3.1 Conceptual Background

In an attempt to accomplish sustained competitive advantages in global marketplaces, MNCs have in recent years turned increasingly to the use of international joint ventures (IJVs). However, the intercultural and interorganizational nature of IJVs results in enormous complexity, dynamics, and challenges in managing this cross-border, hybrid form of organization. One popular argument is that inter-partner comparative or configurational features, variously termed as strategic symmetries, interfirm diversity, or complementary resources and skills, create inter-partner 'fit' that is expected to generate a synergistic effect on IJV performance.

It is assumed that firms establish IJVs only when the perceived additional benefits of exercising the IJV option outweigh its expected additional costs. One of the key notions in the IJV literature is that these additional benefits will accrue only through the retention of a partner who can provide the four 'Cs': compatible goals, complementary skills, cooperative culture, and commensurate risk. Partner selection determines an IJV's mix of skills, knowledge, and resources, its operating policies and procedures, and its vulnerability to indigenous conditions, structures, and institutional changes. In a dynamic, complex, or hostile environment, the importance of local partner selection to IJV success is magnified because the right partner can spur the IJV's adaptability, strategy-environment configuration, and uncertainty reduction.

Local partner selection is critical to the success of IJVs investing in newly emerging economies, most notably China. On the one hand, such economies have in recent years become major hosts of direct investment by MNCs because these rapidly expanding economies, characterized by an exploding demand previously stifled by ideologically based government interventions, provide tremendous business opportunities which MNCs can preempt. On the other hand, transnational investors in such economies face the challenges of structural reform, combined with weak market structure, poorly specified property rights, and institutional uncertainty. Although some economic sectors have been decentralized and privatized, governments in these economies still hinder industrial and market structure adjustments. Indeed, the 'invisible hand' in the reform process often causes unexpected social, political or economic turmoil that may go beyond the tolerance level of the government or society. Under these circumstances, the visible hands of administrative, fiscal, and monetary interventions are called to the rescue. The administrative option is often the most expedient, allowing for swift action that will be promptly reflected in the market. In this situation, local partners can be of great value to foreign firms. They can make investing in restricted industries possible and help MNCs gain access to marketing channels, while meeting government requirements for local ownership. In addition, having recourse to an IJV as a means of reducing political risks or achieving political advantages is a logical choice for many MNCs operating in strategic sectors in such economies. Moreover, local partners can assist foreign partners in obtaining insightful information and country-specific knowledge concerning governmental policies, local business practices, operational conditions, and the like. Furthermore, the IJV form helps MNCs gain access to, or secure at a low cost, locally-scarce production factors such as labor force, capital, or land.

During the process of IJV formation, foreign parent firms must identify appropriate criteria for local partner selection as well as the relative importance of each criterion. They are divergent depending on firm, setting, and time. Broadly, the criteria can be classified into three categories related to: (i) tasks or operations; (ii) partnership or cooperation; and (iii) cash flow or capital structure. Operation-related criteria are associated with the strategic attributes of partners including marketing competence, relationship building, market position, industrial experience, strategic orientation, and corporate image. Cooperation-related criteria often mirror organizational attributes such as organizational leadership, organizational rank, ownership type, learning ability, foreign experience, and human resource skills. Cash flow-related criteria are generally represented by financial attributes exemplified by profitability, liquidity, leverage, and asset management. A partner's strategic traits influence the operational skills and resources needed for the joint venture's competitive success, organizational traits affect the efficiency and effectiveness of inter-firm cooperation, and financial traits impact the optimization of capital structure and cash flow.

Conceptually, strategic, organizational, and financial attributes are all crucial to IJV performance. A partner with superior strategic traits, but lacking strong organizational and financial characteristics, results in an unstable joint venture. The possession of desirable organizational attributes without corresponding strategic and financial competence leaves the joint venture unprofitable. A partner with superior financial strengths without strategic and organizational competencies can lead to an unsustainable venture. From a process perspective, the linkage between partner selection and IJV success lies in inter-partner fit. While strategic attributes may affect strategic fit between partners, organizational traits are likely to influence organizational fit, and financial attributes will impact financial fit. Figure 3.1 schematically summarizes these relationships.

This three-fold classification scheme (strategic, organizational, and financial) may be of interest to both theory and practice. Although this study uses China as its analytical setting, such scheme and key components may be applicable to other contexts. The literature on partner selection has paid little attention to the systematic categorization of various partner attributes. Such classification is imperative because each group affects a different kind of fit (strategic, organizational, and financial), thus influencing different dimensions of IJV performance. Moreover, most previous studies in the area have not yet incorporated financial attributes into the framework. Such attributes are important because cash flow positions, financial strategies, and capital structures of partner firms impact the degree of both financial and operational synergies derived from venturing activities. Further, some strategic and organizational attributes such as strategic orientation, relationship building, learning ability, organizational leadership and rank remain under-researched in the study of partner selection. We addressed these variables using an integrative approach with an aim to include all relevant attributes that may influence IJV success in the scheme. In the selection process, international managers may use this scheme to examine the strengths and weaknesses of the potential partners and to determine whether partner attributes fit their own in strategic, organizational, and financial arenas.

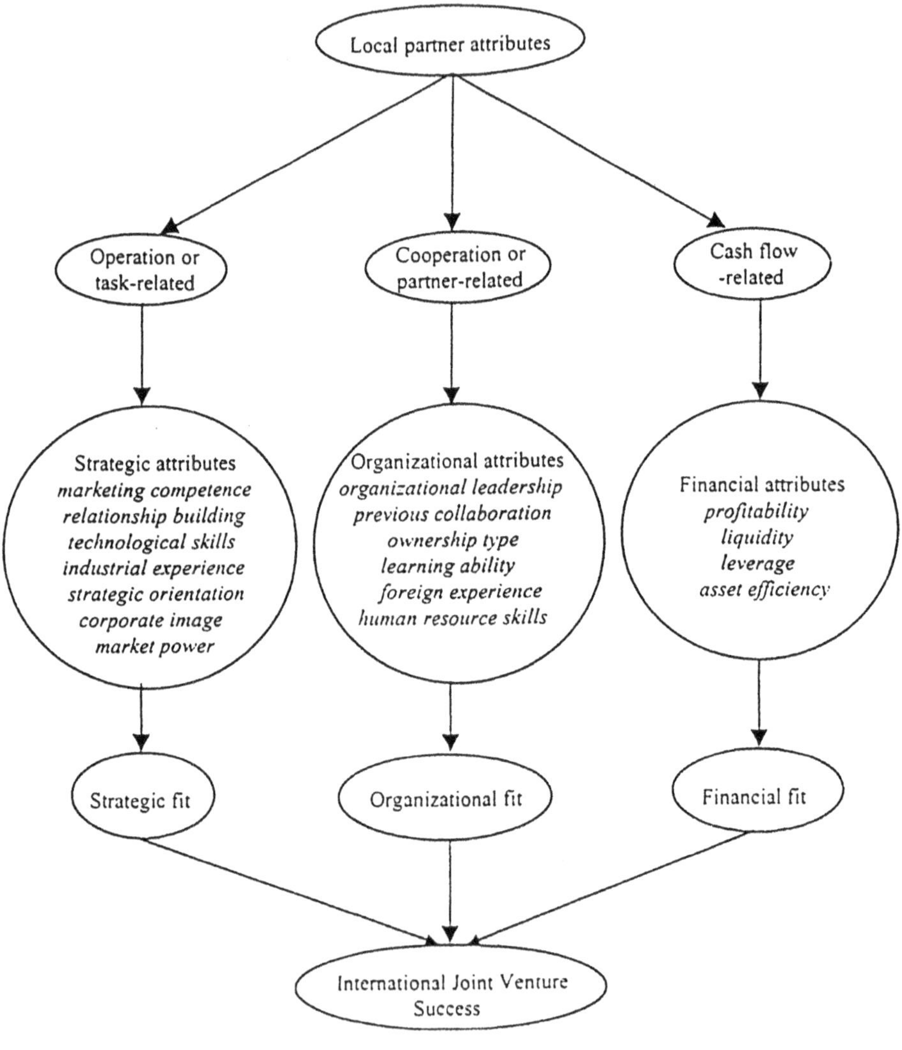

Figure 3.1 Partner Attributes and Joint Venture Success: Three-Fold Classification Scheme

3.2 Strategic Attributes

It is important to note that different strategic, organizational, and financial traits may have a heterogeneous effect on different aspects of IJV performance. MNCs need to discern not only important partner selection criteria in general but also which ones are crucial to their specific strategic goals. We sought to address the performance implications of each attribute as specific as possible throughout the article. The specific performance effects include profitability, market growth, cost minimization, stability, risk reduction, export growth, and the like. The term of 'IJV success' is generally defined as the accomplishment of the parent firm's strategic goals from the venture.

Marketing Competence

As far as the composition of GNP is concerned, China has already become a market economy. Government-instituted distribution, wholesale, and retail systems under the central planning regime have been essentially dismissed. Instead, competitive pressure from both local rivals and other foreign competitors has become increasingly strong in all deregulated industries. In this new environment, a local partner's marketing competencies in distribution channels, promotional skills, knowledge about local business practices, and relationships with major buyers, wholesalers, and relevant governmental authorities are fundamentally important for foreign companies seeking market position and power in China. Because Chinese society is built around a complex social and business web, the costs of establishing distribution channels or business networks in China by foreign businesses are likely to outweigh the potential benefits. Moreover, establishing such a network can be such a long process that foreign companies may be unable to seize market opportunities or align with contextual changes in a timely fashion.

On the other hand, a partnership with a local firm with superior marketing competence enables a foreign company to quickly establish its market position, organizational image, and product reputation in the Chinese market. This also helps the foreign company increase profitability, reduce uncertainty, and boost its competitive edge in the host country. Shenkar (1990) suggests that a foreign company's technological strengths and a local partner's marketing competence creates operational synergies that are mutually beneficial to both parties. Luo (1995) observed an importance of such marketing competence, particularly skills in personnel direct marketing, to the market performance of IJVs in China. As one of the well-established and well-reputed Chinese auto firms, Shanghai Automotive Industry Corp. has utilized its marketing expertise and resources to help its joint venture, Shanghai Volkswagen AG, quickly establish distribution channels, after-sale service centers, and high-quality image recognition nationwide. Today, it is the largest foreign-invested enterprise in China with regard to total sales, and has a market share of more than 50 percent of domestically manufactured passenger cars in China.

Relationship Building

Foreign companies can gain an edge over their competitors in the Chinese market if they have a superior *guanxi* network with the business community (e.g. suppliers, buyers, distributors, and banks) and government authorities (e.g. political governments, industrial administration departments, foreign exchange administration bureaus, foreign trade and economics commissions, commercial administration bureaus, and taxation departments). *Guanxi* refers to the concept of drawing on connections in order to secure favors in personal or business relations. It binds thousands and thousands of Chinese firms into a social and business web. Rather than depending on an abstract notion of impartial justice, Chinese people and businesses traditionally prefer to rely on their contacts with those in power to get things done. Personal connections and loyalties are often more important than organizational affiliations or legal standards. Whenever scarce resources exist, they are mainly allocated by guanxi rather than bureaucratic rules. Guanxi provides a balance to the cumbersome Chinese bureaucracy by giving individuals a way to circumvent rules through the activation of personal relations.

Although foreign companies can establish and maintain their own guanxi networks by themselves, the more efficient and effective way is certainly to utilize the local partners' existing business or personal connections. This is because guanxi cultivation is a highly complicated social investment process that can be costly, unstable, and unreliable if the relationship is constructed inappropriately or with the wrong people. A local partner's guanxi network constitutes strategic assets for all IJVs regardless of their strategic goals, orientations, or objectives. Such networks help foreign companies obtain scarce production factors, facilitate value chain contributions, promote relationships with various governmental institutions, and increase the effectiveness of market penetration. Recently, various studies have found that the utilization of local firms' guanxi connections significantly facilitates IJVs' financial and market-based performance measures such as ROI, sales growth, and risk reduction (e.g., Luo and Chen, 1996; Shenkar, 1990). For example, the well established guanxi networks of China Postal and Telecommunication Corp. (CPTC) have given a tremendous boost to the amazing growth of Shanghai Bell Telephone Equipment Manufacturing Co., currently one of the China's top ten most profitable Sino-foreign joint ventures. Because this industry remains controlled by the central government, CPTC's superior relationship with top Chinese officials, including Jiang Zemin and Zhu Rongji, has substantially contributed to the venture's success in preempting and dominating China's vast telecommunications market. In 1996, it had 40 percent share of China's telephone digital switching market, with Ericsson at the second place only taking 15 percent.

Market Position

Because a major objective of foreign investors in the Chinese market is to preempt market opportunities and business potential, a local partner's market power is a key asset. In China, market power is often represented by a local partner's industrial and business background, market position, and established marketing and distribution networks. Market power also enables the firm to influence some industry-wide restrictions on output, increase bargaining power, and offer the advantages of economies of scale. Over the last few years, the Chinese government has relinquished control over a growing number of industries. The rapidly expanding Chinese economy, together with high market demand, has made market positioning extremely important for the success of any business in the country. In such circumstances, a Chinese partner's market strength is key to the IJV's financial return and indigenous market growth. Moreover, strong local market power can strengthen the IJV's commitment to local market expansion. This commitment will make the IJV less inclined to increase exports in its business operations. Furthermore, strong market power can lead to greater bargaining power with the local government. This can help the IJV reduce political risks and business uncertainties.

These benefits have been confirmed in a recent study by Luo (1997) who found that the market power of a local partner is significantly and positively associated with an IJV's profitability, sales growth, and risk reduction. Many case studies also support the above argument. For instance, Avon Products, Inc.'s local partner, Bureau of Light Industry in Guangzhou (BLIG), manages 140 factories and dominates the Southern China market for many light industry products including fashion jewelry, cosmetics, apparel, gifts, collectible and home furnishings, to name a few. Because Avon's primary market focuses on Southern China, the market position of BLIG fits Avon's strategic needs. In 1995, Avon sold $40 million dollars worth of products in China, nearly doubling its sales of 1994. The business in China has gone so well that the company ranks the China market among their leading expansion markets and expects its China sales to reach $250 million by the year 2000.

Industrial Experience

When operating in a transitional economy characterized by weak market structure, poorly specified property rights, and institutional uncertainty, an IJV seeking efficiency and growth needs an adaptive orientation, a solid supply relationship, comprehensive buyer networks, and a good organizational image. The local partner's market experience and accumulated industrial knowledge are of great value to the realization of these goals. In China, a local partner's established history and strong background in the industry often result in a good reputation or high credibility in the market. Lengthy industrial/market experience signifies that the local firm has built an extensive marketing and distribution network, a badly needed competence for IJV market growth.

In addition, since China has a stronger relationship-oriented culture compared to industrialized market economies, the business activities of IJVs in China can be greatly facilitated by local partners' connections in the domestic business scene and good relations with influential persons. Local firms with longer market experience are expected to have developed a better business relationship network. Goodwill and superior contacts constitute country-specific knowledge or what the resource-based view calls the 'resource position barrier' (Wernerfelt, 1984) which enhances an IJV's competitive advantage, economic efficiency, and risk reduction capability. According to Luo (1997), a local partner's industrial experience has a favorable influence on the IJV's market growth and operational stability. A good case example is Esquel Group Co.'s investment in China. The company's major local partner, Changzhou No. 1 Garment Manufacturing Co., has operated in the industry for more than fifty years. Although this local partner is not an extremely large firm, its long presence and market experience in the industry has created prestigious company and product reputations, and solid marketing and supply channels. These superior attributes helped Esquel Group become one of the leading foreign investors in China's garments and fabrics industry. Recently, its annual output exceeded 1 million dozen garments and 24 million yards of quality cotton fabrics.

Strategic Orientation

The strategic orientation (i.e., prospector, analyzer, or defender, see Miles and Snow, 1978) of local firms is important to venture success because how well it matches that of its foreign partner influences inter-partner consistency in terms of strategic goals and behaviors, cooperative culture, and investment commitment. These in turn affect the formulation and implementation of technological, operational, financial, and managerial policies at various levels including corporate, business, functional, and international. As strategic orientation determines organizational adaptability and innovativeness, it may affect not only the local firm's strategic but also organizational behaviors such as managerial philosophy and style and long-term orientation, which may in turn influence mutual trust and collaboration between parties.

In order to reap benefits from market demand, a defensive orientation (i.e., defender strategy) may be too conservative for firms seeking market expansion in China. However, it is not realistic to orient Chinese firms in a highly proactive direction (i.e., prospector strategy) because this could lead to vast operational and contextual risks and innovative and adaptive costs in a complex, dynamic, and hostile environment. An analyzer orientation fits the environmental traits in a transitional context where environmental sectors are fundamentally complex and dynamic, information is not codified, and regulations are not explicit. Under this orientation, the partner candidate should be innovative and adaptive but not extremely aggressive and risk-taking when the market changes. They should allocate most of their resources to a set of reasonably stable environments while at the same time conducting somewhat routinized scanning activities in a limited product-market area. They monitor market situations, and carefully apply previously developed product and market innovations. This analyzer strategy reduces the likelihood of outright failure and creates upper limits to success. In general, Chinese firms with the analyzer orientation are ideal candidate partners for foreign companies pursuing both profitability and stability. For example, Shanghai Instrument Industry Co., the local partner of Foxboro Co., is extremely skillful in scanning and analyzing environmental changes and balancing market effectiveness and cost efficiency. Today, Shanghai Foxboro Co. has become one of the leading electronic process control instrument manufactures in China.

Corporate Image

A superior corporate image usually implies a superior product brand, customer loyalty, or organizational reputation. Corporate image may be unusually critical in China because Chinese consumers are particularly loyal to the products made by the companies maintaining a superior image in the market. For instance, when purchasing household appliances, Chinese people tend to attach more importance to corporate image than to the physical attributes of the products. In deciding whether to buy a joint venture's products, they are used to evaluating not only the reputation of the joint venture itself but also the goodwill of Chinese partners in the past. Therefore, it is essential for foreign investors to collaborate with those Chinese businesses that have maintained a good organizational reputation and product image. This selection will significantly benefit the market power and competitive position of the joint venture in the relevant industry. For example, Panda Electronics Group, the local partner of Philips in Nanjing, is one of the most famous Chinese giants in various electronics products in terms of high quality and customer responsiveness. This image helped the joint venture's products quickly become pervasive and popular in the Chinese market. Today, their joint venture, Huafei Colour Display Systems Co. Ltd. is one of the top twenty foreign-invested enterprises in terms of total sales.

A superior company image in China also implies better relationships with the local government, as well as with suppliers and distributors. These relationships are crucial for firms pursuing a market share and competitive position in the industry. Recently, the State Council of the P.R.C. has decided to form business groups as part of the reform focus for the next five years. It is deemed that a firm with a superior corporate image will be more likely to be the leading or core unit in the group. Such business groups, which will soon become new market-driven oligopolists in related industries, will become the ideal local partners for MNCs in the future.

3.3 Organizational Attributes

Organizational Leadership

Leadership in Chinese state-owned businesses is a fairly complicated issue because upper level government authorities assign top-level management positions. Moreover, the communist party representatives in the firm, normally remaining out of sight, are politically the real bosses of the firm. On the other hand, leadership is fundamental to venture success in China. The relationships with leaders often outweigh the contractual terms and clauses agreed upon by both parties to an IJV, because law enforcement in China has been weak for many decades as a result of tradition, the public's poor concept of law, and habitual working practices. The leadership of the Chinese partner also critically influences the cooperative culture between the two partners, which in turn affects their mutual trust. In addition, the partner's relationships with the government are largely determined by the interpersonal relationship between its management and government officials. These personal connections, or guanxi, can be the most important factor for a joint venture's competitive edge, especially if the venture has to rely upon the government in acquiring approvals, materials, capital, and other resources or in securing various kinds of support and assistance for dispute resolution, infrastructure access, distribution arrangements, and taxation holidays or allowances. As a result of continuous industrial decentralization and economic reforms, which further increase the autonomy and authority of corporate-level managers, the effect of a Chinese partner's leadership appears to be even more fundamental to the joint venture operation today. The successes in China of Celanese Corp. (with Jiangsu Tobacco Co.), Hewlett-Packard (with Beijing Computer Industry Corp.), McDonnell Douglas (with Shanghai Aviation Industrial Corp.), and Wang Computer (with Shanghai Computer Co.) all suggest that a partner's superior leadership can strongly enhance venture performance. To evaluate the leadership of Chinese businesses, foreign investors should scrutinize such areas as educational background, relationship with government authorities, innovativeness, international experience, managerial skills, length of previous leadership, and foreign language skills.

Organizational Rank

Organizational rank includes both business level and class in China. Chinese organizations, including state-owned and collectively owned enterprises, are generally ranked by upper level government into the following levels: national, provincial, city, county, and so on. At each level, especially the national and provincial levels, firms may be further classified into different classes. For instance, the Panda Electronics Group in Nanjing, Jiangsu Province, is a national-level first-class company, while the Nanton Bicycle Factory in Nanton, Jiangsu Province is a provincial-level first-class business. In general, different levels of firms imply various kinds of autonomy and authority offered by the government. The higher the organizational level, the greater the power delegated to the firm and the greater the support it attains from the government. However, these are often achieved at the expense of increased government interference. For foreign partners, the solution to this trade-off largely depends upon their strategic goals and organizational capabilities in the strategy-environment alignment in the host country. Unlike organizational level, business rank by class is more closely associated with the efficiency and effectiveness of the company. The higher-class firms generally have superior product quality, better internal management, quicker customer responsiveness, and superior organizational performance. Thus, foreign companies seeking high financial and market outcome in China should closely examine the level and class of potential Chinese partners. The successes of Xerox and Johnson & Johnson (both in Shanghai) illustrate this point. Although not extremely large, Shanghai Shenbei Office Machine Co., Xerox's partner, was ranked municipality-level but first class. Shanghai Daily Chemical Industry Development Co., Johnson & Johnson's partner, was approved as a state-level first-class business. Both joint ventures are now among the top 50 foreign businesses in China with respect to total sales.

Ownership Type

Economic transition in China has given birth to a new diversity of organizational forms. The spectrum spans the continuum from state-owned to non-state-owned (private and collective) businesses. A Chinese partner's organizational form influences not only its motivations for forming an IJV but also its commitment and contribution to operations, which in turn affects the IJV's local performance. During structural reforms in the Chinese economy characterized by a weak market structure, poorly specified property rights, and strong governmental interference, state-owned firms have the advantage in gaining access to scarce resources, materials, capital, information, and investment infrastructure. In addition, state-owned organizations usually have an advantage over privately or collectively-owned firms in terms of industry experience, market power, and production and innovation facilities. Moreover, it is fairly common for state-owned enterprises to have privileged access to state-instituted distribution channels. These channels play a dominant role in product distribution in the Chinese market. State-owned businesses are also treated preferentially by the government when selecting market segments. This organizational form may hence facilitate the market growth in new domains. Finally, hierarchical state firms tend to have a better relationship with various governmental institutions. This relationship is expected to result in greater problem-solving capacity for these firms. For all these reasons, state-owned organizations may contribute more to an IJV's local market expansion than non-state-owned organizations. Luo (1997) empirically confirms this. To name two case examples, Otis Elevator Co. and Smithkline Beckman Corp., both in Tianjin, selected state-owned firms: Tianjin Lift Co. and Tianjin Pharmaceutical Industry Corp., respectively. The aforementioned advantages for state businesses are certainly among key factors making the two ventures dominate their respective markets and become two of the top sixty foreign-invested ventures since 1991.

Private or collective enterprises are typically operated and managed by entrepreneurs. They have fewer principle-agent conflicts and greater strategic flexibility. The existence of many unfulfilled product and market niches in the Chinese economy increases their chance for survival and growth. Their simple structure and small size have positioned them for speed and surprise, giving them greater ability to react quickly to opportunities in the environment and proactively outmaneuver more established firms. In addition, private and collective businesses are pressed by hard budgetary constraints, forcing them to be more efficient and profit-oriented. In contrast, state firms lack self-motivation and operational autonomy, while being highly vulnerable to bureaucratic red tape. It is reported that over 60 percent of state-owned enterprises in China have shown a loss whereas private or collective businesses have been showing continuous profit. IJVs with efficiency-oriented private or collective partners are thus likely to enjoy superior returns on investment. This proposition has been supported by a recent analysis of China's top 100,000 companies which finds that firms with defined property rights (collective or private firms) are more productive and profitable than state-owned enterprises (Li, Gao and Ma, 1995). Two joint ventures in Shanghai, Chia Tai (Thailand)'s Da Jiang Co. and Schowel (U.S.)'s Great Wall Zipper Co., both have collectively-owned local parent firms (Songjiang Feeding Co. and Zhoupu Village Industrial Co., respectively). But, today, they both are market leaders in their respective industries and maintain high product reputations. Shanghai Da Jiang has been one of the biggest twenty foreign ventures in terms of sales since 1991.

Learning Ability

It has been noted in the IJV literature that complementary needs create interpartner 'fit' which is expected to generate a synergistic effect on IJV performance (Buckley and Casson, 1988). However, complementarity is not likely to materialize unless a certain threshold of skills is already in place. Chinese businesses in joint ventures generally seek technological, innovational, and managerial skills from foreign partners. The success of an IJV's local operations and expansion in this market will largely depend upon its local partner's learning capability, or its ability to acquire, assimilate, integrate, and exploit knowledge and skills. The firm's ability to process, integrate, and deploy an inflow of new knowledge and skills closely depends on how these relate to the skills already established. This skill base is expected to influence strategic fit and organizational fit between IJV partners, which in turn influence the IJV's accomplishment in terms of both financial and operational synergies. As a result, a Chinese partner's learning ability will contribute to the IJV's profitability and sales growth. For instance, Motorola's partner in Southern China, Nanjing Radio Factory, has the highest R&D intensity and the largest number of engineers in China's radio industry. It has also received government awards several times for advanced innovative or organizational skills. These skills have fundamentally contributed to its superior learning capabilities. In 1995, Motorola (China) Electronics Co. was the second best seller among all foreign ventures in the country, with about US$100 million sales in the local market and an 154 percent asset turnover.

Foreign Experience

A local partner's previous foreign experience is critical to the success of intercultural and cross-border ventures. Foreign experience affects the organizational fit between partners in the early stages of the joint venture and how well they remain matched as the venture evolves over time. Because the business atmosphere and commercial practices in China are quite different from those in developed countries, mistrust and opportunism have often taken place in the course of IJV operations. A Chinese firm's foreign experience, through import and export business or cooperative projects with other foreign investors, proves to be a very desirable attribute since this represents superior knowledge, skills, and values regarding modern management methods. Contact with foreign companies and business people can sharpen sensitivity toward competitiveness in the international market. A long history of business dealings with foreign markets can increase receptivity toward maintaining quality standards, customer responsiveness, and product innovation. As foreign experience is accompanied by exposure to foreign (Western) values, it also increases a Chinese business's ability to effectively communicate with its foreign partner. This acquired knowledge stimulates the trust and collaboration between partners. As a consequence, a Chinese partner having international experience will contribute more to the IJV's financial return, risk reduction, and sales growth in the domestic as well as export markets. This effect is empirically supported by Beamish (1987), Luo (1997), and Shenkar (1990). Many success stories about Western joint ventures in China such as Brown & Root International (China), Beijing Jeep, Shenzhen Konka Electronics, Guangzhou Procter & Gamble, China Schindler Elevator, Shanghai Squibb, Shanghai Ruby & Johnson Cosmetics, and Xi'an Janssen Pharmaceutical, to name a few, all indicate the importance of local partners' international experience in facilitating interfirm trust, forbearance, commitment, and collaboration, which in turn promote joint venture success.

Human Resource Skills

In an IJV, people with different cultural backgrounds, career goals, compensation systems, and other human resource baggage often have to begin working together with little advance preparation. Unless the ground has been smoothed, this 'people factor' can halt the joint venture's progress, sometimes permanently. Because of the existence of cultural barriers, the use of a large workforce, and the reliance of Chinese people in the ventures' most managerial functions, human resource management skills of local partners are key to the goal accomplishment of foreign companies. These skills are reflected not only in blending of cultures and management styles with their foreign counterparts, but also in job design, recruitment and staffing, orientation and training, performance appraisal, compensation and benefits, career development, and labor-management relations. Among these attributes, the abilities to surpass cultural barriers, recruit qualified employees, and establish incentive structures are particularly imperative.

In recent years, foreign companies have encountered increasing pressure from local government agencies to hire redundant or unqualified people, from trade unions to set minimum or maximum wage rates, and from labor departments to obey bureaucratic stipulations over human resource management. Under these circumstances, a foreign company needs a local partner which is skillful in managing the workforce and dealing with unions while externally handling labor departments and other governmental authorities. It is important to create a corporate culture that contains some aspects of Western management style and is, at the same time, acceptable to the Chinese staff. Therefore, a local partner should also be knowledgeable about Western human resource management wisdom. Several lessons for foreign companies include: (1) avoid taking too many employees from a single source, as this can heighten the risk of hiring a lot of people who will reinforce similar bad habits; (2) practice patience and flexibility when looking for high-quality personnel; (3) resist pressures to overhire by Chinese authorities; (4) find a local confidante among the local managers who has experience in dealing with the bureaucracy and is trustworthy; (5) mold the right individuals according to the needs of the company. The success of Shanghai Mitsubishi Elevator, Guangzhou Procter & Gamble, Beijing Toshiba Color Kinescope, Tianjin 3M, Shengzheng Epson Electronics, Fujian Hitachi TV, and Shekou Sanyo Electric Machines has to be attributed largely to the local partners' superior skills in human resource management.

3.4 Financial Attributes

Profitability

A local partner's profitability will directly influence its ability to make a capital contribution, fulfill financial commitments, and disperse financial resources to the joint venture. These in turn affect the joint venture's profit margin, net cash inflow, and wealth accumulation. The profitability attribute will also indirectly influence the joint venture's capital structure, financing costs, and leverage. As in developed countries, less profitable firms usually have to pay higher interest rates or accept shorter terms in order to attain bank loans in China. In recent years, a sustained tight monetary policy, reflected in increased interest rates and reduced bank lending and money supply (the 'credit crunch') has resulted in liquidity problems for many Chinese businesses, particularly those heavily relying on bank loans. Moreover, in a recent step, the Chinese government began separating bank functions from policy directing. This measure led banks to more strictly control those loans made to less efficient, less profitable firms. As a large proportion of capital contribution by Chinese partners to joint ventures comes from bank loans, this new measure substantially constrains the capacity of Chinese partners to meet their financial commitments.

Viewed from the operational perspective, a less profitable business often implies organizational weaknesses in the technological, operational, and managerial spheres. To Chinese consumers, an unprofitable business normally means poor product quality, poor management, and/or slow customer responsiveness. If this poorly performing business is a state-owned enterprise, reasons may include a 'class struggle' within management, organizational rigidity, and/or conservative leadership. If the poorly performing business is a collectively-owned or privately-owned enterprise, the underlying factors may also include weak competitive advantage, little market power, underdeveloped distribution channels, and/or lack of guanxi with the business community or governmental authorities. In sum, lack of profitability of local partners can be symbolic of internal weaknesses in financial, technological, operational, organizational, and managerial arenas. Foreign investors should be wary when scrutinizing a possible local partner's ability to make profits. Indicators of profitability include the gross profit margin, net profit margin, return on assets, and return on equity, among others.

Liquidity

A local partner's liquidity is critical to IJV operations because it directly affects the venture's ability to pay off short-term financial obligations. In the international business literature, it is commonly understood that foreign investors attain financial synergies from the optimization of operational cash flows. A foreign venture can reduce the default risk and uncertainty of operational cash flow, but this depends on the correlation of the pre-cooperation cash flow of the two firms. A larger joint venture will have better access to capital markets and lower financing costs, other things being equal. Given the partial segmentation of national economies and markets, this benefit is even greater for IJVs than for domestic joint ventures. Ideally, in an attempt to achieve the maximum financial and operational synergies, two partners should be complementary not only in capital structure but also between their financial and competitive strengths.

Liquidity is extremely low in most Chinese firms, particularly state-owned enterprises. Many firms have a current ratio even lower than 1. In harsh contrast to the equity status of Western businesses, the initially contributed capital and accumulated retained earnings, called 'retained funds' in China, account only for a very small percentage of the capital resources needed for operations. Consequently, most Chinese firms have to depend heavily on short and long term loans. This is the major reason why Chinese firms are so vulnerable to changes in governmental monetary policy and the 'credit crunch'. International investors should realize that the poor liquidity of Chinese firms and the tight monetary policy will continue for a long time during the economic transition. This is inevitable because the pressure of high inflation and necessity to maintain social stability during a time of economic boom and transformation leave no option but a more tightly controlled monetary supply and vigorously confined capital reinvestment for state-owned businesses. Foreign partners seeking cost and risk sharing or pursuing the reduction of operational cash flow uncertainties should be particularly cautious to ensure that they have a thorough grasp of their Chinese partners' liquidity.

Leverage

As a consequence of the fundamental lack of equity necessary for many business activities, the leverage level of most Chinese firms is markedly low. This is reflected in the high level of various leverage ratios such as debt-to-assets ratio, debt-to-equity-ratio, or long term debt-to-equity ratio. It is well known today that many Chinese firms are encountering a 'triangular debt' problem, whereby the firms owe large sums of money to each other but have no cash with which to settle their accounts. Accounts receivables open more than 180 days are very common, often representing a substantial part of a Chinese company's liquid resources. Apart from the aforementioned 'credit crunch', this situation can be attributed to cultural factors. Preferential terms of payment, particularly temporal extension of payment deadlines, are widely used in China as a primary marketing tool. In a country where guanxi is painstakingly nurtured and the maintenance of harmony is of paramount importance, sellers will do their utmost to avoid embarrassing customers who may be temporarily unable to pay.

In selecting local partners in China, foreign investors should choose those who are less vulnerable to the 'triangular debt' and have a strong leverage position. This superior position often implies that the firms (i) are more conscientious about credit screening and investigations, and thus have maintained a network of customers/buyers with a superior leverage position, and (ii) have better asset management or superior organizational skills. It is essential for the firms in China to establish clear-cut working policies, both internal and external, that will promote the best cash turnover possible and maximize benefits from the economics of accounts receivable. Because these issues significantly influence growth and survival in the Chinese market, foreign investors should attach utmost importance to the leverage level of local firms during the selection process.

Asset Efficiency

The asset efficiency of a local partner is critical to the effectiveness of the joint venture because it is a mid-range construct for maximizing return on investment. The net gains from resource contributions depend in large part on the management of assets, especially inventory, accounts receivable, and fixed assets. A partnership with a local firm, which manages its total assets skillfully and efficiently, is surely beneficial to the foreign investor pursuing either short term profitability or a long term competitive position in the market.

Asset efficiency has become particularly important for the evaluation of Chinese business performance in recent years. Prior to economic reform, a firm's incentives to enhance asset efficiency were rather low because of blurred intellectual property rights and a rigid central planning system. Today, however, firms have much higher autonomy in allocating and utilizing various assets. Thus, the level of asset management mirrors the degree of advancement of managerial skills and the extent of effectiveness of corporate administration. Although a large local firm helps the joint venture increase the economy of scale and gain better access to capital markets or commercial loans, the net size effect on the firm's financial and market performance virtually relies on asset turnover. Foreign investors should research and analyze a local partner's asset efficiency indicators such as turnovers in inventory, fixed assets, accounts receivable, and total assets. Additional insights may be obtained by comparing these indicators longitudinally to see how much improvement the local partner has made over time, and by comparing the indicators with those of other local firms in the industry to see to what extent the partner outperforms its major competitors.

To conclude, it is essential to venture success in China that the potential partner possess complementary skills and resources, and share compatible goals and a cooperative culture. Using reliable sources of information (see below), foreign companies should examine the following attributes of a local partner candidate: (i) *Strategic traits*, including marketing competence, relationship building, market position, industrial experience, strategic orientation, and corporate image; (ii) *Organizational traits*, including organizational leadership, organizational rank, ownership type, learning ability, foreign experience, and human resource skills; and (iii) *Financial traits*, including profitability, liquidity, leverage, and asset efficiency.

3.5 Empirical Evidence

In my previous study (Luo, 1997), the analysis of 116 IJVs established as of the end of 1986 in Jiangsu, China suggests that local partner attributes are important not only for overall performance of international expansion of foreign businesses (multivariate effect), but also for several different aspects of IJV performance such as financial return, local market expansion, export growth, and risk reduction (univariate effect). The results indicate enormous differences in the effect that different criteria have on IJV's overall and unidimensional performance. Each selection criterion affects individual dimensions of IJV performance differently. Overall, cooperation-related criteria, or organizational traits (such as organizational collaboration and international experience), are found to be important for an IJV's overall performance and have a positive effect on uncertainty reduction and profitability. Operation-related criteria, or strategic traits (such as absorptive capacity, product relatedness, and market power), are found to be more important for an IJV's sales growth and financial return. Some country-specific criteria such as organizational form are also linked with some aspects of IJV performance.

The major findings can be summarized as follows. First, product relatedness and market position are critical strategic traits affecting all the major dimensions of IJV performance. Related product linkage between local partners and IJVs outperforms unrelated diversification in terms of both financial return and sales growth. The superior market position of local partners is an essential determinant for IJV success in accomplishing economic efficiency, risk diversification, and market growth. Second, the strategic fit between partners depends not only upon the resource complementarity they actually contribute, but also on the absorptive capabilities of partners. A local partner's high capacity to absorb and assimilate its counterpart's tacit knowledge will lead to better overall performance in general and better ROI and local sales in particular for the IJV. Third, a local partner's organizational experience is of utmost importance in facilitating strategic or organizational fit between partners and hence contributing to the IJV's efficiency and effectiveness. A local firm's market and international experience are both found to have a favorable influence on the IJV's risk reduction, market development, and accounting return. Fourth, the greater length of inter-partner collaboration in the past leads to superior overall performance and in particular to risk reduction, export sales, and profitability. This collaboration spurs fruitful inter-firm trust and mutual forbearance, which in turn result in a better operational outcome and serve as a stabilizing device for venturing activities in a dynamic and complex environment. Finally, organizational form and size are not found to be significant to an IJV's overall performance. Nevertheless, hierarchical state enterprises can assist IJVs greatly in enhancing market power and facilitating market development. Organizational size in terms of the number of employees positively influences IJV local sales.

At a more practical level, this study offered some implications for MNCs operating in newly emerging economies that have become major hosts for MNCs' offshore investments. Based on this study's findings, MNCs will be able to determine what criteria they should use in opting for local partners and what criteria are vital to their goal accomplishment. For example, those investors seeking local market expansion should select those local partners that have rich industrial experience, superior market position, high absorptive capacity, and/or related product diversification. Those seeking profitability and stability should select local firms that have superior international experience, longer inter-partner collaboration in the past, and/or greater market power. From the standpoint of MNCs, the critical partner-selection criteria can ensure partner-traits that are favorable for the achievements of their strategic goals. The host government or local partners, on the other hand, can try to make these traits available to attract more stable and profitable foreign direct investment.

More specifically, the following lessons may be advisable for international managers who are active in the Chinese market. First, partner selection should be integrated with the strategic goals of the foreign company. A foreign investor cannot, nor will it need to, find a local partner possessing superior attributes in all of the above. Indeed, the superiority of every attribute in all three categories (strategic, organizational, and financial) is favorable to the IJV's overall success and should be thoroughly evaluated in the selection process. Nevertheless, the importance of specific attributes within a category is dependent on what the foreign company wants to pursue from the venture. If a foreign company seeks long term market growth, the importance of a local firm's marketing competence, market position, industrial experience, organizational rank, and asset efficiency may outweigh other attributes. If a foreign company seeks cost minimization via export, such attributes as learning ability, foreign experience, and ownership type may be more critical than others. If a foreign company seeks short-term profitability, it should attach higher value to a local partner's relationship building skills, strategic orientation, profitability, and liquidity. Lastly, if a foreign company seeks reductions of financial risks and operational uncertainties, more weight may be placed on attributes such as corporate image, organizational leadership, human resource skills, and financial leverage. The real magnitude of each attribute's influence on an IJV's various aspects of performance is, of course, an empirical question, and should be taken up by future studies.

Second, obtaining as much information as possible about the potential partner is well advised. Get a copy of its business license, which will tell you about its legal capacity to contract with a foreign investor, its registered capital, its business scope, and the name of the legal representative who is legally authorized to sign any joint venture contract. It is also necessary to obtain a copy of the company's brochure and find out about the industry and the candidate's competitors (this can be another good source for potential partners). If the candidate received any award from upper level government authorities, the foreign investor should get a copy. Such an award may include the Chinese party's ranking in terms of size, production, quality, reputation, or economic efficiency as recognized by the industry in a particular province or in the nation.

Third, a site visit is imperative. Social activities, which almost invariably will be pressed on investors during the visit, should be left until the deal is signed, sealed, and delivered. Politely rejecting such offers will not, as many Westerners mistakenly believe, hurt the relationship or cause your potential partner to lose face. It might even earn you respect for taking your business seriously. Diligent work is more, not less, important for IJVs in China than for those in other countries. Reliable information can often be obtained only from such a visit. During the site visit, investors should try to observe employee attitudes and talk to managers, from the lowest to the highest ranks. Do not shy away from asking questions about the operation, employees, finance, technologies, cash flow, and other relevant matters.

Fourth, it is always important to check whether or not your Chinese partner shares your investment objectives, or at least is able to reconcile his objectives to yours. If your partner puts his own interests, benefits, and political advancement above those of the joint venture's, or if his management style differs substantially or completely from yours, or if he wishes to base the venture's potential success on his political clout, you have cause for concern. In general, foreign partners are interested in market access, cheap labor, and lax rules on pollution control; the Chinese side is interested in capital and technology as well as promoting their exports. When these priorities are at odds, coordination between the joint venture partners becomes very poor. As the Chinese phrase goes, they are 'sleeping in the same bed but having different dreams'. Beijing Jeep typified one of these clashes over priorities between foreign and Chinese partners. With a strong interest in absorbing technology, the Chinese felt that AMC had reneged on the terms of their contract, which called for joint design and production of a new Jeep, when exhaust system, noise controls, and speed failed to meet international standards.

Lastly, while recognizing the importance of a local partner's ability to build relationships, we should note that guanxi alone cannot ensure venture success at all. Guanxi is not a substitute for basic organizational fundamentals such as the various strategic, organizational, and financial attributes examined above. Guanxi cannot make customers buy the IJV's products, cannot make the quality of those products acceptable to overseas buyers, and cannot increase the productivity of workers. If guanxi is improperly used to obtain approvals or resources, and if the impropriety is discovered, there may be negative repercussions resulting in revocation of the approvals and a taint on the foreign investor's reputation which will affect his future investment opportunities. All in all, do not place undue reliance on guanxi and particularly beware of someone who claims nothing but guanxi in China. Another pitfall emerging recently in locating a suitable Chinese partner is that some potential candidates are in serious financial trouble. They perceive joining forces with a foreign partner as a way to rejuvenate their dying organization. William Mallet of Tianjin Otis Elevator, China, advises that, 'foreign investors should not try to resurrect worthless organizations. They should link with ones that were strong financially, because that will provide a solid investment foundation'.

Nevertheless, many MNCs have had success stories in finding suitable Chinese partners. A good Chinese partner can be very helpful in a number of ways. They can significantly cut the cost of production, help break entry barriers to the targeted market, and even enhance the technology of the parent company. The operations of the McDonnell Douglas cooperative venture and the Johnson & Johnson venture in Shanghai are two examples of success among many illustrated above. In both cases, the Chinese partners played a key role in promoting their products in the Chinese market.

For both academics and managers alike, the following key areas concerning partner selection await further examination necessary to deepen our understanding of the requirements for joint venture success in China. First, interpartner cooperation antecedents and dynamics should be diagnosed. While partner selection determines the *possibility* of IJV success or failure, partner collaboration determines the *realization* of such possibility. China's dynamic, complex environment characterized by structural transition, industrial property reform, and central authority transformation makes this cooperation both of paramount importance and enormously difficult. Those foreign companies pursuing a long-term market position should attach utmost value to the ways their Chinese partners develop, maintain, and improve their evolving collaboration.

Second, the integration of partner selection with other investment strategies such as location selection, entry timing, and sharing arrangement needs to be investigated. Given the economic, cultural, and historical diversity of China, foreign companies cannot use homogenous criteria in evaluating and selecting local firms for projects in different regions. The importance of each criterion to a foreign company may also differ according to timing of investment, given the changes in the environment and strategic intent and needs of the investor over time. Because the degree and scope of control needed for a planned venture are an important factor underlying partner selection, a local firm's attributes may have different effects on a foreign company's goal accomplishment within different equity arrangements.

Third, more evidence about the evolution of IJVs in China is needed. Partner cooperation in the operational and managerial process has largely been unexplored. Undoubtedly, many IJVs there do not have inter-parent fit in strategic, organizational, and financial areas in the formation stage, but they survive, sustain, and evolve in the country. In other words, we need to longitudinally and dynamically examine how partners maintain fit or adjust mis-fit over time for the attainment of mutual benefits. We have seen a variety of studies focusing on investment strategies such as equity control, timing of entry, and industry selection for Chinese IJVs, but very little examination of business and operational aspects of interfirm cooperation. As a large number of IJVs have moved to the second stage in China, with about ten years of operations, their evolution remains a key issue for us to investigate.

Lastly, the implications of recent economic policies enacted by the Chinese central government for foreign businesses should be assessed. For example, the 'holding big, relaxing small' policy in reforming state-owned enterprises may create more choices and freedom for foreign companies selecting small or medium state-instituted businesses. However, a few large state firms in oligopolistic sectors are likely to be better protected and supported by the central government, implying that joint ventures with such firms may more readily succeed in preempting scarce resources and maintaining market power in the industry. In addition, the permission to establish 'umbrella' investment companies for foreign investors may necessitate such attributes of a local partner that not only fit strategic needs of the IJV but also operational requirements of other integrated subunits with a foreign investor's network. Moreover, the deepening transformation of Chinese industry structure may imply that firms in different industries will encounter idiosyncratic pressure from market demand and industrial competition, and face varying governmental policies and institutional support. Joint ventures operating in different industries may demand different criteria in selecting local partners. In other words, it is vital to have a match not only between a foreign company's goals and a local partner's attributes but also between an industry's characteristics and a local firm's characteristics. Furthermore, China may postpone the convertibility of RMB and tighten monetary control for several more years due to the impact of the recent Asian financial crisis. This implies that foreign investors should attach utmost importance to the local firms' ability to earn foreign exchange, cultivate relationships with financial institutions, and maintain strong leverage and liquidity positions.

3.6 Practical Examples: Mini-Cases

Minicase 1: Chevron's Partner Selection

Chevron is one of the world's largest integrated petroleum and chemical companies, with businesses in more than 90 countries and employing about 34,000 people worldwide. Chevron is involved in exploration and production, transportation, refining, retail marketing, chemicals manufacturing and sales. Headquartered in San Francisco, California, Chevron is the third largest producer of natural gas in the United States. In 1997, Chevron's net income increased 25% from the previous year to a total of $3.26 billion. Chevron Overseas Petroleum Inc. has established sites in 23 countries, where it explores for and produces crude oil and natural gas. China is one of four countries with Chevron operations in the Asia/South Pacific Region.

In 1995, Chevron Overseas Petroleum Limited signed a 2-year geophysical agreement with the China National Offshore Oil Corporation (CNOOC) to explore the South China Sea. Because the technical results turned up positive, Chevron negotiated a petroleum agreement with CNOOC. Wang Yan, president of CNOOC, said of the occasion, 'Chevron has commendable technical expertise to use in advancing sustainable development for China. This new agreement is sure to benefit the growing industry base in southern China in an environmentally sensitive way while strengthening the working relationship between our company and one of America's leading energy firms'.

Then in 1996, Chevron acquired exploration interests in two offshore areas in the northern Bohai Gulf, located about 200 miles east of Beijing. Operations in this year produced about 100,000 barrels a day in the Pearl River Delta, making the consortium the largest offshore oil producer in China.

Recently, Chevron Overseas Petroleum Limited signed a production-sharing contract with China National Petroleum Corporation. The contract will allow Chevron to explore for crude oil in a 695 square-mile tract in the Shengli Field Complex in China's Shandong Province.

Chevron's purpose for establishing international joint ventures in China is to gain complementary skills, competencies, or capabilities from local partners that can help it obtain its strategic goals. A local partner will boost the joint venture's adaptability and strategy-environment configuration.

Chevron has evaluated the objectives of each of its local partners and decided their objectives are compatible to its own. In addition, Chevron's management styles and cooperative culture has affected mutual trust and respect with its partners, contributing to successful partnerships. A certain level of risk is also becoming increasingly necessary for joint ventures to be successful. If there is no risk, there is no reason to keep the partnership going. If Chevron were to learn more than its Chinese partner, risks will no longer be in balance and the venture will dissolve, leaving Chevron with a substantial disadvantage.

One of the three criteria for partner selection is the operation-related attribute. The ability of the local partner to acquire, assimilate, integrate, and exploit knowledge and skills from Chevron is crucial. CNOOC seeks technological and innovational skills from Chevron to gain new knowledge relevant to the oil industry. Absorptive capability is more important in capital-or technology-intensive projects, especially in China's local markets.

CNOOC holds over a 51% interest in the Pearl River Delta project, a very attractive incentive to foreign investors like Chevron. CNOOC's market strength in China is key to the venture's financial return, market growth, and commitment to local market expansion.

The next important criterion is organizational size, which contributes to economies of scale, market power, and organizational image. It also helps the foreign investor's ability to overcome entry barriers in the foreign country. The organizational size of a Chinese firm is linked to its strong bargaining power with local authorities and helps lower the cost of financing. Thus CNPC (China National Petroleum Corporation) and

CNOOC's solid reputations help Chevron create better market power in the Asia region.

Finally, financial attributes create profitability, which directly influences the local partner's ability to make capital contributions, fulfill financial commitments, and disperse financial resources to the joint venture. Chevron's global financial standing and partner selection techniques have allowed it to expand profitably into foreign countries. For example, Chevron's 1998 second quarter report shows that its international exploration and production income nearly triples its U.S. net income.

Foreign investors face the challenges of structural reform, weak market structures, poorly specified property rights, and general uncertainty in the foreign country. Fortunately, Chevron does not seem to have encountered these obstacles with the Chinese government in establishing partnerships with CNOOC and CNPC. Chevron has been careful to evaluate market access, government relations, scarcity of resources, and gain culture-specific knowledge.

In conclusion, investors seeking expansion opportunities in China should look for local companies with a superior market position and related product diversification and that are able to maintain an industrial range of experience. Also, profitability, stability, and greater market power are important traits. Chevron Overseas Petroleum Inc.'s success in the Pearl River Delta and Bohai Gulf has depended on its strong relationships with CNOOC and CNPC.

Minicase 2: DuPont's Partner Selection

DuPont is the 15th largest U.S. company and is currently doing business in over 70 countries worldwide. DuPont is committed to improving the quality of life and the vitality of the communities in which it operates. Its slogan is 'Committed to better things for living'. The goal of DuPont is to be the world's most successful chemical company, dedicated to creating high quality, innovative materials.

DuPont has been a major force in the chemical industry worldwide for many years. One of its newer markets is China. DuPont is slowly increasing its presence in China because of the potential for high revenue. DuPont's strategy is to pursue alliances, joint ventures, and acquisitions that offer significant potential for growth, profitability, and strengthened competitive position. All of DuPont's acquisitions are linked to its core businesses.

DuPont has formed joint ventures with various companies in China as well as with foreign companies located in China. The Shanghai Asia Pacific

Chemicals Group, the China Worldbest Development Corporation, the Thai Container Group, and the BASF Corporation are examples of DuPont's partners in China. With careful selection, DuPont has formed ventures with companies that are also focused on strengthening their business in the Asia Pacific region by increasing market share as well as market size.

Another factor that determines DuPont's partner selection is seeking complementary skills. DuPont hopes to merge its marketing, technological, and manufacturing skills with its foreign partners. The China Worldbest Development Corporation is one of the leading chemical companies in the world with strengths in science and the process of innovation. This partnership enabled DuPont to use CWDC's science and innovation expertise along with its own skills in manufacturing, marketing, and technology to produce better products and also gain market share.

Both companies are making a long-term commitment determine the actual success of a joint venture. Du Pont has formed several joint ventures that are contracted for a minimum of 50 years. This shows the amount of commitment made by both parties.

Equity control is important to foreign investors. DuPont maintains more than a 50 percent stake in all of its joint ventures in China. For instance, DuPont has a 90 percent stake in its partnership with CWDC and an 80 percent stake in the joint venture with Shanghai Asia Pacific Chemical Group.

Cooperative culture is dependent on whether or not senior managers are cooperative. Usually, younger senior managers tend to be more cooperative than older ones. DuPont seeks partnerships with companies that have been successful in China for many years. DuPont formed a joint venture with the Shanghai Chemical Holding Company, the largest chemical company in China. Since it has been active in China for many years, it has already developed a culture similar to DuPont's. Another example is DuPont's joint venture with BASF. BASF is the largest foreign investor in the Chinese chemical industry. BASF has also been involved in the Asian market for more than 100 years. This shows that its has adopted a culture which is cooperative with the Chinese market. Both DuPont and BASF have business cultures that are successful in the Chinese market, which means they are compatible with each other. BASF is also a financially capable partner. Today, BASF has capital expenditures in China of almost $700 million. Within the next 15 years, BASF intends to triple its sales in Asia from $3.8 billion in 1995 to more than $10 billion while doubling its market share. BASF possesses technological skills which DuPont may not already have - a large market share, and the type of strategic orientation to which DuPont is attracted. BASF is a prospector company. It has high R&D intensity, makes high investment, is highly innovative and adaptive to the environment, and is a risktaker. These features of its strategic orientation are virtually identical to that of DuPont, again making these two companies very compatible partners.

DuPont chooses partners with experience in China that will improve its products. All of its partners have had considerable industrial and market experience in China, including the Asia Pacific Agricultural Chemical Company, the Shanghai Photomask Precision Company, Thai Container Group, Foshan Hongji Plastic Packaging Materials Company Ltd., CWDC, and BASF. DuPont's partners must also be willing to learn and provide information. An example is the Thai Container Group which not only brings many benefits but also purchases a large amount of supplies from DuPont. DuPont reciprocates by providing valuable information on how to improve its manufacturing processes and the quality of its products.

Minicase 3: Toyota's Partner Selection

The Toyota Motor Corp. has set up a joint venture with Chinese Tianjin Automobile Industrial (TAI) Group Co., Ltd. to make 1.3 liter auto engines. In 1998, production of the small engines that power cars like the Daihatsu Charade began. Output is expected to reach 15,000 units per year. The main partner in this joint venture is the Tianjin Automobile Chassis Parts General Works (TACP), a subsidiary of TAI that up until now has been producing steering parts and propeller shafts for the Charade, Hijet, and other vehicles manufactured by TAI. This is one of four Toyota production ventures in China that will be in operation by the end of 1998. Management at Toyota views local production of engines as a big step toward vehicle production in China. In addition to the engine plant, Toyota has invested in Chinese ventures to produce constant-velocity joints, steering components, and forged parts. Previous investment in parts companies in Tianjin are the Tianjin Toyota Forging Co., Ltd., Tianjin Jinfeng Auto Parts Co., Ltd. and Tianjin Fengjin Auto Parts Co., Ltd.

Tianjin Jinfeng Auto Parts Co., Ltd. was established in July 1997 with 104 million yuan capital and 1,130 employees. It produces steering parts and propeller shafts. Tianjin Fengin Auto Parts Co., Ltd. was established in December 1995 with 230 million yuan capital and 200 employees. It produces constant-velocity universal joints. Tianjin Toyota Motor Engine Co., Ltd. was established in May 1996 with US$248 million capital and 1,500 employees. It produces 1-3 liter engines. Tianjin Toyota Forging Co.,

Ltd. was established in February 1997 with 245 million yuan capital and 50 employees. It produces forged parts.

Toyota Motor Corporation's total investment in these four companies amounts to about 1.5 billion yuan. Moreover, with the recent establishment of Tianjin Asian Automobile Parts Co., Ltd. on July 14, companies in the Toyota Group and related parts makers will have a combined 10 joint ventures or technical assistance projects in the Tianjin area.

Toyota selected Tianjin Automobile Industrial as its joint venture partner because TAI is a large-scale, state-owned automobile manufacturer. It is an economic entity performing the functions of manufacturing, supplying, sale, scientific research, and after-sale service. Also, TAI has an established history and strong background in the automobile industry in China. It has a good reputation and high credibility in the market. Its long market experience implies that it has already developed a good business network. Moreover, TMC can utilize its existing distribution channels, product image, industrial experience, and production facilities. In addition, since China has a stronger relationship-oriented culture compared to industrialized market economies, TMC's business activities can be greatly facilitated by using its local partners' connections in the domestic business scene and good relations with influential persons. TAI can help TMC develop a better relationship with the government, gain access to scarce production factors, increase administrative efficiency, and reduce financial and operational risks from either related or unrelated product diversification.

TMC will also incorporate the Toyota Motor Technical Center (China) Co., Ltd. as a Chinese base for jointly developing vehicles. The Toyota Motor Technical Center is a strategic addition to Toyota's global network of technical centers. The new company resulted from incorporating and expanding Toyota's existing technical center in Tianjian. It will work closely with Toyota's local partners in developing parts and vehicles to be produced in China.

President Okuda commented that Toyota's operations in China could be likened to the triple jump in sports. There was an 'approach run' from the mid-1980s to the early 1990s, when TMC supplied technology to Shenyang Jimbei Passenger Vehicle Manufacturing Co., Ltd., set up the Toyota-Golden Cup Technician Training Center of China Automobile Industry, established the Toyota Driver Training School of the Shouqi Group, and conducted joint research with national organizations. The first jump phase, or the 'hop', lasted from the early 1990s to the present day and corresponded to preparations for the parts production business. Today, it has entered the second, 'step' phase by starting Tianjin Toyota Motor Engine

(TTME) production and establishing the new technical center. Okuda expressed Toyota's hope for the Chinese venture by saying that it wants to continue this progress by moving to the final 'jump' phase as soon as possible. Specifically, it will continue efforts to obtain approval for jointly developing small passenger cars to be produced in Tianjin. It will also do its best to continue developing its business and contributing to China's social and economical growth.

With the goal of becoming an engine plant with internationally competitive, state-of-the-art facilities, TTME has been improving its technology since its May 1996 founding. The company has installed the latest computer-controlled machine tools, including numerically controlled and ultra-high-speed units in all major processes such as machining cylinders, camshafts, and crankshafts. Existing facilities have been improved in order to integrate and effectively apply production know-how for Toyota Type A engines. In software, TTME has introduced the world-acclaimed Toyota Production System for quality, production, and plant management applications. In addition, the company sent more than 120 core production employees to Japan for training. On their return, training results were disseminated within the production group in order to raise TTME's overall technological level; trainees continue to receive ongoing support from Toyota training resources in Japan. Meanwhile, TTME has implemented QC circles as well as an employee suggestion system. TTME also plans to introduce an employee skill certification process, as well as an integrated education program targeted to newcomers, experienced employees, and middle management levels.

Minicase 4: NEC's Partner Selection

NEC is a Japanese corporation recognized as a worldwide leader in high technology. NEC offers a full spectrum of products and systems, including semiconductors, electronic devices, telecommunications, computer peripherals, imaging, and computers. NEC is poised to play a vital role in the multimedia age.

Since 1972, NEC has supplied China with telecommunications systems, computers, and electronic devices. It began direct investment in China in 1989 through a joint venture strategy. NEC's total investment so far is about 53 billion yen and it employs 2,300 staff members. This investment ranks NEC among the largest Japanese companies doing business in China. NEC now has twelve joint venture companies in China. It owns more than 50 percent shares in seven of its joint ventures. Also, NEC has a wholly-owned subsidiary called 'NEC (China) Co., Ltd.' which serves as the strategic, umbrella center for NEC's business in China, invests in newly established subsidiaries, and increases the capital of existing joint venture companies.

NEC's twelve joint venture companies in China have been set up in Tianjin, Beijing, Wuhan, Huizhou, Benxi, Shanghai, and Guilin. Their major businesses include installation and maintenance of switches, and production and marketing of semiconductors, public switching systems, fiber optic transmission systems, mobile phones, pagers, PBX equipment, PCs, peripherals, microwave radio communications systems, and digital microwave communications systems.

NEC's most recent joint venture is the Beijing Hua Hong NEC IC Design Co., Ltd., which was launched with Beijing Hua Hong Integrated Circuit Design Co., Ltd. in March 1998. It was set up to provide support infrastructure for a new chip fabrication plant. It is the second joint venture between NEC and Hua Hong. NEC only contributed 28.6% of equity in the first joint venture with Hua Hong, the Shanghai Hua Hong NEC, which was set up in July, 1997 to make semiconductor devices. NEC holds a 60% share in its second joint venture. Its overall investment in Beijing Hua Hong NEC will amount to US$30 million, while capitalization will amount to US$20 million, with 41% contributed by the NEC Corporation in Japan, 10% from NEC (China) Co., Ltd., and 9% from Shougang NEC. The total share of the NEC group is thus 60%, while the remaining 40% comes from Chinese partner, Beijing Hua Hong Integrated Circuit Design Co., Ltd.. Shougang NEC was set up in late 1991 by NEC and Shougang Electronics to produce and market semiconductors. NEC holds a 51% share in the venture. NEC dominates this joint venture since it holds more than half of the share. Since NEC has greater degree of equity, it has greater control over the company so it can protect itself. However, it may mean greater risks and commitment to be faced later on.

The Beijing Hua Hong Integrated Circuit Design Co., Ltd. was set up in February, 1998, capitalized at 140 million RMB. It has 45 employees. It is also a joint venture company between Shanghai Hua Hong Electronics and Beijing Electronic Information Industry (Group) Co., Ltd. Shanghai Hua Hong contributes 85.7% of equity, while Beijing Electronic Information Industry contributes 14.3% of shares.

Beijing Hua Hong NEC is due to be established in June, 1998 and begin operations in January 1999. Overall investment in the company will be $30 million. It will have approximately 120 employees by 1999 and 260 employees by 2001. The venture will design microcomputers, applications specific ICs, IC cards, and other semiconductor products for use in applications such as digital video and still cameras, consumer electronics and mobile communications equipment. Seeking to further develop the market in China, the company will also aim to develop System On a Chip (SOC) devices that combine the functions of several semiconductors into one chip. The new joint venture company strengthens NEC's commitment to its participation in the Chinese Government's '909 Project' aimed at promoting development of the semiconductor industry as a key part of the nation's ninth 5-year economic plan. NEC's joint venture partner is closely linked with the Chinese Ministry of Electronics Industry. Accordingly, NEC could benefit from favorable *guanxi* between Hua Hong and the Chinese Ministry of Electronics.

Beijing Hua Hong and NEC have compatible goals, as stated in their agreement. Moreover, Beijing Hua Hong has its own market power and a strong background which are useful to NEC. As Beijing Hua Hong is a local company, it already has good market distribution, market knowledge, and supplier relations. NEC can take advantage of these complementary skills. In addition, NEC and Beijing Hua Hong are sharing development and operating costs and risks.

Beijing Hua Hong also has a wide range of electronics businesses in China and its own manufacturing facilities and offices in some cities. Not only does Hua Hong have a good relationship with the Chinese government, it also has good strategic attributes such as market competence, technological skills, accumulated industrial experience, corporate image, and market power. Hua Hong's good reputation and high credibility in the Chinese market are valuable to NEC.

With the addition of Beijing Hua Hong NEC to the NEC Group, NEC will offer more complete products to better serve its customers. From design and manufacturing to sales and service, it will have the ability to support significant development in China's industry. Furthermore, NEC believes that it will double its semiconductor manufacturing capability in China within a few years.

Minicase 5: 3Com's Partner Selection

The 3Com Corporation is the world's largest organization dealing with local area network (LAN) and wide area network (WAN) based infrastructures, with over 100 million network connections. 3Com stands for Computer, Communication, and Compatibility, words which basically sum up 3Com's business. Its mission is to bring information and communications to all people anytime, anywhere.

3Com has been doing business for a number of years in China. It has managed to gain a dominant 31% market share for its networking devices, beating out its nearest competitors, Cisco Systems, Inc. and Bay Networks, Inc. 3Com's largest leap into the Chinese networking and telecommunications market occurred just recently, in July 1998, when it made public that it would invest over $100 million U.S. dollars in China over the next two years.

3Com has a great reputation as an outstanding partner, so it has its pick of thousands of prospective partners in China. 3Com must evaluate each company's capability in creating top-quality products, complementary skills, compatibility in terms of goals, commitment to joint ventures, and cooperative culture at both the corporate and national levels. 3Com's recent joint ventures with three Chinese companies in summer 1998 illustrates this choice-making process. The object of these joint ventures is to help China expand and improve its networking infrastructure. The three companies are Beijing Kuanguang Telecommunications, Beijing Guochuang Information Technology, and Beijing Yuguangtong Science and Technology Development Center.

All three companies have superior local marketing competence and want to increase the level of technology in China, making it easier for 3Com to gain a market advantage over Cisco and Bay Networks. Each local company is a leader in systems integration and networking providers, but specializes in different areas. Beijing Kuanguang Telecommunications specializes in asynchronous transfer mode (ATM) switch technology, Beijing Guochuang Information Technology works directly with one of the leading Internet Service Providers in China, and the Yuguangtong Science and Technology Development Center specializes in systems integration. With these partnerships, 3Com's already impressive organizational image and product reputation can only grow greater.

Since each of the three Chinese companies is a market leader in a different aspect of the computer industry, putting all four companies together to form one joint venture company will provide the new company with the expertise to greatly increase China's network infrastructure. 3Com will provide new technology and consult the other companies. The three other companies will control the actual integration of the infrastructure systems. Although none of the companies specialize in the networking industry, their skills complement 3Com's networking superiority.

3Com's overall commitment to this new joint venture is most evident in the amount it has planned to invest. Of 3Com's $100 million dollar total planned investment in China, several million dollars will be invested on this infrastructure project alone. 3Com's total investment is significant because in 1997 its total sales was only about $150 million dollars.

Another important aspect that should not be overlooked is whether the corporate and national cultures of these Chinese companies are cooperative with 3Com's culture. U.S. companies such as 3Com should understand the cultural differences existing in foreign countries. In China, it is important to have a good relationship with the government, as well as with leading local companies. This will lead to foreign products becoming more desirable to the Chinese people because they will feel assured that the company and its products are of good quality. 3Com has built good relationships with both the Chinese government and local companies by understanding that it takes time for good faith and trust to be realized. In fact, Eric Benhamou, CEO of 3Com, met with Chinese Vice Premier Wu Bangguo and the Deputy Minister of the Ministry or Information Industry, Zhou Deqiang. At this meeting, 3Com made investment plans attempting to open manufacturing facilities in China, either with this joint venture or as a subsidiary of it. None of 3Com's closest competitors in China have manufacturing facilities so far.

Minicase 6: CAI's Partner Selection

As China opens up and makes its cheap workforce available to MNCs in exchange for the transfer of knowledge and monetary funds, such big name companies as AT&T, Motorola, Dell Computer, Hewlett-Packard, IBM, Ford Motor Company, General Electric, Phillip Electronics, and General Motors have set up business there. The one thing all of these companies have in common is that they all use electronic components in manufacturing their products. They are all experiencing difficulties, however, in acquiring quality materials with which to build their components.

A joint venture has been set up to address this problem. Partners include Cal-Aurum Industries (CAI), the Electronic Stamping Corporation (ESC), and Ningbo Radio Specialty Equipment Plant. The new company is named NBESCAL Electronics Co. Ltd. It will be an electronic components service and manufacturing facility in Ningbo, China, about 200 miles south of Shanghai. Its business function is to provide the electronics components manufacturers, both Chinese and foreign owned, with metal stamped products and electroplating services. These products are used in a wide variety of electronic products such as TVs, VCRs, computers, printers, and automobiles.

Many manufacturers are experiencing difficulties with freight costs and delays brought on by the lack of infrastructure and uncooperative customs authorities. Ningbo is a major seaport and has the Zhungqiao Airport and a major railway network. These transport facilities help with the distribution of goods and materials. Ningbo is also located within manageable proximity of many of NBESCAL's customers in Xiamen, Shanghai, and Shenzhen. By building a local factory to manufacture electronics components, along with stamped and plated leadframe materials, NBESCAL has created a niche market for itself. For example, one of its customers located in Xiamen, 400 miles south of Ningbo. This customer has an annual production volume requirement of 2 billion leadframes which equates to $1.5 million in sales for just that one component.

This joint venture did not happen over night. The process was started in 1984 by Mr. Hang Up Moon but a contract was not signed until 1995. In 1984, Mr. Moon, President of Tridus International, an overseas trading company, established many contacts within the national government in Beijing and Ningbo. He invited a delegation from Ningbo to visit the U.S. to discuss a joint venture with American firms who had the expertise they were looking for. The delegation proposed the joint venture to the CEC, Chinese Electronics Committee, which approved the proposed project. However, the city of Ningbo was unsuccessful in finding a company in their jurisdiction to consummate the joint venture. From 1985 to 1992, Mr. Moon was busy with many projects in China and the U.S., where he purchased the Electronic Stamping Corporation. In March 1995, Guo Fang Sun, Deputy Director of Ningbo Municipal Economic Commission, along with Guo Ming Long, Director of Ningbo Radio Specialty Equipment, visited Mr. Moon and Paul Grinder, President and CEO of Cal-Aurum Industries. The group discussed the possibilities of establishing a joint venture located in the Ningbo Economic Development Zone. They developed a letter of General Agreement to run a feasibility study. The agreement stated that Mr. Guo would build a 50,000 square foot facility, designed by CAI and ESC, and would invest $800,000 cash in return for a 30% ownership position. CAI and ESC would be responsible for supplying equipment for stamping, tool making, plating, waste treatment, and testing and provide technology and employee training. They would also invest $1,850,000 cash in return for a 70% ownership position. In May, 1995, after lengthy negotiations the contract and general provisions were signed and the company officially opened in October, 1996.

Although it took a long time to set up, both Chinese and American parties receive matching benefits from the venture. First, there are substantial risk reductions. The Chinese partner does not have to invest in all the new equipment necessary and in training all its employees. The

American partner overcomes governmental mandates, bureaucracy, and trade barriers and avoids having to build a plant in an unknown country. They also attain economies of scale by using the comparative advantages of each partner to lower costs. Lastly, there is vertical quasi-integration through access of materials, technology, labor, distribution channels, and capital.

The NBESCAL joint venture is a great example of finding a niche or sub-industry within a major industry. Rather than trying to compete with all the different manufacturers in China, the partners found a common bond in tackling a problem that concerned all the companies. Because of the lack of technology in manufacturing and for maintaining the tooling for the stamping process and the chemical make up and processing capabilities for electroplating, NBESCAL has virtually no qualified competitors. It is hoping to expand its capabilities to open new markets for its services by bringing in new equipment not yet used in the Asian market.

Minicase 7: Nokia's Partner Selection

Since the early 1980s, Nokia has established several joint ventures in China to supply mobile phones and mobile and fixed telecommunications networks. One of its first joint ventures was established in 1994 when Nokia partnered with the Hang Xing Machinery Manufacturing Company to form a new entity called Beijing Nokia Hang Xing Telecommunications Systems Ltd., or BNT for short. The equity joint venture produces DX 200 fixed switching systems, mobile switching centers, and base station controllers.

Beijing Nokia Mobile Telecommunications Ltd. was formed in April 1995. This 50/50 joint venture between Nokia and Beijing Telecommunications Equipment Factory 506 manufactures digital cellular telecommunications products, and distributes, markets, and services mobile telephones and network products.

During the same year, another joint venture was established. Nokia and the Cable-Wire Group of Shanghai formed Shanghai Nokia Optical Cables to produce optical cables. Nokia holds a 65% share of equity and the Cable-Wire Group of Shanghai receives 35%.

In addition, Nokia and the Fujian Post and Telecommunications Administration signed an agreement to establish a new joint venture in China. The contract covers technical support, specialized training, and network planning and optimization of large cellular networks.

Recently, Nokia signed an agreement with the Chongqing Telecommunications Bureau and Chongqing PTAC for the establishment of a new joint venture, Chongqing Nokia Telecommunications Ltd. The venture will provide a full range of services and will manufacture and supply products for fixed networks.

In addition to forming partnerships with China's government, Nokia has also formed strategic alliances with foreign distributors. One was with CellStar Corporation, a wholly owned foreign entity with extensive retail experience and distribution networks. It is the world's largest wholesaler and retailer of wireless phones and wireless communications products with worldwide operations. Another strategic alliance was made with Brightpoint Inc., a leading provider of distribution and value-added logistics services to the wireless communications industry. Both corporations were appointed as Nokia's authorized distributors of phones and accessories in China.

Since Nokia has formed many partnerships with Chinese telecommunication companies, this minicase will focus on just one, Nokia's partnership with the Beijing Telecommunication Administration. Nokia and Beijing Telecommunications have goals that complement each other and allow both companies to advance technologically. Beijing Telecommunications wants to expand its GSM network as an important advance in Chinese networks. It also feels that China's networks need to become standardized and unified to better administer the telecommunications market.

Nokia also has high expectations for growth in China's telecommunications market. Nokia wants to deliver infrastructure equipment in order to meet the needs of the telecommunications operators. As previously mentioned, Nokia is the largest supplier of the GSM network. Nokia's partnership with Beijing Telecommunication allows both companies to meet or exceed their goals of expanding and advancing China's telecommunication networks.

The joint venture between Nokia and Beijing Telecommunications is a fifty-fifty partnership. In addition to the joint venture, Nokia has supplied Beijing Telecommunications with millions of dollars worth of GSM networks since 1994. The most recent contract between Nokia and Beijing Telecommunications in December 1997 was worth $70 million. The contract made Beijing Telecommunications' network the largest city-wide GSM network in China, with the amount of subscribers increasing from five 540,000 to 1,115,000. The contract between Nokia and Beijing Telecommunications was also important for Nokia as it significantly increased Nokia's GSM network revenues and helped it set up an important referral site.

Beijing Telecommunications and Nokia have similar corporate cultures. Nokia has four core values. The first is customer satisfaction. To keep customers satisfied with its products, Nokia promptly applies new technologies. Its second core value is respect for the individual. Nokia thinks of its employees as its greatest asset. It shows respect for its employees by using a non-hierarchical structure so information flows in all directions. This allows Nokia to make decisions quickly because the information can go from the CEO straight down to the individual that it affects without any hold up by middle management. The third value is achievement. As previously mentioned, Nokia tries to keep up with technology. It wants to integrate values into its performance management system and encourage employees to focus on internal cooperation. Nokia's final core value is continuous learning. Nokia has training programs for induction, skills, technology, and leadership. Training lasts from four to thirty days a year, with new employees receiving the most.

Like Nokia, Beijing Telecommunications' primary focus is on its customers. It wants its customers to have the best service available. In order for Beijing Telecommunications to accomplish this, the company has trained its employees well. Training includes team leader morality training and post qualification examinations for service personnel. The employees at Beijing Telecommunications have an instrumental role in the success of the company. A career-oriented spirit and desire to complete projects and serve customers enhance their political, cultural, and technical skills. The similarity of cultures at both Nokia and Beijing Telecommunications in terms of focusing on employees and customers will prove an important aspect of joint venture success. Top level managers with similar philosophies will have enhanced relationships.

Another important aspect of partner selection is commitment. Nokia strives for continued leadership in the global telecommunications segment. In 1997, Nokia made a significant advance in the future of wireless networks when it developed a Wideband Code Division Multiple Access (WCDMA) network which allows operators, manufacturers, and users new network systems. Nokia is also dedicated to the emergence of data in all areas of communications. The CEO of Nokia, Jorma Ollila, feels that the "inclusion of Internet Protocol based services into public networks will change the nature of communications, both in fixed networks as well as on the wireless side". For Nokia to maintain its success in the future, it plans to continue improving its competitiveness in its current business, as well as identifying, creating, and entering new opportunities in mobile and fixed communications industries.

Beijing Telecommunications has the same commitment towards technology as Nokia. It wants to use international resources to develop telecommunications capabilities, optimize networks and introduce advanced technology and equipment to China. Beijing Telecommunications is planning on accomplishing this by strengthening services of general interest, maintaining contacts, and promptly developing communications networks in Beijing.

Nokia and Beijing Telecommunications have also demonstrated a commitment to each other. Nokia has signed numerous contracts with Beijing Telecommunications to expand its GSM Network. In fact, Nokia has been an integral part of all of Beijing Telecommunications' expansions since 1994.

Beijing Telecommunications provides about one million people in China with communications capabilities. Its GSM network has become the largest city-wide GSM network in China. Nokia is the world's largest supplier of the GSM 1800 network and one of the two largest suppliers of the GSM 900 network. The ability for Nokia to supply Beijing Telecommunications with the GSM Networks is another reason why this partnership is so successful.

The most important aspect of partner selection is capability. Local partners need technological and innovative skills from their foreign partners. Nokia can provide this by looking at its partner's corporate image, market power, and strategic orientation. In China, it is important to form partnerships with companies that have a good reputation and product image, as perceived by Chinese customers. If a company has these qualities, it also implies a good relationship with the government. Nokia has built a reputation as a leading brand in communications. This is crucial for securing a good position in the telecommunications industry. Ollila states that Nokia is "now the undisputed leader as a preferred brand in mobile communications" in many parts of Asia. Beijing Telecommunications also has a good image in China.

If a company can form partnerships with local companies that have strong market power, then there is a better chance for market expansion. Nokia is the world's largest manufacturer of mobile phones with profits increasing by 85% in the third quarter of 1998. Also, Nokia is the world's largest manufacturer of the GSM network. Beijing Telecommunications has significant market power in the Chinese market.

Nokia has an analyzer orientation. Nokia's partner should therefore be innovative and adaptive but not extremely aggressive or likely to take many risks when the market changes. Beijing Telecommunications fits this orientation very well. Beijing Telecommunications is focused on growth and improvements to a network that is always in place. This is shown by its continuous expansion of the GSM network even though other networks, like the CDMA, might provide superior service.

In closing, Nokia and Beijing Telecommunications are closely aligned in many respects. This correlation is what makes the partnership so successful.

Mini Case 8: BNP and China's Industrial and Commercial Bank

The French based Banque Nationale de Paris (BNP) holds a unique position in Asia by offering the scope of a truly transnational bank in combination with services tailored to meet the needs of regional (local) markets. BNP has offices in Beijing, Shanghai and Guangzhou, and branches in Shenzen and Tianjin. BNP has now embarked upon the first ever Sino-foreign joint venture bank with the Shanghai branch of the Industrial and commercial Bank of China (ICBC). This new Bank is known as the International Bank of Paris and Shanghai. BNP's international expertise and breadth (80 countries) is a natural fit with ICBC's domestic experience and tacit knowledge. Moreover, this joint venture allows BNP to continue to diversify its product and service line outside of its staple trade finance into merchant, corporate and private banking. This allows it to evolve with the changing market environment and better meet the needs of its clientele, while at the same time enlarging its geographic scope.

ICBC brings several operations and task-related attributes to this marriage. Strategically, it offers increased market power, high product complementarity, huge domestic industrial expertise, and a respectable corporate image. In addition, its strategic orientation as a defender/analyzer could potentially provide a great synergistic fit with BNP's prospector orientation. Its huge size would contribute to the joint venture's market power, which would help meet and reduce competitive challenges. BNP's experience in Asia is obviously behind its choice of a partner with extensive local know-how. This will certainly smooth the road and help overcome barriers for BNP in the marketplace and in governmental and regulatory areas, as well as assist in its adaptation to local management and organizational patterns and processes.

Synergy seems to be the key word in this case. This marriage gives BNP greater access to markets, faster entry and payback (a risk reducing factor) due to increased efficiency of products and processes, and a high degree of complementarity of assets. The increased size of the Bank will improve negotiating strength and economies of scope and scale, while reducing risk through both product portfolio and geographical diversification. Further, the marriage will provide BNP with access to labor, brand recognition, and links to ICBC's major clients, in addition to allowing it to draw on a preexisting fixed marketing establishment as well as other vertical quasi-integration factors.

The local partner also brings organizational and cooperational attributes. Their size and leadership position and rank are invaluable here. As stated earlier ICBC's defender/analyzer orientation could be a perfect synergistic fit with BNP's prospector orientation, but it could also become the source of trouble. BNP's extensive experience in Asia and around the globe could, however, mitigate against conflict. BNP has never abandoned an Asian partner and obviously understands the importance of sensitivity to indigenous culture. It would appear that BNP is ready and willing to adapt. This high level of adaptability and commitment is probably just what will make these two very different organizations fit well together.

BNP brings many attractive characteristics or attributes to the joint venture. Strategically, BNP offers a huge absorptive capacity, as it is backed by the French government as well as its own massive asset base. BNP's market power is truly global and its product portfolio universal. This global product portfolio is precisely what ICBC was after in the partnership. More accurately, it was after the technical expertise and knowledge required to manage a portfolio of such international scope and variety.

It is no secret that China is cautiously, moving toward a free market global economy. The value of the explicit and tacit technical knowledge that can be gained through a partnership with a world class player such as BNP cannot be overstated. The pragmatic shift from the strategic orientation of defender to prospector is one clear example; this simply can not be done without a mentor. ICBC sought a huge private world leader with vast international expertise and a history of successful past collaborations. These cooperative and organizational attributes abound for BNP. BNP's ability to meld with its local partners has already been extolled. The value of the experience gained by this world leader over the centuries that it has been engaging in foreign enterprise cannot be overstated.

BNP also brings with it a 'five star–AAA' corporate image, not only around the globe but especially in Asia where image, reliability, track record and reputation are of the utmost importance. BNP further brings enormous cash flow and financial attributes. It is a world leader with solid profitability, asset efficiency and liquidity. This stability in combination with ICBC's financial ranking grants this joint venture image, prestige, credibility, and leverage that any firm would envy.

There should be little doubt about the likelihood of success of this joint venture. The synergies which exist between a huge transnational bank with a broad global network and demonstrated local cognizance, and a local partner with particular expertise in that local market cannot be overestimated. Both partners share the risk reduction gained through product portfolio diversification, dispersion of fixed costs, lower capital investment and quicker payback. Likewise both share in the lower costs of doing business granted by increased economies of scale. BNP will gain local expertise from ICBC, while ICBC will gain international expertise from BNP. This joint venture will block competitive threats for both while co-opting a formidable opponent for BNP. BNP gains much in the way of overcoming any government or trade barriers by partnering with an established local firm. It also gains access to necessary inputs such as labor, permits, distribution networks and channels, and the benefit of brand recognition in a foreign land. Both partners gain access to links and networks with each other's present client base. By pooling complementary resources, learning new business techniques, and gaining market power through synergy and reduction of potential industry overcapacity, both partners are certain to grow from this experience.

References

Beamish, P. W. (1987), Joint ventures in LDCs: Partner selection and performance, *Management International Review*, 27: 23-37.

Beamish, P. W. (1993), The characteristics of joint ventures in the People's Republic of China, *Journal of International Marketing*, 1(2): 29-48.

Brouthers, K. D., Brouthers, L. E. and Wikinson, T. J. (1995), Strategic alliances: Choose your partners, *Long Range Planning*, 28: 18-25.

Buckley, P. J. and Casson, M.C. (1988), The theory of cooperation in international business, In F. Contractor and P. Lorange (eds), *Cooperative strategies in international business*, 31-34, Lexington, Mass.: Lexington Books.

Contractor, F. and P. Lorange (1988), Why Should Firms Cooperate? Strategy and Economic Basis for Cooperative Ventures, In F. Contractor and P. Lorange (eds), *Cooperative Strategies in International Business*, 31-34, Lexington, Mass.: Lexington Books.

Geringer, J. M. (1991), Strategic determinants of partner selection criteria in international joint ventures, *Journal of International Business Studies*, First quarter: 41-62.

Goldenberg, S. (1988), *Hands across the ocean: Managing joint ventures*, Boston: Harvard Business School Press.

Hamel, G. (1991), Competition for competence and inter-partner learning within international strategic alliances, *Strategic Management Journal*, 12 (Special issue): 83-104.

Hamel, G., Doz, Y. L. and Prahalad, C.K. (1989), Collaborate with your competitors-and win, *Harvard Business Review*, 67: 133-139.

Harrigan, K. R. (1985), *Strategies for joint ventures success*, Lexington, MA: Lexington Books.

Killing, J. P. (1983), *Strategies for Joint Venture Success*, New York: Praeger.

Kumar, B. N. (1995), 'Partner-Selection-Criteria and Success of Technology Transfer: A Model Based on Learning Theory Applied to the Case of Indo-German Technical Collaborations', *Management International Review*, 35 (special issue), 65-78.

Li, S., Gao, Y. and Ma, G. (1995), Picking the winners in profitability and productivity, *China Business Review*, July-August: 31-33.

Luo, Y. (1995), Business strategy, market structure, and performance of international joint ventures: The case of joint ventures in China, *Management International Review*, 35: 241-264.

Luo, Y. (1997), Partner selection and venturing success: The case of joint ventures in China, *Organization Science*, 8(6): 660-676.

Luo, Y. (1998), Timing of investment and international expansion performance in China, *Journal of International Business Studies* (in press).

Luo, Y. and Chen, M. (1996), Managerial implications of guanxi-based business strategies, *Journal of International Management*, 2: 293-316.

Miles, R. E. and Snow, C. C. (1978), *Organizational strategy, structure, and process*, New York: McGraw-Hill.

Park, S. H. and Ungson, G. R. (1997), The effect of national culture, organizational complementarity, and economic motivation on joint venture dissolution, *Academy of Management Journal*, 40: 279-307.

Parkhe, A. (1991), Interfirm diversity, organizational learning, and longevity in global strategic alliances, *Journal of International Business Studies*, 22: 579-601.

Schaan, J. L. (1983), *Partner Control and Joint Venture Success: The Case of Mexico*, Unpublished Ph.D. dissertation, University of Western Ontario.

Shenkar, O. (1990), International joint ventures' problems in China: Risks and remedies, *Long Range Planning*, 23: 80-90.

Tallman, S. and O. Shenkar (1994), 'A Managerial Decision Model of International Cooperative Venture Formation', *Journal of International Business Studies*, 25, 91-114.

Wernerfelt, B. (1984), A resource-based view of the firm, *Strategic Management Journal*, 5: 171-180.

Yan, A. and Gray, B. (1994), Bargaining power, management control, and performance in United States-China joint ventures: A comparative case study, *Academy of Management Journal*, 37: 1478-1517.

4 Partner Selection: A Chinese Parent Perspective

Chapter Purpose

This chapter discusses and analyzes what Chinese firms are looking for from foreign partner contributions. It elaborates how Chinese firms should appropriately evaluate foreign firm's critical capabilities and identifies strategic, organizational, and financial attributes that are important to Chinese business satisfaction with the performance of international joint ventures. This chapter presents a conceptual framework on the relationship between dynamics of Chinese firms and their needs in selecting foreign investors. The major findings from a recent study of 122 Chinese firms are introduced and discussed. It shows that a foreign partner's strategic attributes, namely technological capability, foreign market power, and international marketing expertise, and its organizational attributes, including managerial skills and organizational reputation, are positively associated with IJV performance as perceived by Chinese firms. Different from foreign firms in organizational contingencies and institutional constraints, Chinese firms are asymmetrical with foreign firms in terms of strategic needs for IJV formation and partner selection criteria.

4.1 Evaluating a Foreign Investor's Critical Capabilities

Many Chinese firms do not know how to properly evaluate critical capabilities of foreign companies. This section addresses this issue in a general context, that is, to identify such capabilities that are important for regular Chinese companies when they select foreign candidates in a general environment. Critical capabilities can be defined as an MNE's business and organizational competencies as well as various forms of intellectual property such as patents, trademarks, software technology, and other non-patented but exclusive technological products and processes. Economic rents are created when the business, organizational, and technological process skills of a firm are enhanced by or interwoven with key industrial or intellectual property such as brands or patents. Examples of technological capabilities may include design for manufacturing, time to market, patents and intellectual property, low cost manufacturing, quality management, and technology in general. Examples of strategic capabilities include fully exploiting worldwide capabilities, acting on changing globalization drivers, product life cycle management, customer service, speed and flexibility, and making moves against competitors around the world. Financial capabilities may include transfer pricing, capital structure optimization, cash flow management, foreign exchange risk reduction, economic exposure reduction, tax avoidance, and the like. Lastly, examples of organizational capabilities may include developing talent and leadership for innovation and renewal, leveraging global capabilities effectively, partnering and alliance skills, hiring and developing international managers, structuring optimal global performance, nurturing global management talent, transferring excellent practices, stimulating transfer of critical capabilities, international negotiating, contract building, and relationship cultivation. Resource-based view suggests that MNEs make strategic choices based on their ability to exploit firm-specific resources or capabilities in international environments. Firm-specific resources must fulfill the requirements of value, rarity, inimitability, and non-substitutability and be operationalized at the level of the firm.

Technological Capabilities

A recent survey shows that MNE CEOs identify new product development and technology as their companies' most critical capabilities (Conn and Yip, 1997). One important feature of the cross-border network is transfer of product development and design capabilities, in addition to the conventional transfer of production facilities. Capability transfer goes beyond the usual technology transfer. It involves transfer of human capacities that generate dynamic technological changes. In addition, the cross-border network facilitates transfer of procurement and coordination capabilities. Coordination and control of information are carried out within a region in response to a corporate strategy of setting up autonomous regional headquarters or centers. Organizational arrangements are critical to generating dynamic capability. Technological capabilities such as patents or proprietary designs are more difficult to diffuse across national and cultural borders than within a national industry and are greatly affected by differences in supporting industries and demand patterns. Therefore, this type of capability is more likely to yield a sustainable advantage internationally than in a purely domestic context. Sharing technologies is difficult, which suggests that strategies that rely on shared resources, such as mergers, acquisitions, or joint ventures, will not be used. Much of the rationale for such strategies is based on the possible synergies, often technological, that may be achieved by combining the resources of two or more firms. If such synergies are technically incompatible, the incentives to use such arrangements are limited. Therefore, the greater the dependence on home country specific technologies, the more likely that firms will either rely on market (export or licensing) arrangements or expand through wholly-owned greenfield ventures. Export arrangements allow firms to avoid substantial technological makeovers, licenses place development burdens on the licensee, and the wholly-owned greenfield operations permit firms to internally transfer technology that has already been tested.

The process of creating an industrial product involves both technological accumulation and technical change. Technical change involves both (a) the introduction of technology embodied in new products and/or new plants through major investment projects, and (b) incremental adaptation and improvement of existing production capacity. The first involves incorporation of new technology in relatively large lumps through investments in new production facilities. The second incorporates strands of new technology into existing facilities through incremental changes. In order to bring about technical change, technological capability is a significant factor. Technological capability is a resource needed to generate and manage technical change. It comprises knowledge, skills, and experience, and institutional structures and linkages within a firm, between firms, and outside firms. Technical capabilities have to be acquired and accumulated through learning.

There are several forms of technical accumulation that create technological capability: (i) some are derived from trial and error and experience rather than formal R&D; (ii) some are tacit, uncodified and embodied in people or institutions; it is acquired and improved only with experience; (iii) some are centered in firms by learning from operating experience and development of production systems; technological accumulation may be a part-time activity in a smaller firm, under the name of design or production engineering; (iv) some technological accumulation is generated out of the complex interactions of firms, suppliers, and customers; the process of acquiring technological capability involves building various kinds of institutional structures within which firms can interact in creating and improving the technology they use; and (v) technical learning is cumulative; there are cross-country differences regarding technological efficiency; it cannot be changed rapidly, and it has long-term implications for competitiveness and comparative advantage.

Strategic Capabilities

A firm's marketing competencies in distribution channels, promotional skills, knowledge about local business practices, and relationships with major buyers, wholesalers, and relevant governmental authorities are fundamentally important for foreign companies seeking market position and power in the host country. Foreign companies can gain an edge over their competitors in the host country if they have superior relationships within the business community of suppliers, buyers, and distributors. Networking with other players in the business community affects value creation as well as profit margin. The costs of establishing distribution channels or business networks in a host country market are often likely to outweigh the potential benefits. Moreover, establishing such networks can be such a long process that foreign companies may be unable to seize market opportunities or align with contextual changes in a timely fashion. Comparatively, indigenous firms have natural advantages in networking with the local business community. Thus, MNEs need to strive to either establish their own supply and distribution networks in the local context or build up strategic alliances with local firms. Relationships with various government authorities are also critical to gaining a competitive advantage in a foreign country. Governmental regulations concerning market activity, such as antitrust laws, significantly affect the degree of competition among firms. The intense competition of multiple competitors in Japan compared with the stagnation of government supported or owned national champions in Europe provides an example of how national policies influence global competition. The role of political actors, such as the Ministry of International Trade and Industry (MITI), in influencing business to focus on new technologies of national significance has been widely described as critical to the rapid development of Japanese multinationals. A good relationship with host and home country governments usually enhances a firm's market and financial performance.

Because a major objective of international expansion is to preempt market opportunities and business potential overseas, a firm's market power in the global marketplace is a key asset. This power is often represented by the firm's industrial and business background, market position, and established marketing and distribution networks. Market power also enables the firm to influence some industry-wide restrictions on output, increase bargaining power, and offer the advantages of economies of scale. Market power in the global marketplace propels the firm's ability to preempt emerging opportunities in some foreign countries, coordinate vertical integration among geographically dispersed subunits, and increase profit margins from economies of scale, transfer pricing, and reductions of communication, transportation, and transaction costs.

Organizational Capabilities

Organizational capabilities are developed from diverse legal, political, and cultural traditions that create different administrative heritages among firms from different nations. Organizational capabilities include a firm's reporting structure, formal and informal planning systems, controlling and coordinating systems, and informal relations among groups within a firm and among different firms. Organizational resources involve firm-specific routines, that are regular and predictable behavioral patterns rather than specific product skills or knowledge.

The historical development of different routines and systems in firms from different nations is important for understanding why firm-specific invisible resources vary. Even within a culturally similar setting, such resources are generally difficult to substitute or imitate due to the socially complex nature of their development. At the international level, given widely varying firm cultures, organizational resources are particularly insulated. Consequently, these resources are considered to be a major source of sustainable competitive advantages. Organizational resources affect strategic choices concerning the product market and the ability to coordinate globally dispersed operations and use of alliance arrangements.

Broadly, an MNE's human resource system is also part of organizational resources. In many foreign subunits of an MNE, people with different cultural backgrounds, career goals, compensation systems, and other human resource baggage often have to begin working together with little advance preparation. Because of the existence of cultural barriers, the use of a large workforce, and the reliance on local managers, human resource management skills are key to the goal accomplishment of foreign companies. These skills are reflected not only in blending with the cultures and management styles of foreign colleagues, but also in job design, recruitment and staffing, orientation and training, performance appraisal, compensation and benefits, career development, and labor-management relations. Among these attributes, the abilities to surpass cultural barriers, recruit qualified employees, and establish incentive structures are particularly imperative. Building and maintaining a multinational cadre of senior executives and middle managers strongly boosts a firm's competitive edge. International development and rotation of managers will increase their adaptability to the value systems of other cultures. Recruitment, training, and reward systems are parts of the global approach to managing business.

Organizational routines are also a critical aspect of organizational capability since firm capabilities are embedded within their regular ongoing activities. This premise, popularized by the resource-based view of the firm, represents a significant shift from the industrial organization perspective of competitive advantage that regards firm performance as a function of how it is positioned within its industry. Instead, this new perspective views firm performance as a function of how capable firms are at deploying their resources through ongoing routines. Routines are the source of a firm's differential and inimitable capabilities. For MNEs, overseas knowledge leveraged through their routines is an important factor driving up global product development capabilities. With increasing globalization of markets, the capability of developing new products for multiple markets is of growing significance. MNEs leveraging tacit overseas knowledge may gain greater global product development capabilities. Thus, an MNE's organizational capability can derive the regular activities through which it uniquely leverages its knowledge resources. Tacit, as opposed to explicit, knowledge is difficult to codify; it consequently poses significant challenges in trying to transfer it across borders. These challenges make tacit overseas knowledge a unique resource that is difficult to imitate. Not all firms are able to transfer and leverage such knowledge. As a result, those MNEs that effectively leverage this resource are rewarded with greater benefits such as worldwide product development and global coordination abilities.

Organizational learning has become increasingly important to international expansion. It concerns the capacity or processes within an organization which maintain or improve performance based on experience. In the learning process, well-developed core competencies serve as launch points for new products and services. It is also imperative to support continuous improvement in the business's value-added chain. Moreover, firms should be able to fundamentally renew or revitalize themselves over time. As a dynamic, non-linear process, learning includes several stages, namely: knowledge acquisition (the development or creation of skills, insights, and relationships); knowledge sharing (the dissemination of what has been learned); and knowledge utilization (the integration of learning so it is broadly available and can be generalized to new situations). Kogut and Zander (1993) define MNEs as social communities that specialize in the creation and internal dissemination of knowledge. They arise out of their superior efficiency as an organizational vehicle that creates and transfers knowledge across borders. In these social communities, firms use their relational structures and shared coding schemes to enhance the transfer and communication of new skills and capabilities. Learning capabilities serve as efficient mechanisms for the creation and transformation of knowledge into economically rewarding products and services. Such capabilities constitute ownership advantages for the firm, which help mitigate the liabilities of foreignness in international expansion. Further, the capacity to speed the internal transfer of a technological or production capability to new foreign markets is also of fundamental significance in a competitive environment.

Organizational learning is stimulated both by environmental change and internal factors in a complex, iterative manner. Organizational learning cannot be created or eradicated by varying external stimuli. Organizations affect learning processes and outcomes. Strategy plays a proactive role in stimulating the competitive accumulation of learning. MNEs need to have the ability to purposefully adopt structures and strategies that encourage learning. They can proactively seek to influence the environment in which they learn. As complex organizations, MNEs are characterized by a multiplicity of learning processes: each individual, group, and subunit within the network has its own knowledge base and learning capability. Therefore, learning is one of the major activities which needs coordination. Mechanisms used to achieve such coordination play a central role in shaping the organizational learning process and determining its outcome. Of these mechanisms, the structure of the MNE defines the way in which these processes interact and give rise to organizational learning. Although research and development is a major source of organizational learning, the processes and outcomes of learning can be facilitated drastically by other mechanisms such as multi-media, information transfer, and training. Learning occurs throughout the activities of the firm.

Because corporate culture is the language that communicates a company's mission, the ability to transplant that culture from one country to another is critical to the success of an international business. No matter what the type of corporate culture, when business goes global the culture must be translated overseas. It mixes with the host country culture and changes. Those MNEs that are sensitive to local attitudes and customers are bound to be more successful. A firm's ability to transplant cultures across borders is reflected in clear mission and vision statements, supportive human resource management systems, appropriate compensation and recognition structure, and advanced communication networks. In an international setting, attitudes, cognitive functioning, and beliefs are not randomly distributed in the population but tend to vary systematically with demographic variables, especially nationality. Thus, an expected consequence of increased cultural diversity in foreign companies overseas is the presence of different perspectives on problem solving, decision making, and creativity. Organizations wishing to maximize the benefits and minimize the drawbacks of cultural diversity, in terms of group cohesiveness, interpersonal conflict, turnover, and coherent action on major organizational goals, must create multicultural organizations.

Information technology simultaneously drives and facilitates global business. Worldwide networks of computers are inexorably transforming the nature of business even as firms seek to harness this technology to the task of managing that transformation. The winners in this global environment will be firms that can align worldwide information systems with integrated global business strategies. The synergy that develops from a close strategic linkage between information technology and business strategies will be critical to success in highly competitive global markets. The ability to create and utilize information technology to facilitate communications, reporting, and decision making within a globally integrated network will affect the competitive advantages of the firm in the global marketplace. Information technology can drive a firm toward globalization in a number of ways. Using computer and communications technologies, firms can extract information components from tangible products, or substitute knowledge for materials, and then instantly transport the electronically represented information or knowledge throughout the world. Value can be added or an information-based product can be used at the most economically advantageous location. The time delays, high costs, and lack of customer responsiveness associated with transportation, reproduction, and inventory can be reduced or even eliminated.

Financial Capabilities

The ability to execute strategy rapidly across the globe requires financial capability. Financial capability enables the organization to put into place its corporate mission. Today, financial capabilities extend far beyond the traditional tasks of raising and managing funds. Financially capable MNEs tap global markets to get the best possible terms, and seek out windows of opportunity and the right market conditions. Fund deployment involves the financial appraisal of strategic investment opportunities and the control and monitoring of working capital. Financial managers increasingly participate in solving corporate strategic issues. The globalization of competition in product and factor markets and the deregulation and integration of world financial markets are major forces shaping these changes. In such an environment, financial capabilities can add value, in addition to its basic role of evaluating and funding investment opportunities, through the exploitation of pricing distortions in financial markets, reduction of taxes, and mitigation of risks. Reallocating them among different parties can bring diversification benefits, create managerial incentives, and reduce costs of financial distress.

Investment assessment and capital budgeting ability is critical to international expansion. Without this ability, MNEs would be unable to allocate financial resources to global projects in such a way as to get the highest returns. Projects in different countries face not only different business or commercial risks, but also variable political risks. Financial managers need to be able to gauge the total risk of a foreign capital project and to develop appropriate risk-adjusted discount rates to be used in assessing the project. MNEs must develop investment estimates and the net cash flow generated by proposed foreign capital projects. They should also gauge the riskiness of these cash flows, and summarize the cash flow and risk analysis information into a measure of desirability for the project such as the net present value. As a consequence of an increase in the complexity of investment opportunities and the potential for management error in international expansion, the firm's ability to evaluate, analyze, and budget overseas investment opportunities becomes increasingly crucial.

Risk management ability is imperative to international expansion because global operations encounter various levels of exposure, uncertainty, and risk. Risk reduction in the form of hedging and risk sharing largely determines a firm's stability and pattern of growth. During the international expansion process, currency fluctuations can accentuate the volatility of earnings and cash flows. Such volatility can in turn distort management information systems and incentives, hinder access to capital markets, jeopardize the continuity of supplier and customer relationships, and even put the company into bankruptcy. For such reasons, MNEs overly exposed to exchange rates, interest rates, or commodity prices may benefit by dispersing these risks to other firms or investors that have smaller or perhaps even opposite exposures. Under global competition, exchange rate fluctuations affect not only the dollar value of the firm's foreign profits, but also its overall position relative to its global competitors. Managing foreign exchange risks often calls for changes in operating variables such as pricing, output, and sourcing. It may also involve strategic changes such as shifting ownership of assets to other investors, relocating plants, and changing the internal organizational structure to improve the corporate-wide ability to respond to exchange rate shifts. Such strategic and tactical responses to exchange rate shifts will require far greater integration of finance into the once largely separate strategic and operating domains of MNEs. This implies that risk management and other financial capabilities bring financial perspectives to bear on business policies and strategic decisions, thereby enhancing overall success of international expansion.

Hedging exposure has become increasingly complex. This is because economic and operational exposures are more long-term than typical foreign exchange transactions. They arise from movements in real exchange rates (relative prices) as distinguished from nominal exchange rates. Moreover, they are not based on explicit commitments; thus, hedging these exposures may be subject to speculative rather than hedge accounting under FASB No. 52. Short-dated forwards and options do not offset the effect of long-run cumulative exchange rate movements on operating profits. If a firm uses long-dated or forward options, then it will be exposed to differential movements in real and nominal exchange rates. The company should also develop an effective system for hedging foreign exchange exposure and reducing the possible risks from foreign exchange fluctuations. This system should be able to forecast exchange rates, project and track exposure, track hedging options and costs, and implement exposure management policies.

While tax evasion is illegal, tax avoidance or reduction helps maximize net cash flows from geographically dispersed sources. This capability is essential to the prosperity of an MNE during international expansion. Relative to domestic firms, MNEs are generally in a better position to create financial synergies from transfer pricing. While some of these synergies occur through transfer pricing of real inputs and outputs, the pricing of interaffiliate financial transactions also provides great opportunity and flexibility for reducing taxes. Facilities jointly used by multiple subsidiaries on a global scale can also help reduce corporate income taxes. Furthermore, an MNE may reduce taxes through structure interaffiliate commercial and financial dealings as well as hedging the risks of individual subunits through external transactions, so as to minimize the change that any of its corporate components will experience losses on its tax account and, as a result, have to carry forward some of its tax shields. In sum, an environment of increasingly global competition puts MNEs under much greater pressure to match the lowest tax burden obtainable by any firm in the industry while increasing their flexibility in locating and coordinating activities. An MNE's financial ability in tax reduction will make the difference in its net income, cash flow, capital structure, and operational growth.

An MNE's financing and capital structure optimization capabilities are of significance to international expansion because they determine optimum composition of debt and equity that will minimize costs and risks. Such capabilities also affect the firm's liquidity, working capital structure, leverage, and cash positions, all of which influence a firm's financial position and structure. An MNE's capital structure optimization is much more complicated than that of a domestic firm because the former has to make its foreign subsidiaries' capital structure consistent with its parent company's overall capital structure with some modifications based on specific conditions in the markets and specific corporate financial strategies. To make the most of the advantages multinationality confers, financing strategy of the MNE should be global in scope. Sources for an MNE's financing include global equity markets, global debt markets, trade-related financing such as trade finance, project finance, and cross-border leases, local financial markets where a firm has subsidiaries, and the internal financial system of the MNE for unit-to-unit funds transfer. In general, the objective of a global financing strategy is to meet the funds needs of the various global units of the firm at the lowest possible cost, with due regard for the currency and political risk engendered by the financing strategy and with provisions for flexibility in meeting unanticipated financial needs without excessive delay or cost.

An MNE's ability to manage and mediate cash flows within a globally integrated network is a major source for improving its working capital management and financial synergy generation. Moving fund from one subunit to another within the MNE is by no means an easy task because there are many barriers hampering funds movement across borders. More importantly, such movements must be integrated with other financial and operational strategies. Funds move between the parent firm and subsidiaries along the following channels: (i) initial capitalization from the parent may be in the form of capital investment in subsidiary equity or parent loans to the subsidiary; (ii) the subsidiary returns funds to the parent via repayment of loans, return of capital, payment of interest on loans, and payment of dividends; (iii) royalties, licensing fees, and management fees; (iv) leads and lags and movements arising from alteration in the transfer prices on inter-unit transactions; (v) inter-unit loans including direct loans, back-to-back loans, and parallel loans. Governmental restrictions and taxation considerations are two major complicating factors for MNEs in developing a system for global cash management. In this management process, firms should have a high ability to determine an appropriate level of dividend payment by subsidiaries. Among the most important factors include: (i) the relative needs of the subsidiary and parent for funds; (ii) the exchange rate prospects of the local currency; (iii) the effect of the dividend on the firm's global tax bill; and (iv) short- and long-term attitudes of local authorities and legal restrictions on the level of dividend payments.

Overall, financial capabilities play an increasingly strategic role in the evaluation of corporate investment, whether in capital, technology, or product programs, and in the enhancement of financial synergies and cash flow optimization, whether in the form of transfer pricing, lead and lag, taxation reduction, funds movement, or financing. The growing interaction between an MNE's corporate and financial strategy is perhaps most visible in the case of corporate takeovers, restructuring, and strategic alliance formations which have been pervasive in recent years. Many MNEs are now using financial strategies as one of the major instruments balancing global integration and local responsiveness. Financial capabilities are important not merely to the realization of financial strategies but also to the implementation of global corporate strategies and international operational strategies.

4.2 Theory on Chinese Firms

The ever-greater roles played by markets and pecuniary incentives, and the increasing decision-making authority of localities, enterprises, and individuals, have been central elements of China's economic reforms. China may be seen today as on its way to establishing a socialist market economy in which state and collective ownership forms are predominant. It is also well along the path to a radical transformation of property rights, including a *de facto* private agriculture, massive foreign investment, stock markets, and the growth of private enterprise (Naughton, 1995). As in the former Soviet Union and Eastern Europe, economic reform initiatives in China seek to increase productivity by introducing elements of market-oriented policies and institutions into an economy formerly dominated by state planning. China remains in a transformative stage from redistribution to market coordination, which shifts sources of power and privilege to favor direct producers (firms) relative to redistributors (governments). This shift, in general, improves incentives for direct producers, stimulates the growth of private markets, and provides entrepreneurs with an alternate path for socioeconomic mobility. A widely implemented contract obligation system further increases managerial discretion and reduces the bureaucratic costs embedded in hierarchical firms. When the responsibility for output decisions is shifted from the state to the firm, and when firms are allowed to retain more of their profits, managerial autonomy and power in state enterprises are strengthened. Accordingly, their economic rationality and managerial discretion escalate (Guthrie, 1997). Considering the dominance of state (fully owned by the state government) and collective (dominantly owned by a community government in town or district) enterprises in the Chinese economy, as well as in partnerships with foreign businesses, these are the types referred to as 'Chinese firms' in this study.

Despite the progress discussed above, Chinese firms involved in IJVs are still institutionally constrained. They are only quasi-marketized during economic transformation (Nee, 1992), meaning that they are hybrid between hierarchical and market institutions. Property rights ambiguity and the incentive asymmetry between government and management means that these firms are unable to stand alone, operate independently, and isolate themselves from constant governmental hindrance (Groves, Hong, McMillan and Baughton, 1994). Transaction costs become less important to top managers when ambiguous property rights provide them an easy channel to acquire compensation from the state for their operating losses (Boisot and Child, 1988). Although the government seeks to fiscally delink firms from state or local governments, the soft budgeting system remains effective (Walder, 1992). This implies that firms, irrespective of performance, are financially protected in various ways under the umbrella of the national fiscal system (Guthrie, 1997). Hyper-unemployment pressure, in the absence of a well developed social welfare system, makes the central government preoccupied by sociopolitical stability and therefore unable to harden the budget system and eliminate fiscal support. The dual track price system (one market determined and the other centrally planned) for regulated products leads to dependence upon governmental subsidization for Chinese firms. As the state planning prices are drastically lower than those determined by the market, producers cannot generate profit (Boisot and Child, 1988). Since no governmental agency can discern exactly which loss is policy-induced and which is not, losses incurred because of mismanagement are likely to be subsidized. Under this soft budgeting system, managers are not very cost-sensitive.

Under such constraints, increased managerial discretion spurs firm expansion rather than minimization of transaction costs. After suffering from low productivity, poor technology, lack of organizational skills, and isolation from the outside world for over two decades, firms are choosing the IJV as a popular strategic vehicle and effective organizational choice for fulfilling their needs to expand and redress organizational deficiencies. To maximize the value of expansion, Chinese firms look for productive resources and capabilities from foreign partners that can satisfy their strategic needs. Interfirm resource complementarity is important only when they believe that foreign firm contributions will meet their demands. While transaction cost reduction may not be their major rationale for forming IJVs, interpartner learning is a critical motivation. Having been designated or appointed by the upper level government, the political careers of top managers rely upon firm growth in general and market and size expansion in particular (Naughton, 1992). They attach greater importance to maximizing expansion value rather than minimizing transaction cost, through improving organizational deficiencies, strategic weaknesses, and corporate image so that firm expansion flourishes. Chinese managers thus view the IJV as a means by which they acquire foreign technologies and partner knowledge to stimulate their expansion. Because it is difficult, if not impossible, to find other Chinese firms which can provide what they need, they turn to collaborating with foreign firms rather than employing conventional expansion strategies such as acquisitions, mergers, or joint ventures with other local firms.

This behavior is further compounded by the institutional externalities facing Chinese firms. A critical difference in economic reforms between China and the former Soviet Union and Eastern Europe resides in governmental policies which support domestic firms acquiring knowledge from Western businesses. While the former Soviet Union and Eastern European countries did not distinguish institutionally between firms investing in IJVs from other local firms during their economic transitions, the Chinese government has continuously provided preferential treatment such as lower income taxes (or longer tax breaks), favorable financing terms, priority of access to scarce resources and infrastructure, and exemption from value-added taxes to those firms collaborating with foreign companies which bring advanced technology and superior organizational skills to IJVs. These institutional privileges stimulate the efficiency and effectiveness of acquiring and absorbing foreign knowledge for local partners. They also shorten the political distance between firm and state priorities.

Heterogeneous organizational dynamics and different institutional constraints between IJV parties give rise to various rationales underlying venture formation and asymmetric considerations behind partner selection. The criteria for selecting foreign partners by Chinese firms should differ from selecting Chinese partners by foreign companies, as identified in the literature. Luo (1998) proposes that IJV partner attributes can be categorized into three clusters: strategic (operation-related), organizational (cooperation-related), and financial (cash flow-related). These in turn affect strategic fit, organizational fit, and financial fit between foreign and local partners. He further suggests that every category of local partner attribute is important to foreign companies who seek profitability, stability, and sustainability in a dynamic host market. We argue that these three categories may not all be important to Chinese firms, given their different rationales and needs.

Specifically, when Chinese firms are little concerned with transaction costs, the financial attributes of foreign partners become insignificant. This is because the minimization of transaction and production costs is more dependent on financial than other attributes. Financial attributes directly affect cost control, expense reduction, asset allocation, and working capital management, thus impacting transaction cost economies. If partner selection is driven by transaction cost reduction, a partner's financial capabilities can help improve a venture's investment analysis, financing policy, accounting budget, tax avoidance, liquidity control, debt management, and cash flow balance. These attributes become unimportant, however, if a firm is not concerned with minimizing these costs and risks. When firms are motivated to acquire foreign knowledge for expansion, they will naturally attach a higher importance to a foreign investor's strategic and organizational qualifications (Inkpen and Beamish, 1997). Superior strategic attributes committed by a foreign partner can improve a local partner's operational skills and competitive resources, technological and production capabilities, and market power and competitive position. The superior organizational attributes contributed by a foreign company may help spur a local partner's managerial efficiency, organizational legitimacy, and corporate reputation. This suggests that Chinese firms look for strategic or organizational attributes but not financial competency in choosing foreign partners. In the absence of a theoretical or empirical foundation, this argument is raised as a research question to be tested:

> *Do Chinese firms seek strategic and organizational attributes rather than financial attributes in potential foreign partners?*

Market expansion in both domestic and international domains represents the central, predominant element of firm expansion through international cooperation for Chinese firms. This implies that firms aim not merely to learn and acquire foreign technologies but also to obtain and benefit from foreign partner capabilities and resources involved in market development. Market expansion in international territories is of particular importance as Chinese firms investing in IJVs are politically required and financially encouraged to export IJV products to their foreign partner's home or other international markets (Lardy, 1995). At minimum, the export must be sufficient to allow the IJV to balance its foreign exchange expenditure with foreign exchange earnings. The more the firm exports, the greater the benefits in terms of tax reductions or refunds, lower financing costs, and priority of access to scarce resources, as offered by the central or local governments. Institutionally, expanding a firm by extending its market domain to worldwide is preferred to local market expansion by the government. It ensures that state socialism will be able to generate foreign exchange reserves, import strategically vital materials, and implement its export-orientation policy. Under this bounded rationality, Chinese managers will choose appropriate foreign partners based on how well they meet strategic and organizational criteria that stimulate market expansion across borders and are able to upgrade technological or managerial skills.

Importance of Strategic Attributes

Strategic attributes involve operation-related competencies that bolster firm growth and sustain a competitive advantage. If strategic attributes are complementary between partners, they can create operational synergies for partnerships. These synergies may translate into increased financial and market performance of IJVs. From the perspective of Chinese firms, a foreign partner's technological capabilities, foreign market power, and international marketing expertise are important strategic attributes to look for. This is because these attributes make up for deficiencies in Chinese firms that need to be improved through international collaboration. Despite cost advantages, Chinese products have been short on competitiveness in the global marketplace for decades, largely attributable to lack of innovation and technological capabilities (Rawski, 1994). In contrast to foreign companies which often aim at market penetration in China, many Chinese firms are eager to export more to international markets. Thus, a foreign partner's position and power in the home and international markets becomes particularly crucial to its Chinese counterpart. Since Chinese firms lack international presence, experience, and distribution channels, the successes of their export strategies significantly depend on their partners' marketing expertise when dealing with international distribution and promotion. A foreign company that is equipped with these superior attributes is expected to promote IJV performance which is defined in this study as the degree of a Chinese partner's satisfaction with its goal fulfillment behind IJV formation.

Technological Capability

Under the former centrally planned regime, firms did not have to dedicate themselves to research and development because all outputs were marketed within a geographically dispersed but nationally integrated redistributive system controlled by the government (Nee, 1989). When they began to target international markets after they were permitted and encouraged to export, Chinese firms started realistically pursuing technological improvement through ventures with foreign firms, particularly those from industrialized countries, to compensate for their weaknesses in product differentiation and process innovation (Shenkar, 1990). At the organizational level, most Chinese firms do not have a R&D division. At the national level, the technological capability to produce consumer products is low, attributable to the absence of well established commercialization and intellectual property rights systems (Jefferson and Xu, 1991). A foreign partner's advanced technological competence helps improve a Chinese firm's operational weakness and stimulate its product and process innovation in domestic or international markets. Such competence will directly contribute to IJV performance as perceived by a Chinese partner, and indirectly enhance the Chinese partner's technological development. IJV performance as perceived by Chinese firms is thus likely to be a positive function of a foreign partner's technological skills. Therefore, we hypothesize that *a foreign partner's technological capability will be positively associated with a Chinese firm's satisfaction with IJV performance (H1).*

Foreign Market Power

A foreign partner's market power can be defined as its competitive strength and position in its home or international market. Because export businesses have been monopolized by a few state-controlled foreign trade corporations since 1949, most Chinese firms do not have knowledge and experience about foreign markets. The market power of foreign partners in home or international markets becomes a key asset for increasing foreign exchange yields for Chinese firms. Strong power often implies a firm's strong industrial background, superior market position, and well established networks with suppliers and buyers. It also gives the firm an ability to shape market competition and transaction value. Because such power is an organizationally embedded strategic asset, it elevates a foreign firm's bargaining power stemming from its resources on which a Chinese firm depends. As long as this dependence remains, a Chinese firm will behave collaboratively, which is often conducive to IJV performance (Osland and Cavusgil, 1996). When a foreign firm maintains strong market power, it tends to make a strong commitment to export IJV products. This provides the firm with an additional opportunity to enhance joint or private profits and its own bargaining power through leveraging existing competencies. From the view of Chinese firms, high market power of foreign counterparts fulfills their needs and helps increase IJV performance. Therefore, we expect that *a foreign partner's foreign market power will be positively associated with a Chinese firm's satisfaction with IJV performance (H2).*

International Marketing Expertise

A foreign investor's marketing expertise, that is, its ability to distribute, promote, and customize products in its home or international markets is important to Chinese firms. When Chinese firms use IJVs as a platform for creating foreign exchange earnings, the marketing expertise of foreign partners becomes critical. Before establishing IJVs, most Chinese partners did not have any distribution networks or marketing skills necessary for entering the global market. Although they excel in production promotion in China, such knowledge is not transferable across borders, especially between developing and developed nations. Chinese firms must rely on their foreign partners' marketing experience to boost IJV exports. As IJV products made in China are often new to international markets, marketing efforts must be undertaken to substitute for the disadvantage of product newness in a highly competitive environment. The importance of a foreign partner's marketing expertise is further amplified when an IJV's product quality and customer responsiveness are considered. Chinese IJV products are often less competitive in international markets than those made by their major rivals from industrialized countries (Nolan, 1996). They have the liability of foreignness in reaching and satisfying the end-users of their exports. To compete in this context, the marketing expertise equipped by foreign partners is likely to be a determinant of IJV performance as perceived by Chinese companies. This expertise also helps improve marketing effectiveness in the Chinese market. Therefore, we propose that *a foreign partner's international marketing expertise will be positively associated with a Chinese firm's satisfaction with IJV performance (H3).*

Importance of Organizational Attributes

A foreign partner's managerial skills, international experience, and corporate reputation are expected to be fundamental to IJV success as perceived by Chinese firms. This is because these competencies are particularly complementary to the strategic needs of Chinese firms and stimulate improvement of organizational weaknesses. Acquiring organizational competencies from foreign partners and then integrating them with China-specific dynamics has been recognized as the most effective and efficient way to ameliorate low productivity, poor management, and outmoded administration in Chinese businesses (Rawski, 1994; Shenkar and Von Glinow, 1994). Under the former redistribution structure of state socialism, managerial skills had little significance because top managers lacked both the power and incentives to enhance organizational efficiency. This deficiency immensely deters firm growth and business evolution during economic reform (Walder, 1992). Having been isolated from the outside world for decades, Chinese firms engaged in IJVs are critically concerned with their partners' international experience and organizational reputation. These attributes are perceived by Chinese firms as stimulating their own reputations in both domestic and foreign markets. When this is achieved, top managers are much more likely to be politically promoted, which is often their predominant incentive (Groves, et al., 1994).

Managerial Skills

Poor managerial skills have hindered product competitiveness and operational efficiency and been a big headache for both firms and the state for decades (Jefferson, Rawski and Zheng, 1992). A Chinese firm with better organizational and managerial skills tends to be more innovative, productive, and adaptive (Jefferson and Xu, 1991) and grows faster than others (Nolan, 1996). Thus, a foreign investor's contribution of advanced managerial skills is strategically complementary with its Chinese partner's organizational needs and dynamics (Lardy, 1995). This increases interpartner organizational fit, which may in turn generate synergetic rents as perceived by Chinese firms. Managerial skills are reflected not only in human resource management skills, effective organizational structure, active employee participation, and managerial efficiency, but also in blending of cultures and management styles between partners. Thus, a foreign partner's managerial skills also have strong implications for interfirm collaboration and conflict resolution (Khanna, Gulati and Nohira, 1998). This reinforces Chinese business satisfaction with IJV performance. Therefore, we predict that *a foreign partner's managerial skills will be positively associated with a Chinese firm's satisfaction with IJV performance (H4).*

International Experience

International experience includes not only transnational and regional experience but also experience in operations in China and cooperation with Chinese firms. International experience affects the organizational fit between partners in the early stages of collaboration and the changes of fit over time as the venture evolves. A Chinese partner can avail itself of a foreign firm's experience to learn more about international operations as well as business strategies concerning these operations. A foreign party's experience can also add value to an IJV's reputation and product image in both host and international markets. More importantly, accumulated experience and increased familiarity with different national cultures are conducive to overcoming mistrust, attenuating opportunism, and facilitating cooperation. Since the business atmosphere and commercial practices in China vary substantially from those in other countries, a foreign investor with considerable international experience will be seen as culturally knowledgeable and cooperative by a Chinese partner. This in turn facilitates effective communication and mutual trust between partners. Therefore, we postulate that *a foreign partner's international experience will be positively associated with a Chinese firm's satisfaction with IJV performance (H5).*

Organizational Reputation

Organizational reputation can be defined comprehensively as a corporate reputation in the home and host country, international market, and industry. Superior organizational reputation implies a superior product brand, customer loyalty, or corporate image. It is an important intangible asset sustaining competitive advantages and represents both an internal resource and a means to secure external resources. Having long suffered from counterfeiting and inferior products, Chinese consumers tend to be loyal to IJV products which are jointly made by prestigious foreign companies. This reputation represents a critical distinctive competency fostering an IJV's competitive advantage and enhancing a Chinese partner's reputation in the local market. Internationally, a foreign firm's organizational reputation can help promote IJV exports and foreign exchange gains, and stimulate brand image and firm expansion. This reputation is a form of relational or social capital which can add additional value to Chinese firm satisfaction. It escalates trust and fosters relationship building with business community and government agencies both domestically and internationally. Therefore, we propose that *a foreign partner's organizational reputation will be positively associated with a Chinese firm's satisfaction with IJV performance.*

4.3 Research Methods

This section reports methodological issues involved in my recent study on how Chinese firms perceive partner selection for their IJVs. Specifically, this study was designed to test the above hypotheses and find the systematic relationship between foreign partner attributes and Chinese parent satisfaction with IJV performance. These methodological issues include the research background, data collection, and variable measurement.

As the world's largest emerging economy and fastest-growing market, China accounted for almost half of the total FDI in all developing countries and close to 20 percent of the worldwide total in 1997. Transfixed by a vast emerging economy with 1.2 billion consumers, foreign investors have pumped more than $100 billion into China since economic reform efforts were redoubled in the early 1990s. About 70 percent of these investments are in the form of IJVs. Real growth in GDP has averaged 9 percent per year since 1981. By the year 2000, China's consumer market will be larger than the United States or Western Europe. In many ways, China is taking steps toward a market economy, creating tremendous opportunities for foreign businesses. The average growth rate of industrial sales and profits has reached 32 percent and 25 percent, respectively, over the past years. More than 200 million Chinese are expected to have purchasing power in excess of an annual $1,000 by the year 2000. At the same time that finding competent foreign companies is important to Chinese firms, knowing Chinese firms' needs is imperative to ensure payoffs for foreign firms.

A nationwide mail survey of general or deputy general managers representing the Chinese party in Sino-foreign joint ventures was undertaken in 1998. Our sample list was drawn from the *Directory of Foreign-Invested Industrial Enterprises*, compiled by MOFTEC, China, in 1996, and the *Almanac of China's Foreign Economic Relations and Trade* (1993-1996). We sent the questionnaires to 500 randomly selected manufacturing IJVs, each three years or longer in operation. These had all been established by non-private Chinese parents (state or collective-owned). Questionnaires were sent through an independent contractor (a distinguished international business professor in China). The geographical focus was the Yangtze River Delta (Shanghai, Jiangsu, and Zhejiang provinces) and the Pearl River Delta (Guandong and Fujian provinces). These regions are major hosts of foreign investment; they represented 61 percent of the total value of FDI nationwide at the end of 1995. In a pilot test, the preliminary Chinese version of the questionnaire was sent to fourteen senior managers representing Chinese parties in IJVs in Nanjing. They were asked to identify any ambiguities in the terms, concepts, or issues raised. Face-to-face interviews were later conducted. The questionnaire was adjusted based on their comments. After three rounds of reminders, there were 122 complete responses, including 109 equity IJVs and 13 contractual IJVs. Seventy were formed by state firms and 52 by collective enterprises. The foreign sources of investment mainly originated from the U.S., U.K., Japan, Germany, Hong Kong, France, Italy, Australia, and Singapore. The respondents were asked to frame their responses over the most recent three years.

In order to alleviate the possibility of 'politically correct' responses to our survey, we left the respondents unidentified. Previous research has found that when guaranteed anonymity managers in China are more willing and likely to provide accurate information. In order to provide triangulations with some of the mail survey results and between respondents within the same company, twenty senior Chinese managers in IJVs in Nanjing (two from each firm) were interviewed semi-structurally and asked to identify the strength of foreign partner attributes and other questionnaire items right after the questionnaires were collected. The reported results demonstrated a high consistency with their answers on the questionnaires and between the two interviewees from each firm (correlations all at $p<0.0001$).

The possibility of nonresponse bias was checked based on information obtained from the *Directory of Foreign-Invested Industrial Enterprises* and *22,000 Businesses in P.R.C* (published by China International Business Investigation Co. in 1996). From these resources, we were able to compare some firm attributes between responding and non-responding firms, identified from the code number we had stamped on each questionnaire. The mean differences between respondents and non-respondents with respect to the number of employees, length of operations, sales, and net profit were tested using an unpaired *t*-test. The results demonstrated that all *t* statistics were insignificant. In order to check the representativeness of the sample, the mean of the project size of the sample firms was compared with those of the population nationwide, using information obtained from the *China Statistical Yearbook* (1996). The *t*-test results were insignificant, suggesting no significant bias from the population in terms of investment size. In an attempt to check the threat of common method variance, we followed the *post hoc* procedural method suggested by Podsakoff and Organ (1986). In early 1999, we sent the same questionnaires to 29 randomly selected senior managers who had responded to the early round. The correlation analysis of 22 responses exhibited strong consistency in surveyed items between the two different periods (all at $p<0.0001$).

As detailed in the Appendix, each attribute in the strategic, organizational, and financial categories was defined as a multidimensional construct measured by respondent assessments of their foreign partners' actual strength in relevant aspects of that attribute. The Appendix shows the resulting measurement after modification based on the content validity check conducted during our pilot test with fourteen IJV Chinese managers. We did this by asking them to judge the extent to which the relevant dimensions of each attribute reflected the content of that attribute. Those dimensions rated ≤ 2 on a 5-point Likert scale were deleted in the final version of the questionnaire. In addition, the convergent validity of each attribute was examined using a confirmatory factor analysis. The test indicated that standardized factor loadings of all of the observed dimensions measuring every attribute were significant at least at the .05 level. Construct reliability for every attribute ranged from .76 to .93, all exceeding the level of .70 as recommended by Hair, Anderson, Tatham and Black (1992:460). In aggregating the scores of individual dimensions to arrive at attribute scores, we used the standardized factor loadings, found in the confirmatory factor analysis, as weights.

This study defined IJV performance as a multidimensional construct measured by the Chinese informant's assessment of an IJV's fulfillment in six areas: domestic sales, export growth, risk diversification, cost minimization, profitability, and knowledge acquisition. We chose these dimensions because they had been recognized as major strategic goals underlying IJV formation for most firms (Contractor and Lorange, 1988). Since the perceptual importance of each of these dimensions differs between Chinese firms and foreign companies, and probably among Chinese businesses themselves, this construct was measured by the average of these six dimensions, *weighted* by the importance of each dimension as perceived by the same respondent (see Appendix). As far as this importance, the result shows considerably high means of knowledge acquisition and export growth ($\mu \geq 5.86$, st.d≤ 1.17), marginally high mean of domestic sales ($\mu = 3.88$, st.d$=1.26$), and low means of risk diversification ($\mu = 2.24$, st.d$=0.78$), cost minimization ($\mu = 1.93$, st.d$=0.57$), and profitability ($\mu = 2.78$, st.d$=0.74$). These descriptive statistics from the sample firms confirm our early argument concerning Chinese firms' rationales underlying IJV formation. That is, market expansion (particularly foreign market) and knowledge acquisition, rather than minimizing transaction costs/risks or maximizing profits mainly drive them. If knowledge acquisition is a vehicle to accomplish ultimate financial or market performance, it seems to be a critical means for achieving market expansion rather than financial performance. Chinese businesses attach greater value to expanding market internationally than domestically.

In examining the IJV performance predicted by foreign partner attributes, we controlled for relevant factors in the model. First, the industry effect may shape operation outcomes and influence organizational needs.

This variable was measured as the geometric average of the 3-year profit of an industry in which an IJV operated during 1995-1997. The data were obtained from the three-year editions of the *China Statistical Yearbook* compiled and published by the State Statistical Bureau. Second, the type of an IJV (a dummy variable: 1 if equity; 0 otherwise, i.e., contractual) may affect the underlying rationale of IJV formation and partner selection criteria. Third, governmental intervention over IJV formation and operations, measured by the respondent's assessment on a 5-point Likert scale, may impact either the partner selection process or subsequent operations. Lastly, the ownership of Chinese firms (a dummy variable: 1 if state-owned; 0 otherwise, i.e., collective-owned) was included because it may be associated with different incentive structures, which may in turn influence managerial needs that have to be fulfilled by partner attributes.

4.4 Analysis and Results

This section presents the major findings from the analysis of the above survey. Table 4.1 shows the descriptive statistics and Pearson correlation matrix pertaining to all variables involved in this study. Overall, the level of IJV performance and foreign partner attributes as perceived by Chinese firms is moderately above average. Most strategic and organizational attributes are significantly correlated with Chinese business satisfaction at $p<.001$ level, whereas financial attributes are either insignificantly or only moderately correlated with this satisfaction. In order to assess the importance of proposed attributes in relation to Chinese partner satisfaction, we conducted a standardized multiple regression in which various categories of attributes are both individually and collectively tested (Table 4.2). VIF (variance inflation factors) values in Table 4.2 models range from 1.11 to 3.22, which implies the nonexistence of a multicollinearity threat among all predicting variables. A modified Kolmogorov-Smirnov test was performed to validate the assumption of normality of each variable in these models. The results (0.05-0.08, $p>0.10$) confirm the normality of all relevant variables.

As shown in Table 4.2, all strategic attributes possessed by foreign partners (technological capability, foreign market power, and international marketing expertise) are significantly and positively associated with Chinese partner satisfaction at $p<.05$ or lower in both before (model 1) and after controlling for other factors (model 4). Similarly, the two organizational attributes, namely, managerial skills and organizational reputation have a strong and favorable influence on satisfaction from Chinese businesses (models 2 and 4).

Table 4.1 Descriptive Statistics and Pearson Correlation

$N = 122$

Variables	Mean	S.D.	1	2	3	4	5	6	7	8	9	10	11	12	13
1 ICV performance	4.73	1.03													
2 Technological capacity	4.77	1.24	.48***												
3 Market power	4.41	1.19	.56***	.46***											
4 Marketing expertise	4.47	1.06	.45***	.37***	.27***										
5 Managerial skills	4.45	0.96	.41***	.24**	.13	.21*									
6 International experience	3.69	1.02	.19*	.15	.17	.19*	.18*								
7 Organizational reputation	4.87	1.04	.31***	.21*	.18*	.09	.26**	.28***							
8 Cost reduction	4.97	1.12	.16	-.06	-.08	.12	.20*	.11	.13						
9 Capital allocation	4.88	1.13	.21*	.02	.11	.07	.25**	.09	.07	.24**					
10 Asset management	5.13	1.18	.20*	.15	.06	.10	.29***	.12	.13	.30***	.23**				
11 Industry growth	9.24	3.61	.18*	.03	.11	.07	.03	-.08	-.04	.16	.08	.16			
12 Chinese ownership	0.57	0.50	-.15	-.08	-.07	-.13	-.12	-.04	-.09	-.06	-.06	-.21*	-.02		
13 Govt. intervention	5.18	0.75	-.32***	.05	.09	.06	.11	.10	.02	.07	.05	.12	.22*	.20*	
14 ICV form	0.90	0.30	-.01	-.14	-.15	-.09	-.06	-.06	-.08	-.01	-.04	.01	-.03	-.01	-.06

* $p < 0.05$; ** $p < 0.01$; *** $p < 0.001$.

Table 4.2 Foreign Partner Attributes and Chinese Business Satisfaction with ICV Performance: Standardized Multiple Regression (N=122)[#]

	Model 1	Model 2	Model 3	Model 4
Strategic Attributes				
Technological capability	.32***			.31***
Market power	.29**			.16*
Marketing expertise	.28**			.18*
Organizational Attributes				
Managerial skills		.25**		.21*
International experience		.14		.13
Organizational reputation		.22*		.28**
Financial Attributes				
Cost control			.14	.08
Capital allocation			.19	.09
Asset management			.09	.07
Control Variables				
Industry growth	.03	.11	.04	-.03
Chinese ownership	-.05	-.06	-.07	-.15
Govt. intervention	-.26***	-.21**	-.16**	-.27***
ICV form	.13*	.09	.12	-.05
Model F	24.31	20.85	11.33	27.07
$p <$	.001	.001	.01	.001
Adjusted R^2	.56	.38	.17	.69

[#] The entries in the table are the standardized β_s where * $p<.05$; ** $p<.01$; *** $p<.001$.

International experience, nevertheless, is insignificantly related to IJV performance. It suggests that Chinese firms do not highly value this experience in relation to their private payoffs. Such experience may not necessarily be able to help Chinese partners achieve their goal of expansion in the local market, given that Chinese firms are generally more familiar with this market than are foreign partners. Moreover, this experience may not necessarily mirror market power in international markets, which is sought by Chinese firms, because this power depends more on product, process, and managerial innovations in a competitive environment. Foreign partners with little experience but distinctive competitive advantages can also fulfill Chinese firms' needs in generating foreign exchange earnings. The above evidence lends support to our early hypotheses except for H5. As Table 4.2 shows, financial attributes of foreign partners including cost control, capital allocation, and asset management are not important to IJV performance as perceived by Chinese partners (models 3 and 4). When firms are not concerned with minimizing transaction costs and financial risks, partner attributes in financial aspects become insignificant. In this case, no financial synergies and cash flow optimization benefits accrue for both parties and the venture itself. For a truly private business in a competitive environment, the success of long-term firm expansion and growth is in fact influenced by its financial capability of cost reduction, capital allocation, and asset utilization. For state or collective enterprises surrounded by a quasi-protected institutional environment, however, the 'expansion' they are concerned is primarily market-based rather than efficiency-driven, and essentially shortsighted rather than long-run based.

The above results answered our early research question, that is, Chinese firms seek strategic and organizational attributes rather than financial attributes in potential foreign partners. Different categories of attributes are not necessarily homogeneous in terms of the importance in relation to a Chinese partner's satisfaction with IJV performance. Chinese firms perceive foreign partner competence in the strategic and organizational aspects as significantly critical to achieving their goals from IJV formation. Financial attributes are not fundamental factors affecting their satisfaction. As far as the statistically explanatory power is concerned, the strategic category ($R^2=.56$) has a greater impact on IJV performance than the organizational category ($R^2=.38$, see Table 4.2).

Among the control variables, governmental intervention over IJV formation and operations is found to be significantly and negatively related to Chinese partner satisfaction with IJV performance (see Table 4.2). Previous studies agree that host governmental intervention often hampers IJV development from the point of view of foreign businesses (Beamish, 1993). This study shows that, even from the perspective of Chinese firms, such intervention hurts IJV performance. How to use market or fiscal levers in lieu of administrative interference to boost foreign direct investment and monitor subsequent activities seems to be an important lesson for the Chinese government and perhaps those in other transition economies as well. Other control variables including the ownership type of a Chinese firm (state vs. collective) and the form of an IJV (EJV vs. CJV) are insignificantly related to a Chinese firm's satisfaction.

4.5 Discussion and Conclusion

This study explores which attributes of foreign partners importantly affect Chinese business satisfaction with performance of ICVs in China. It diagnoses three categories of firm attributes, namely, strategic, organizational, and financial. The analysis of 122 sample IJVs supports our research question. That is, Chinese firms select foreign partners based upon organizational learning considerations and the need to acquire knowledge from partner firms, rather than transaction cost concerns. It validates a related assumption that strategic (technological capability, market power, and marketing expertise) and organizational (managerial skills and organizational reputation) attributes of foreign firms are strongly associated with Chinese partner satisfaction with ICV performance whereas financial attributes (cost control, capital allocation, and asset management) are not. These strategic and organizational competencies accommodate the organizational needs of Chinese firms and improve the internal deficiencies largely caused by a bureaucratic, cumbersome, centrally planned regime lasted for decades. These findings about Chinese perspectives differ from previous studies which observed the significance of strategic, organizational, and financial attributes of Chinese partners to foreign business satisfaction (e.g., Luo, 1998). Further, needed attributes under strategic or organizational categories are asymmetrical between Chinese and foreign partners. For foreign firms, Chinese partners' organizational form, absorptive capacity, industrial experience, and foreign experience were found to affect IJV performance (Luo, 1997). This study shows that Chinese firms pursue different attributes (e.g., managerial and technological skills, marketing expertise and reputation) and perceive differently the importance of common attributes such as industrial and international experience. This concludes that Chinese firms have idiosyncratic needs from partner contributions and maintain asymmetric rationales behind partner selection and IJV formation. Chinese firms are primarily expansion-driven rather than focused on minimizing transaction costs or maximizing profits.

Asymmetric needs and criteria underlying partner selection between foreign and local firms can be attributed mainly to different organizational dynamics and various environmental contingencies. In contrast with foreign companies, the majority of Chinese partners are either state-owned or collectively-owned. Different ownership structures have variable influences on managerial motivation, agency cost, administrative autonomy, decision power, growth strategy, and strategic orientation. The absence of a powerful market mechanism for both output and production factors dispels external competition and propels internal inertia amongst Chinese firms. The soft budgeting system which financially links the state and firms attenuates organizational incentive, discretion, and the power to operate efficiently and effectively. The dual track price system reinforces governmental control, fosters discriminatory policies toward different firms, and weakens business innovation and adaptation. Under these constraints, Chinese firms commonly lack technological and organizational skills to cope with an increasingly competitive environment both domestically and internationally. Because extending the local market to the international domain and creating foreign exchange earnings are governmentally preferred and institutionally encouraged strategies, Chinese firms need foreign partners' market power, marketing expertise, business experience, and corporate image, all pertinent to international operations, to redress their organizational deficiencies and stimulate goal achievement.

Knowing what local firms need from foreign firms may enrich our understanding of interfirm complementarity dynamics, particularly in terms of which dimensions of knowledge are complementary between foreign firms in the developed world and local businesses in a developing country. Relative to vigorous studies in the literature on interpartner learning from the perspective of foreign firms (e.g., Hamel, 1991), our understanding of this issue from the local firm perspective is inadequate and incomplete. This study shows that Chinese firms attach utmost value to their partners' technological and organizational skills that can spur their goal achievement in firm expansion. Because foreign exchange earnings underlie the major motivations of both the state and firms, local firms are more concerned with market expansion internationally than domestically. This explains why they highly value those attributes that raise product or marketing effectiveness in the international market. This concern may differ critically from the goal of many foreign companies which are pursuing market positions and business expansion within the Chinese market. Some foreign investors do not want to see this backfire in their home yards or other established international markets, which could happen if IJV exports increase competition with parental products in the same market. Resource complementarity rather than goal complementarity enhances the likelihood of IJV success (Osland and Cavusgil, 1996). While resource complementarity boosts joint profitability, goal congruence improves IJV stability (Inkpen and Beamish, 1997). Foreign firms should verify not only whether their capabilities satisfy or fit Chinese business needs, and vice versa, but also if their objectives agree with those of their counterparts, and, if not, whether they can tolerate this.

Knowing the performance implications of foreign partner attributes as perceived by local firms may enable us to identify important sources of resource dependence and bargaining power that foreign businesses can employ to improve their position in skewing negotiation outcomes, controlling venture operations, protecting intellectual property rights, and exploring more benefits from financial and operational synergies. The technological and organizational capabilities contributed by foreign companies are generally markedly superior to those of local firms. Because of limited absorptive capability and a weak infrastructure for technological advancement, Chinese partners hardly become major rivals competing for foreign firms' innovative products after dissolution of IJVs. It is hence advisable for foreign firms to contribute strategic and organizational resources, such as those we found above, to venture operations. This can increase the likelihood of both parties receiving a payoff and foreign firms achieving private rents if they successfully transform their superior resources into greater bargaining power and organizational control.

From both the theoretical and practical view points, the management literature needs to pay more attention to examining Chinese firms, especially their strategic behavior, economic rationales, and business policies. In essence, current studies on Chinese domestic firms remain in the infant phase, lagging behind practice and several other disciplines such as sociology and economics. Just as transaction cost theory cannot necessarily be applied to explaining Chinese firm rationales for partner selection, other theories or paradigms in management may not be generalizable to Chinese firms as well. Now with a half million enterprises in various industrial sectors, Chinese firms are playing an increasingly important part in shaping the world economy. This study suggests that Chinese firms are expansion driven, rather than focused on maximizing returns or minimizing costs. Thus, the key assumptions of an economic perspective may not hold in analyzing these firms. Moreover, the assumption of a complete market mechanism in Western theories apparently does not hold true in China, which undermines the applicability of these theories to this context. The differences of Chinese firms in terms of property rights ownership, organizational forms, institutional protection, and hardness of the fiscal-budget system increase the complexity of applying existing theories to Chinese firm behavior and strategies. The constant changes of the institutional environment and unexpected dynamics of structural transformation additionally heighten this complexity. This study represents only one effort to appreciate this issue from the partner selection perspective. It remains to be seen whether our findings can hold longitudinally as China takes further steps toward a market economy.

References

Beamish, P. W. (1993), 'The characteristics of joint ventures in the People's Republic of China', *Journal of International Marketing*, 1(2): 29-48.

Boisot, M. and J. Child. (1988), 'The iron law of fiefs: Bureaucratic failure and the problem of governance in the Chinese economic reforms', *Administrative Science Quarterly*, 33: 507-527.

Buckley, P. J. and M. C. Casson. (1988), 'The theory of cooperation in international business', In F. Contractor and P. Lorange (eds.), *Cooperative Strategies in International Business*, 31-34, Lexington, Mass.: Lexington Books.

Conn, H. P. and G. S. Yip. (1997), 'Global transfer of critical capabilities', *Business Horizons*, 40(1): 22-32.

Contractor, F. and P. Lorange. (1988), 'Why should firms cooperate? Strategy and economic basis for cooperative ventures', In F. Contractor and P. Lorange (eds.), *Cooperative Strategies in International Business*, 31-34, Lexington, Mass.: Lexington Books.

Groves, T., Y. Hong, J. McMillan and B. Baughton. (1994), 'Autonomy and incentives in Chinese state enterprises', *Quarterly Journal of Economics*, 109(1): 193-209.

Guthrie, D. (1997), 'Between markets and politics: Organizational response to reform in China', *American Journal of Sociology*, 102(5): 1258-1303.

Hair, J. F., R. E. Anderson, R. L. Tatham and W. C. Black. (1992), *Multivariate data analysis with readings*, New York: Macmillan.

Hamel, G. (1991), 'Competition for competence and inter-partner learning within international strategic alliances', *Strategic Management Journal*, 12 (Special issue): 83-104.

Inkpen, A. C. and P. W. Beamish. (1997), 'Knowledge, bargaining power, and the instability of international joint ventures', *Academy of Management Review*, 22: 177-202.

Jefferson, G. H. and W. Xu. (1991), 'The impact of reform on socialist enterprises in transition: Structure, conduct, and performance in Chinese industry', *Journal of Comparative Economics*, 15: 45-64.

Jefferson, G. H., T. G. Rawski and Y. Zheng. (1992), 'Growth, efficiency, and convergence in China's state and collective industry', *Economic Development and Cultural Change*, 40: 239-266.

Kogut, B. and U. Zander. (1993), 'Knowledge of the firm, combinative capabilities, and the replication of technology', *Organization Science*, 3(2): 383-397.

Lardy, N. R. (1995), 'The role of foreign trade and investment in China's economic transformation', *The China Quarterly*, 144: 1065-1082.

Luo, Y. (1997), 'Partner selection and venturing success: The case of joint ventures with firms in the People's Republic of China', *Organization Science*, 8(6): 648-662.

Luo, Y. (1998), 'Joint venture success in China: How should we select a good partner'? *Journal of World Business*, 33(2): 145-166.

Naughton, B. (1992), 'Hierarchy and the bargaining economy: Government and enterprise in the reform process', In Lieberthal, K. G. and D. M. Lampton (eds.), *Bureaucracy, Politics, and Decision Making in Post-Mao China*, 245-279.

Naughton, B. (1995), *Growing out of the plan: Chinese economic reform 1978-1993*, New York, NY: Cambridge University Press.

Nee, V. (1989), 'A theory of market transition: From redistribution to markets in state socialism', *American Sociological Review*, 54: 663-681.

Nee, V. (1992), 'Organizational dynamics of market transition: Hybrid forms, property rights, and mixed economy in China', *Administrative Science Quarterly*, 37: 1-27.

Nolan, P. (1996), 'Large firms and industrial reform in former planned economies: The case of China', *Cambridge Journal of Economics*, 20:1-29.

Osland, G. E. and S. T. Cavusgil. (1996), 'Performance issues in U.S.-China joint ventures', *California Management Review*, 38(2): 156-171.

Peng, M. W. and P. S. Heath. (1996), 'The growth of the firm in planned economies in transition: Institutions, organizations, and strategic choice', *Academy of Management Review*, 21: 492-528.

Podsakoff, P. M. and D. W. Organ. (1986), 'Self-reports in organizational research: Problems and prospects', *Journal of Management*, 12(4): 531-544.

Rawski, T. G. (1994), 'Chinese industrial reform: Accomplishments, prospects, and implications', *American Economic Review*, 84: 271-275.

Shenkar, O. (1990), 'International joint ventures' problems in China: Risks and remedies', *Long Range Planning*, 23(3): 82-90.

Shenkar, O. and M. A. Von Glinow. (1994), 'Paradoxes of organizational theory and research: Using the case of China to illustrate national contingency', *Management Science*, 40(1): 56-71.

Walder, A. G. (1992), 'Property rights and stratification in socialist redistributive economies', *American Sociological Review*, 57: 524-539.

Williamson, O. E. (1985), *The economic institution of capitalism,* New York: Free Press.

Yan, A. and B. Gray. (1994), 'Bargaining power, management control, and performance in United States-China joint ventures: A comparative case study', *Academy of Management Journal*, 37: 1478-1517.

Appendix: Selected Items from the Questionnaire

Part 1: General Information

1. Type of ICV (equity vs. contractual)
2. Major industry and products
3. Ownership of Chinese parent (state vs. collective)
4. Degree of governmental hindrance and intervention over your ICV formation and operation (5-point Likert scale)

Part 2: Strategic Attributes: As a senior manager representing the Chinese party, how do you rate the foreign partner's actual strength in each of the following areas (7-point Likert scale: 1 very weak-7 very strong)?

1. Technological capability:
a. product development and innovation skills
b. process design and innovation skills
c. technological development skills
d. quality control skills
e. transparency of technology transfer

2. Foreign market power:
a. quantity and diversity of customers
b. economy of scale
c. competitiveness in home and int'l markets
d. market share in home and int'l markets
e. ability and efficiency of product differentiation

3. International marketing expertise:
a. distribution channels in home and int'l mkts
b. product promotion skills
c. customer service
d. customer loyalty
e. relationships with home and international distributors, wholesalers or retailers

Part 3: Organizational Attributes: As a senior manager representing the Chinese party, how do you rate the foreign partner's actual strength in each of the following areas (7-point Likert scale: 1 very weak-7 very strong)?

1. Managerial skills:
a. human resource management skills
b. effectiveness of organizational structure
c. level of employee participation in mgt
d. managerial and administrative efficiency
e. blending of cultures and management styles with partners

2. International experience:
a. experience in transnational operations
b. experience in investment and operations in Asia
c. experience in investment and operations in China
d. experience in cooperation with Chinese firms
e. experience in the industry in which the ICV was established

3. Organizational reputation:
a. organizational reputation in the home country
b. organizational reputation in the int'l mkt
c. organizational reputation in the Chinese mkt
d. organizational reputation in the industry
e. organizational reputation in interfirm cooperation

Part 4: Financial Attributes: As a senior manager representing the Chinese party, how do you rate the foreign partner's actual strength in each of the following areas (7-point Likert scale: 1 very weak-7 very strong)?

1. Ability to reduce cost:
a. cost control ability
b. expense reduction
c. tax avoidance ability

2. Ability to allocate and utilize capital:
a. ability to allocate and use working capital
b. financing ability
c. ability to use and control debts

3. Ability to manage assets:
a. ability to manage acc'ts rec. & cash flows
c. ability to manage inventory and fixed assets
d. ability to manage intangible assets

Part 5: Performance: From the perspective of the Chinese party you represent, how do you rate (1) the importance, and (2) your satisfaction with actual fulfillment, of the following aspects of an ICV's performance (7-point Likert scale: 1 very low-7 very high)?
a. domestic sales and local market expansion
b. export growth and foreign market expansion
c. risk diversification
d. cost minimization
d. profitability
e. knowledge acquisition from foreign partner

PART III
MNEs IN CHINA: CASE STUDIES

Introduction to Case Studies

Part III presents ten case studies which offer insights into how some Western MNCs enter and operate in the Chinese market and how they select and collaborate with Chinese partners. These case studies include Atlantic Richfield, Intel, PepsiCo, Xerox, Otis, Kodak, Coca-Cola, Microsoft, Boeing, and KFC. In addition to analyzing both external and internal environments, these case studies illuminate a number of strategic issues such as entry mode, timing of entry, location selection, product diversification, competitive strategy, partner selection, equity arrangement, joint venture management, and operational strategies. All these issues are important decisions and determinants that will affect the evolution and success of international expansion.

At the turn of this century, China is emerging as one of the major players in world economy. Most notably, it becomes the prominent and popular site attracting worldwide MNCs to invest and market. Today, most large MNCs have entered the new stage of operations in China: engaging increasingly complex activities (technology, product, and market) in a multitude of businesses situated in dispersed regions through diverse entry modes and numerous partnerships. These case studies cast some light on investment patterns, entry and cooperative strategies, and operational characteristics of this new generation of MNCs in China. Other companies may be able to draw some lessons and implications from them.

These cases are prepared by myself based on publically available information and solely for the purpose of class discussion rather than to illustrate either effective or ineffective handling of an administrative situation.

Case Study 1: Atlantic Richfield

Executive Summary

The Atlantic Richfield Company (ARCO) began in the United States as an oil refining and marketing company. The company's primary businesses are oil and natural gas. At one time, it diversified into chemicals and coal, but more recently has begun to spin-off or sell these two product divisions. Atlantic Richfield now wants to concentrate on the core business of exploring, producing, refining, and marketing oil and gas. Although Atlantic Richfield is not one of the top oil companies in terms of size or sales, it is a leader in the industry in its use of cutting-edge technology which has enabled it to obtain greater efficiency in draining oil and gas fields.

ARCO originally focused its business in the western states of California, Oregon, Nevada, Washington, and Arizona. It has oil reserves in Alaska, refining facilities in Washington and California, and retail outlets throughout the west coast of the U.S. Besides its domestic operations, Atlantic Richfield now operates in many countries worldwide. Its four main international operations are in Algeria, China, Indonesia, and the United Kingdom. Atlantic Richfield has made significant inroads into the Chinese market by controlling the Yacheng natural field off the coast of Hainan Island. Because of the significance of its international operations, ARCO mixes global and multidomestic strategies. It uses joint ventures as well as strategic alliances when dealing with host country firms. This gives Atlantic Richfield the control it wants while obtaining necessary local knowledge from its local partners.

Mission Statement and Company Introduction

Mission and Goals

ARCO's mission statement details its policies on domestic and international labor relations and the standards it sets for its suppliers. Two main statements govern its international operations in developing countries: its 'Principles of Business Conduct' and 'Standards of Business Conduct for International Operations'. ARCO holds its foreign suppliers to the same strict labor standards of the U.S. Of special concern are the workplace environment, worker health and safety, environmental protection, and discrimination. ARCO has conscientiously addressed the issues of human rights, financial accountability, business ethics, and legal compliance in its business statements.

ARCO's main goals are to maintain superior execution of its core businesses while pursuing new opportunities. In order for ARCO to achieve its goal of becoming a truly global company, it has focused on the core businesses of oil and natural gas refinement and marketing in the United States and key global markets. It has also acquired assets that it believes will enhance and help expand its business worldwide.

Major Business/Core Products

ARCO's major business is in the petroleum industry. The two core business segments that characterize ARCO are resources and products. The resources segment includes exploration, development, production, purchase, and sale of petroleum liquids and natural gas. It has also been involved in coal production, but is currently trying to sell off this part of its resources. The refining, marketing, and transportation of petroleum products make up ARCO's product segment. The sale of intermediate chemicals and specialty products was once included in this segment. In the mid-1990s, ARCO exited the plastics business and sold the ARCO Chemical Company to its spin-off, Lyondell Petrochemical. ARCO has a 49.9 percent stake in Lyondell.

Corporate History/Development

The Atlantic Richfield Company is a merger of two oil companies, the Atlantic Petroleum Storage Company and the Richfield Oil Corporation. The Atlantic Petroleum Storage Company was founded in the mid-1800s in Philadelphia by Charles Lockhart and his partners. It was later sold to John D. Rockefeller's Standard Oil Trust. After three decades of control, Standard was dissolved by federal court, and Atlantic was left to survive on its own. Steadily, it built up its assets of crude oil, pipelines, refineries, and service stations. In 1915, Atlantic opened its first service station in Pittsburgh. During WWI, ARCO's gasoline powered Allied planes. In 1963,

Atlantic acquired a small oil producer in the western states, Hondo Oil and Gas Company. Hondo's owner, Robert O. Anderson, became a member of the Board of Directors and eventually the chairman of Atlantic. Anderson, along with president Thornton F. Bradshaw, was instrumental in the creation and growth of Atlantic Richfield.

The Richfield Oil Corporation was founded in 1905 and quickly became one of the leading gas marketers in the western U.S. Its first service station was in Los Angeles. It faced trouble during the Depression era in the 1930s, but was able to reorganize to become a leading oil company. On January 3, 1966, Atlantic and Richfield merged to become the Atlantic Richfield Company. The two companies blended extensive exploration operations and producing properties. Another significant merger occurred in 1969 between the newly formed ARCO and Sinclair Oil Corporation, which had been founded in 1916 by Harry F. Sinclair. ARCO was Attracted by Sinclair's chemical and refining operations as well as its pipelines.

ARCO's production of crude oil grew significantly following these acquisitions. Its operations were also expanded following the discovery of a large oil reserve in Alaska. This reserve is estimated to contain 13 million barrels of recoverable crude oil. In 1989, ARCO introduced the first environmentally engineered fuel, the EC-1 Regular. This clean-burning reformulated gasoline was credited with reducing the pollution from cars and trucks in Southern California.

In 1972, the company moved its headquarters from New York to Los Angeles in order to focus its main production on the West Coast and Alaska. It also expanded its refining and marketing facilities in the western U.S. Through acquisitions of other companies, ARCO became a complete 'earth resources' company. In 1985, it divested its major operations in the East Coast. The divestiture, valued at $3.2 billion in assets, included all petroleum refining and marketing operations east of the Rocky Mountains and hundreds of oil and gas producing properties. ARCO's operating costs were subsequently reduced by $700 million.

ARCO underwent a second restructuring starting in the early 1990s, when it divided its mainland U.S. oil and gas businesses into four business units: ARCO Permian, ARCO Western Energy, ARCO Long Beach, Inc., and Vastar Resources, Inc. The restructuring caused the elimination of 1,300 jobs and included the sale of the company's Dallas, Texas headquarters.

Major International Markets

Atlantic Richfield has numerous exploration and production operations around the world. The four pillars of its international operations are Algeria, China, Indonesia, and the United Kingdom. ARCO has also started operations in Ecuador, the United Arab Emirates, Brazil, Mozambique, and Zimbabwe.

ARCO established its commercial relations with China in 1978; it became the first foreign company to sign an offshore oil contract with China in 1981. In 1983, ARCO discovered a gas field in the South China Sea, near Hainan Island, known as Yacheng 13. It set up China's first natural gas field production facility there. The gas field required two subsea pipelines, one to Hong Kong and one to nearby Hainan Island. The pipeline to Hong Kong is the second largest in the world, stretching nearly 500 miles. The gas is piped to the Castle Peak Power Company in Hong Kong for refining and processing in order to meet the growing demand for energy in the Asia-Pacific region. The gas piped to Hainan Island is used for power generation and fertilizer plant feed stock. ARCO began selling gas from Yacheng 13 in 1996.

ARCO formed another partnership in 1997 with the China National Offshore Oil Corporation for the development of the Ledong natural gas fields. The two companies had cooperated previously in developing Yacheng 13-1. For the Ledong project, they combined complementary resources to determine the economic viability and possible development of the gas fields.

Besides the Yacheng 13 and Ledong gas fields, ARCO has several other stakes in China. ARCO has concessions in the San Jiao and South Hedong coalbed methane blocks located in northeast China. It also has ties with the Zhenhai Refining and Chemical Company, in which it purchased a 10 percent interest in 1994. In 1996, it purchased convertible bonds that gave it a 20 percent interest. ARCO is also considering several joint projects with Zhenhai.

The ARCO Coal Company and China's Shenhua Group, Inc. formed a partnership in 1996 which illustrates the importance of compatible goals and complementary skills between partners. The partnership had the main objective of evaluating the economic viability of various coal mine/power plant projects in north central China. It was understood that in the future there would be the possibility of cooperation in the development of such projects. Both companies complemented each other. As one of the largest coal companies in the U.S., the ARCO Coal Company provided expertise and resources. It operates surface and underground coal mines in both the U.S. and Australia. The Shenhua Group is in charge of the development and operation of the Shenfu/Dongsheng coal field in Shaanxi and Inner Mongolia provinces. It is also involved with related railways, power plants, Huanhua Seaport, and other auxiliary businesses and projects.

In 1998, ARCO and the China United Coalbed Methane Corporation signed production sharing contract. They will evaluate the commercial potential of three coalbed methane projects in the Shanxi Province. The three projects are known as Sanjiao, Sanjiao Bei, and Shilou. All three cover about 1,930 miles and are located in the Hedong Coal Basin. ARCO has been in the coalbed methane business for more than ten years and has the most efficient project in the San Juan Basin/Four Corners area of the United States. The China United Coalbed Methane Corporation was established by the Ministry of Coal Industry, the Ministry of Geology and Mineral Resources, and the China National Petroleum Corporation. The company's primary objective is to supervise and administer the development of the coalbed methane industry in China.

External and Internal Environment (SWOT)

Atlantic Richfield faces a variety of environmental factors, both internally and externally, that affect how it does business and at what levels it competes. The company's strengths are centered on its use of cutting-edge technology to drain oil fields. Its focus and vision as a company should allow it to remain competitive in the integrated oil industry. Its main weakness is its inability to compete on a global scale with Exxon or Royal Dutch Shell. This weakness is somewhat mitigated by its focus on those regions of the world in which it can be a dominant player. The best opportunities come from Southeast Asia, where developing economies require more of ARCO's products and services. The main threat is from its inability to set the prices on its products.

The various factors affecting ARCO in China are described in greater detail below. The external analysis looks at how the company deals with competition at the industrial and national levels. The development stage of the industry and political, socio-cultural, and economic factors also affect the company. The internal analysis includes an assessment of the company's financial, organizational, technological, and operational capabilities.

External Environment

Industrial Level ARCO is involved in the integrated oil industry. The company locates and develops petrochemical reserves, making oil resources into finished goods or semi-finished commodities. Atlantic Richfield refines natural chemicals and sells them through over 1500 retail outlets in California, Oregon, Nevada, Washington, and Arizona.

ARCO's decision to continue with its core business in China can be analyzed using the Five Forces model. The first force is the threat of potential competitors. ARCO's major competitors worldwide include Exxon, Mobil Corp, Chevron, Texaco, and Shell Oil. The oil industry is considered an oligopoly with the top four companies controlling 58.5 percent of the market as measured by sales. The threat of new entrants is low, however, due to the intensive capital required by the oil industry. ARCO spent over $2.25 billion on exploration and development in 1997 alone. A start-up company must obtain sufficient technology and capital to do efficient explorations. The cutting edge technology needed for detailed research is expensive. Once a potential well is found, site development costs are tremendous. Building oil rigs and pipe systems can run into the billions of dollars.

The second force is supplier bargaining power. In this case there are no real suppliers for component parts for ARCO products. The raw materials for its products come from the earth itself. ARCO itself supplies its downstream industries by refining crude oil into other useful materials. Supplier bargaining power is therefore fairly low. ARCO's main cost is leasing the land from various nations, some of which require joint ventures with local companies or extensive bureaucratic red tape before being cleared to do business. National governments may in this sense be considered suppliers. Since every nation is different, the level of the bargaining power of each is also different. Their bargaining power also depends on the size and quality of their petroleum reserves, their political situation, and the proximity of their reserves to a refinery.

Consumer behavior, level of development in emerging economies, and the weather all affect oil demand, but buyer bargaining power remains weak since the only things that affect oil prices are weather conditions and OPEC policies. Consumers have almost no power in this industry. When OPEC allows production by member nations to exceed demand, the price of oil drops. In 1997, the price of oil was $21.28 per barrel. In the same quarter in 1998, the price had dropped to $14.17 per barrel. When OPEC tightens the oil supply, corporations gain bargaining power, as during the 1973 oil crisis in America.

The threat of substitutes has the potential to be stronger in the future. Coal, hydrostatic power, wood, and nuclear power are potential threats. Luckily, these substitutes are either inefficient (wood), disliked by the public (nuclear) or polluting (coal). The threat of competition from substitute products in the near to intermediate term is therefore minimal. As technology improves, however, nuclear power may be made safer or chemicals may be developed that are perfect substitutes for petroleum and natural gas.

The threat of rivalry is fairly large because natural resources are limited. In this mature industry there is a rush to discover oil fields and be the first to start production. Once a company gains the rights to exploration and production, other companies are prevented from capitalizing on newly discovered oil fields. OPEC countries can present potential problems as the leading oil producers affect global crude oil prices.

National Level In China, the petroleum industry is undergoing rapid growth. In 1995, China produced 149 million tons of oil, the fifth largest production capacity in the world. In 1996, China became a net importer of oil, which was used to fuel industrial growth. Some of the major players in the industry (through joint ventures with China National Petroleum Corp.) are Atlantic Richfield, Exxon, Texaco, Chevron, and Royal Dutch Petroleum. ARCO does not face any direct competition from the other companies since its main focus in China is natural gas. China is currently an exporter of ARCO's products, but will eventually become a major consumer. Being the first entrant will help establish ARCO before this transition takes place.

Perhaps the most important national factor is China's political/legal environment. Recently, the government has been pushing for economic expansion; it has allowed many Western companies to enter China to do business either in the form of joint ventures or strategic alliances. The Chinese government's ninth five year plan (1996-2000) shows planned infrastructure spending of $35-45 billion on oil and gas products and exploration, $35-45 billion on increasing refinery capacity, $30-40 billion on roads, $40-45 billion on rail transportation, and another $15 billion towards developing sea ports and airports. This type of spending bodes well for the exploration and development aspects of the integrated oil business, as well as for refining and marketing. Since ARCO has already set up a $1.13 billion project with the Chinese government, it is uniquely positioned to benefit from future capital expenditures.

From a macroeconomic standpoint, China's projected 7.5 percent GDP growth is very strong, as is typical of an emerging economy with expanding industry. Such growth requires stable sources of energy, the most feasible of which are nonrenewable resources.

A foreign exchange reserve of $140.9 billion puts China in a good position to prevent devaluation of its currency, especially when compared to a mere $20 billion in short term foreign debts. Since one of China's goals is to become a major player in the global economy, devaluation of its currency would be counterproductive. Macroeconomic factors therefore make China an attractive place for ARCO to invest.

The technological level of the country is almost irrelevant for ARCO as it does not take a well-developed infrastructure to prospect for oil and natural gas. The demographic factors will become increasingly favorable as more of China's population becomes affluent. As people attain a higher level of disposable income, they take part in more leisure activities such as travel and become able to afford motorcycles and cars. This means that the consumption of oil and gas will increase, providing a local market for ARCO's products.

Internal Environment

Finances ARCO's financial statements provide an insight into a company that is being effectively restructured to meet the vision of its management and satisfy its shareholders. The company's gross profit margin increased from 13.74 percent in 1995 to 14.57 percent in 1996 to 15.40 percent in 1997. The net profit margin showed a comparable increase over the same time period. The company's return on assets and return on equity also increased over the same period, providing increased total returns on investments for stockholders.

The company's liquidity ratios have dropped, with the current ratio moving from 1.5 in 1995 to 0.8 in 1997. The quick ratio also dropped from 1.26 in 1995 to 0.54 in 1997. Normally this would be a red flag for people looking at the balance sheet, but further analysis shows that the reason for the drop in current assets is due to retirement of expensive high coupon debts. This is reflected in the leverage ratios. Debt to assets dropped from 0.72 in 1995 to 0.66 in 1997, while debt to equity decreased from 2.57 to 1.92.

The activity ratios reflect ARCO's increasing efficiency. Inventory turnover rose from 13.88 in 1995 to 14.55 in 1997. Fixed asset turnover remained virtually the same over these three years. The average collection period dropped from 39 days in 1995 to 31 days in 1997, showing that the company is becoming better able at collecting on its account receivables in a shorter period of time.

From a tax efficiency standpoint, the company has done well. It is keeping its effective tax rate at about 32 percent while raising revenues and net income. The company increased its quarterly dividends of 4 percent to $0.712 in 1997. Its dividend payout ratio is 50 percent, which compares favorably with the industrial range of 35-55 percent. The dividend yield of 3.6 percent is very good considering that the S&P 500's yield is about 1 percent. Overall, the company is committed to shareholder value enhancement, as it reiterated at a recent meeting for security analysts.

Organization The leadership at ARCO has been more focused since Mike Bowlin took over as CEO in 1994. He, along with his management team, turned around a company that seemed dead in the water four years ago. At that time, ARCO was liquidating its businesses and lacked direction or momentum. Bowlin's vision for ARCO includes greater commitment to becoming dominant in specific regions of the world and particular businesses. This direction has led to the return to the core business of the company and the disposing of unneeded operations. The money from the sale of ARCO Chemical will be used to finance acquisition of Union Texas Petroleum. This move will increase the economies of scale from which ARCO can benefit. ARCO is also increasing its reserves in Indonesia, Pakistan, North Africa, Alaska, the United Kingdom, and Venezuela. It should be able to reduce overhead and exploration costs by $85 million after taxes every year.

ARCO may be categorized as a transnational organization. The company is structured around two divisions, resources, which includes exploration and production, and products, which includes refining and marketing. The exploration and production division oversees the development of fields in the United States, United Kingdom, Indonesia, China, Algeria, Tunisia, Dubai, Quatar, and has interests in Kazakhstan and Turkey. This division had net earnings of $1.35 billion in 1997. The exploration of new fields enabled ARCO to replace 164 percent of its production with new reserves. The refining and marketing division turns petroleum liquids into motor fuels and other products at the company's two US refineries, located in Washington and California. This division had net earnings of $325 million in 1997.

Technology From a technological standpoint, ARCO has to be considered an industrial leader. It has traditionally relied on its state-of-the-art technology to prolong the lives of older fields. In its Alaskan operations, the company reduces costs by using amplitude-versus-offset 3D seismic scanning to see medium and small traps. The company also uses geo-steering for designer wells to improve its ability to drain fields at lower cost. It also uses satellite imaging to explore areas where there appear to be large reserves. All of these technologies can be applied to its international operations to increase efficiency overseas.

In 1997, the company spent $120 million on research and development, compared with $106 million in 1996 and $104 million in 1995. New technologies include the Immersive Visualization Environment, in which a viewer wears 3D goggles to 'see' inside hydrocarbon traps whose images are projected onto the floor and walls of a room. This tool will change the way teams choose, evaluate, and develop prospective fields. The technologies that are developed can only improve process innovation.

Operations ARCO's operational efficiency is best seen in the refining and marketing division, where it markets auto fuels in the Western United States. The ARCO gas stations are known to provide the best buying experience for their customers. Customers can purchase gasoline using either cash or credit cards at island cashiers, allowing the customer to avoid lines. The company has a special training program for its customer-contact employees. It also provides 24 hour convenience stores/fast food restaurants at each gas station. Such convenience stores are becoming a larger part of the gasoline business. The prevalence of such dual-purpose businesses grew 12.2 percent nationally in 1997, while traditional convenience stores only grew by 3.2 percent.

In the exploration and production division, most of the natural gas reserves are sold by contract before production begins. The marketing for this division is focused on industrial users in the region in which the products are being produced. Production efficiency is a hallmark of ARCO. The recent acquisition of Union Texas Petroleum and the proximity of its reserves to the company's existing reserves will allow for even greater efficiency in terms of equipment and facilities usage. ARCO's acquisition of UTP was a strategic international move. ARCO already had fields in

Venezuela and Indonesia, but they are not yet ready for production. UTP's fields in the same areas are already productive and come with established business and government contacts. The acquisition will allow ARCO to bring its products to market more immediately.

Corporate-Level Strategy

Geographic Diversification

In deciding on its corporate-level strategies, ARCO considered two issues of diversification. The first concerned geographic diversification. Using Michael Porter's Diamond model, ARCO examined five areas before choosing a location. It analyzed factor conditions, firm strategy, demand conditions, related and support industries, and governmental and industrial FDI policies.

China is estimated to have over 20 billion metric tons of petroleum reserves. Most of China's petroleum reserves are located offshore. This factor help in their exploration because it is much more difficult to obtain permits to search reserves on land. Another factor condition China possesses is a cheap labor source. Using Chinese labor will only cost a fraction in wages of what it would be in the United States.

Second, since ARCO is an internationally integrated petroleum producer, it must travel worldwide looking for petroleum reserves. ARCO was the first foreign company to win rights to explore oil and gas fields off the coast of China. This meant it had no rivals as it sought pockets of natural gas. It was therefore the first to capitalize on these resources. Its strategy as first mover has proved successful.

Before ARCO could drill and extract gas from the field in Yacheng, it needed to make sure its products would be in demand locally. Natural gas is too expensive to liquefy and export. Luckily, demand for natural gas exists in China's growth centers. Eighty percent of China's power generation plants use coal, of which China has a rich reserve. The problem with coal is that it produces a lot of pollution and is expensive to transport. In places like Hong Kong, where there exists a dense population that uses motor vehicles and other polluting machinery, there was a huge demand for clean burning natural gas. Natural gas also has uses in the household to heat homes and as fuel to cook food. As China grows and the population demands more power, pollution producing fuels like coal are going to be substituted with cleaner, environmentally friendlier fuels like natural gas. It is also energy efficient and cheaper to transport than coal. The other alternative, nuclear power, is not a popular choice of the public.

China's related energy industry is looking for cheaper, more energy efficient fuels. The electricity industry is always looking for better fuel, which opens the door to companies like ARCO. Other industries also take an interest in ARCO's products. The chemical industry, for example, uses natural gas to produce fertilizers and other products. The steel industry is also considered a support industry, as steel is used in the construction of gas rigs and pipelines.

The Chinese government is open to joint ventures by foreign companies, provided technology is transferred to China and taxes are paid to the government. ARCO contracted with the China National Offshore Oil Corporation that has been entrusted by the State Planning Commission to do studies on petroleum and natural gas development in China. The CNOOC has a majority 51 percent share in the Yacheng gas venture.

Aside from the Diamond model factors, ARCO also considered macroeconomic factors such as the Asian financial crisis. The weak Asian currencies may actually help ARCO. The money it pays to its workers is usually denominated in the home currency while the petroleum products in the world market bring in dollars. With a strong dollar and weak local currencies, ARCO has the potential to gain even higher profits than expected. It is unable to take advantage of the economic crisis at the Yacheng field because it only serves China's domestic market, but as it continues to find and develop other petroleum fields it may be able to take advantage of the foreign exchange situation.

Product Diversification

The second diversification strategy ARCO had to consider was what industry to focus on in China. The exploration and development of natural gas and petroleum is ARCO's core business segment, but it had to decide whether this was appropriate for the Chinese market. The results of analysis using the five forces model were discussed in detail in the previous section on the external environment at the industrial level. The political/legal environment also influences choice of industry. Since the Chinese government had authorized the China National Offshore Oil Corporation to make natural gas a major source for energy in China, and since this company has a major equity holding in its joint venture with ARCO, ARCO had an easy time breaking into the Chinese market.

Another important factor is the demographic environment. As provinces like Guangdong, Fujian, Jiangsu and Hainan grow, their energy needs also grow, as does the problem of pollution. As noted earlier, natural gas is a clean alternative.

Taking all factors into consideration, the petroleum/natural gas industry is an appropriate choice for ARCO in China.

Business-Level Strategy

The four building blocks of competitive advantage that lead to strategic decisions are quality, customer responsiveness, innovation and efficiency. The first factor is irrelevant to ARCO since it operates in a standardized raw materials industry. All oil goods are equal substitutes. Product differentiation usually occurs only at the level of price competition, which is where ARCO is focusing.

Customer responsiveness also plays only a minor role in ARCO's business level strategy. ARCO is mainly concerned with the delivery process. For the Yacheng field, ARCO constructed a $1.1 billion pipeline connecting its rigs to Hong Kong. Getting the product to where it is wanted is the extent of ARCO's responsiveness.

Innovation, by contrast, is key to the oil game. Cutting edge technologies make it easier for ARCO to determine a project's life span and economic returns. Extensive research helps cut costs and avoid errors. ARCO's innovative exploration and production technologies, such as coiled tubing and multilateral drilling, have made ARCO a pioneer in the industry while contributing to its efficiency and low cost production.

Although market forces determine the prices of products such as natural gas and oil, the Yacheng gas price was negotiated with ARCO's buyer, the Black Point power plant. ARCO had to offer reasonable prices and then depend on efficiency to cut costs and guarantee profits.

ARCO's competitive strength lies in its efficient, innovative techniques. This strength allows ARCO to pursue a low cost focused strategy in China. Its goal has been to target customers close to production sites. These customers are Chinese power plants that are looking for a more efficient fuel. Although ARCO originally went to China in hopes of discovering a petroleum field that could provide exportable products, it has ended up selling domestically. This strategy has worked only because there is sufficient demand in China and ARCO products can be delivered efficiently.

International Entry Strategies

Before any firm decides to sell its products or services beyond its domestic market, it must plan an international strategy, by identifying opportunities and potential incentives in the international marketplace. Although ARCO has been in the petroleum industry for many years and is the seventh largest oil company in the United States, it must continue seeking new opportunities for expansion if it hopes to remain competitive.

Entry Mode Selection

Entry mode selection is an important step in a corporation's international strategy. There are basically five types of entry: exporting, licensing, strategic alliances, acquisitions, and wholly owned subsidiaries. ARCO is mainly involved in strategic alliances, acquisitions, and new wholly owned subsidiaries or greenfield ventures. Entry mode selection depends upon country, industry, firm, and project specific factors. Analysis of these four types of factors helped ARCO choose its various entry modes in China.

Country-specific factors included potential demand for ARCO products and services and China's strict governmental policies. ARCO International Oil and Gas is the division of ARCO in charge of exploring, developing, and producing oil and gas outside the United States. In 1978, high-ranking officials of the Chinese government met with ARCO CEOs to discus China's interest in developing its oil, natural gas, and coal resources effectively and quickly. China needed to cooperate in a joint venture with a firm outside the country that could supply the know-how and services it needed. This obvious demand provided a great opportunity for ARCO. In part because of the government's interest in developing its natural resources, ARCO did not have to deal with as many tough governmental policies and corruption as did other foreign companies attempting to enter China. For this reason, Chinese dubbed ARCO the 'lucky company'. By 1982, the ARCO China subsidiary became the first foreign company to be awarded offshore oil exploration rights.

One industry-specific factor that concerned ARCO was competition. After lengthy discussions with officials from China's Ministry of Foreign

Affairs and other participating departments, ARCO agreed to a contract in which it would finance resource exploration, jointly develop and produce the fields, and then transfer operations to the Chinese in exchange for a share of the profits. ARCO was also required to train a number of Chinese managers who would be able to handle operations after ARCO's withdrawal. ARCO agreed to such broad terms because it gave it first mover advantages including a considerable edge over future competitors.

ARCO had some difficulties with China's tax laws and industrial regulations that had not been set up to handle foreign firms. Laws had to be developed for each specific situation, which made the whole negotiation process much more time-consuming. One difficult rule was that major joint ventures were expected to generate enough hard currency to be self-sustaining. Despite these problems, the first contract between ARCO and China, signed on September 19, 1982, gave ARCO a 70 percent interest in the 2.2 million-acre Yingge Hai block. Sante Fe Minerals was the junior partner, with a 30 percent interest.

ARCO had to determine its firm-specific objectives before any type of planning could be implemented. Its interest in China is primarily for growth opportunities, to increase the size of its potential market as well as achieve a higher rate of return. Another objective is gaining access to China's resources. Originally, ARCO went to China to find oil but initially found other forms of natural resources like gas and coal. The Yacheng 13-1 project has approximately three trillion cubic feet of recoverable reserves and a projected field life of twenty years. There are also ongoing projects in northeast China in San Jiao and South Hedong coalbed methane blocks, and in the Ledong natural gas fields in the South China Sea. China clearly met one of ARCO's objectives.

Other factors it had to consider were firm experience and knowledge. ARCO had no problems in this respect, since it has been in operation since 1966 and has an excellent history of finding and developing natural energy resources. Its experience and technical knowledge increases its chances of successful expansion overseas.

Project-specific factors include project size and partner availability. The most significant project in China is the Yacheng 13-1 gas field, discovered in 1983. It is China's first productive offshore gas field. It cost about $1.1 billion to develop, requiring the construction of two offshore production platforms, as well as onshore receiving facilities. A 480-mile subsea pipeline was also built to transport gas from the site to Hong Kong. It is the world's second longest offshore gas pipeline and the project altogether is the largest energy investment in China. Three firms, the China National Offshore Oil Corporation, ARCO China, Inc., and Kuwait Foreign Petroleum Exploration Company, jointly developed the Yacheng 13-1 project. Partner availability was not, therefore, a major problem for ARCO.

ARCO first entered China in cooperation with the Chinese government through the Chinese National Offshore Oil Corporation by forming a strategic alliance with Santa Fe Minerals. Later, ARCO made acquisitions and then created a new wholly owned subsidiary, ARCO China, Inc., which now has headquarters in Hong Kong. This subsidiary, in turn, has partnered with other companies in some of the largest natural resource development projects in the world.

Entry Timing

ARCO's early entry into China poses many advantages as well as disadvantages. As the first foreign company in its industry to establish a foothold in China, it gained an immediate competitive edge over future rivals. As the first foreign company awarded offshore oil exploration rights, it was also able to preempt resources.

The major disadvantage it faced was a high level of risk due to political uncertainty. ARCO had to comply with many of conflicting rules and requirements. The poor infrastructure in China also posed a threat. Finally, partner selection was constrained; ARCO was required to cooperate with the Chinese National Offshore Oil Corporation.

Location Selection

The existence of resources is one factor in deciding on location. Two fields were discovered in the South China Sea near Hainan Island. Another location determinant is demand. There is a strong demand for the processing of energy in Hainan and on Mainland China. Energy is in such demand because cities like Guangzhou are desperately short of reliable electricity. Factories are sometimes forced to operate only half days. Where ARCO located its projects and built pipelines depended in part on servicing these needs.

There were many other reasons for locating in Hainan. Facilities and support industries already existed for the development of energy. A 60-mile pipeline was built from the Yacheng field to a shore base on the island. The island had several downstream petrochemical facilities. In addition, three large chemical plants are planned by the year 2000 and an oil refinery is also under consideration. Hainan is also both China's largest and most under-performing special economic zone. Foreign investments are encouraged and provided preferential treatment in these zones. The potential of growth in the region was another attraction for ARCO.

International Strategies

Sharing Distribution and Control

As a national protectionist measure, host Chinese firms in partnership with foreign companies generally maintain control and a larger share of the equity distribution in the joint venture. The Yacheng project provides a fairly typical example of the kind of sharing distribution ARCO is involved in China. The China National Offshore Oil Corporation has a 51 percent interest, Kuwait Foreign Petroleum Exploration Company has a 15 percent interest, and ARCO has 34 percent. Although ARCO does not usually have majority equity, it is looking for opportunities to increase its share in most projects. For example, ARCO started with 10 percent interest in Zenhai Refining and Chemical Company in 1994. Then, in late 1996, ARCO purchased convertible bonds that will give them 20 percent interest upon conversion.

China maintains such controls in part to prevent transfer of new technology to other countries. In the early stages of ARCO's involvement in China, it set up operations headquarters in Zhenjiang. None of the work developed there could be taken out of the country, however. This meant that ARCO employees could not process data at the more advanced laboratories in the U.S. China also wanted ARCO to develop projects that would be later turned over to the Chinese and ARCO trained Chinese managers. This further maintained Chinese control over joint ventures.

International Strategy

International operations are essential to ARCO as oil reserves in the U.S. dwindle. Since ARCO conducts business in many foreign countries, it has relied on a transnational strategy, a mixture of global and multidomestic strategies, to meet its goals. This strategy has been adopted for several reasons.

First, ARCO's main products are standardized commodities. Standards are set by the oil industry itself or by governmental regulations, with little deviation amongst industrial competitors. The standardization of oil products combined with ARCO's well-developed experience curve in the oil industry illustrates its global strategies.

ARCO also utilizes multidomestic strategies. Differentiated local markets require ARCO to customize its petroleum products locally. For example, in the United States there are strict environmental regulations banning pollution. California has one of the strictest pollution controls in the world, so ARCO must modify its petroleum products to comply with governmental regulations. On the other hand, China and most of Asia are lax on pollution controls. Although there are environmental laws on the books, they are seldom enforced. This is because economic growth has taken priority over the environment. What this means to ARCO is that it does not have to process its petroleum products as significantly to meet environmental laws in those areas.

Even though ARCO uses both global and multidomestic strategies, its global strategies are more heavily emphasized because of the standardization of the product. Since there are no real substitutes for oil and the world depends on oil, ARCO is able to carry out a global strategy without impairing its international operations.

Business Structure

In line with ARCO's transnational strategy, the company's international business structure is characterized by the global products/divisions model. ARCO's organization was divided into five main divisions; Oil and Gas; Business Development; Refining, Marketing and Transportation; Chemical; and Coal. (The Chemical and Coal divisions are now being sold off or phased out.) One reason for the use of this structure is the nature of the oil product. The basic processes of oil exploration, extraction, and refining are common knowledge in the industry. By organizing its company into products or divisions, ARCO allows each division to focus on its own product area and specific international operations. In this way, the Oil and Gas division can concentrate on exploring new oil fields and create better methods of extracting oil. The Refining, Marketing and Transportation division only has to concentrate on operating efficiently.

The second reason ARCO is organized according to the global product/division model is the competitiveness of the oil industry. As mentioned previously, the oil industry is an oligopoly, with the top few companies controlling the majority of the market. ARCO is considered a large company, but it is not the largest in comparison with competitors such as Exxon and Royal Dutch Shell. In order for ARCO to compete effectively it must integrate its products globally. A global product/division structure allows ARCO to do this.

Operational Strategies

Human Resources Management As mentioned in ARCO's mission statement, the company is greatly concerned with its employees health and safety and the work environment. The company has stated that it will create a positive work environment by fostering mutual respect and freedom from harassment. ARCO has also promised to abide by environmental, health, and safety laws and regulations.

ARCO has consistently hired talented and productive personnel by tapping into the best colleges in the United States. The main recruits hired by ARCO are MBA's, engineers and exploration geoscientists. Knowing that training is an ongoing process, ARCO further educates its new personnel. The company has three development programs for its three different recruits. The Financial Development Program is designed to allow new recruits to directly influence senior management, to gain a valuable, diverse experience base, and to work throughout the global operations of ARCO. Some of the typical assignments given to a recruit are strategic planning, evaluating capital investments, performance analysis, and marketing analysis. Los Angeles, Anchorage, and the Latin American region are typical starting locations.

The Engineering Development Program is mainly designed to give the new engineer work experience in the oil and gas business and establish company-wide and industrial contacts.

All new exploration geoscientists in the Exploration Geoscience Development Program are assigned mentors. Besides a mentor, a new exploration geoscientist works with his or her supervisor and training coordinator to develop a three-year plan in order to learn the exploration process. The exploration geoscientist also attends Exploration School for 3-4 weeks. During that time, the exploration process is taught and a basis of networking within the company and industry is started.

Marketing The ARCO Products Company handles ARCO's marketing activities. This company is responsible for ARCO's petroleum refining, distribution, and refined products marketing. Its major operations are in the Western part of the United States, but it has begun to expand internationally. ARCO is well positioned to expand because of its reputation for high quality products and consistency as well as its commitment to protecting the environment.

Finance ARCO's chief interest in the finance area is risk management. Because of currency fluctuations around the world, ARCO uses a variety of financial instruments to hedge against the effects of interest rate and foreign currency fluctuations. To minimize the effects of commodity price fluctuations, ARCO and its subsidiaries use forward and futures contracts, and swaps and options. To hedge the effects of interest rate and foreign currency fluctuations, ARCO uses derivatives, which are placed in major financial institutions. Only senior management is allowed to authorize hedging activities; policy controls are used to limit the dollar amount of any particular financial strategy.

Conclusions

ARCO's involvement in joint ventures, strategic alliances, and wholly owned subsidiaries has seemed beneficial to the company. The company's transnational strategy has worked well in the past, but as the world's oil reserves begin to decrease competition among the existing oil companies will become fierce. In order to survive, oil companies are likely to merge. When Atlantic and Richfield merged in 1966, they did so because Atlantic felt that it needed a partner to increase its reserves of oil and gas, which Richfield could provide. As oil companies compete in emerging markets there will be even more of a tendency for larger oil companies to acquire smaller companies. Currently, countries such as China do not allow foreign oil companies to have majority control over joint ventures. But as the cost of starting up and operating oil or gas facilities increases, one of two options will occur. Either the Chinese government will allow foreign partners to acquire joint ventures as a subsidiaries or it will force foreign firms to divest all interest in joint ventures after the local firm has obtained the knowledge needed to operate oil or gas facilities.

Meanwhile, increased competition will spur oil companies to enter emerging markets like China. Although there are both advantages and disadvantages of entering a market early in the game, the advantages outweigh the disadvantages. As an early mover into an emerging market, the infrastructure of a country is usually inadequate. The cost of upgrading the infrastructure is considerable. But in the long term, the rights to scarce resources will more than compensate for these initial costs. Being an early mover also allows a company to establish its position in the new market, as ARCO has demonstrated in China.

ARCO is well prepared for the future of international business. The company is strong financially, organizationally, technologically, and operationally, ARCO is committed to enhancing shareholder wealth as well as protecting worker health and safety. The company has begun to concentrate on its core businesses of oil and gas. Focusing on core business increases the company's operating efficiency. Its use of technology in the extraction of oil and gas helps the company prolong its oil and gas fields. ARCO's retail business will experience phenomenal growth as the use of automobile and other gas-powered vehicles increase in emerging markets such as China. With these favorable factors, Atlantic Richfield's future is positive.

Table c1.1 Selected Financial Ratios of Atlantic Richfield Company

	1997	1996	1995
Profitability			
Gross Profit Margin	15.40%	14.57%	13.74%
Net Profit Margin	10.11%	8.94%	8.70%
Return on Assets	7.40%	6.70%	5.70%
Return on Equity	22.90%	22.80%	21.30%
Liquidity			
Current Ratio	0.80	1.00	1.50
Quick Ratio	0.54	0.84	1.26
Leverage			
Debt to Assets	0.66	0.70	0.72
Debt to Equity	1.92	2.30	2.57
LTD to Equity	0.51	0.72	0.59
Activity			
Inventory Turnover	14.55	14.20	13.88
Fixed Asset Turnover	1.10	1.15	1.03
Average Collection Period	31.02	38.01	38.86

Case Study 2: Intel's Entrance into China

Executive Summary

Intel is renowned worldwide for excellence in the production of computer chip technology. This report discusses Intel's domestic and international presence, with a focus on Intel's efforts in the Chinese computer market. This market has treated MNCs unfavorably in the past.

Current changes in Chinese foreign investment policies as well as positive market approaches made by Intel have afforded this company great opportunities in one of the fastest growing economies in the world. Examination of the company, including internal and external environmental factors, corporate and business level strategies, international entrance and cooperative strategies, and global integration objectives will provide useful lessons to other companies involved in international expansion.

Company Introduction

Mission

Intel's mission is to become the preeminent building block supplier to the global computing and telecommunications industries. This is accomplished through formation of strategic alliances with major corporations as well as equity participation in early stage companies. Developing products jointly with software companies is high on the list of Intel's goals, as it increases its ability to directly meet the needs of its product users.

Intel plans for growth and profitability are premised on going from a position of industrial supplier to industrial leader. Until recently, Microsoft has been a leader in the computer industry by developing continually more sophisticated software packages requiring high speed computer processing capabilities. Intel has not been a market leader, but a follower. Intel's current ventures are intended to guide the computer industry rather than simply meet the demands of software companies. Intel has made large investments in research and development (over US$2 billion in 1997) with an intention of leading the industry by doubling processor speed every 18 months.

Intel is guided by five initiatives. Intel's Small Business Initiative strives to provide cutting-edge computing and communications technologies to help small companies become more productive and profitable. Small and medium sized companies make up 75 percent of the world's business entities. Although consulting is not one of Intel's core products, it realizes that unless customers can understand and utilize the increasing capacity of its products, its market potential will be limited. If Intel focused only on the individual consumer market, it would run out of customers within a few years. Concentration on the small business market, however, provides a customer base that will continue to demand the superior processing capabilities Intel offers.

The Wired for Management Initiative is geared toward reducing the cost of running PCs for business while maintaining performance and flexibility. Intel realized that the cost of using and maintaining an up-to-date computer system within a small company is high relative to the results obtained from continual upgrades. Intel is therefore working on platform development, to make future advancements in processor technology more cost effective for those firms which are most likely to comprise more than 70 percent of its market in the near future.

The third goal for Intel is called the Visual Computing Initiative which aims at providing a more intuitive computing experience for users. This initiative was spurred by the relatively lackadaisical approach of PC owners towards using the Internet. Intel began to focus on advancing the potential of Internet capability in order increase the demand for its core product (accelerated computer processors). Departments involved in this initiative include PC Imaging, Accelerated Graphics Port, DVD, and Intel's Open Arcade Architecture Initiative.

Intel Technologies, the fourth initiative, focuses on new frontiers in computer industry development, including Plug and Play technologies, connectivity Solutions, automobile PCs, and intelligent I/O solutions. The last looks at all components of the I/O structure to engineer more congruous development of all information platforms including wiring, communication, hardware, and software conformity.

The Mobile Computing Initiatives includes mobile manageability, power, and connectivity. This is perhaps the most essential of Intel's communication-oriented goals. In an age where maintaining continual connections is important, a company that aspires to lead the telecommunications and computer industries must provide solutions that have not previously been available. Continual connectivity requires advanced digital cellular and pager products. Intel is stepping into communications at the time when the need for greater communications technology is at its apex.

Intel's core product is the computer microchip, or microprocessor, for which it holds approximately 75 percent of the worldwide market. Intel's processors are in over 80 percent of PCs. The variety of chips produced by Intel has grown enormously since the founding of the company. Intel currently offers Pentium microprocessors for low and high-end personal computers, Pentium Pro microprocessors for Internet servers and high-powered workstations, and mobile processors for portable computers. Other products include Flash memory chips for cellular phones, digital switches, and the like; communication equipment for Internet development, including processors designed for LAN/WAN systems; and video conferencing workstations for international companies

It might seem initially that Intel has set goals that take it away from its core product. However, its future lies in building markets that can take advantage of its original proprietary designs. Thus, Intel continues to concentrate on its core microchip products by designing new ways in which to use them as stipulated in the five mandates.

Corporate History

Two visionary engineers, Bob Noyce and Gordon Moore founded Intel in 1969. Noyce invented the integrated circuit. Moore coined Moore's law, which predicted that the speed of the microprocessor would double every eighteen months, as is still true today.

With only twelve employees, Intel began producing SRAM (static random access memory) chips in 1970. Its first year revenues were $2,672. In the following year, Intel received a contract from a Japanese firm to produce twelve custom chips for calculators. Ted Hoff, an Intel engineer, suggested that instead of making twelve separate chips, they should work on a single chip that would do all twelve functions. This was the birth of the processor named 4004. When the calculator company ran into financial problems, Intel bought back the proprietary design and introduced it on the open market in 1971.

This was followed by different versions of the 8000 series in quick progression. In 1980, IBM marketed its first round of Personal Computers using Intel's 8088 processor, at a cost of $2,495 each. In 1982, the 80286 or 286 chip was introduced. This chip contained 134,000 transistors and provided three times the performance of other 16-bit processors at the time.

This chip was used in IBM's PC-AT. The 80386 was set loose in 1985. This chip had 32-bit architecture and contained 275,000 transistors, allowing the chip to perform a staggering five MIPS (million instructions per second). In 1989, Intel released the 486 and product development was booming. By 1993, it introduced the Pentium Processor, which had five times the performance of the 486, and a processing speed of 90 MIPS. It performed at 1,500 times the level of the initial Intel 4004. The current products that maintain Intel's market dominance are the Pentium Pro and the Pentium II chips.

International markets for Intel include all major economies, developed and emerging, in Asia, Europe, the Americas, and Africa. Market size as well as potential for computer technology determines the major markets. North America accounts for 42 percent of Intel's sales, followed by Europe with 28 percent, the Asia-Pacific region with 18 percent, and Japan with 12 percent.

Intel is currently making inroads into foreign markets that show great potential for growth in the computer industry. Brazil's current demand for Intel products is growing at 42 percent per annum because of Brazil's youthful consumer population. In China and India, Intel is working to build a solid customer base by providing public events to showcase the capabilities of its microprocessor-based PCs. It also donates equipment and software to select organizations. Due to decreased prices in China, Intel has already garnered about 80 percent of the Chinese microprocessor market.

China is expected to surpass Japan in demand for computers and computer-related equipment in the next decade.

SWOT Analysis

External Environment

Industry Level The semiconductor industry has grown tremendously in the past twenty years. According to World Semiconductor Trade Statistics (WSTS), in 1980 global semiconductor sales were $13.1 billion. By 1990, global sales had reached $50.5 billion; last year they surpassed $137 billion. This amazing growth is expected to continue due to strong worldwide demand for consumer electronics and rapid increases in communications and networking devices. By the year 2002, WSTS predicts that global sales will reach over $245 billion. This growth will present many opportunities for firms within the industry. Although the semiconductor industry is very competitive, the threat of new entrants is relatively low, buyers and suppliers have minimal bargaining power, and there are no substitute products.

Intel continues to dominate the industry with little threat from competitors. Its semiconductor revenues are more than twice that of the next leading manufacturer. Last year, Intel's semiconductor revenues increased 20 percent to $21 billion, while NEC remained second in the industry with semiconductor revenues up 2.2 percent to $10.7 billion. The third leading manufacturer was Motorola with revenues of $8.1 billion. Texas Instruments, Toshiba, and Hitachi followed in fourth, fifth, and six places with semiconductor revenues of $7.6 billion, $7.5 billion, and $6.5 billion respectively.

Korean manufacturers Samsung and Hyundai, normally among the top producers, were particularly vulnerable last year due to currency devaluation and falling chip prices.

Intel initially gained market share in China by providing Chinese manufactures with motherboard designs based on Intel microprocessors. According to the Beijing-based China Research Group, in 1996 Intel commanded an 83.8 percent share of China's CPU market, followed by Advanced Micro Devices with 11.5 percent, and Cyrix with 3.2 percent. Despite Intel's lock on the microprocessor niche, Intel faces competition in other sectors. In 1996, there were over fifty different companies involved in various foreign-invested projects in China's semiconductor sector. Projects include research and development, chip assembly, manufacturing, and testing.

The semiconductor industry presents numerous barriers to new entrants, including extensive capital requirements. Wafer fabrication plants can cost anywhere from $300,000 for a relatively low-tech factory, to nearly $3 billion for a state-of-the-art facility. Manufacturing equipment can account for 70 percent to 80 percent of the total cost of the facility. In addition, the technology required to produce semiconductors is mind boggling. The latest Pentium Pro contains over seven million transistors. Modern photolithography equipment is used to create chips with transistors only .25 microns thick (a human hair is about 80 microns). Furthermore, firms in this industry must continually advance to survive. They cannot rely on acquiring state-of-the-art equipment once and for all.

Although it is extremely difficult for individual companies to enter the industry, these barriers can be overcome with governmental assistance including subsidies, tax breaks, and market protection to aid companies. This was demonstrated two decades ago when Japanese and Korean electronics companies moved into the semiconductor industry. Today, this type of threat comes from China. The Chinese government has focused its Ninth Five-Year Plan (FYP 1996-2000) on micron chip technology. It plans to develop advanced .3 micron chip technology in labs, produce .5 micron chips on a trial basis, and mass-produce the less sophisticated .8 micron chips. Chinese manufacturers are still more than 5 years behind the rest of the world's leading semiconductor manufacturers; however, they will present a considerable force in the future.

Although there are numerous industries which depend on semiconductors (computer, consumer electronics, automobile, and telecommunications), these buyers do maintain some bargaining power with chipmakers. For some buyers, like computer manufacturers, semiconductor components represent up to 50 percent of total costs. In 1996, when consumers began demanding sub-$1,000 PC's, computer makers pressured semiconductor manufacturers to lower their prices. Since all these industries are cyclical, when the demand for these products slows down, it can cause a buildup of semiconductor inventories, which also pressures chip makers to lower their prices. For example, from September 1996 to February 1998, the prices for flash-memory chips alone dropped from $15 to $4 due to oversupply.

Because there are many large semiconductor manufacturers who have an even greater number of relatively smaller suppliers worldwide, the bargaining power of these suppliers is very low. Although many foreign governments require that semiconductor manufacturers purchase a given level of components from local suppliers, there is a great deal of competition both locally and globally among these suppliers. In addition, since a dependable product is critical to semiconductor manufacturers, they exert pressure on their suppliers not only in terms of pricing but also in terms of quality.

There are no substitutes for semiconductors, but firms must remain aware of changes in technology or trends that might lead to obsolescence in the end products semiconductors are used in. For example, the Network Computer (Net PC) is seen as a threat to many microprocessor manufactures because it requires very little processing and could replace many personal computers used today.

National Level Since China opened its doors to the rest of the world in 1979, it has implemented numerous economic, political, and legal reforms which have greatly improved its foreign investment climate. As a result of these reforms, along with a potential market of 1.2 billion people, it has had remarkable success in attracting foreign investment, especially to its coastal regions and special economic zones (SEZ). China has become the second largest recipient of foreign direct investment in the world, after the United States. The Chinese market offers many opportunities for foreign firms due to government incentives and a growing consumer demand. Firms also face a number of threats, however, including a complex regulatory environment, high tariffs, and corruption.

Strong consumer demand fuels China's domestic electronics market. The number of cellular phone users in China is expected to total over 17 million users in 1998, a 1,000 percent increase over the 1994 level. According to China's Ministry of the Electronics Industry (MEI), 1.1 million personal computers were sold in China in 1995, 2 million in 1996, and an estimated 3 million units in 1997. Although most computers were sold to government agencies and commercial businesses, sales to consumers are expected to explode. Currently, less than 2 percent of Chinese families report owning computers, but more than 4 percent have plans to purchase them in the near future. A 1997 report by a presidential commission on U.S. trade and investment in Asia said the semiconductor market in China would quadruple between 1996 and 2000, to reach more than $20 billion. Other sources predict that China will have the world's largest semiconductor market by the year 2020.

In its Ninth Five-year Plan, the Chinese government declared electronics a 'pillar industry'. This status gives electronics firms priority funding and approval for foreign investment projects in several key electronic subsections, including high-end PC's, large-scale integrated circuits, advanced semiconductor materials, and photolithography devices. China plans to spend $71 billion to upgrade its overall electronics technology in the areas of telecommunications, computers, and consumer electronics. China's (MEI) will offer incentives to investors on a per-project basis. The current lack of advanced manufacturing technologies and processes in China presents great opportunities for foreign firms.

Although the Chinese government has made many improvements to its foreign investment climate, a common complaint by many foreign firms is that China has a complex regulatory environment in which various jurisdictions and agencies often overlap and contradict each other. Potential investment projects usually go through a multi-tiered screening and approval process. Foreign investment incentives and import duties are constantly changing as the Chinese government attempts to direct foreign investment into needed areas while simultaneously protecting its domestic industries. For example, in April 1996, China reversed the duty-free exemption for semiconductor equipment imports; this type of equipment is now subject to a

20-30 percent tariff as well as a 17 percent value-added tax. This was done to protect China's infant semiconductor industry and redirect foreign investment.

Corruption is commonly cited by foreign companies as one of the most prominent features of the Chinese business environment. It is an accepted business practice in many Asian, African and Latin American countries to include payments with business documents and applications to ensure that the documents 'receive proper attention'. According to a 1996 survey of multinational companies by Transparency International, China ranked fourth in terms of the level of perceived corruption, behind Nigeria, Pakistan, and Kenya. The most common form of corruption in China is local officials siphoning public funds into their own coffers as a result of dwindling funds from the central government. For example, each of McDonald's 38 restaurants in Beijing is subject to 31 miscellaneous fees, many of which are negotiable; only 2 are spelled out in the legal code. The central government is aware of the problem and has begun an anti-corruption campaign. It reports that it has forced more than 21 provinces and cities to cancel more than 2,800 fees in 1997.

Internal Environment

Financial Resources One of Intel's greatest strengths is its considerable financial capabilities. In 1998, Value Line gave Intel's financial strength its highest rating. Each and every year for at least the past decade, Intel's Revenues and profits have broken new records. In 1995, Intel's profits reached $3.5 billion on revenues of $16.2 billion. By 1996, profits topped $5.1 billion on sales of $20.8 billion, and last year profits were nearly $7 billion on sales of $25.5 billion. Although the semiconductor industry as a whole is quite profitable, Intel's profitability is consistently nearly double the industrial average. In addition, Intel manages its assets efficiently, generating a return that is also nearly double the industrial average. Intel also receives high marks in the area of maximizing shareholder wealth. An investment in 100 shares or $2,300 worth of Intel's stock in 1971 (when the company first went public) would be worth over $2 million today.

Intel is much more financially capable than its closest competitor, Advanced Micro Devices (AMD). Intel is far more liquid and has a greater ability to meet its short-term obligations than AMD. In addition, AMD has almost double the inventory to debt ratio than Intel. Leverage ratios suggest that both companies use about the same degree of leverage and are able to withstand significant losses without impairing the interest of their creditors.

However, AMD finances its operations using significantly more debt than equity compared to Intel. Intel also manages its assets better than the competition. Intel turns its inventory over slightly faster and produces about 20 cents more in sales for every dollar invested in assets than does AMD.

Intel's financial strength has allowed it many advantages. It can invest heavily in research and development. It has been able to build a new wafer fabrication plant about every 9 months. It can purchase companies that have superior technology and invest in small start-up companies. It can withstand downturns in the industry and slash its prices to gain market share or hurt its competitors. It is also able to enter into expensive litigation to defend its patents.

Technological Resources Intel currently employs over 12,000 people worldwide in its R&D department. Last year, Intel spent over $2 billion on research and development, amounting to 9.4 percent of sales. This is close to the industry average of 9 percent. AMD invests about 12 percent of sales in research and development, but because AMD is a much smaller company, the dollar amount last year was only $300 million.

Innovation is deeply imbedded in Intel's corporate culture; it has been the first to develop many new technologies and introduce them to the market. Among other things, it invented the first microprocessors, dynamic random access memory chips (DRAM), flash memory chips. When Intel introduces a new chip, it is able to charge a hefty price (upwards of $900) and then lower the price by more than 50 percent as other competitors develop the chip. It is much more expensive to develop a new technology than it is to merely copy it. It took Intel more than a year and $1 billion to create its 486 microprocessor, but Cyrix was able to produce a clone in just 18 months for only $10 million. Intel continually improves its manufacturing processes to try to stay ahead of the competition.

Business Level Strategies

Quality Management The competition for processors was dominated by Japanese manufacturers in the early 1970s. At that time, Intel's strategy focused on cost effectiveness and product quality. Consequently, it lost market share in Asia to Japanese firms that focused on customer and supplier service. Intel evaluated its business processes against the Japanese benchmarks, then worked to upgrade the quality of its corporate environment and services. It started the Quality Improvement Process (QIP).

The QIP steps involve: (i) having management acknowledge weaknesses; (ii) setting up a team to identify customer requirements and global performance expectations; (iii) developing, implementing, and monitoring the improvement plan; and (iv) standardizing improvements and providing rewards to those who get results.

Intel then turned its attention to external quality efforts, creating partnerships with its suppliers and setting very strict goals. Most of the suppliers embraced the changes because they did not want to lose a valuable customer. Supplier quality is evaluated based on: (i) SPC; (ii) documentation; (iii) productivity improvement; (iv) leadership; (v) total employee involvement; (vi) training; and (vii) supplier relations. Because of this change in philosophy, Intel won the Malcolm Baldridge National Quality Award in 1991.

Customer service was also improved. Intel developed the Vendor of Choice program (VOC). Teams were created to identify what customers thought were important and to rank Intel against all other competitors. These evaluations helped Intel decide what services, technologies, prices, delivery systems, and levels of quality were really in demand. Intel's VOC program proved successful. In 1990, Intel's VOC increased from 50 percent to 75 percent.

Intel's top management is responsible for much of the company's success. Intel's leadership understands the semiconductor industry, knows the company's strengths and how to use them, and is willing to take risks. Intel's management structure is relatively flat; this creates a team environment and fosters creativity from its employees. It has also implemented a management values program designed to coordinate company goals with company values based on a strong work ethic, risk taking, and response to customers. In *Fortune* magazine's 1998 survey of America's most admired companies, Intel's quality of management ranked second behind Coca-Cola and ahead of General Electric. In 1997, CEO Andrew Grove won *Time* magazine's coveted 'Man of the Year' award for successfully guiding Intel through turbulent times in the industry and for realizing the innovative potential of microchips.

Intel continued to focus on the quality of its products as well. Since the delivery window was decreasing, Intel reduced its design-to-sample time by 50 percent in 1988, even though product complexity had increased by 100 percent. At the same time, it reduced defects per unit. In 1991, NEC gave Intel a zero-defect score, even though NEC has one of the strictest defects rating systems. Intel's brand name is therefore synonymous with quality and reliability. In 1997, *Financial World*, ranked Intel the eighth most valuable brand in the world. Intel uses this power in its marketing campaign which encourages consumers to demand products that contain the 'Intel Inside' logo. PC manufacturers across China are participating in the Intel Inside co-op marketing program. Program licensees gain the benefits of having the Intel Inside logo on their products along with some marketing development funds, while Intel gains greater profits and market share. Intel has become the dominant supplier of processors and logos for most systems manufacturers in China.

Product Diversification Intel takes both backward and forward approaches to product diversification. The forward approach depends on expanding its technological achievements. Its development of flash memory chips that retain information after the power is turned off is an example of this. These chips are used in products like PCs, voice recorders, digital cameras and mobile phones. Intel also expanded on its Pentium II chips to create the Pentium IIII chip, targeted at the workstation market segment.

Intel took a backward approach to product diversification by breaking down its technologies into smaller products. The Celeron chip is a slimmed down version of the Pentium II chip that lacks the level 2 cache. This chip is aimed at the lower end of the market to meet the rising demand of customers with PCs valued under $1,000. While the chip is slower than the Pentium II, it has enough processing power to operate low end PCs efficiently.

Supporting China's Technological Development Since opening its first office in China, Intel's goal has been to build a facility that would lead the industry in terms of cost, delivery, quality, and environmental and health safety. Intel planned to support local PC manufacturers, multinationals, smaller PC assemblers, and software developers in closing the technological gap in China. For example, Intel works with local PC manufacturers such as Legend, Great Wall, Creation and Tonturu to make their hardware 'Platform enabled'. Platform enablement gives manufacturers the engineering knowledge and technology to integrate Intel's processors, networking, and other products into their PCs and servers. The scope of Intel's operations in China further includes applied research, supporting the Chinese software industry, manufacturing, marketing and demand generation, purchasing, and academic relations programs.

In May 1998, Intel announced it would invest about $50 million over the next five years in establishing a new research center in Beijing. The Intel China research center will focus on applying research towards developing information technology for the Internet and speech recognition systems for

Chinese PC usage. This center will become part of Intel's global $2.8 billion R&D commitment, which involves 700 researchers in the US, Israel, Russia, and China.

Intel's Shanghai-based Architecture Development Laboratory has more than 80 engineers working with local and international software vendors to develop and deliver consumer and business applications to PC users in China. The lab's charter is to accelerate technological acceptance in the PRC. In May 1998, Intel announced it would provide $1.5 million worth of 350 and 400 MHz Pentium II processor-based development systems to leading Chinese software developers to assist them in bringing advanced software to local and international markets. The developer support program provides companies with application engineering support, software engineers, and seminars and training. Matchmaking events are conducted regularly to introduce local software developers to international software firms and distributors. Intel also supports China's electronics industry through purchasing. In 1997, it purchased $142 million worth of electronics from Chinese manufacturers. By the end of 1998, it expects this to have increased to around $160 million.

Intel's first flash memory assembly and test factory, located in Shanghai, became operational four months ahead of schedule. Opened on May 1998, the $198 million dollar factory makes memory for PCs, digital cameras, and other consumer electronic devices. The facility currently employs 400 people, a number that will grow as the factory increases production. The factory meets Intel's strict quality specifications by training local employees and managers in global manufacturing and business practices.

Intel's marketing program in China reflects Intel's belief that China will be the world's third largest PC market by the year 1999. Its marketing strategies include advertising, channel programs, cooperative marketing, and interactive marketing. Intel's website is one of the most visited sites in China, containing information for every level of computer user and developer. Intel is the most extensive technology advertiser in China in terms of media investment, geographic reach and TV presence. These approaches create end-user awareness of the benefits of computing for home and business. Intel's focus on children as future computer users also creates greater demand for PCs. It also supports higher education. Over the last four years, Intel has donated $1.3 million worth of equipment to China's leading universities, including Tsinghua, Beijing, Fudan, Jiaotong, and UEST. The academic relations program includes scholarships, research funding, technology, and conference sponsorships.

Entry Strategies

Choosing the right entry strategy plays an important role in the success or failure of firms penetrating a new foreign market. Firms need to know how, when, and where to enter a new market most effectively. To make the right choices, firms must analyze many firm-, country-, industry-, or project-specific factors.

Firm-Specific Factors

Intel's strategic objectives are clearly defined for the Chinese market. It intends to support the success of local PC manufacturers, multinationals and smaller PC assemblers, and software developers in closing China's technology gap. Intel views its investments as being more strategic than financial. In short, it invests to broaden its market rather than take over smaller rivals.

Country-Specific Factors

Since 1980, the Chinese government has created special economic zones that provide tax incentives to foreign companies. Some companies, such as Intel, get further preferential treatment and even lower taxes (15-24 percent). The political relationship between China and the US has become smoother at the same time as Chinese governmental policies on international business, foreign investment, and intellectual property rights have been updated and improved, reducing the risk of doing business in China. Intel has taken advantage of these changes by diversifying geographically into China.

Intel believes that the Chinese demand is both enormous and favorable to US semiconductor companies. A reported early in 1982, most of China's semiconductor manufacturing equipment consists of versions of old US and Japanese models along with obsolete Eastern European equipment. To upgrade this equipment, the Chinese are looking to obtain American know-how while avoiding reliance upon Japanese equipment. In the future, China is expected to become the biggest market in the world for information technology, surpassing the US by 2010.

Industry Specific Factors

Although Intel is the biggest chipmaker in the world, with little fear of competition from new entrants, a late start might put the company behind others who have already penetrated the China market. For instance, other semiconductor manufacturing, assembly, or sales firms in China include Texas Instruments, SGS-Thomson, Hyundai, Mitsubishi, Advanced Micro Devices, Samsung, Matsushita, Harris, Goldstar, Lucent, NEC, Philips Semiconductor, and Northern Telecom. Makers of passive components and connectors, such as AMP and Molex, as well as producers of semiconductor production and assembly equipment, component distributors, and others have also begun operations, including joint ventures or partnerships. The Chinese computer market is now mature, with a high demand for brand name products.

Project-Specific Factors

An Intel spokesman explained that Intel tends not to see a direct relationship plant location and market share. It feels that customers buy its products based on quality and price, not where the plant is located. In other words, Intel will not construct extremely expensive factories in China for every product it plans to sell there. Nevertheless, Intel has invested a lot in the Chinese market. Between 1996 and 1998, Intel put down US$198 million to build a flash memory chip assembly-test plant factory in Shanghai. In addition, it has several sales offices in Chinese cities. Most of the chips will be exported, with some of them being sold within China. Intel believes its Shanghai plant will reinforce its presence in China, preparing the way to gain a greater market share in a country with enormous potential demand.

During the next five years, Intel plans to invest another US$50 million to build an applied research center in Beijing. While continuing its advanced comprehensive integrated circuit technology projects, Intel will also cooperate with Chinese companies to design and produce desktop computers and service adapters.

Entry Mode Selection

To understand Intel's choice of entry mode of Intel in China, it is helpful to analyze Intel's movements from the beginning of its involvement in China (see Table c2.1). By studying milestones, one can recognize specific changes in choice of entry mode during different periods.

Intel first established its representative/branch offices and joint ventures. The reasons for this strategy are simple and applied universally. Like other firms, Intel wanted to reduce risks at the beginning when the Chinese market was uncertain and governmental policies and laws unclear. It was crucial for Intel to study the market and culture, to learn from other firms' successes and failures, and to familiarize itself with Chinese business practices before preparing for its next move.

In the period 1990–1995, Intel established wholly owned foreign subsidiaries in China. Intel wanted full control over its operations in China in order to protect its technological know-how.

In the present period, 1996–1998, Intel has continued to establish wholly owned subsidiaries along with cooperative join ventures. Intel's wholly owned foreign enterprise test and assembly facility was begun in the Waigaoqiao Free Trade Zone, Pudong area of Shanghai. Intel then agreed that the Great Wall Group would have rights to master design technologies provided by Intel, and could then produce and sell its personal computer systems using new generations of the Pentium processors.

Timing of Entry

Intel is not the first company in its industry to operate in China. In fact, Intel is the third US chip making company in the China market. Rather than depend on first mover advantages, Intel has approached China with all the aplomb of a poker player holding a royal flush. With a highly valued reputation and image, Intel has a competitive advantage over other chip making companies. It chose to make a late start as part of a strategy of waiting for the right moment.

Location Selection

Location is the next important issue for foreign firm to consider when they operate in China. Selecting the right location requires firms to compare the advantages and disadvantages of one location over another according to various aspects. These include cost of doing business, taxation, labor skills, infrastructure, and supportiveness of local governments. Understandably, developed cities are often the first choice.

Currently, Intel has offices in Beijing, ChengDu, ChongQing, Fuzhou, GuangZhou, Harbin, JiNan, Nanjing, Shanghai, ShenYang, Tianjin, WuHan, and Xian. These coastal and inland cities are all involved in strategic-project development plans set up by the Chinese government. Intel's experiences have so far been positive, despite a misunderstanding over the location of its flash memory chip plant in Shanghai. Its first purchase of a factory site turned out to be in a prohibited zone, so it was forced to purchase a different site.

International Cooperative Strategies

Partner Selection

Some clear lessons have been emerging on what divides the winners from the losers in China. Profitable firms have been those who have become smarter about picking Chinese partners or are daring to go it alone. Intel has shown its high commitment to doing business in China by mainly choosing the government and state owned enterprises for its partnerships.

Intel joined forces with China's Ministry of Electronics Industry (MEI) in an agreement to expand China's computer industry. Under this program, Intel and MEI will join hands to improve the viability and competitive strength of China's computer and software manufacturers. Educational and multi-media applications are also in the works. MEI will help develop desktop computers and service adapters using energy-efficient, high-density Pentium processors. MEI has encouraged Chinese computer manufacturers to cooperate with Intel, stressing cooperation, improved technology, and customer service.

Intel has also signed an agreement with the Great Wall Computer Group to provide China with technological guidance and standards on motherboard designs.

Intel also signed a Memorandum of Understanding (MOU) with Shanghai. Under the terms of the MOU, Shanghai officials will recommend Intel's Pentium processors for personal computers in a broad variety of projects. Intel and the city's commercial, research, and academic institutions will cooperate on other personal computer technology advancements for Shanghai.

Intel's partnership strategies in China can be explained according to three key factors. First, Intel and the Chinese government share compatible goals. China wants to upgrade its computer industry, and Intel wants to invest in China to gain market shares. It is willing to help close the technology gap in order to achieve this goal. Second, Intel and its Chinese partners have complementary skills. Intel provides capital and technological know-how while its partners handle manufacturing, distribution, and educational programs. Finally, both the Chinese government and Intel have show that they have made a strong commitment to their business marriage. Intel's heavy investments and donations to Chinese universities show its intention of helping Chinese users catch up with current technology. The government's commitment to Intel is shown through including Intel in its ninth five-year-plan (1996-2000) and in encouraging Chinese people to become familiar with Intel technology.

Sharing Distribution and Control

Because most of Intel's operations in China are wholly owned subsidiaries and cooperative joint ventures, Intel has majority control over its operations. Intel owns 100 percent of its shares and responsibilities. This enables Intel to guard its technology, and increases the likelihood of a high return on investments. It also means greater risks if there are any changes in Chinese policies on foreign investment in the future.

Global Structure

Intel's headquarters in Silicon Valley originates all major developmental decisions. Major R&D decisions, financial choices, and company goal formation occur at the corporate level. Intel's business structure relies on a hierarchy of foreign representatives to provide insight into local market climates, including both opportunities and threats. Representatives handle country-specific decisions like local marketing, resource allocation, government and industry PR, and development of new territories within specific countries. Thus, Intel's global business strategy is closer to a global matrix or hybrid structure than a global product or matrix structure. Products are not differentiable among markets. Likewise, geographic distinctions have little impact on the levels of control within the organization.

This framework ensures that the company's global objectives are adhered to while benefits from the development of individual markets are maximized. Intel's presence in China is a prime example of a market in which Intel operates within a dichotomy between corporate and regional objectives.

Global Integration and Control

Intel has, to date, successfully established multiple area representative offices, a research facility, and a manufacturing base in China. Similarly, Intel established an early base in the European computer market with representative offices in nearly all major European cities. The company then built manufacturing and research facilities in countries such as Ireland, Spain, and France.

By utilizing the resources of multiple international research markets, Intel is able to take advantage of the innovative talents of many nations. Through the establishment of country-specific representative offices, Intel has been able to gain important information about potential markets. By establishing manufacturing facilities within easy reach of major international markets, Intel is capable of interacting in regional trade as a local facilitator rather than as a foreign threat. This international framework is a measure of the thoroughness of Intel's global strategy. It is a major reason for the company's continuing success in the global marketplace.

Global Strategy

Intel provides building block products to the computer and communications industries. To successfully export these products to many economies, Intel pursues international growth with a global strategy.

One reason this is an effective strategy is the homogeneity of Intel's products. Products developed for the American market are equally suitable in foreign markets. Consumer demand for computing speed and ability is not determined by cultural or national tastes. Rather, foreign market constituents who hope to keep up with the American computer technology eagerly accept new developments in processing power provided by Intel and other market leaders. Along with this homogeneity of products, Intel is able to take advantage of a high degree of global integration, mastering high profits by concentrating on core products that do not require differentiation according to local requirements.

Second, Intel is able to exploit the experience curve. Intel, a long time innovator, is currently boosting development through research and development spending. The company is working to establish new and improved research facilities in countries such as China. Intel already knows how to make chips, however. It stays ahead of the game by continually producing products with greater performance. Intel takes advantage of past successes which provide a proven track record on which to base future innovations.

Finally, Intel has the ability to exploit the benefits of location. By making early investments in the Chinese markets through the establishment of representative offices in major Chinese cities, Intel established ties with local government and industry officials. This has greatly enhanced Intel's ability to enter the market successfully. As Intel continues marketing in China, its initial investment in learning local customs and laws will aid future expansion.

Conclusions

Intel will celebrate its thirtieth anniversary in 1999. Intel's domination over the domestic market in the past can be attributed to product excellence. Intel's future, however, is threatened by increasing competition by companies such as AMD and Cyrix, lack of applications using the ever increasing speed and ability of Intel chips, and the split in the PC market between low-end and high-end users.

Intel has successfully established many platforms from which to confront these threats. The reliability of Intel's chip technology, as recognized by NEC and the Malcolm Baldrige Award will sustain the company's reputation for high quality products and thwart competition.

The five initiatives, which guide Intel's goals for future growth, aim at creating new markets that will use Intel's new products. Development of the Celeron chip will appease the low-end market, while advanced Pentium development will fuel the high-end user market.

Internationally, Intel has developed a framework of successful global strategies, emphasizing knowledge of local markets. Intel's entrance into China is a prime example. Through initial investment in regional representative offices, Intel gained valuable knowledge regarding local market potential and impediments to development. Intel has successfully followed its initial market research efforts with investment in the development of markets for its products.

In China, Intel has stimulated the local computer manufacturing industry by providing engineering data on current technologies. Intel instills growth in the local software industry by hosting software developer conferences and providing technical support, which will help to spawn future software applications capable of taking advantage of Intel technologies. Market demand is stimulated by interactive demonstrations for the public and donations to educational institutions. The local computer companies will begin producing technology-rich computers that will utilize the superiority of Intel chips. Software developers will produce software packages that require Intel chip processing ability.

Lessons

The lessons to be learned from studying the Intel success story are attention to the core product, to the industry, and to key markets. Intel still produces the best microprocessor chips in the world market. Intel has never neglected its core product.

Intel has become a market leader rather than a follower. The company follows initiatives based on creating markets for its increasingly superior technologies. With research and development investments increasing 40 percent between 1995 and 1996, Intel has provided proof that it strives for a greater realization of potential for advancement than is currently shown in the marketplace. With concentration on advancement in small business computer integration and feasibility, mobile computing technologies, communications, and I/O levels of computer architecture, Intel creates new frontiers for its core product, the microchip.

Finally, Intel knows that true growth in the international computing market will occur in countries with an increasing level of industrial and capitalistic development. Such economies provide incentives for FDI and represent large consumer markets. By establishing an early presence in such countries as China, India, and Brazil, Intel ensures that when these markets are ripe and the countries mature, it will lead these markets.

Companies interested in expansion into emerging economies such as China should likewise make an effort to understand the intricacies of the local marketplace. They should confront challenges prevalent in the industry while remaining committed to reliance on the strengths inherent in their core products.

Table c2.1 Intel's Milestones in China

- 1985: Representative office opened.
- 1988: Joint Venture with ICT (Intel Computer Technology) to manufacture 16- and 32-bit microcomputers for industrial control applications (iRMX, MultiBUS).

- 1994: Donated Pentium(r) processor high performance computers to Tsinghua and Beijing Universities for the establishment of educational labs.
- April 1994: Established nation-wide Intel Advanced Network Reseller (iANR) program to provide training, technical assistance and marketing services support for Intel brand networking products.
- September 1994: Established Intel Architecture Development Co, Ltd. in Shanghai, a wholly owned foreign entity of Intel.
- March 1995: Daqing Petroleum acquired the first Paragon Supercomputer in China, which is the first Intel Scaleable Supercomputer in China. The Paragon system will be used for seismic data processing at the Daqing oil fields.
- September 1995: Microcontrollers tested and assembled by the Huajing Electronics Group qualified for the Intel world-class standard and quality guarantee.
- November 1995: Pentium(r) Pro processor launched; first ever to introduce a new generation of products in China around the same time as the US and Europe.
- May 1996: Signed Memorandum of Understanding (MOU) with the Ministry of Electronics Industry of China on accelerating growth of PC computing in hardware and software development in China.
- May 1996: Dr. Andrew Grove, president and chief executive officer of Intel Corp, presented "The Connected PC" in Beijing.
- October 1996: James Jarrett, President of Intel China, arrived in Beijing.
- November 1996: Breaking ground for Intel's wholly owned foreign enterprise test and assembly facility began in the Waigaoqiao Free Trade Zone, Pudong area of Shanghai.
- May 1997: Dr. Craig Barrett, president and chief operating office of Intel Corp, presented "Connected PC in Business" in Shanghai.
- May 1997: Dr Craig Barrett met with Chinese President, Mr Jiang Zemin.
- May 1997: Intel successfully accomplished the first Chinese/English webcast from China for Craig Barrett's presentation in Shanghai.
- June 1997: Intel launched regional children's campaign in Shanghai to disseminate PC knowledge and promote PC use in China.
- September 1997: Paul Otellini announced Intel's PC education initiative in China jointly with local OEMs.
- October 1997: Intel announced US$99 million second phase investment its assembly/testing facilities in Pudong, Shanghai, bringing the total investment to US$198 million.
- May 1998: Dr Andrew S Grove, Intel Chairman visits China.
- May 1998: Dr Grove announces a new applied research center called the Intel China Research Center, to be established in Beijing.
- May 1998: Dr Grove officially opens Intel's Shanghai flash memory assembly and test facility, four months ahead of schedule.

Case Study 3: PepsiCo

Executive Summary

PepsiCo, Inc. is among the most successful consumer products companies in the world, with annual revenues of over $20 billion and about 140,000 employees. Some of its brand names are nearly 100 years old, although PepsiCo is a relatively young corporation.

PepsiCo has a record of continual growth. This has been achieved due to its high performance standards, distinctive competitive strategies, and the personal and professional integrity of its staff, business practices, and products. PepsiCo's primary strategy is to concentrate resources on business expansion, both through internal growth and acquisitions within businesses. This strategy is continually adjusted to address the opportunities and risks of the global marketplace.

PepsiCo has achieved a leadership position in each of two major packaged goods businesses: beverages and snack foods. The beverage segment markets and distributes Pepsi-Cola, Diet Pepsi, 7UP, Diet 7UP, Mountain Dew and other brands worldwide. Principal international markets include Argentina, Brazil, China, India, Mexico, the Philippines, Saudi Arabia, Spain, Thailand, and the UK. The snack food segment manufactures, distributes, and markets salty and sweet snacks worldwide. Its principal international snack markets include Brazil, Mexico, the Netherlands, South Africa, Spain and the UK.

PepsiCo's overriding objective is to increase the value of its shareholders' investments through integrated operations, investments, and financing. The corporation's success reflects its commitment to growth and a focus on those businesses in which it can create opportunities.

Company Introduction

Mission and Goals

As a consumer product company, PepsiCo's main mission is to reinvent the company so it can win in the marketplace. This mission has worked as a strategy which positions the company for a better future. In order to achieve this mission, PepsiCo has chosen to focus on its strengths, manage for strong cash flow, and invest aggressively in major opportunities.

PepsiCo considers two groups to be the most important contributors to the success of the company: consumers and customers. It is committed to making consumers happy since they are the end-users for its various products. PepsiCo attains this goal by regularly analyzing its marketplace performance. The company continuously evaluates product quality, service, value, brand image, and employee performance. The second critical area for PepsiCo is its customers, which include supermarkets, convenience stores, restaurants, and other businesses. PepsiCo sales teams provide tools and know-how to its customers so they can give better service to its consumers. There is a positive correlation between PepsiCo's growth and profit and having informed customers,

Corporate History

PepsiCo, Inc., is one of the most successful consumer products companies in the world, with annual revenues of over $20 billion and about 140,000 employees. Even though some of PepsiCo's brand names are almost 100 years of age, the corporation itself is relatively young. It was founded in 1965 by Donald M. Kendall, president and CEO of Pepsi-Cola, and Herman W. Lay, chairman and CEO of Frito-Lay, through the merger of the two companies. PepsiCo's aggressiveness was immediately apparent when it entered Japan and Eastern Europe the year after the merger. By 1969, it introduced its signature red, white, and blue packaging. In 1976, the company became the single largest selling soft drink brand sold in U.S. supermarkets.

PepsiCo started out with a commitment to research and development, opening its Research and Technical Center in Valhalla, NY in 1979. PepsiCo is also recognized as one of the most advanced companies in the areas of employee health and fitness, as shown by the opening of the PepsiCo Fitness Center in 1981. The same year, PepsiCo and China reached an agreement to manufacture soft drinks. In 1986, PepsiCo's Board of Directors visited China to mark the opening of its second bottling plant in China. In 1994, China got cheese-less Cheetos, the first time a major snack food brand has been developed by a foreign company to meet Chinese tastes.

In 1989, PepsiCo introduced the SharePower Stock Option program, becoming the first large corporation to award stock options to virtually all full time employees. In 1992, Pepsi-Cola implemented the "Right Side Up" philosophy, where the consumer and front line employees are at the top of the organization. In 1996, Pepsi-Cola launched its first website, called Pepsi World.

Major Restructuring

The corporation took its first step into the restaurant business in 1977 by acquiring Pizza Hut, Inc. It acquired Taco Bell the next year. In 1984, the corporation was restructured to focus on its three core businesses: soft drinks, snack foods, and restaurants. Its early transportation and sporting goods businesses were sold.

In 1986, Wayne Calloway became chairman of the Board of Directors and CEO. Shortly thereafter, the corporation was reorganized and decentralized. Beverage operations were combined under PepsiCo Worldwide Beverages while snack foods were combined under PepsiCo Worldwide Foods. The same year the corporation acquired Kentucky Fried Chicken, 7-Up International, and Mug Root Beer. In 1988, PepsiCo was reorganized geographically into East, West, South, and Central regions, each with its own president and senior management staff.

PepsiCo signed the largest commercial trade agreement in history with the Soviet Union, expecting sales in the U.S.S.R. to double by the end of the century. In 1992, the corporation took an equity position in California Pizza Kitchen. In 1993, PepsiCo acquired East Side Mario's Restaurants, Inc. and D'Angelo Sandwich Shops chain. Pepsi-Cola International then acquired an Indian company, its first big bottling plant in Bombay.

The company then entered into an agreement with Starbucks to jointly develop ready-to-drink coffee beverages. In 1995, Pepsi-Cola International and Kraft Foods International jointly announced the formation of the Maxwell House Beverage Company. The new company will market ready-to-drink canned coffee in Asia. At the same time, the company formed a joint venture with Thomas J. Lipton Co. to develop and market tea-based beverages. In 1996, Roger Enrico succeeded Wayne Calloway as CEO.

In order to concentrate on its core beverage and snack food businesses, PepsiCo decided to spin off its restaurant businesses as an independent, publicly traded company named Tricon Global Restaurants, Inc., in 1997. The international and domestic snack food operations were combined into one business unit named the Frito-Lay Company, with major products including: Fritos brand corn chips, Lay's brand potato chips, Cheetos brand cheese flavored snacks, Ruffles brand potato chips and Rold Gold brand pretzels. Finally, the Pepsi-Cola domestic and international operations combined to become the Pepsi-Cola Company, with its major products including: Pepsi-Cola, Diet Pepsi, Mountain Dew, Slice, Mug Root Beer, Mug Crème, All Sport, Lipton (Partnership), Aquafina, Josta, and Frapuccino. Pepsi-Cola's key international markets include Argentina, Brazil, China, Mexico, Saudi-Arabia, Spain, Thailand, and the United Kingdom. The company also has established operations in the emerging markets of the Czech Republic, Hungary, India, Poland, Slovakia, and Russia.

External and Internal Environment Analysis (SWOT)

External Environment

Industrial level China's beverage industry has already entered the growth stage of the industrial life cycle. The huge nation has exceptional potential; it is already the ninth largest market for soft drinks in the world. Carbonated beverages, mineral water, fruit juice, milk, and summer alcoholic beverages are important categories in China's beverage market. Carbonated beverages are the top category, supplying 32 percent of China's beverage market. Coca-Cola and Sprite share half of China's carbonated beverage market, while local brands only garner 10 percent of the market share. The competitive market makes it relatively difficult for new brands of carbonated beverages to squeeze into the market.

Five Forces (i) existing rivalry: Among the top eight brands in China in terms of market share are Coca-Cola, Sprite, Pepsi-Cola, Jianlibao, and 7-Up. Coca-Cola is Pepsi's main competitor, holding 46 percent of the carbonated beverage market to Pepsi's 21 percent. Coke first entered the Chinese market in 1927. It resumed operations there in 1979. Pepsi entered the Chinese market in 1982. Jianlibao is the largest Chinese soft drink company; its market share is increasing at a substantial rate. There are also over 300 other brands of beverages in the Chinese market, with 154 brands of mineral water making up 7 percent of China's market. Fruit juice, milk, and beer together make up 24 percent of the entire beverage industry in China, with over 100 brands in these categories.

(ii) potential competitors: It is apparent that the Chinese beverage market is relatively competitive. It seems difficult for other companies to enter the market. However, difficulty in entering the market does not imply there will not be any potential competitors. There are certainly some threats, not from the outside, but perhaps within the existing marketplace. Other categories of the beverage market might become strong competitors for both Pepsi and Coca-Cola. For instance, 'functional' beverages, which enhance nutrition or beauty, are presently popular among Chinese consumers. Among the over 130 brands, the most popular are lactic acid free milk, fruit and vegetable juices, and iced tea. This results in a market less dominated by Coke and Pepsi.

(iii) supplier power: PepsiCo currently has 12 bottling plants in China and fairly direct control over its franchises since they have to rely on technology and equipment provided by PepsiCo. Since 1992, PepsiCo has been establishing equity joint ventures, maintaining 45 percent to 60 percent of the equity share in each partnership. This indicates that Pepsi has the advantage of being able to control costs.

(iv) buyer power: At the moment the two giants, Coca-Cola and Pepsi, are trying to supply an increasing demand for their products. Today's Chinese consumers are affluent, with income levels on the rise in urban as well as a few rural areas. Bargaining power is based on consumer consumption patterns. The average Chinese consumer drinks 17 eight-ounce servings of soft drinks each year; many industrial analysts expect that average to grow to 55 servings over the next 15 years. Soft drinks in China are consumed at the point of purchase, usually in restaurants and parks. Take-home volume is small compared to that of other markets. Changing this pattern is very important for increased consumption.

(v) Substitutes: Tea is the primary substitute for the soft drink market. Tea has over 2000 years of history in China; it has become a part of Chinese culture. China is also the largest exporter of tea in the world. Tea has been an integral part of social gatherings, business meetings, and almost every other occasion for centuries. Furthermore, tea is a source of minerals and vitamins. It is also medically proven to help fight cancer. Other substitutes are milk, fruit juice, soup, and traditional Chinese beverages like ginger soup, sugarcane juice, and mineral water.

National Level

Political and Legal Forces Beginning in 1980, when the Pragmatic Reformers led by Deng Xiaoping came to power, the government adopted an 'Open Door Policy' to stimulate the economy. The goal of the reform was to improve resource allocation, raise living standards, and, most importantly, push for faster economic growth. The government invited many overseas investments, encouraged domestic enterprenuership, and adopted a socialist market system. The result of these reforms has made China the third largest economy in the world today.

The primary method by which China attracts foreign investment was through joint ventures, either equity and contractual or cooperative business operations. Both types of joint ventures limited ownership of the equity by foreign enterprises. Duration of joint ventures was initially confined to 30 years, later increased to 50 years, and now may included longer periods with State Council approval.

The major problem faced by foreign enterprises in joint ventures in China is lack of an adequate legal framework. Corruption and abuse of power at the local governmental level are on the rise. Local officials set up their own guidelines, most of which are illegal, to lure foreign investors. Many foreign enterprises that did not prepare and plan carefully were tricked into bad deals. The Chinese even refer to the practice of hooking investors as 'fishing'. Foreign investors were also vulnerable to problems with taxes, accounting, distribution, and other policy issues.

Another major legal issue faced by PepsiCo and many other foreign enterprises involve intellectual property rights. Infringement and piracy on trademarks, patents, and copyrights were prevalent in China in the 1980s. In 1992, under pressure by the international community, the Chinese government promulgated and began to enforce a number of intellectual property laws.

Technological Force Before some of the state-owned enterprises in China became privatized, their technologies were grossly inadequate and obsolete. Factory buildings were badly maintained, machinery was inefficient, and workers were unproductive because they were guaranteed an income (the 'iron rice bowl'). This has changed since the Open Door Policy began. Increasing competition and profit motivation have forced Chinese enterprises to become more technologically advanced. Production has become more efficient with more skilled workers. Joint venture agreements, as in the case of PepsiCo, often stipulate that the foreign partner must contribute technology and equipment, while the Chinese contribute land, buildings, and labor.

Macro-Economic Factors At the present time, the most serious issue in Asia is the financial crisis. Although China's situation is better than that of Japan, South Korea, and Malaysia, the threat of the crisis and its side effects should not be underestimated.

In the early 1990s, China underwent rapid economic expansion and development. Before 1994, the economy had been out of control. Land prices in some coastal cities, especially Shanghai, Guangzhou, Tianjin, Beijing, were skyrocketing. Luxurious hotels, office buildings, and villas were everywhere left empty. Inflation and unemployment were threatening the healthy growth of the economy. Former Vice-Premier, Zhu Rongji, took countermeasures to cool down the overheated economy. Now, however, the slack economy in other parts of Asia threatens China's economic growth. Analysts predict that China's four traditional and major growth engines (consumer spending, foreign investment, exports, and fixed-assets investment) will slow down. If China decides to devalue its Renminbi, the consequences would not only affect exports in other Asian countries, it would also affect U.S. companies. Serious currency exchange problems could negatively influence their profits.

Socio-Cultural Environment Doing business in China is completely different from in Western societies. Western business people must rely upon maintaining relationship networks in the Chinese cultural style in order to remain in business, especially in the absence of a strong legal framework protecting their rights. The Chinese term for these kinds of relationships is 'guanxi'.

Western business people also have to learn Chinese business practices and practice good business ethics. Such behaviors often turn out to be more important than the political and legal influences on business in China. For example, gift giving in China has a long history, with complex rules for different social levels and occasions. In Western societies, gift giving on an expensive scale is considered bribery. In China, however, it is still common for executives of large companies to give major household appliances or electronic equipment to top officials and high-ranking company managers. Chinese law states that individual gifts from foreigners are not to be accepted, but actually it is illegal only for government officials to accept gifts. Furthermore, the law does not distinguish between a small, inexpensive gift and an expensive one. Gift giving helps foreign business people receive preferential treatment from government officials, who are free to interpret many 'unwritten' and fluctuating rules. For Western business people, having a native business partner can be an enormous help in getting them in the 'back door' and helping them understand and adapt to the complicated Chinese business arena.

Demographic Environment The economic reform and rapid growth have transformed Chinese society. Chinese consumers have become increasingly affluent, while desiring foreign, modern products. Income growth has been greatest in large coastal cities and SEZs (special economic zones) such as Beijing, Shanghai, Guangzhou, Tianjin, Shenzhen, Xiamen, and other prosperous cities. The emergence of middle class families in urban areas has stimulated demand for modern consumer goods and services. However, the highly populated inland areas of the country, where it is less economically developed and still mainly agricultural and industrial, do not enjoy the same prosperity as the coastal regions.

With a one child per family policy, children have become the center of attention for each urban household. The Chinese refer to these children as 'little emperors' because they are each pampered by six adults (four grandparents and two parents). Satisfaction of material wants has become a standard expectation of single-child families. A number of products in China are targeted at children. PepsiCo recognizes this trend and has tried to develop brand loyalty among young Chinese consumers.

Internal Environment

Financial Selected financial data from PepsiCo's annual reports (Table c3.1) shows that the company has been in rapid growth with occasional setbacks. Net sales and operating profits increased from 1993 to 1995. In 1996, however, PepsiCo's beverage sales rose only 1 percent and its operating profit fell by a dramatic 57 percent. International sales declined $183 million. This is due to several factors. First, currency rates were unfavorable. Second, volume declined because of fewer shipments to franchisees. This was only partially offset by higher packaged product sales to retailers. The precipitous drop in volume is partially attributable to a series of setbacks in Latin America. The biggest bottler in Argentina was experiencing financial difficulties at that time. Puerto Rican bottling facilities were experimenting with new accounting practices, and PepsiCo lost the Venezuelan bottler to its competitor. The single-digit decline in sales in Latin America was, however, partially offset by double-digit growth in China and India.

Other international operating losses ($846 million in 1996) reflected a broad-based increase in advertising and marketing expenses. $576 million due was to asset write-downs, the disposal of some none-core businesses such as packaging, and personnel reorganization. The sale shortfall reflected price competition in the domestic market and further operational difficulties for international operations.

Table c3.1 Financial Data

	1997	1996	1995	1994	1993
Net Sales	20917	20337	19067	17984	15706
Operating Profit	2662	2040	2606	2506	2141
Total Assets	20101	22160	22944	22533	21628

Net Sales in Industry Segments

	1997	1996	1995
Beverage	10541	10587	10467
Snack Foods	10376	9750	8600

Operating Profit in Industry Segments

	1997	1996	1995
Beverage	1114	890	1309
Snack Foods	1695	1608	1432

Net Sales by Geographic Areas

	1997	1996	1995
Europe	2327	2513	2451
Canada	941	946	889
Mexico	1541	1314	1204
United Kingdom	859	810	751
United States	13878	13408	12401
Other	1371	1346	1371

Operating Profits by Geographic Area

	1997	1996	1995
Europe	(133)	(88)	(7)
Canada	105	116	94
Mexico	214	105	135
United Kingdom	106	159	139
United States	2,567	2,548	2,277
Other	(50)	(342)	103

Financial ratios evaluate the profitability of the company in comparison with its competitors and the industry. PepsiCo's 3 year gross profit margin is weaker than Coca-Cola's over the same period. Similarly, although PepsiCo's net profit margin is much stronger than the industry norm it is still weaker than Coca-Cola. Likewise, compared with the industry average, PepsiCo's return on assets is above the norm, but still behind Coca-Cola. In 1996, non-cash charges were related to investments in unconsolidated affiliates, concentrate-related assets, and assets unrelated to its core international beverages.

Generally, a relationship of at least 10 percent on return on equity is regarded as a desirable objective for providing dividends plus funds for future growth. In 1996, PepsiCo's return on equity was below 10 percent and the industry norm. In 1997, the company got back on its feet after this setback.

The next set of ratios deals with the solvency of the company. The higher the current ratio, the more assurance a company has that current liabilities can be retired. PepsiCo's current ratios were all below the industry average. Coca-Cola's current ratios were even lower than PepsiCo's. This means that both companies have little cash on hand and the turnover rate of their account receivables is low. PepsiCo is, however, more liquid than Coca-Cola. This is shown in PepsiCo's quick ratios, which are usually close to or better than the industry average. The larger the quick ratio the greater the liquidity. Coca-Cola has less favorable conditions because it has too much prepaid expenses. In 1995 and 1996, PepsiCo had a lot of inventory tied up in net working capital, which was undesirable for the company. Coca-Cola had a negative number for this ratio because its current assets were less than its current liabilities.

The third set of ratios deals with the company's capital structure or leverage condition. Since we do not have a specific industrial average for the debt to assets ratio we can only compare the competitors. In general, more debt financing increases risk to the shareholders; it is undesirable if the company's objective is to maximize shareholder wealth. However, financial theory does not set an optimal level for debt financing. Both PepsiCo and Coca-Cola have similar ratios between 25-30 percent. According to the debt to equity ratio, PepsiCo has relatively more debt in its capital structure. In 1995 and 1996, the proportions were quite significant due to the fact that PepsiCo was undergoing some capital acquisitions through bonds. In 1997, debt to equity decreased, but remained much higher than Coca-Cola. Too much debt is undesirable because of the risk of increased financial distress.

PepsiCo's long-term debt to equity ratio is the same as its debt to equity ratio because the company only issues bonds and stocks to make up its capital structure. This is also unfavorable to shareholders because long-term debts are subject to higher risks than short-term debts.

The last set of ratios deals with the company's operating efficiency. A high inventory turnover reflects fast sales generation. PepsiCo's inventory turnover ratio is above Coca-Cola's probably because Coca-Cola only engages in the soft drink business that does not require a large inventory. PepsiCo's snack food business necessitates maintaining more inventory. Nevertheless, between 1995 and 1997 its inventory turnover ratio increased, showing an improving situation.

The higher the fixed-asset ratio the better the position of a company. In 1995, PepsiCo was investing too much in fixed assets; however, the situation became favorable in 1996 and 1997. This resulted from sales of businesses, such as packaging, which enabled PepsiCo to manage its assets more efficiently. Finally, it is undesirable for a company to have a long period of collection; the smaller the average collection period ratio, the faster the company gets cash. Compared with the industrial norm, PepsiCo has an overly long collection period. However, the collection period has also been high for Coca-Cola. This may be attributed to the credit policies of both companies.

Organizational Today's corporate success can be attributed to sound management and genuine leadership. Wayne Calloway, CEO from 1986 to 1996, played a key role in positioning the company for growth. He orchestrated a major restructuring of PepsiCo's operations to concentrate on the three businesses of beverage, snacks, and restaurants. He also built a management team which empowered employees. PepsiCo became the first major corporation to award stock options to all full-time employees.

Mr. Calloway received wide praise for his accomplishments. In 1991, Chief Executive Magazine named him CEO of the Year. Industry Week magazine also named him one of America's best CEOs. A panel of financial, academic and business experts assembled by Business Month magazine twice named PepsiCo one of the best-managed companies in America. In a survey of business executives and securities analysts published by Fortune magazine in 1993, Mr. Calloway was ranked the sixth most admired CEO in the U.S. Although he passed away recently, the corporate culture he developed is deeply rooted in the company. While leadership and corporate strategies have changed, PepsiCo has maintained its reputation for superb business practices employees with personal and professional integrity.

Technological PepsiCo has been active in promoting environmental protection through package recycling, source reduction, and solid waste prevention. Across North America and in a number of international markets, the company is working with suppliers to develop reusable boxes for its distribution system. Worldwide, it has worked to make its packaging more environmentally friendly.

PepsiCo recently launched new product production for Pepsi One, the first ready-to-drink beverage in the U.S. to contain a new sweetener. This new product has been created specifically for the U.S. market. The new formula has one calorie per serving but still retains the cola taste. If this product is able to win over the U.S. market, PepsiCo will eventually introduce it internationally.

Operational Pepsi is putting its marketing priority on product image as well as taste. Its brand image is the focus for every advertising campaign, aimed at the 'New Generation' (teenage audience) with the 'Change the Script' logo. Pepsi advertisements use celebrities like Cindy Crawford, Claudia Schiffer, and Andre Agassi.

This focus is an attempt to wrest away some of Coca-Cola's market share. While Pepsi was diversifying, its rival gained strength in the international markets. For instance, Pepsi once monopolized the soft drink industry in Russia. It later lost the competition with Coca-Cola because it failed to strengthen its distribution system. In many developing countries, including China, infrastructure and distribution systems are still primitive. Coca-Cola has put more emphasis on developing and improving direct distribution through route sales and establishing sales centers in smaller cities. Pepsi is now trying to compete by putting more force behind its marketing campaigns.

Corporate-Level Strategy

Geographic Diversification

PepsiCo was pulled into China because of the attractive market. It has decided to focus an estimated $400 to $500 million in international beverage investments in emerging markets where it is likely to hold a profitable number two position. Emerging markets are long-term investments. It is believed that China will be the largest soft-drink market in the world in 15 years. With more money to spend and less time to shop and cook, processed foods and beverages are appealing to the Chinese. Increasing numbers of fast-food restaurants suggest Pepsi sales will also increase because Chinese consumers usually drink at the place of purchase. Although PepsiCo faces competition from more than 300 beverage firms in China, most of these only produce non-cola drinks and many new firms fail. It does face stiff competition from Coca-Cola, however.

PepsiCo is also confident in investing in China because joint ventures there grew by 70 percent in 1994 despite concurrent aggressive investments in the emerging low per-cap markets. The macroeconomic environment is therefore favorable as consumers have increasing bargaining power.

The government attitude toward growth and opening the market is positive. When PepsiCo initially entered the Chinese market in 1982, the government allowed only cooperative joint ventures. By 1992, however, it began to admit equity joint ventures. It has also established Special Economic Zones (SEZs) which encourage foreign direct investment by providing incentives in the form of taxes, land, and labor. Foreign enterprises within SEZs pay a 15 percent income tax compared to the 30 percent levied in areas outside the zones. If contractual agreements set a term of ten years or more, the firm can have an additional two-year tax holiday and a 50 percent reduction in taxes for the following three years. Rents to industry projects are also lower in SEZs. Finally, higher wages in these zones tend to attract more skilled labor. Nevertheless, these wages are still low compared to other countries. Thus, SEZs make available many production factors. In addition, 98 percent of the materials needed for beverage production is available in China.

Product diversification

In 1965, Pepsi-Cola and Frito-Lay joined to form PepsiCo. PepsiCo expanded from its soft drink and snack businesses into restaurants with the acquisition of Pizza Hut, KFC, and Taco Bell. It then grew to include nearly 25,000 company-owned, joint venture, and franchised outlets in some 90 countries. In 1986, PepsiCo sold two unrelated businesses, the Wilson Sporting Goods Co. and North American Van Lines Inc. As a result, PepsiCo is now involved in related, horizontal product diversification. The advantages of related diversification are market power, economies of scale, customer loyalty, and a competitive edge. PepsiCo's loyal consumers are indicated by its number two market position. Pepsi and Frito-Lay utilize the same computerized barcode system for packages and cartons to improve economies of scale.

When Roger Enrico succeeded Calloway in 1996 as CEO, he saw the restaurants as a distraction from Pepsi's core businesses of drinks and snacks. He decided to separate the beverage and snacks division from the restaurant division. Restaurants have shrinking profit margins and massive capital requirements. It is also difficult time to expand their customer base. Because other fast-food chains considered PepsiCo restaurants a threat, they refused to carry PepsiCo beverages, decreasing the potential clientele for the company. This was a significant internal weakness.

Enrico decided upon a simple strategy for building international markets through partnerships with major bottlers. Sustaining good relationships with hundreds of small bottlers has never been easy for Pepsi. In the past Pepsi had pumped untold amounts of cash into its bottling operations and joint ventures, which drained both capital and management energy.

Given its number two position worldwide, PepsiCo does have the skills and resources necessary to succeed in the beverage industry. Initially, Chinese partners contributed land, building and labor to the venture, while Pepsi contributed technology and equipment that would revert to its Chinese partner in 10 to 15 years. Although the arrangement has meant that Pepsi's investment is disproportionate to its return, these ventures have enabled Pepsi to establish a share in the rapidly growing Chinese market. This approach also gives equity partners significant management control and shows the market and government that PepsiCo is a serious investor.

Industrial Life Cycle

The beverage industry is decentralized in China, which means less rigidity and bureaucracy than is faced by other industries. In general, quality, progress, and consumption are also better in the beverage industry. PepsiCo is only limited by local regulations. PepsiCo can introduce quality products without worrying about government intervention. Moreover, it can set up better distribution systems that will increase consumer familiarity with PepsiCo products.

At this stage in the growth cycle, the beverage industry must focus on bringing new products to market as quickly as possible. At its plant opening, Pepsi introduced Pepsi Free and Diet Pepsi Free, China's first caffeine-free soft drinks. PepsiCo also introduced new products such as colorless soda and tea- and fruit- based drinks. Currently, Pepsi holds a 21 percent share of the carbonated soft-drink market in China.

The growth cycle influences the five forces model. Presently, buying power is low because Chinese consumers only drink 17 eight-ounce servings of soft drinks annually. Due to low supplier power, Chinese consumers do not have a large selection of soft drinks to choose from. Moreover, PepsiCo has only 12 bottling plants in China. There are, however, few substitutes for PepsiCo beverages in China, since most other firms produce non-carbonated drinks.

Structural Attributes

The period between 1988 to 1991 was a pivotal period in China in which many industries were in the operational stage. Furthermore, most laws, rules, and regulations had already been established. This period therefore reflects current conditions. For these reasons, the structural attributes of the beverage industry in China are discussed here in detail based on this period (Table c3.2).

Table c3.2 Structural Attributes

	No. of Firms	Net Output	Sales Revenue	Net Fixed Assets	After Tax Profit	Comprehensive Growth Index	
1988-1991						Mean	Standard Deviation
Beverage	-3.39	30.37	21.79	18.97	-11.42	10.81	14.55
Standard Deviation	4.31	8.20	9.19	6.15	81.58	15.38	
1990-1993							
Beverage	-1.18	33.98	16.93	22.23	114.83	36.48	36.90
Standard Deviation	16.28	17.14	19.69	11.87	515.60	89.05	

The growth in the number of enterprises is -3.39 compared to the standard deviation of 4.31. The negative number indicates that there are no new competitors entering the market. Nevertheless, the growth in net output is 30.37 percent. This number indicates that Chinese customers are buying more beverages from companies already in the market. Sales revenues have, however, grown by only 16.93 percent. Material costs may have increased, which means profits have been relatively steady.

The beverage industry has a relatively high level of net fixed assets compared to its standard deviation. A high asset intensive industry requires large capital or resource investments. New firms are therefore discouraged from entering. An increase in after tax profits of -11.42 (1988-1991) to 114.83 (1990-1993) indicates growth in the beverage industry. Finally, the comprehensive growth index attests to the strong potential of the beverage industry.

Business-Level Strategy

PepsiCo's competitive strategy has always been product differentiation. The Pepsi Challenge promotes taste difference and comparative image advertising. In China, however, PepsiCo mainly wants to supply demand for its product. It is less preoccupied with the marketing platform and product differentiation, more with affordable packaging and distribution. Wholesalers, rather than direct store delivery (DSD), are the backbone of Pepsi's Chinese bottle-and-can distribution network, while its fountain business is serviced by in-store merchandising. The franchiser hopes to refine its delivery system for greater customer responsiveness.

Four building blocks

Superior quality Two illustrations of quality marketing are Pepsi's commercials dubbed 'Matriarch' and 'Electron Microscope'. In the 'Matriarch' commercial, an 80-year-old woman explains that she drinks Coke because it has been around for a long, long time. She dismisses Pepsi as 'for kids', gesturing through the window from which loud music is heard. When she shouts for quiet, the 'kids', revealed to be young-at-heart 60-year-olds, crank up the volume instead.

The 'Electron Microscope' commercial supposedly shows submolecular differences between Coke and Pepsi. At first the droplets reveal the same man and his lawn-mowing wife. A close up shows that the Coke wife is dowdy, while the Pepsi wife is Cindy Crawford.

These two commercials humorously reveal quality differences between Coke and Pepsi. Pepsi suggests that drinking Coke is boring, while Pepsi is refreshing and fun.

Superior customer responsiveness PepsiCo's 'global brand' strategy is key to leveraging cross-border synergies. One of the components of this strategy is responsiveness, that is, customizing products to fit the unique needs of individual customers or groups. In 1995, brand managers at Guangzhou

Frito-Lay launched a cheese-less version of Cheetos snacks. After six months, the brand became a sellout, with plant capacity shifting to overdrive to meet demand. This is remarkable given that, although snacking is growing as a global pastime, the per-capita consumption rates and expenditures on snacks is still nearly zero in China (compared to $52 annually in the U.S.).

Cheetos was originally a cheese-flavored snack puff. However, the main ingredient was eliminated because cheese is not a staple of the Chinese diet. Following consumer tests of nearly 600 different flavors, the company settled on a popcorn-like 'Savory American Cream' flavor and teriyaki-style 'Zesty Japanese Steak' flavor. Cheetos in China is PepsiCo's bid to understand new markets and adapt product characteristics to local tastes. Flexibility also increases its revenue.

Superior innovation and efficiency To achieve superior innovation, a company must closely integrate R&D with marketing. A company should also minimize the time it takes to get new products to market and ensure good product management.

The key target market for PepsiCo's beverage and snack businesses are China's 300 million children. Chinese children have influential power as direct customers spending pocket money, as well as through 'pestering' their parents to buy products and as change agents. Children learn of new products through friends or television; they are usually the ones to introduce products into the household. PepsiCo regards mothers as important gatekeepers, however, by virtue of controlling the purse strings.

PepsiCo decided to introduce a new children's beverage in China within one year. Given that China is an emerging market, there was an advantage to being a first mover. It was an ambitious goal, however, because brand development usually takes 3 to 5 years and Pepsi did not yet have a children's drink anywhere in the world. Because of the image in China of carbonated soft drinks (CSDs) being only for adults, Pepsi decided that it would introduce a fruit juice. The PepsiCo team conducted research on different types of packaging preferences amongst six- to twelve-year-olds in Shanghai and Guangzhou. The study indicated that tetra packs were preferable because they were unbreakable and easy to handle. The study also showed that Chinese children: (i) are able to distinguish amongst brands of CSDs and juices; (ii) distinguish products by packaging; (iii) tend to repeat the health concerns held by their parents concerning CSDs; (iv) find the personification of a fruit ('Fruitman') as novel and interesting; and (v) are powerfully motivated by the texture of a drink in their taste preferences.

PepsiCo decided to name its new drink FruitMagix to heighten a sense of excitement and fantasy. It also printed fun, educational information on the drink, since Asian mothers place a lot of emphasis on children's education. FruitMagix was launched in early November 1995 in Guangzhou, 44 weeks after development. The core concept was 'fun', carried out in every element of the brand launch: in its television campaign, by having Fruitman visit schools, and in coloring contests. FruitMagix was expanded from an initial orange flavor to other flavors. FruitMagix is now sold in 45 percent of all beverage outlets in the city.

In conclusion, research must be used as a decision support system. A cross-functional task force helps maintain focus on the end objective. PepsiCo not only encourages innovation in its products, but also in the process by which it develops new brands.

International Entry Strategies

In 1982, PepsiCo began its operations in China. PepsiCo entered the Chinese market by forming a cooperative joint venture with local partners. In 1992, the Chinese government permitted Pepsi to start equity joint ventures with Chinese partners. Shenzhou Happiness Soft Drink Factory was the first joint venture that PepsiCo set up with a domestic partner. Its local partner was the Shenzhen City Food Company located in Shenzhou in the province of Guangdong. PepsiCo has invested $3,600 million in this project, while the local Chinese partner has made a $4,400 million investment. Pepsi-Cola has a 45 percent equity share in this case, compared to Shenzhen City Food Company's 35 percent. The duration of this project was designated for 15 years so it is still operational today. The core objective of this venture was bottling Pepsi-Cola soft drinks.

Entry Mode Selection

PepsiCo chose the joint venture mode partly because of the government at that time only allowed this entry mode. Other underlying country- and the industry-specific factors support this decision.

Country specific factors include a big cultural distance between the United States and China. Having a partner in China mitigates the liabilities of foreignness. Besides that, the infrastructure condition in China is not as well-developed as in the U.S. Setting up an effective distribution channel depends strongly on having good relationships with different distributors, which were provided by the local partner. The Chinese government also imposes strict policies on foreign business operations; the local partner helps the joint venture deal with such policies most efficiently since the joint venture operates as a local entity due to the presence of local partners. Since the intellectual protection laws are not enforced in China, a joint venture also allows PepsiCo to maintain more control over its products and soft drink formulas.

PepsiCo also considered some industry-specific factors before choosing the joint venture entry mode. One of these factors was competition. PepsiCo is not the first foreign beverage company to enter the Chinese market. It had a major competitor in Coca-Cola, and numerous small local competitors. Relationships with suppliers and buyers also play an important role in the beverage industry in China. By using the networks of its local partners, PepsiCo ensures access to reliable suppliers and buyers.

The joint venture provides the benefit of risk reduction while giving PepsiCo greater global integration and strategic flexibility. Its cooperative joint venture has no limits on the duration of the contract nor is PepsiCo prohibited from withdrawing its registered capital during the contract term. Therefore, management, its asset structure, and the organization of its production processes are all more flexible.

PepsiCo also benefits from product portfolio diversification and dispersion and reduction of fixed costs. This results in a lower total capital investment and faster entry and payback. As a cooperative joint venture, PepsiCo is exempt from paying transfer taxes and duties on equipment that is imported and used for setting up the joint venture operations.

Another advantage is that PepsiCo can learn from its local Chinese partners while building on their established markets. The networks with the government, suppliers, buyers, and customers provide the joint venture with better access to materials, technology, labor, capital, and distribution channels.

Entry Timing

China has been isolated from the rest of the world for many decades. Foreign firms have described the Chinese market as uncertain and difficult to enter. On the other hand, it presents many potential business opportunities and a large market for foreign companies to explore. Since PepsiCo was not the first entrant to the Chinese market, it did not have the brand image advantage Coca-Cola enjoys and faced a lot of competition. It has, however, benefited from the first entrants through environment-stabilization and learning. First movers reduce the risk of structural industry or market instability as well as macroeconomic or political uncertainty.

As the second largest foreign soft drink company to enter the Chinese market, PepsiCo must remain innovative and adaptive to be competitive in the vast Chinese market.

Location Selection

PepsiCo chose to locate in southern China (in Guangzhou, Fuzhou, and Shenzhen) because these provinces are closer to the more entrepreneurial Hong Kong. PepsiCo's market orientation was to target its product for the local market. The process is made easier in the southern provinces where lifestyles are similar to those in Hong Kong, which means consumers there are more open to new products. Locating in these regions makes it easier for PepsiCo to penetrate the market.

These provinces are open economic regions with greater autonomy to conduct their economic affairs. They provide more Western-style business facilities and a favorable cultural atmosphere for international business activities. Joint ventures in these areas enjoy preferential treatment in terms of income tax and other fees. Foreign invested enterprises are also excluded from paying the Industrial and Commercial Consolidation Tax (ICCT) for imported production equipment and facilities, export products, and imported raw materials and components or packing materials for the production of export products. Since these provinces are industrialized, their infrastructures are also better than in other provinces. Moreover, workers from the southern provinces tend to be better qualified.

As an SEZ, Shenzhen has provincial-level power over its economic administration. Special policies pertaining to PepsiCo's joint venture in this city include increased credit loans, retention of all newly increased revenues for a given time period, and exemption from tariffs for materials required for building up the zone.

PepsiCo picked Guangdong and Fujian for two joint ventures because they contain Economic and Technological Development Zones (ETDZs). ETDZs are usually locations near a harbor that have the basic infrastructure for the establishment of new ventures. Within an ETDZ, FIEs can take advantage of reduced taxes and fees (the Enterprise Income Tax (EIT), Customs Duties, the ICCT, and land rent). The central government also allows Guangdong and Fujian special policies and flexibility in conducting foreign economic activities. They receive more financial support. They are also two of the 14 coastal port cities that were opened and granted more autonomy to attract FDI in 1984.

International Cooperative Strategies

Partner Selection

Partner selection is the most crucial process in forming a joint venture. According to the Six-Cs Scheme for partner selection, the first criterion PepsiCo had to consider was whether its goals were compatible with its prospective Chinese partners. The local Chinese companies' goals were to gain capital, profit, and new technology. PepsiCo's goal was to enter the Chinese soft drink market. Their long-term goals for the joint venture were therefore compatible. This ensured a high degree of commitment by both PepsiCo and its Chinese partners.

The third factor to be analyzed was whether the Chinese partners had complementary skills. PepsiCo provided mainly upstream factors (equipment, technology, organizational skills, and other factors related to production) in the value chain while the local Chinese companies were providing downstream factors (land, buildings, and labor; pricing, customer and government relationships, marketing and promotion).

A cooperative culture is also important; it indicates whether the partner will be mutually compatible. Significant differences in corporate culture or managerial policies would probably lead to dispute in the future. PepsiCo values its workers. This idea is similar to the ethics of China's collectivistic society in which management is not completely task-oriented. Therefore, PepsiCo and its Chinese partners had a cooperative culture.

The strategic capability of the joint venture was another consideration. Both PepsiCo and its Chinese partners are analyzers, and therefore compatible. Analyzer companies tend to practice both cost efficiency and a product differentiation strategy.

The local partners that PepsiCo chose were State Owned Enterprises (SOE) and therefore had strong relationships with the local government. These were also experienced local companies, with strong local images, customer loyalty, and networks. PepsiCo is also able to obtain better market knowledge from these local partners.

Sharing Distribution and Control

Pepsi-Cola possesses the majority of the equity in its joint ventures with Chinese companies. PepsiCo probably expected external antecedents such as environmental uncertainty and complexity. A larger share in the joint venture would provide more control and protection in the face of these hazards.

Internal antecedents include its strategic objectives. PepsiCo entered the Chinese soft drink market to gain market share. A majority of equity better supports this goal. It also gave the company protection of its proprietary competencies and stronger bargaining power in the face of dependence on local partners. Majority equity helps PepsiCo balance its ventures between the two imperatives of global integration and local responsiveness.

Other International Strategies

International Strategy

PepsiCo practices a transnational strategy in its joint ventures in China. This is a hybrid strategy that allows local ventures to customize products and marketing to suit the needs of customers while coordinating activities with the parent company and benefiting from global learning. PepsiCo's transnational strategy places a little more emphasis on the multi-domestic side. It tends to decentralize power to local ventures in order to increase local responsiveness. PepsiCo takes an active strategic role in its joint ventures, however, with a high degree of both localization and integration. The local joint venture partners and the parent company closely coordinate their activities and decisions. Its local ventures are thereby able to learn from PepsiCo headquarters.

PepsiCo confronts a relatively diverse market structure in China, with a complex business and political environment. There are many regulations and unique business policies that must be followed. Giving more power to local managers within its transnational strategy provides them with greater flexibility to make necessary changes. The cooperation of a local management team and its ability to network with local firms and the government is crucial for the realization of PepsiCo's expansion goal.

Global Business Structure

PepsiCo uses a global regional structure. It has different regional subsidiaries under the control of PepsiCo headquarters in New York. In 1988, PepsiCo was reorganized along geographic lines into four major regions. Each region has its own president and senior management staff.

Operational Strategy

PepsiCo strongly believes in the importance of marketing. It has used many different slogans to market its products. Celebrity marketing is PepsiCo's favorite method, but it relies even more heavily on music. Commercials featuring Michael Jackson in the early 1980s combined these two approaches.

PepsiCo also uses entertainment marketing strategies in the international market. It signed Hong Kong singer/movie star Aaron Kwok to represent its soft drinks in China in 1998. Again, PepsiCo combined music with celebrity. The company hired a Hong Kong advertising agency, Ogilvy & Mather, to produce a music video that was widely shown on TV throughout China and Hong Kong for three months. The commercial features the same song in either Mandarin or Cantonese languages depending on the region in which it is being shown. PepsiCo has continued this campaign with promotion of Kwok's latest music album. The album cover includes Pepsi's signature blue and red colors and the album's title is 'Generation Next', which is PepsiCo's current slogan. Other promotional activities include large display boards featuring Kwok in major cities such as Shanghai and organizing charity concerts for Kwok with the obvious purpose of promoting the brand.

Conclusion and Suggestions

There are many compelling reasons for U.S. companies to expand abroad. Revenues and profits are modest at home and in much of the industrialized world, while spending on consumer goods is rising significantly in many other parts of the globe. There is intense competition in many product categories in the U.S. A rise in private labels and store brands is also taking a toll on MNC profits. U.S. companies are therefore turning to developing markets in their aim for double-digit growth.

A promising market does not always guarantee profit growth, however. Moving into a foreign market can prove difficult and costly for newcomers. In China, political and distribution issues offer daunting logistical challenges. For example, delivery vehicles in China usually have two wheels rather than eighteen. Cultural and business practices are different from those in the U.S. Building relationship networks is crucial, but takes time and is not easy. Finally, local taste preferences can be quite specific, as PepsiCo found in adapting Cheetos to China. Overall, there are many risks and obstacles in the foreign market.

Foreign companies desiring expansion into the Chinese market should evaluate the their own strengths and weaknesses, thoroughly research the host country market, choose reliable partners and make careful plans before entry, develop relationships with members of the central and local governments, and study China's cultural practices.

Several suggestions derive from PepsiCo's experiences. PepsiCo has had major problems with inefficient distribution networks and problems with its international bottlers. The creation of a separate business entity overseas would help it improve distribution, reduce costs, and increase operating profits.

Along with its core products of soft drinks and snacks, the restaurant business proved too much for PepsiCo to handle. It decided to spin off the restaurant business into another independent company. It needs to follow this action through to completion rather than continuing to spend too much time, energy, and capital diversifying. In other words, PepsiCo needs to refocus.

The need to redesign its image is critical to the future success of the company. PepsiCo is perceived as outdated in many countries. It needs to reposition its products as refreshing, 'cool' soft drinks. It has already taken a step in this direction by hiring singer Aaron Kwok to represent its beverages in China. Directing its efforts towards young consumers is another wise decision. Recent advertising campaigns have been quite expensive, however, and their success is difficult to measure. PepsiCo should find new ways to examine the effectiveness of its various marketing strategies.

Case Study 4: Xerox

Executive Summary

Xerox was founded in 1906 as the Haloid Company, a distributor and manufacturer of photographic paper. Today, Xerox Corporation is one of the leaders in the industry of document production and management. Since the mid-1960s, Xerox has been conducting business in countries outside of the U.S., integrating entrance into foreign markets with its corporate strategy. Under the guidance of C.E.O. David A. Allaire, Xerox currently operates or sells its products in more than 150 countries. In 1997, Xerox earned $18.2 billion in revenues, with a net profit of $1.5 billion, from operations in the United States, Canada, Latin America, and Europe. Fuji Xerox Co., Ltd. of Japan brought in another $7.4 billion in revenues in the same year.

Company Introduction

Corporate Development

In 1938, Chester Carlson, a patent attorney and part time inventor, created the world's first copier. The prototype was to be a replacement for carbon paper, but it was large and messy. Carlson attempted to sell his technology unsuccessfully for nine years. IBM and General Electric were among the companies that ignored his invention. After refining his technology, Carlson finally licensed his copier to The Haloid Company of New York in 1947.

Haloid coined the term 'xerography', derived from Greek words meaning 'dry' and 'writing'. The company shortened xerography to Xerox as a trademark for the copiers. The copiers were so successful, that The Haloid Company changed its name, first to "Haloid Xerox", then to "Xerox" in 1961.

Xerox began conducting business in Asia in the 1960s by exporting its copiers. Since then, it has opened manufacturing plants and research centers and established joint ventures worldwide. The following timeline covers Xerox's substantial dealings in Asia, with a concentration on China.

1962 - Xerox's first joint venture with a company on the Asian continent was established with Fuji Photo Film Co., Ltd. of Japan. The venture is named 'Fuji Xerox'.

1964 - Xerox began selling copiers and other document processing equipment in Hong Kong as 'Rank Xerox (Hong Kong) Ltd.'.

1969 - Operations department opened in Macau.

1971 - Fuji Xerox purchased Iwatsuki and Takematsu manufacturing plants in Japan.

1979 - Fuji Xerox won the Deming Prize, Japan's highest award for quality.

1987 - Its joint venture with China Computer Systems Engineering Corporation opened an electronic printing center in Beijing. A second joint venture with Shanghai Movie Photo Industry Corporation (SMPIC) and the Chinese Bank of Communications was formed to make copiers in China.

1991 - Xerox and Fuji Xerox formed Xerox International partners. Based in Singapore to serve nine Asia-Pacific countries, the company markets low-end printers worldwide.

1994 - The Xerox Quality institute was established as a strategic alliance between Hong Kong Productivity Council and Xerox.

1995 - Xerox (China) Ltd., a subsidiary of Xerox, was formed to oversee marketing and manufacturing in China.

As the time line illustrates, Xerox's most recent activities in Asian markets have taken place in China. This trend marks the importance of China as potentially one of the most lucrative markets in the world. Xerox first established operations in Hong Kong; it has further entered the Chinese market by establishing joint ventures with existing Chinese firms and banks.

Xerox's goal for its operations in China is to become the leading supplier of document products to the Chinese economy by the turn of the century. It is estimated that by the year 2000, China will be the third largest economy in the world. Xerox China is already one of the fastest growing entities within the Xerox Corporation.

Major Businesses

Xerox's mission statement is to become the leader in the global document market. Prior to the release of a new marketing strategy in 1994, Xerox was known for its copiers. The correlation was so strong that the name Xerox nearly became the generic term for photocopying. This prompted the adoption of the stylized X as Xerox's trademark along with the reinvention of Xerox as 'The Document Company'.

Xerox and Fuji Xerox offer the broadest selection of document products and services in the industry. Xerox currently sells publishing systems, copiers, printers, scanners, fax machines, and document management software in more than 150 countries. The purpose of Xerox International Partners, a joint venture between Xerox and Fuji Xerox, is to sell printers to equipment manufacturers for resale.

The Xerox Services Division handles facilities management, corporate security, and employee health services. Other operations include the Xerox Credit Corporation, which finances purchase of Xerox business equipment, and the Xerox Realty Corporation, which develops land for commercial use.

Xerox's Alliances

Xerox currently engages in joint ventures, corporate alliances, and over 300 third party agreements with other companies. The primary reason Xerox gives for establishing alliances is to increase compatibility between its products and those of its competitors. Xerox strategically selects partners who specialize in technological development. By allying with innovative companies, Xerox ensures that its products will be compatible with the latest technology. Xerox currently has alliances with companies such as Adobe Systems Inc., Compaq Computer Corporation, IBM, and Microsoft Corporation. Adobe helps Xerox provide customers with document production systems for all levels of the enterprise. Xerox works with Compaq to create integrated products at lower costs. Xerox is exploring opportunities on the Internet for its document services with IBM. The alliance with Microsoft is to facilitate future compatibility between Xerox and Microsoft products.

SWOT Analysis: External Environment

Industrial Level

Existing Competitors The office equipment and supplies industry is moderately competitive. One of Xerox's major competitors in China is Canon Inc. Xerox has been able to stay competitive, however. In 1991, it held a slightly smaller market share of 18 percent, compared to Canon's 27 percent. In recent years, Xerox has surpassed Canon by gaining a 29 percent market share.

Firms involved in the office equipment and supplies industry deal with many barriers to entry. Quotas, import licensing, tariffs, and various taxes are just a few of these barriers, along with government regulations regarding project approval. Such barriers cause delays in project implementation that can cost firms money. One method of diminishing these barriers is by establishing joint ventures with local Chinese firms. This entry mode allows foreign firms to share the burden of imposed governmental regulations and gain knowledge from local firms about the local culture, business etiquette, and business networking. Both Canon and Xerox have used partnerships to create new opportunities and increase their profit potential in China.

Potential Competitors The threat of new entrants into the Chinese market is fairly low because of high capital requirements. China is considered an expensive locale to operate in, including high rental rates and tariffs. Most small firms cannot produce the capital necessary for entering this market and being innovative enough to stay competitive.

Power of Buyers Since there are few competitors in this industry in China, consumers do not have much bargaining power. The majority of buyers come from institutions like the government. They are faced with constraints on purchases and the need to get purchasing approval that limits their choices and further reduces their bargaining power.

The Chinese government has imposed certain restrictions on Xerox products. For example, it requires companies to register their copiers with a governmental security agency.

Substitutes In the office equipment industry there are few substitutes for the copier, printer, and fax machine. The Internet and e-mail both provide methods of copying and transferring data. However, copiers, printers, and fax machines provide the only means for creating hard copies of data. The lack of comparable substitutes increases the marketing power of companies such as Xerox, making this a desirable market.

Power of Suppliers The marketing power of suppliers in China is a moderately low threat to Xerox mainly because of the low number of competitors in the industry. Because Xerox is larger than any of its suppliers, it has greater bargaining power. It is able to set the terms on details of payment, product specifications, and delivery arrangements, even if it is limited to doing business with only a few vendors due to governmental restrictions. Furthermore, because of its technological requirements, Xerox often manufactures or imports its supplies.

National Level

Demographics China has one of the largest pools of unskilled labor in the world, with a surplus of 150 million rural workers. This labor is inexpensive. In China, the average wage is US$0.25 per hour, even cheaper than countries such as Indonesia, which average US$0.30 per hour. Since minimum wages in the United States range from $4.00 to $7.00 per hour, a company can save millions of dollars in employee expenses alone by doing business in China.

Political/Legal Generally, the Chinese government's attitude towards foreign investors has been positive because it understands the vital role companies from abroad play in improving the economy. The government does tend to favor domestic firms and goods, however. For example, Xerox is required to use government-approved vendors in its four main joint ventures. Although Xerox still has bargaining power over its suppliers, the number of suppliers is limited.

Another legal constraint Xerox faces is that copiers must be registered with the Chinese security agency. The government is attempting to prevent document and currency counterfeiting.

In recent years, the government has set up special economic zones to attract foreign investment as part of its economic reform program. Companies that have factories and offices in these zones are granted incentives such as special tax rates. The majority of these zones are located along the coasts (coastal city zones and eastern seaboard zones) which are also the most industrialized areas in China.

Technological Because China is not as technologically advanced as other countries, the government is making an effort to gain know-how and new technology. It has allocated approximately $340 billion dollars to fulfill its modernization plans, including importing equipment and building a better infrastructure. The improved infrastructure and technology may decrease the need for outsourcing by companies such as Xerox, thus reducing their expenses.

Although foreign firms are not required by law to share their technology with local firms, they are encouraged and even pressured to do so. Because information exchange is highly valued by the Chinese government, joint ventures are favored. Xerox has been able to profit from these joint ventures with development of new technology.

Macroeconomic factors Although some experts say that China has one of the worst economies because of barriers like high costs and tariff rates, China is still the seventh largest economy in the world. Along with Hong Kong and Taiwan, China is the biggest emerging market in the world. Its potential for growth is shown by its 1997 GDP rate of 9.3 percent. This rate has been increasing despite a slowly growing inflation rate. In addition, due to an increase in foreign activities such as exports, the Chinese currency has remained steady despite the strong U.S. dollar. There has even been a slight increase in the value of the Chinese currency, from RMB 8.31:$1(U.S.) in 1996 to RMB 8.28:$1(U.S.) in 1997.

The Chinese government has been working to increase fair treatment of foreign firms under its 'National Treatment' policy. Under this policy, both domestic and foreign firms are treated the same. For example, foreign firms now enjoy a standard 33 percent tax rate rather than the earlier 50 percent. If they do business in special economic zones, they receive the lower tax rate of 15 percent.

SWOT Analysis: Internal Environment

Financial

Financially, Xerox is fairly competitive. It has a slightly higher profitability than Canon and is better able to cover its operating expenses (a 49.9 percent gross profit margin compared to Canon's 44.6 percent). Xerox also yields a more profitable return on sales and investments than Canon. Its liquidity is not as good as Canon's, however, as shown by its current and quick ratios. It is not as efficient as Canon when it comes to paying off short-term creditors. This may be due to higher investments in R&D, as shown by its leverage ratios. Xerox has double the percentage of funds invested in its operations than does Canon. This is due to its effort to remain innovative by investing in new technology. Also, Xerox uses a high amount of inventory to generate revenue, with an inventory turnover ratio of 3.26 versus Canon's ratio of 2.71. Xerox's ability to take financial risks in order to reach long term goals is one of the reasons it has become a leader in its industry.

Technological development

Xerox believes that the key to staying competitive and remaining a market leader is innovation. Its R&D spending is highly intensive ($1.7 billion in 1997 alone). Over the years, Xerox has invested larger percentages of annual sales in the development of new technology than any of its competitors. In 1993, it allocated 6 percent of its sales to R&D, while Canon only allocated 5.7 percent.

Xerox uses its joint ventures to develop new products and improve customer service. In 1996, it established the Xerox Industry Development Co. Ltd. in Shanghai. This company was developed to create new methods of servicing and distributing Xerox products in China. In the same year, working with Adobe and Changzhou SinoType Technology, Xerox created the first Adobe PostScript color laser printer capable of printing Chinese fonts. Xerox has therefore been focusing in on the Chinese market through product differentiation.

Organizational Capabilities

Xerox prides itself on having a diverse and open organization. It welcomes people from different backgrounds and encourages them to voice new ideas. This helps keep Xerox on the cutting edge. Xerox understands the value of its employees and works with them to create a balance between their family and work lives by offering options such as flexible hours and job sharing. By treating its employees with respect, it more effectively taps their potential.

Operational Capabilities

Xerox also believes in tapping the resources and knowledge of local firms. All of Xerox's manufacturing plants are joint ventures, including partnerships with the Shanghai SMPIC Corporation and the Shanghai Jiushi Corporation. Xerox works with local firms not only to manufacture goods, but to share ideas and know-how on marketing and distributing products in China.

Xerox deliberately contributes to China's infrastructure and economy. It established the first Document Technology Center in Beijing in 1996 to develop technology needed to modernize document processing. The technology created there both benefited Xerox and various sectors in China such as the government, banks, and the educational system. In December 1996, Xerox set up the Industry Development Co. Ltd. in Shanghai's Pudong New Area Wai Gao Qiau Free Trade Zone. This venture has helped improve the service, reliability, and timeliness of supply shipments. Projects like these help to improve relations with the Chinese government and business circles by showing Xerox's willingness to share knowledge.

Corporate-Level Strategy

Geographic Diversification

Increasing potential markets by expanding internationally is particularly attractive to firms whose domestic markets have limited growth opportunities. The copier industry in the U.S. is already flooded because the U.S. enjoys a high degree of technological development.

The decision to enter China was made on the basis of several factors. First, as noted above, the Chinese Economic Area (China, Hong Kong, and Taiwan) is the biggest emerging market worldwide. It had a combined GDP of $783.7 billion in 1994. Second, the demand for copiers is booming because business in China is booming. Today's generation requires computers, fax machines, and copiers for even basic business functions. Xerox products are virtually a necessity in China. Third, competition in the copier industry was far from intensive. Firm rivalry was weak enough to allow Xerox to penetrate the market full force. Furthermore, government taxation policies favored investment, especially in special economic zones. Thus, although economic factors were not initially positive, Xerox knew the potential was enormous. Presently, Xerox China is one of Xerox's fastest growing subsidiaries.

Xerox was also attracted to China for the abundant availability of many production factors such as cheap labor, materials and low land rent. Xerox chose to expand into areas that would strengthen the local business economy. This in turn increased jobs and stabilized the demand and supply factors, creating an even more favorable business environment.

When Xerox established its first joint venture in China, the value of the Chinese Yuan against the US dollar was competitive. This helped Xerox gain an initial market share. One negative factor was the introduction of government purchase controls, as part of the government's austerity policy. This led to a far smaller market than Xerox had originally envisioned. In order to purchase a copier, a prospective buyer (from a large agency) first had to obtain permission from several government agencies. Because Xerox was mainly interested in penetrating the business market, this policy negatively affected its production costs.

Related and support industries are also important factors for a foreign company doing business in a developing country. Since Xerox is primarily concerned with gaining long-term acceptance in China, it accepted a stipulation by the Chinese government that 70 percent of components would be sourced locally by the end of 1992. Xerox developed close working relations with the Shanghai Foreign Investment Commission, which provides funding to local companies to enable them to upgrade their plants. Cooperating with the Shanghai Foreign Investment Commission also gave Xerox an opportunity to learn appropriate ways to conduct business in China.

Product diversification

Xerox China's strategy is categorized as both low-cost leadership and product differentiation. Xerox needs to combine both competitive strategies to succeed in the imaging industry in China. The international low-cost strategy is likely to progress in a country where there is high demand for new products, as in China.

Xerox offers the broadest array of document products and services in the industry, including copiers, printers, fax machines, scanners, desktop software, digital printing and publishing systems, supplies, and comprehensive document-management services from the running of in-house production centers to the creation of networks. Xerox decided to specialize in the photo/imaging industry within China because that is what

Xerox does best. It had already achieved success in this industry in other countries overseas.

Xerox is a related, vertically integrated corporation. Such corporations tend to be seen as specialists. As a specialist in the copier industry, Xerox has invested a lot of money on research and development to create the most efficient, economical, cutting edge machines in the world. Because Xerox has concentrated on perfecting one core product, it has developed a worldwide brand name trusted for quality. When the corporation diversifies its core product to suit local needs, loyalty to the company increases further. This provides greater market power.

Business-Level Strategy

Geographic Diversification

As a related, vertically integrated company, geographic diversification provides other advantages. Xerox gains economies of scale while exploiting core competencies across its various international markets. This allows resource and knowledge sharing between units across country borders. Xerox shares its knowledge (via patents, engineers, marketing, etc.) with subsidiaries in 130 countries. Sometimes it is able to share facilities and machinery with joint partners as well. Through joint ventures with other leading, technologically advanced companies, Xerox's competitive advantages have been heightened.

Vigorous quality standards, extensive dealer networks, and aggressive and skillfully executed advertising campaigns accompanied with reasonable prices have allowed Xerox China to become the number one copier seller in China. In 1989, Xerox China had gained 32 percent of the Chinese desktop copier market; by late 1990 it had 45 percent.

Building Blocks

A company capable of successfully implementing an integrated low-cost/differentiation strategy should be positioned to adapt quickly and effectively leverage its core competencies across business units and product lines. The major building blocks of Xerox's business strategy have been superior quality, customer responsiveness, and innovation.

Quality Xerox is renowned throughout the world for its quality products. It chose a Shanghai partner that also had a reputation for quality in China. All components used by Xerox China are subject to the same standards of quality established by Xerox Corporation. The parent company also instituted its corporate quality control culture in the venture to ensure that Xerox China's output is on par with Xerox products manufactured in other countries. Quality in Xerox China is thus instilled not only by the Chinese government but also by the corporation. Xerox reinforces the concept of quality at all levels, not just in interactions with the end user.

A Customer Satisfaction Review Board was established by Xerox to ensure that its reputation would remain high in China. As a result, the Shanghai municipal government awarded the venture the Shanghai Quality Award in 1989 and 1990, and Xerox Corporation awarded it an in-house quality award in 1990.

Chinese components still tend to be produced at costs above the world market average, which forces up the final cost of Xerox China copiers. Although the prices of Xerox products in China are more than in the U.S., Xerox China products are still priced competitively against Japanese brand name copiers. Customers are willing to pay a little more for Xerox's products because of its excellent reputation for reliability.

Responsiveness Xerox believes that success comes from satisfying customers. Xerox China is the fastest growing division in the Xerox corporation, which indicates that this strategy has been effective in that market.

In today's evolving marketplace, customer satisfaction can be associated with the environmental, health, or safety impact of a product or the performance of the corporation as a whole. Environmental considerations are now designed into products from the beginning, rather than as an afterthought. Manufacturing engineers are designing source separation centers into assembly and disassembly lines and packaging engineers are designing reusability into the vendor specifications for shipment of Xerox parts and assemblies. Programs have been implemented which survey the environmental requirements of customers in the US, Canada and Europe. The results will be used in designing future products. Designing environmental attributes into products gives Xerox a strong marketplace presence through enhanced customer satisfaction.

Innovation Xerox spends hundreds of thousands of dollars to create innovative products for the business world. In 1998, Xerox released two software tools incorporating the Internet Printing Protocol (IPP) designed to promote universal printing standards set by a consortium of industry leaders. Use of this software will enable swifter, simpler, higher quality printing from the Internet. The company provided this software free of charge to developers of printer, print-service, and network-operating products. With this move, Xerox took initiative, using creative research to meet the needs of today's dynamic, high-tech business environment.

International Entry Strategies

Entry Mode Selection

The sheer size of the Chinese population and the availability of cheap labor have made China an attractive location for international business expansion. When Xerox entered China in the early 1980s through export, Japanese manufacturers such as Canon, Minolta, Ricoh, and Toshiba dominated the copier market in China. Xerox chose to enter the export market through a joint venture, believing it would give Xerox an advantage in dealing with the Chinese community. The Chinese government responded with loyalty towards Xerox products, while outside businesses also benefited by associating with Xerox and its network. The company's dominant position in a restricted market undoubtedly reflects official support of the joint venture mode.

Numerous pitfalls faced any company desiring to commit financial as well as capital investments to China. The legal system left much to be desired. Intellectual property rights were rarely enforced. Local managerial practices were outdated. Taking into consideration all these risk factors, Xerox opted for the export mode in order to capture the copier market while avoiding the risks of equity investment. Exporting allowed Xerox to test the viability of the copier market and maintain control over the quality of the products it sold in China.

Xerox soon took a different look at China as a strategic market. Its competitors, such as Canon, Minolta, Ricoh and Toshiba, had already been exporting to China and had a long history of serving the Chinese market. Xerox, however, was the first copier manufacturer to establish a joint venture there. To make up for lost time and capture a larger share of the growing copier market, Xerox began to contemplate a greater involvement in the copier market in China. Xerox decided to establish an equity joint venture with Shanghai Movie and Photo Industry Corporation (SMPIC) and Bank of China in 1987. The new entity was named Xerox Shanghai.

Xerox's strategic choice seemed optimal for several reasons. First of all, contributions from its partners reduced its financial burden. They also provided plants, equipment and personnel. Xerox was therefore able to reduce the amount of its capital investment and had a ready labor pool. It also reduced the losses it might incur in the event that the joint venture failed. With SMPIC and Bank of China holding a total of 49 percent share of the joint venture, Xerox was assured of a certain level of business vigilance from its two partners. Cooperation was more likely to be forthcoming and business decisions based on the bottom line rather than cronyism or favoritism.

The joint venture would also allow Xerox to utilize its the market expertise of its partners, learn about local market conditions and business practices, and share in a wider distribution network for the joint venture products. This helped Xerox penetrate the market with relative ease and get its products to the market faster. With the copier market projected to grow by as much as 20 percent each year, the joint venture would allow Xerox to capitalize on potential economies of scale. Affiliation with a local copier firm also increased Xerox's market presence relative to both foreign and domestic competitors. The combined resources of the joint venture also served as an entry barrier to other prospective competitors.

An established social network was important for meeting the demand for products outside the Shanghai area. Xerox Shanghai established a nationwide distribution, sales, and service network, including over 100 dealerships. The nationwide network helped Xerox build good relationships with the Chinese community while gaining introductions to every business and person interested in the technological field. Xerox also set up three representative offices in Beijing, Guangzhou, and Shanghai to provide additional dealer support in areas such as training, inventory, and advertising.

Xerox generally collaborates with leading companies to better serve its customers in today's high-tech, fast-changing global marketplace. Cooperation allows each company to concentrate on its core strengths and still provide customers with unified solutions to complex information needs.

Firm-Specific Factors International business expansion has always been an important part of Xerox's overall corporate strategy. Its overseas operations in Europe, Asia, and Latin America account for over half of the company's total revenue in most years. The joint venture preference in China was further motivated by Xerox's substantial experiences and success with overseas joint venture operations in Australia, Brazil, Germany, Great Britain, India, and Japan.

The driving force behind Xerox's foray into China was the strategic intent to become the leader in the copier industry in China by the year 2000. This objective was especially daunting since most of its formidable competitors were already on the scene when Xerox decided to enter the copier market. To capture a greater market share, Xerox needed to serve the market better than any of its competitors. This required better understanding and information about the local market, a readily accessible distribution network, and appropriate *guanxi* for helping the business operate smoothly. Only through a local partner could Xerox hope to achieve these benefits.

Country-Specific Factors In entering the photo/imaging industry in China, Xerox had to research the country's governmental industrial and foreign direct investment policies. China's top political leaders are strongly supportive of foreign business investment in China, realizing that foreign investment plays an integral part in supporting the country's modernization drive. To ensure modernization, the government needs a constant inflow of foreign investment to help develop infrastructure and technology. To attract foreign investment, the Chinese government often gives preferential treatment to foreign companies interested in setting up joint ventures in China. Such preferential treatment includes tax exemptions, loans for working capital, priority in obtaining basic utilities and facilities, and exemptions from land fees. The government is also concerned that excessive foreign investment will bring about foreign domination of the local economy, however. To secure capital inflow without compromising national security, the Chinese government favors establishment of equity joint ventures over other entry modes. Accordingly, it is generally easier to meet the requirements for joint venture establishment. A joint venture thus allowed Xerox faster, easier access to establishing manufacturing facilities in China.

China's leadership is also attempting to reform the legal system to rationalize the various sets of regulations governing commercial activity. China has a complex system of trade and investment incentives and disincentives, some of which may work for exporters and investors, and some which count against them. Its service sectors are open only on an experimental basis. One of the challenges inherent in entering China is that, since its economy is in the midst of reform, rules and regulations are ambiguous, subject to change, applied inconsistently, and non-transparent. U.S. firms have been hindered in bidding on major projects in China by opaque bidding procedures. Although open and competitive bidding is increasingly used for both domestic and foreign-funded projects, the great majority of government procurement contracts are handled through domestic tenders or direct negotiation with selected suppliers. Foreign suppliers are routinely discriminated against in areas where domestic suppliers exist. Projects in certain fields require government approval, usually from several different organizations and levels. Even if a project meets the government's investment screening requirements, it may still be rejected if the contract is deemed unfair, its technology is available elsewhere in China, or if there is already sufficient production capacity for a particular product.

One factor, which prompted Xerox's choice of joint venture rather than technological transfer agreement, was concern over the dismal record of intellectual property right protection in China. A joint venture helps ensure that Xerox's desktop office copier technology is solely transferred to the newly founded partnership, rather than to a local partner.

Xerox's strategy in China is primarily to target its product of mid-range to low-end copiers at the domestic market. Yet the Chinese government would rather have the majority of joint venture outputs exported. A compromise was reached whereby Xerox got its wish in exchange for a stipulation that 70 percent of the venture components would be sourced locally by 1992.

Industry Specific Factors Since copier manufacturing is a capital intensive industry, going it alone would have required Xerox to make substantial financial and capital investments. At the same time, the profitability of business ventures in China is unpredictable given the unstable political environment. A joint venture enables Xerox to share high start-up costs and reduce the risk of losses. The highly competitive copier market made the need for a joint venture more necessary. Joining forces with SMPIC helped Xerox establish a nationwide distribution, sales, and service network in China. Moreover, being the number one seller of copier machines in China, SMPIC also had unique knowledge of buyer needs and a close relationship with suppliers. This benefited Xerox in terms of designing products that better met the needs of buyers and securing a reliable source of supplies. These factors helped Xerox gain a competitive advantage, capturing 32 percent of the market share and making Xerox Shanghai the leader in the copier market two years after establishment.

Project-Specific Factors Xerox's joint venture in China was estimated at $30 million in 1987. While this would not be considered a tremendous amount of money, given Xerox's strong financial resources, this was only an initial investment. Xerox's commitment to China was made on a long-term basis. Further augmentation of this investment was inevitable. Xerox chose to partner with local firms to share the costs as well as risks of the project.

Timing of Entry

As the first copier company to form a joint venture in China, Xerox gains the advantages of quick access to supplies and market, establishing its products as the industrial standard, and building customer loyalty. All these combine to give Xerox a competitive advantage, increasing the possibility of higher economic returns for the company.

As the first copier company to form a joint venture in China, Xerox could develop a close relationship with dealers and suppliers, helping it obtain priority, sometimes exclusive, rights to getting supplies and access to the market. SMPIC's reputation as the only local copier machine company in China and its unique knowledge of market demand and understanding of cultural nuances enables Xerox to design products that better meet the needs of consumers. This helps establish Xerox Shanghai copiers as the industrial standard in China. Xerox let its partner establish a dealer network to make joint venture products available in most major Chinese regions. This further promotes the product's prominence amongst Chinese consumers, cultivating a positive brand image and building customer loyalty. Finally, the combined assets of Xerox, SMPIC, and the Bank of China, created an entry barrier that discourages other copier manufacturers from entering the copier market.

Location Selection

Xerox located its first joint venture in the Minhang Economic and Technological Development Zone (ETDZ) in Shanghai. The location was selected for lower tax rates, amongst other benefits. The Minhang ETDZ offered Xerox an incentive of a five-year property tax exemption and an exemption from local income taxes until the end of 1995. Minhang also has a well-developed infrastructure capable of providing fully functional telex, telephone, water, and sewage treatment services. Particular attractive to Xerox is Minhang's uninterrupted supply of electricity, a rarity in other parts of China.

Xerox also had official support for locating in Minhang. Approximately 21 Shanghai government offices are represented in Minhang, including a customs house that facilitates the passage of goods, equipment, and materials. Minhang is characterized by the presence of many well-known multinational companies, including Shanghai Squibb Pharmaceuticals, Grace China Ltd., and Shanghai Ingersoll Rand Compressor Ltd. The proximity of other large foreign companies provides Xerox with opportunities to save through cooperative sourcing and coordinating purchases and shipping. These geographical, logistical, political, structural and social advantages combined to influence Xerox to locate the joint venture in Minhang ETZD in Shanghai.

Shanghai is also an ideal location because of the large concentration of component suppliers and skilled laborers in the area. The Shanghai Economic Commission assists supplier companies in upgrading their factories and purchasing new technology. Shanghai's port is in a large, well-protected harbor near the mouth of the Yangtze River. It can handle heavy cargo traffic and serve as a gateway for international business. Located at the base of China's longest internal waterway, Shanghai provides a convenient access to raw materials located in China's interior.

With its high-tech based products, Xerox requires the availability of a more educated workforce. Shanghai has a comparatively strong science and technology base, with 711 research institutes, 108 scientific and technological associations, and three top-notch universities (Fudan, Jiaotong, and Shanghai Scientific and Technology) which have helped create an active research and educational environment. 55,000 science and technology personnel, as well as 400,000 technicians, reside in Shanghai. These attributes have made it easier for Xerox to recruit skilled labor.

International Cooperative Strategies

Partner Selection

After four years of negotiations, Xerox chose two state-owned enterprises as its partners. The Bank of China (BOC) is a profitable financial institution, but Shanghai Movie and Photo Industries Co. (SMPIC) consists of more than ten enterprises dominating the domestic market by supplying copier machines and office supply related equipment. Xerox selected a Shanghai partner because of the high reputation of Shanghai-based products.

Proof of Xerox's success in attaining high quality with its partners came when it won the Shanghai Quality Award in 1989 and 1990, and was awarded an in-house quality award in 1990 by the parent firm. These awards proved that Xerox was doing an excellent job at attaining the high quality that the Chinese community expected and helped Xerox spread the reputation of its products. An analysis of Xerox's partner selection follows:

Compatible Goals Even when acquiring capital and technology transfers from joint ventures, local firms prefer export-oriented productions. This would have hindered Xerox's goal of market penetration in China. Fortunately, this dispute was settled during contract formation. Local firms promised the products would primarily serve domestic needs, while Xerox would localize production by as much as 70 percent by the year 1992.

Complementary Skills Each firms' unique skills offset the other's limitations. Since SMPIC is the number one copier machine producer in China, Xerox could take advantage of its image and successful distribution channels to better target the Chinese market. Inversely, the poor industrial infrastructure of the local firm demonstrated an urgency to acquire high technology from a foreign firm. Xerox, as a well-known high-tech copy machine producer in the United States, served this need.

Commitment Since economic reform began, highly market-oriented economic behavior has been injected into Shanghai state-owned enterprises (SOEs). Profit maximization has become the heart of firm operations. Along with increased managerial autonomy in decision-making and work incentives, the performance of SOEs such as SMPIC and BOC has greatly improved.

SMPIC has also formed joint ventures with many other well-known foreign companies such as Polaroid of Shanghai Ltd., Shanghai SMPIC Brother Industries, Ltd., Shanghai SMPIC Electronics Co. Ltd., and Shanghai Universal Center and Commercial Building Co., Ltd. High levels of international experience increased SMPIC's degree of commitment and willingness to adapt to foreign operating styles.

Cooperative culture Chinese management style is family oriented. Chinese workers, regardless of rank, treat each other like brothers and sisters. Such an enjoyable work environment contributes to the success of cooperative efforts that every firm needs. This fits perfectly into Xerox's cooperative culture.

Strategic Capability Guanxi dictates a firm's ability to do business successfully in China. SMPIC's good relationship with the Chinese government, as well as suppliers, explains aspects of Xerox Shanghai's achievements. As a subsidiary of the Shanghai City Light Industry Bureau, SMPIC is strongly supported by President Jiang Zemin and Prime Minister Zhu Rongji, who also promoted the Xerox Shanghai joint venture.

Under the "Open Door Policy" of 1979, most products are required to follow the supply and demand function of the marketplace. SMPIC's power in the domestic market is demonstrated by the fact that it has number one sales volume in various productions, like copiers, instant cameras, typewriters, mimeograph machines, document shredders and numbering machines. SMPIC also possesses vertical production lines for producing special cameras, education equipment, office supplies, optical and quartz glass, optical fiber and cables, carbon products, measuring instruments and medical equipment, and so on. This further demonstrates SMPIC's advocation of innovation. Xerox's success in building a dealer network throughout China proves it chose the right partner.

Organizational Capability Shanghai SOEs have adopted the 'Modern Enterprise System', which imitates a Western management style, including setting up boards of directors to represent owners and oversee operations. Such a system ensures easy coordination and collaboration between SMPIC, as a typical SOE, and its foreign joint venture partners. SMPIC's high involvement in joint venture activities further strengthens its successful organizational capabilities.

Financial Capability Both the BOC and SMPIC obtain high profit margins. The BOC possessed 442 billion Ren Min Bi (RMB) in 1988. The BOC has branches in most major Chinese cities and several foreign countries such as the United States and Japan. By November 1988, BOC had offered 5.1 billion RMB, equivalent to 1.2 billion U.S. dollars, to roughly 3,000 Sino-foreign joint ventures. In 1995, the sales revenues at SMPIC amounted to RMB1.4 billion and its foreign exchange earnings from exports ran US$40 million.

Sharing Distribution and Control While Xerox holds 51 percent of the venture by providing $15 million capital, BOC has 5 percent of the venture ($10 million investment contribution) and SMPIC owns 44 percent of the venture by offering existing plants, equipment, and personnel estimated at about $5 million.

The primary goal of market expansion drives Xerox to obtain majority equity shares in its joint ventures. However, Xerox decided to take as small a portion of the share as possible while still maintaining a majority because of the lack of intellectual property protection in China and uncertainty of the market environment. To minimize the risk of technology outflow while maintaining high control, Xerox selected this optimal equity holding ratio. Since the local firms hold of similar stakes, their commitment is strengthened.

To preserve greater control of Xerox Shanghai, Xerox requires that all components are subject to quality standards set by the parent company. Despite the fact that 70 percent of components are locally outsourced, Xerox retains control over key components imported from the U.S.

International Operational Strategies

Marketing

To secure the reputation of Xerox Shanghai products, a Customer Satisfaction Review Board was established. Representatives from the marketing, service, distribution, management, engineering, and quality control departments meet monthly to analyze complaints from customers and the results of surveys.

Xerox Shanghai utilizes SMPIC's distribution function to establish a dealer network throughout China. As a result, Xerox Shanghai gained 32 percent of the Chinese desktop copier market in 1989 and 43 percent in 1991. Moreover, in 1987's advertising campaign, Xerox Shanghai successfully created a brand name representing worldwide acceptance of the cooperation between American technology and Shanghai production.

Human Resources

Although technology is improving in China, the lack of expert personnel in a majority of local suppliers seriously hinders quality component production. Xerox has transferred technology and provided technical support to sixty suppliers, mostly in Shanghai. Besides providing supplier training and materials management and handling, accounting skills are taught.

Xerox Shanghai requires high standards within the organization. A top down approach system, called 'LUTI' (Learn, Use, Teach, and Inspect), is applied to all levels of management. High level managers teach low level colleagues and new employees. This smoothes cooperation and coordination between departments and firms.

Conclusions

The scope of business being conducted in China today is probably far beyond what the senior management at Xerox believed possible. As one of the first and strongest entrants in this market, Xerox is well established and has a reputation for quality, which is an especially important attribute to most Asian consumers. Taking into consideration the future growth of China's economy and technologies, Xerox is currently in an advantageous position to become even more integral to the evolving Chinese business community.

Xerox should continue to expand the scope of its operations in China. There are several possible avenues that are yet unexplored. One of these is the use of the Internet as a business tool in China. Chinese web addresses are increasing as more users attempt to establish identities on the Internet. Xerox could pursue this quickly developing market by having its joint venture collaborate with one of its other partners, such as Sun Microsystems, which specializes in the Internet and Java programming language.

Xerox is well advised to continue allying with companies who meet certain criteria such as innovation and complementary assets. One of the guarantors of success in this era is maintaining consistency with emerging technologies. This is especially important for Xerox as the global business and private communities move from being paper oriented to a digital world. Granted, China is not as advanced as other first world countries, but it is changing rapidly and its Internet usage has already exceeded expectations.

Xerox often participates in community activities in the United States. On a global level, Xerox has supported the summer Olympics for approximately fifteen years. In order to build a healthy relationship with its host country, Xerox should find ways to contribute to the welfare of its people. This may be particularly important given that operating in foreign countries always involves a certain level of risk. Currently, China is welcoming towards the Xerox Corporation. While there are no signs that predict that this may change in the future, it is important to build a solid relationship with the host government in order to secure a safe position. Xerox should therefore promote a cooperative corporate culture in China that extends past the boundaries of office buildings and into the communities through the *guanxi* network established with its partners.

Case Study 5: OTIS

Executive Summary

Otis Elevator, a wholly owned subsidiary of United Technologies Corporation, is the world's largest manufacturer and servicer of elevators, escalators, moving walkways, and shuttle systems. These products are quite profitable in China, the world's largest elevator market. Otis Elevator has captured a notable 25 percent of this market and expects growth to continue.

Despite dominating the elevator industry, Otis has not become complacent. It has an aggressive training and recruitment program and a worldwide product strategy. Otis was quick to realize the advantages of joint ventures and has chosen partners wisely.

Economies of scale have enabled Otis to enter and dominate the market despite existing competitors. Its huge capital investment on research and development has paid off in the form of innovative products such as its Early Car Announcement (ECA) technology.

Otis is considered a financially strong company; its revenues for 1997 exceeded $5.5 billion dollars. Otis Elevator is the most profitable subsidiary of United Technologies Corporation (UTC). The majority of its revenues are derived from servicing old elevators rather than selling new ones, a strategy that has contributed to Otis's continued profitability.

As a result of committing to quality, customer responsiveness, and employee satisfaction, Otis Elevator's goals of maintaining worldwide recognition and increasing market share are likely to be attained, propelling it into the 21st Century as an industry leader.

Company Introduction

Corporate History

In 1853, Elisha Graves Otis invented the safety elevator. His invention sent buildings soaring upward and helped transform agrarian communities into industrial centers. In 1975, Otis became a wholly owned subsidiary of United Technologies Corporation. Today, it is the conglomerate's single most profitable operating unit, accounting for 29 percent of its profits. Otis aims to keep it that way.

In 1982, Otis was granted approval by the Chinese government to begin operations in China. By 1984, Otis established its first manufacturing joint venture there: China Tianjin Otis Elevator Company, Ltd. (CTOEC). The venture not only manufactures a full range of products, but also uses its extensive distribution network to install and service these products throughout the country.

Otis second joint venture in China, Beijing Otis Elevator Company, Ltd. (BOEC) was formed in 1992. BOEC, a partnership between Otis, CTOEC, and Beijing Equipment Installation Engineering Company, installs, services, and modernizes elevators and escalators in the Beijing area. Also in 1992, the Guangzhou Otis Elevator Company, Ltd. (GOEC) was formed to capture the increasingly important southern market.

In 1993, Otis established Shanghai Otis Elevator Company, Ltd. (SOEC), the first foreign joint venture elevator company in Pudong. It is a partnership between Otis, CTOEC, and Shanghai SITICO Enterprises Company, Ltd.

Core Products

Otis Elevator's core products include elevators, escalators, moving walkways, and shuttle systems. Each year Otis sells approximately 42,000 elevators worldwide. Its long-term profits come not from selling new elevators, however, but from servicing older ones. As in the appliance industry, it only sells new equipment to augment its service base. Consequently, Otis worldwide services more than one million elevators and escalators.

Otis's goal is to become the premier elevator company by supplying the highest quality products and services. In order to achieve its mission, Otis employs a worldwide product strategy aimed at global seamlessness. It chooses to obtain component parts from whichever manufacturing facilities have the most global supply advantages. Otis reduces manufacturing costs by shipping parts to each site where elevators will be assembled and eventually operate. It achieves world-class efficiency by using this 'just-in-time' manufacturing approach.

Major International Markets

Otis offers its products in 222 countries and maintains 28 major manufacturing facilities in 17 countries: the United States, Mexico, Brazil, United Kingdom, France, Germany, Italy, Spain, Japan, China, Taiwan, India, Malaysia, Czech Republic, Ukraine, Korea, and Russia. Despite being headquartered in the United States, 80 percent of Otis's revenues are generated elsewhere. Its European and Transcontinental operations contribute more than 50 percent of total sales, with North America responsible for about 25 percent, the Pacific-Asian operation contributing 19 percent, and the balance derived from Latin America. Combined, these regional operations enable Otis to permeate the market.

External Environment

Industrial Environment

Factors affecting Otis's industrial environment all fall within Porter's Five-Forces Model. The five forces are: competition, suppliers, consumers, new entrants, and substitution.

Competition The Chinese market for elevators, escalators, and other equipment (moving a potential 1.2 billion people a day) is enormous. Just a few years ago, experts claimed that China's elevator market could easily increase by more than 10 percent per year until the turn of the century. The Chinese market is therefore large enough to accommodate all of the world's elevator manufacturers.

Considering the vastness of the market, the 25 percent market share that Otis possesses is overwhelming. Otis's presence in the market is so predominant that its two most threatening competitors, Schindler and Mitsubishi, combined only share another 25 percent, making the market oligopolistic. Aside from these two, Otis leads 123 registered elevator manufacturers in China, the majority of holding only single digit percentages of the market. Although Otis dominates the industry, it has not become complacent or allowed production and morale to diminish. It remains focused on product innovation.

Suppliers Otis's 1997 cost reduction plan includes a supply management program. The overall plan is targeted to help its parent company, United

Technologies Corporation (UTC), save $750 million by the new millennium by consolidating 80 percent of UTC's supplier population, while requiring suppliers to undergo the same reengineering and quality assurance processes that have been used by UTC over the past five years.

Since Otis can demand that its suppliers adopt certain methods, its suppliers have little bargaining power. Otis's profitability and supplier services are therefore enhanced.

Consumers Otis's primary customers are: mechanical and building contractors, building owners and developers, and architects and building consultants. As the nation's business environment increases, more buildings are being produced, providing greater demand for Otis products. The demand for elevators is so enormous that at the close of 1997, Otis had a backlog of services that amounted to over $3 billion. As a result of this high demand, Otis's customers have little bargaining power.

New Entrants New entrants into China's market do not pose any threat to Otis. Being oligopolistic, the market may turn away any newcomer hoping to obtain a large percentage share.

Substitutions Since there is no equipment that can take the place of elevators, escalators, and moving walkways, there is no threat of substitution. Unless a new invention emerges, the elevator market will continue to prosper in its growth stage.

National Environment

Although China has the largest elevator market in the world and Otis holds the biggest portion of that market, Otis is not invincible. Its success is dependent on national economic factors. Fluctuations in commercial construction can affect new equipment installations. Labor costs also have an impact on the service and maintenance margins on installed elevators and escalators. Changes in foreign currency rates can affect the profitability of exchanging its returns into U.S. dollars. Finally, Otis is influenced by changing legislation and governmental regulations.

Internal Environment

Financial

Otis is efficient in its use and allocation of resources. However, when compared with its counterparts, Otis is not very liquid. The following analysis was performed using Standard and Poor's market average ratios.

Profitability ratios were computed to ascertain how much more profitable Otis is compared to the industrial average. These ratios emphasize the company's efficiency in using its resources. The return on assets shows that Otis is more efficient at using economic resources than the rest of the industry. The return on sales, also known as the net profit margin, illustrates that the company efficiently controls costs and expenses in relation to sales. The return on net worth provides proof that Otis's stockholders received higher returns on investment than its market counterparts.

Liquidity ratios demonstrate how quickly Otis can repay its creditors. The quick ratio indicates that Otis and other firms share about the same ability to repay short-term debt obligations without having to sell inventory. The current ratio says that Otis cannot repay its current debt as well as others in the industry, due to the fact that inventory is involved in the calculation. The ratio further implies that Otis's inventory is fairly difficult to sell. Lastly, the inventory-to-net worth ratio provides evidence that Otis has much more working capital invested in its inventory.

Leverage ratios render a favorable picture of Otis's position in the market. The debt-to-asset and debt-to-equity ratios reveal that the company uses more debt to finance its operations compared to others in the industry.

Activity ratios indicate Otis's efficiency in using its short-term resources. Inventory turnover proves that Otis is far more efficient at using inventory to generate sales. Its fixed-asset turnover says that Otis utilizes its plant more efficiently. Finally, the average collection period of accounts receivable is about the same as for others in the industry.

One of Otis's strengths is its sales figures, which alone would discourage potential competitors. 1997 revenues were over $5.5 billion, a decrease of 1 percent from 1996 (because of exchange rate fluctuations). Its operating profits reached over $4.6 million, a decrease of 11 percent. If translation is excluded, revenues increased by 7 percent, while operating profits would have decreased only 2 percent. This translation problem is a weakness for almost every global corporation.

As for hedging activities, instruments utilized by Otis are viewed as risk management tools that involve little complexity and are not used for trading purposes. The instruments include swaps to manage certain foreign currency exposures. The company also holds risk sensitive instruments, including cash, debt, and derivative instruments. A value at risk model, which uses a variance/covariance methodology, applies statistical analysis to the company's market risk sensitive instruments utilizing historical market data, volatilities, and correlations.

Organizational

With goals of maintaining worldwide status and increasing market share, Otis does not need to chase cheap labor outside of the U.S. Otis is aware that higher wages draw increased skill and knowledge. Otis has implemented a worldwide Employee Scholar Program to increase the company's intellectual resources and company morale. The program pays for all tuition and related costs, provides time off from work, and awards 100 shares of UTC stock when an employee receives an undergraduate or graduate degree. Enrollment in the program has reached over 10,000 employees worldwide. The Employee Scholar Program is touted by employees as being the best benefit the company has ever provided.

Operational

To employees, downsizing is seen as a company's weakness, an indicator that the company is not doing too well. But in Otis's case, downsizing means being more efficient with resources relative to demand. Downsizing is a strong part of its broad restructuring plan. It means that out of 19 worldwide engineering centers, 13 will be eliminated and about 2,000 employees will lose their jobs.

Otis is also a safe and ethical place to work. The company follows a permanent improvement policy, which includes: proactive participation in national working groups on safety; an internal audit program; identification and control of emissions, reduction and safe disposal of waste; and continuous training programs on risk elimination and prevention.

Additionally, Otis is committed to the highest standards of ethics and business conduct. This encompasses its relationships with customers, suppliers, shareholders, competitors, and the Chinese communities.

Technological

Although the elevator is not seen as a technologically demanding product, Otis knew that there was a potential threat from Japanese manufacturers who tend to be technologically intensive. Otis took the opportunity to advance its own technology. It invested $1 billion in R&D, the largest investment of any elevator corporation in the market. The investment paid off handsomely when Japanese competitors introduced a cutting-edge technology known as fuzzy logic. Fuzzy logic can identify the closest elevator to a particular floor. Otis's version of fuzzy logic is known as Early Car Announcement (ECA). ECA lets passengers know which elevator will respond as soon as they push the elevator hall button. Otis claims this technology makes passengers feel more at ease by reducing the anxiety associated with waiting and improves boarding efficiency.

To increase its internal efficiency, a flexible manufacturing system has been implemented, with the goal of having suppliers provide parts on a just-in-time basis using bar codes. The system not only increases efficiency, but also flexibility and responsiveness in customer handling. It raises productivity, lowers costs, and increases product quality and reliability. As a result, employees become more motivated.

Finally, to further increase internal efficiency, a website has been set up providing thousands of registered users with customized reports and statistics.

Corporate-Level Strategy

Geographic Diversification

The main factors that have led Otis to specific regions of China have been intense demand conditions, favorable Chinese FDI policies, and good factor endowments. Otis's successful entry into China has been the result of three factors. First, it entered the nation at the earliest possible moment with a strong national partner who had deep local roots. Second, it uses a multi-domestic approach that ensures that its companies will become an essential part of each nation's industries in which it does business. Finally, Otis is able to provide products and services that are tailored to meet the needs and requirements of local markets.

China is the largest elevator market and one of the top three elevator-manufacturing countries in the world. Since China's reforms and implementation of an open-door policy, the building industry has become one of its fastest developing industries. China's total building projects now take up nearly one-fourth of the world's total. Since the 1980s, the flourishing of hotels and office buildings has created a high-rise rush in China. High-rise complexes are located in large- and medium-sized cities; some cities even have the ambition as to build the highest buildings in Asia. In Beijing, there are eight high-rises over 100 meters high. Shopping mall, hotel, and office building construction creates a huge market for high-quality, high-speed elevators and escalators.

China's elevator manufacturing has achieved rapid development since 1990, revealing that the elevator industry in China is in its growth stage. About 28,000 elevators and escalators were manufactured in 1994. However, only about 10,000 units were produced in 1990, 12,000 in 1991, 16,000 in 1992 and 24,000 in 1993. The increase was 1.8 times as in 1990, with an annual increase rate of over 29 percent.

China's elevator installations have also increased rapidly in recent years. In 1994, about 34,000 elevators and escalators were installed. The total number of existing elevators and escalators is now over 200,000.

It is predicted that from 1996 to 2000, the average annual rate of increase for elevators will be over 10 percent. During this period, the state will highlight apartment construction. Its investment accounts for about 13 percent of the total on the fixed assets, mainly for the construction of medium- and high-rise apartments. In some big cities, the construction of 20- to 30-story high-rise apartments will be given priority. China is now carrying out many large-scale communication projects, such as airports, railway stations and subways, which also need numerous elevators, escalators, and passenger conveyors. Otis definitely entered China because of the pull factor of increasing demand.

As an FDI, Otis receives favorable treatment from the Chinese government. Otis projects falls into the technologically advanced category. The company is therefore seen as a major partner in helping China to become industrialized. Benefits such as low corporate and income tax rates, rent deductions, tariff cuts, and utilities expense cuts are just a few of the many benefits that are enjoyed by FDIs in this category. Although these policies are not the driving force behind Otis's expansion into China, they certainly have made it easier.

Otis's local joint venture partners were all companies that were already in the manufacturing industry. Some, like Nanfang Elevator Company in Guangzhou, were actually elevator companies to begin with. There are many advantages for Otis in forming joint ventures with these types of companies.

First, the local company already has existing connections with suppliers and customers. By using these connections, Otis avoids the cost of developing these networks. Second, the local company already has skilled employees that are knowledgeable in the manufacturing industry. Although Otis still invests heavily in training its workers, the major costs of teaching basic skills are averted.

While Otis experiences the benefits of joint ventures, it also see benefits from production factors in China. The availability of resources in China is abundant. Labor, supplies, and land are all tangibles that are in vast supply in China. For a highly technological company like Otis, these factors are essential to business. Their low cost adds to Otis's low cost strategy.

Product Diversification

Otis vertically integrates its products within related product diversification. One of the major advantages of vertical integration is market power. Otis has earned a worldwide reputation for innovation and quality of work. Market power along with economies of scale from vertical integration has given Otis a strong competitive edge as well as customer loyalty.

Otis faces the challenge of designing, manufacturing, and servicing a standard elevator while satisfying worldwide customer demand for customization. This is accomplished by including minor changes inside the cab of the elevator, while the main part of the machine remains standardized. This strategy is no big secret to Otis's customers, yet because of dedication to the standard the company only stands to gain. The knowledge curve continues to increase.

Otis's strategy is simple, since there are only 3 types of elevators. There is the hydraulic elevator that is used in low-rise buildings of about 3 stories. It consists of a single hydraulic cylinder that pushes the elevator in each direction. Ropes connected to a motor drive a geared elevator. This type of elevator operates in mid-rise buildings. Lastly, there is the gearless elevator for high rise buildings. This elevator operates at high speeds with the use of a motor to regulate travel.

In the past, Otis designed its products in certain areas of the world to suit that area. A product would be designed for Europe where it is cold and dry. These products were not useful in new markets, such as Malaysia, where the climate is very hot and humid. Consequently, Otis would have to start all over again on the design. Now, Otis engineers its products with all of the requirements of the world in mind. Codes governing elevator construction have followed Otis's lead. National and local codes are giving way to regional, even global code standards. These global standards will help perfect global design.

The demand from the Chinese market has attracted every world famous elevator company. Otis, Schindler, Mitsubishi, Hitachi, Toshiba, and Thyssen have established joint-venture companies and manufacturing facilities in China, contributing much to Chinese technological improvements. Presently, half of production comes from these joint ventures, which supply almost all the high-grade, high-speed elevators. Even with all of these competitors entering the Chinese market, demand exceeds supply.

Business-Level Strategy

Otis Elevator enjoys a competitive advantage through maintaining a low-cost strategy. Otis has strong motives for eliminating costs while sustaining quality in its products. The importance of a price-sensitive product is everything in an increasingly competitive global environment. Even though it is the largest elevator and escalator company in the world, it still only has a 24 percent share of the world elevator market. It faces competition on all fronts. At the low end of the market, small local companies are manufacturing hydraulic elevators and escalators. At the high end, global competitors like Schindler, Hitachi, Thyssen, and Mitsubishi are increasing their global presence. The second motive for a low-cost strategy is the fact that Otis Elevator is a part of the family whose parent is United Technologies. Among the children, Otis is by far the most profitable unit; it would like to sustain this ranking.

In 1995, the company went through a major restructuring. Previously, Otis had been a mixed bag of joint ventures, start-ups, and local licensees. The setup was not very centralized. The new goal has been to create 'global seamlessness' by changing administrative, accounting, and management systems. Global design has maintained high standards of quality, but at a cheaper cost realized in product design.

Otis also sees the need for product differentiation, even in an industry where the products are essentially the same. The reason for a product differentiation strategy is for the sake of the customer. If Otis can convince its customers that along with having the best-known, highest-quality elevator on the planet, that they can also come in any shape or size required, then its competitors will have to watch out.

Efficiency has been improved with better employee training. The 1997 Employee Report states that Otis employees receive 50 percent more training than others in the industry. The results: 60 percent decrease in lost time accidents, and 70 percent decrease in days lost from work. These figures reinforce Otis's desire to maintain superior efficiency.

Superior innovation has been the foundation on which Otis built its whole business. From the first safety brake to the Odyssey system, Otis's innovations have defined the elevator industry. One of the first things Elisha Graves Otis did as owner of Otis Elevator was to add the safety brake to the elevator. In the more recent past, Otis Elevator has shown superior innovation in both its products and in the technology used for various functions of production. For example, in 1997 Otis received numerous awards for engineering processes, safety innovation, product development, and new technologies. On July 24, 1996, Otis introduced perhaps the greatest innovation since the invention of the elevator, the Odyssey, an Integrated Building Transit System. What this system allows is the building of larger, taller buildings using interconnected structures, dictated configurations, performance, and dispatch characteristics. The Odyssey has lower construction costs and larger interior volumes; the system eliminates hoistways and machine rooms that consume valuable rental space.

A little history shows the real significance of this innovation. In 1956, famous architect Frank Lloyd Wright sketched the Illinois, a mile high building. The Illinois would have 528 stories, 100,000 inhabitants, and parking for 15,000 cars. There would be two heliports with 50 helicopters each, 18,462,000 square feet gross, and 13,047,000 square feet net rental space. The cost of this building, in 1956 dollars, would be $60,000,000. The Illinois could have been built in 1956. All technologies were available at that time except one: a viable transportation system. Conventional roped elevators couldn't service buildings higher than 300 meters. Cable weight, as well as the complex spaces needed for hoistway systems, made these kinds of elevators impractical. Even with a feasible elevator system, a complex dispatch plan would be needed to manage long wait and travel times. Also, horizontal travel would also be necessary to alleviate long walks on a five to ten city block square. Today's Odyssey system will make buildings as tall as the Illinois become a reality.

Otis has demonstrated its dedication to superior customer responsiveness through increased safety records, customer response systems, and more efficient service. For its North American Operations, new equipment installation times are down to a record level. A new system called Remote Elevator Monitoring constantly tracks critical operating parameters, automatically calling for service as necessary. The potential of these automated systems is being unlocked on a worldwide basis. Remote diagnostics and other sophisticated tools will allow Otis to deliver better service faster and more economically.

International Strategies

After Otis Elevator decided to enter the Chinese market, it had to consider many factors that would contribute to its future success, including location, mode of entry, business partners, and time of entry.

Otis's first entry into the Chinese market occurred in 1984, but this was not its first business interaction with China. Otis Elevator began selling elevators to China in 1900. In 1907, it began installing elevators there. During these early years, its activities were frequently interrupted due to the formation of the P.R.C. Prior to making any foreign direct investments in China, Otis Elevator set up branch offices to study the factors involved. Establishing local branch offices allowed it to be in the local market without having to commit to it. As of now, there are 35 branch offices throughout China.

Finally, in 1982, Otis Elevator was granted approval for operation. The Chinese government was pleased by Otis Elevator's presence in China, because it believed that additional competitors to China-Schindler Elevators would promote competition in the elevator business, which would ultimately increase quality and efficiency. In 1984, Otis Elevator entered into a partnership with the Tianjin Lift Company and CITIC, and set up its first operation in Tianjin. This was followed by three more joint ventures set up in 1992 and 1993.

Entry Mode

In selecting entry mode, firms typically consider four groups of factors: country, firm, industry, and project. Otis had to analyze all factors tied to China, such as market demand, cultural distance, infrastructure, governmental policies, and risks. In the early 1980s, China's population was rapidly growing and cities were heavily overcrowded. The Chinese government and Otis Elevator realized that skyscrapers were needed in the near future to ease population congestion. Therefore, there were plenty of opportunities for companies like Otis to make a higher return on investment.

The government, seeing the advantages of an open market, encouraged competition within the industry.

Cultural differences between the US and China are also vast. Chinese managers have been trained to produce and manufacture products efficiently but not to maximize profits. Governmental policies protect the interest of Chinese firms; privatization and foreign ownership are controlled. Overall, the risk of doing business in China was high at the time Otis entered the market because the Chinese political system had just recently allowed in foreign direct investment. There were many uncertainties about the role that the government would play.

Firm specific factors included Otis Elevator's prior business experience in China. It did not, however, have any joint venture experience. Project specific factors depend on location of investment and needs of the market which determine such things as project size. The Tianjin joint venture had an initial investment of $5 million dollars. Industry specific factors include entry barriers, competition, structural uncertainty, and relations with suppliers and buyers. At the time Otis entered the market, the Schindler Elevator Company of Switzerland was the only major competitor. There was no fierce competition for small projects, however, because demand was much greater than supply. Since the government wanted new competitors in the elevator business, there were little or no entry barriers. After Otis entered the market, buyers benefited from having more choices of elevator companies to choose from. The relationship with suppliers depends on the bargaining power of local partners. Otis's partner, the Tianjin Lift Company, is a major firm that has established rapport with local suppliers. Therefore, Otis need not worry about supplier reliability.

Besides looking at these four kinds of factors, Otis studied the entry mode selections of previous successful corporations in China. Otis observed the success of a refrigerator company that assembles refrigerators in the local market instead of importing them from the home country, thereby saving the cost of shipping.

As a result of analyzing the four factors discussed above and previous success stories, Otis chose to form equity joint ventures with local companies. This strategy allows Otis Elevator to assemble, manufacture, and service elevators in the local market. Another advantage is that both parties share risks and uncertainties. The disadvantages are that Otis does not have total control over the venture and technology can be stolen easily. In international joint ventures, the majority owner is whichever party contributes the most equity. Regulations often stipulate that foreign companies cannot hold a majority share. In some cases, however, the percentage return for a party might be different from the percentage of its contribution. This logic is based on the idea that minority owners will work harder if they expect to get a bigger piece of the pie.

Entry Timing

Otis Elevator was not the first foreign elevator company to invest in China. Schindler's of Switzerland had entered the market a few years earlier. Otis Elevator is still considered an early mover. It therefore enjoys some of the same advantages as Schindler's, such as establishing a network of subcontractors and distributors. The infrastructure in Tianjin was already well developed, which contributed other benefits. Furthermore, the government wanted more elevator companies in the market and offered many incentives in different regions. A shortage of elevators also presented Otis with a great opportunity. Despite political uncertainty, Otis entered at an ideal time.

After less than 10 years in China, Otis Elevators had four out of its top ten contracts in China. In 1996 and 1997, it received the two biggest contracts in Shanghai, with a combined worth of over $26 million dollars. It beat out Mitsubishi, Toshiba, and Schindler's in vying for these projects. One project is to supply and install 74 units in the Grand Gateway Complex. The second one is a subway project. The timing of formation of the second and third joint ventures was impeccable due to a continual demand for elevators. The Guangzhou joint venture benefited the most from explosive growth and development of shopping malls and department stores in Southern China. The Guangzhou Otis Elevator Company already controls 40 percent of the market, and expects to share 50 percent by the year 2000. The demand for escalators, as of 1994, is increasing at an even higher pace than elevators. The overall market share for Otis Elevator in China, as of 1995, is 24 percent.

Location Selection

A firm should analyze both the micro and macro contexts for factors that determine location choice. The determinants under micro-context are cost/tax, demand, and strategic factors. Analysis of these factors has led Otis to choose four main locations.

The first joint venture was established in Tianjin. Tianjin is the city of choice for foreign investors because of the advantages of its domestic and export markets and its well-developed infrastructure. This quiet coastal city is the third largest industrial city in China. It contains the hub of a network of routes leading to the interior. Tianjin also has many higher level educational institutions specializing. Tianjin is the most important world trade center in China. The cost/tax factors of doing business in Tianjin are low. The corporate tax rate is only 10 percent within designated ETDZs (Economic and Technological Development Zone) within the city, for companies that export 70 percent of their finished products. High-tech ventures get an additional 3 years of 50 percent reduction on corporate taxes. In addition, telephone and escalator fees are lifted and electricity and water charges are reduced in these zones. As in most big cities in China, there is high demand for elevators and escalators. The city is extremely crowded (6 million people according to the 1990 census). The high demand has made Tianjin Otis Elevator the 29th largest joint venture in China as of 1995.

The second location is in Guangzhou. Guangzhou is located in southern region China. The city is over 2000 years old and had relatively few buildings the 1990s. Since the 1950s, the city has been experiencing tremendous growth due to a strong economy based on industries such as shipbuilding, iron and steel, chemicals, machinery, textiles, and rubber goods. Guangzhou's population is the sixth largest in China. As in Tianjin, there are special cost/tax advantages of opening businesses in the region. Businesses get tariff cuts for materials used in producing import substitutes. Firms in this region get a 5-year 50 percent reduction on corporate taxes. They are also exempt from urban construction taxes on high-tech and export ventures. Guangzhou's construction boom began in the 1980s. It made sense for Otis Elevator to form a joint venture with a local firm to meet the sudden high demand for elevators.

The third joint venture is in Beijing, China's capital. This northern city has a population of over 10 million. Since 1949, the city's economy has developed rapidly based on industry and manufacturing. There are enormous incentives to do business in Beijing, including access to high governmental officials a tax advantages. The first high-tech industrial development and experimental zone was set up in Beijing, which enjoys even more preferential treatment than do ETDZs.

Otis's fourth joint venture is in Shanghai, China's biggest market with a population of over 12 million. It is 4 times more densely populated than Manhattan. Shanghai is the greatest commercial and port city in China. U.S. companies have made the majority of investment in China in Shanghai. Fourty percent of all Sino-American joint ventures are located there. At an average of 16.2 percent, American joint ventures receive the highest return on equity in Shanghai. The local government has far more autonomy in managing the city's finances and other activities than do other local governments in China. Businesses located in its ETDZ are exempt from local taxes, receive a 5-year exemption from property taxes on new buildings, and have only a 15 percent corporate income tax with 2 years exemption and subsequent 3 years of 50 percent discount. Finally, there are no tariffs or value-added taxes on imported machinery. Aside from these benefits, the local government recently opened the Pudong area to foreign investment.

International Cooperative and Operation Strategies

Partner Selection

The Tianjin Lift Company was originally considered by Schindler as a potential joint venture partner, but was not selected. This does not mean Tianjin is not a good partner. Each foreign company seeks a partner to complement its own objectives, taking into consideration capability, cooperative culture, commensurate risk, commitment, complementary skills and compatible goals. Of these, the most important factor for Otis is capability. Capability can be broken down into strategic, organizational, and financial attributes.

Strategic Attributes The strategic attributes for all of Otis's joint ventures are similar. Otis Elevator provides technical know-how and capital, while local firms provide experienced industrial workers, infrastructure, and capital.

The Tianjin Otis Company has two local partners, the Tianjin Lift Company and CITIC (China International Trust and Investment Corporation). Otis Elevator sought a partner that had the capability to manufacture high quality elevators and escalators. The Tianjin Lift Company was willing and able to provide labor, equipment, infrastructure, and capital. It also shared a common interest with Otis in wanting to dominate the elevator business. Its management was willing to adopt Otis Elevator's management style while Otis agreed to provide training for Tianjin workers to raise their technological skills. Similarly, Otis invested $2 million dollars in building a training facility in Guangzhou. The partners in the Guangzhou Otis Elevator Company are Otis Elevator and the Guangzhou Nanfang Elevator Factory, which is a lift manufacturer operating under the Guangzhou Bureau of Mechanical and Electrical Industry.

CITIC has also been an important partner because it is the biggest state-owned enterprise in China and its CEO has a good relationship with the central government. Many companies desiring a strong relationship with the government try to form partnerships with CITIC.

Organizational attributes Neither Otis nor the Tianjin Lift Company had prior experience with Sino-American joint ventures. The joint venture is managed according to Otis Elevator's standards in order to maintain quality. The joint venture in Shanghai did have a partner that had previous experience in joint ventures, the China Tianjin Otis Elevator Company. The Shanghai joint venture thus expected to avoid any mistakes the earlier joint ventures had made.

Financial attributes In Shanghai, China, the average return for American joint venture is around 16 percent. The average return for joint ventures in the coastal regions of China average around 11 percent, which is significantly higher than joint ventures in the inner regions. These high returns may be one of reason Otis Elevator formed joint venture with partners near coastal regions.

Sharing distribution and control

Even though in the beginning Otis did not own majority shares in its Chinese joint venture, it has been able to control management because of its technical know-how and reputation. In its first joint venture, it also signed a special agreement allowing it to increase its contribution, and therefore ownership, over time. In the first year of operations in Tianjin, Otis Elevator had a 30 percent stake, the Tianjin Lift Company had 65 percent, and the remaining 5 percent belonged to CITIC. In 1993, Otis's stake was increased to 44 percent. Finally, in 1994, the 10-year anniversary of Otis in China, Otis Elevator invested an additional $12.3 million dollars to increase its stake from 44 percent to 51 percent, giving it majority control over the venture. The increase in capital also allowed the venture to increase its manufacturing capacity and allowed it to become a partner in the new joint venture in Shanghai (the only manufacturing plant in China with ISO 9000 accreditation).

In Guangzhou, Otis Elevator owns 80 percent of the joint venture through its Hong Kong based subsidiary, Otis Far East Holding. The Guangzhou Nanfang Elevator Factory owns the remaining 20 percent.

Joint Venture Cooperation

Local partners, although trained in Western ways of conducting business, still understand and can make use of Chinese ways of doing business. Negotiations are handled by local firms that practice the same kinds of negotiation techniques as suppliers. Since business relationships in China are founded on trust, most Chinese firms are loyal to their partners. Thus, once strong relationships are developed between Otis joint ventures and suppliers, they are likely to continue working with each other for a long time.

Human Resource Management

Motivating local staff to perform well in China can be difficult. Otis originally set up a strategy based on personal responsibility. Motivation was achieved through higher wages; instead of extra titles, salesmen received substantial cash pay incentives. Employees, in return, produced tangible results. Sales rolled in, invoices were error free, and factories were kept clean. Because of the success of this recognition program, Otis extended its results oriented pay system throughout the entire company. In 1992, the pay structure was revamped again. This time, pay raises were only for those who performed well according to three criteria: quality, productivity, and care of the working environment.

Introducing Western management techniques to its joint ventures was one of Otis's prime objectives. Accordingly, technical and management courses are run at the joint venture's Tianjin training facility. Additionally, each year Otis hires 10-15 new graduates from a range of disciplines. They are put through a sandwich course, three years at a local university, one working for Otis on a regular salary and the last back at college. Likewise, managers identified internally as having potential are sent for training in Otis's overseas facilities in the U.S. and Europe.

It is projected that Otis will need several hundred Chinese managers over the next decade. Otis will need to recruit local managers able to train their own staff members. If it continues intensive training and recruitment, it should enjoy continued success in China.

Conclusion

In summary, Otis is a very profitable company. With revenues surpassing those of its competitors and holding the biggest market share in China, Otis is in an excellent position. The Five-Forces model suggests that there are few competitors that will have any affect on Otis's presence in the Chinese market. The model also confirms that both suppliers and consumers have little bargaining power, while providing tremendous demand and enhancing profitability and supplier services. Everything about Otis's external environment is positive.

Internally, Otis is a well-organized, well-run company, prudent with its human resource management. Otis also leads the industry in its dedication to technology.

Although the company has a majority market share, Otis should continue to increase its share without losing focus on its business and abilities. Its competitors are fairly close behind; if Otis should become complacent, another huge company could easily overtake the market.

Otis has been pulled into specific regions in China by market demand, favorable FDI policies, good factor endowments, and dependable joint venture partners. Otis's 25 percent share of the oligopolistic market in China proves that its product diversification strategy is effective. Its competitive advantages have been gained through low-cost as well as product differentiation strategies and customer responsiveness.

Our forecast is that Otis will to continue to lead the field by providing a high quality product through superior innovation, quality, and customer response. It should maintain its aggressive stance in the Chinese market as the major competitor in the industry. Its four joint ventures provide quality service to four major cities. However, China has many more than four large cities; Otis Elevator should expand to other major cities, capitalizing on increasing demand for elevators throughout the nation. Since the majority of the population resides in coastal regions, and return on equity is higher there, it would make the most sense for Otis to continue satisfying demand in these areas before moving inward.

Because of Otis Elevator Company's dedication to meeting the needs of its global customers, it will undoubtedly continue to forge ahead into the next millennium as the strongest contender in its industry.

Case Study 6: Kodak

Executive Summary

Kodak is engaged primarily in developing, manufacturing, and marketing consumer and commercial imaging products. Kodak had sales in excess of $14 billion last year, somewhat short of its 1996 $15 billion figure. 1997 was clearly a disappointing year for shareholders and employees of Kodak; necessary steps will be taken to help Kodak reach solid growth in the years to come.

Kodak has six key growth initiatives: product innovation and differentiation, digital imaging, service, penetration of emerging markets, market access, and selective equipment manufacturing. Kodak also aims to maintain a world-class cost structure. Kodak's fundamental growth objective is to produce an average annual increase in earnings per share of at least 10 percent.

The result of Kodak's activities will be a leaner, tougher, more competitive Kodak, one that truly rewards performance. Kodak believes that 1998 will be a milestone for its management team and will ensure that Kodak remains market-focused well into the 21st century.

Company Introduction

Goals and Values

Kodak's past and future vision is to be the world leader in imaging products by providing its customers with cost-effective, efficient ways to capture, store, process, output, and communicate images to people and machines while maintaining flawless quality. It draws on a team of energetic and talented employees to achieve this mission. It also has a set of values, which defines its corporate culture, including respecting the dignity of individuals, integrity, trust, credibility, improvement, and personal renewal. These values have two primary dimensions. The first is a commitment to social ideals, including building a diverse global work force. This can be seen in Kodak's consistent, aggressive effort to attract, develop, and retain highly skilled people with a variety of perspectives from all cultures and population segments. The second commitment is to the people in its organization. Kodak provides employees with opportunities to contribute, learn, grow, and advance. It wants its employees to feel respected, treated fairly, listened to, and involved and to attain satisfaction from their accomplishments. This is partly done by the use of management assessment reviews and individual recognition and reward mechanisms.

In 1997, CEO George Fisher identified three goals for Kodak. First of all, he wants to significantly reduce the company's total cost structure. Secondly, he wants Kodak to participate more successfully in its equipment businesses and key markets. While its basic strategy is sound, its cost structure should lead to a business model that makes it a more effective global competitor. Lastly, Fisher wants to continue heading for top-line growth to maximize long-term shareholder value. He hopes to produce an average annual increase in earnings per share of at least ten percent over time.

Corporate History

George Eastman originally founded Eastman Kodak. In 1878, he demonstrated the benefits of gelatin dry plates compared to the messy, cumbersome wet-plate photographic method then in use. Dry plates could be exposed and developed at the photographer's convenience. Two years later, he started commercial production of his dry plates out of a rented loft in Rochester, New York. By 1881, he formed a partnership with Henry Strong called The Eastman Dry Plate Company. By 1884, the partnership became a $200,000 corporation with 14 shareholder, called the Eastman Dry Plate and Film Company. Four years later, the term Kodak was coined, and the first Kodak camera was placed on the market with the slogan, 'You push the button, we do the rest'. In 1892, the corporation had changed its name to the Eastman Kodak Company of N.Y. By 1927, its worldwide employment had already passed the 20,000 mark. Worldwide employment reached 120,000 within 50 more years. By 1973, sales surpassed $4 billion. In 1980 Kodak celebrated its 100th anniversary; the next year company sales surpassed $10 billion.

In late 1993, George Fisher, former CEO of Motorola, took over as current CEO of Kodak. He brought many ideas for restructuring and streamlining the company. In 1994, Kodak announced it would eliminate its non-imaging health related businesses, including consisting Sterling Winthrop, L&F Products, and Clinical Diagnostics, so the company could focus all its resources on its core imaging business. Kodak also brought in new senior management, mainly hired from computer companies such as IBM and Apple. In 1996, Kodak entered into an agreement with Danka Business Systems PLC allowing Danka to acquire the sales, marketing, and equipment service operations of Kodak's Office Imaging business, as well as Kodak's facilities management business, Kodak Imaging Services. Late in 1997, George Fisher announced a minimum reduction goal of $1 billion over the next two years from Kodak's total cost structure. Fisher expects to save at least $500 million in 1998 and over $750 million in 1999.

Kodak increased its commitment in other areas. In 1997, it acquired the Wang Laboratories software business for approximately $260 million in cash. It then increased its stake from 12 percent to 50.1 percent in a Japanese camera manufacturing company, Chinon Industries, by consolidating financial statements. Kodak also purchased a 49 percent interest in a Fox Photo Inc. joint venture for $10 million in cash, with a $44 million note due at the beginning of 1999. On December 31, 1997, Kodak and Sun Chemical Corporation formed a joint venture, Kodak Polychrome Graphics, that will supply film, paper, conventional and computer-to-plate solutions, processing chemistry and digital color proofing products to the global graphics arts market. Finally, in early 1998, Kodak announced it would invest more than $1 billion in China over the next several years.

Major Businesses and Core Products

Consumer Imaging (CI) is Kodak's largest business unit. It leads the others in the drive for improved growth in sales and earnings. Some of the recent products launched by CI include Kodak's Select series of 35mm film, Kodak's Gold Max Film, and the Advantix Product Line.

Kodak Professional provides cutting-edge film, paper, cameras, and services for professional customers. Three new innovative films were introduced recently, with Kodak Ektachrome E200 leading the way. The award winning DCS 460 and the professional DCS 520 digital cameras were also introduced last year by this unit.

Kodak's Digital and Applied Imaging unit creates electronic imaging technology that effects all the other business units and customer segments. Key products include the DC 200, DC 210 Zoom camera, and the DC 120 camera, which USA Today called the best digital camera under $1,000.

The Entertainment Imaging unit provides a wide range of products and services which help customers enhance real images or create imagined ones. The major product for this unit is the use of its innovative family of Vision film, used to film the movies *Wag the Dog* and *Titanic*.

Kodak's Health Imaging business provides health care professionals with differentiated high-quality products such as an X-ray machine (Min-R 2000), medical laser printer (9000D), and medical film.

Kodak's Commercial and Government Systems business helps demanding customers use images as tools. Core products are used by the U.S. space program, the military, and other government customers. For example, Kodak provided key digital camera components for the Lockheed Martins satellite imaging system and has built the world's largest optical reflecting surface for the Hobby-Eberly Telescope.

The Business Imaging Systems unit offers film, digital, and hybrid imaging products and services to help businesses and government manage information. The major type of product is software, which includes a newly developed image capture and storage product. With the recent acquisition of Wang Software, now called Eastman Software, Kodak has increased its software capabilities as well as formed a valuable strategic relationship with Microsoft.

Office Imaging concentrates on developing and manufacturing innovative products for business. The major products are large volume copiers, including the award winning models Image Source 70 and 110 copiers.

Kodak also has a Global Customer Service and Support business unit. This unit focuses on anticipating and responding to the needs of all Kodak's customers. Its employees can be reached by phone, fax, email, or in person and can always be relied on to provide superior Kodak servicing to Kodak's various products.

Major International Markets

Kodak has entered and operated in many major international markets including the United States, Europe, the Middle East, Africa, the Asia Pacific region, Canada, and Latin America. A sampling of businesses include a manufacturing plant in England, a wholly-owned subsidiary in France, a distribution center in Canada, a manufacturing plant in Australia, a camera company in Germany, a sensitizing plant in Brazil, a manufacturing plant in Mexico, and two Kodak controlled Chinese stock companies in China.

External and Internal Environment (SWOT Analysis)

External Environment

Industrial China's photographic film market is the third largest in the world, next only to the U.S. and Japan. Consumers bought over 170 million rolls of film at retail stores in 1997, representing 6-7 percent of worldwide film consumption. Kodak's research indicates that a strong pent-up demand for conventional photography in the massive $800 million Chinese photographic and paper market. There is also a high demand for advanced imaging technology for medical and government applications. Kodak's revenue in China approached $250 million in 1997.

The industrial environment in China can be analyzed according to Porter's Five Forces, which includes the threat of new entrants, intensity of rivalry, bargaining power of suppliers, bargaining power of buyers, and threat of substitutes. The barriers to entry in the imaging industry remain high because of high start-up costs. It would take millions of dollars for other firms to enter the Chinese photographic industry and achieve success. Kodak has succeeded where others might have failed thanks to having signed an exclusivity agreement with the Chinese government. This agreement allows Kodak to expand manufacturing and marketing capabilities in China. It also stipulates that over the next four years, the Chinese government will not approve another foreign invested film production venture, which gives Kodak the exclusive right to develop the Chinese photographic industry. This level of exclusivity is unprecedented, and demonstrates the strong relationship, or *guanxi*, Kodak has developed with Chinese leaders. In exchange for this preferential treatment, Kodak will be the first foreign corporation to set up a technological research center in China to help improve the technology sector.

This exclusivity agreement both protects Kodak from the threat of new entrants and significantly reduces the intensity of rivalry. Currently, Kodak's main competitors are Fuji and Lucky Film, with Fuji enjoying a sizable lead in market share for a number of years. Since Kodak signed the agreement with the government, however, this lead has rapidly diminished. Fuji now accounts for roughly 48 percent of the market and Kodak accounts for 40 percent. Lucky Film represents Kodak's only domestic competition. Since 1994, its market share has plunged from 24 percent to 7 percent due to foreign competition. As a result, Kodak currently perceives Lucky Film as an alliance opportunity rather than a threat.

One key factor that cannot be ignored is the bargaining power of Chinese buyers. Chinese people are amongst the world's best savers. It is difficult to convince them to take out money from their saving accounts to purchase consumer goods. Nevertheless, Kodak's conventional 35mm cameras have done surprisingly well in China, with sales up 17 percent in 1997. On the other hand, the bargaining power of suppliers is limited, mainly due to the fact that Kodak supplies the majority of its own products in China. By the year 2000, most Kodak products sold in China will be made in China. As the supplier, Kodak can offer a lot of incentives to retail stores for carrying Kodak products. For example, Kodak pays each retail store $2,000 as enticement to become its affiliate in China. There are currently over 2,000 Kodak affiliated stores in China. The threat of substitute products is marginal for Kodak. Digital imaging and camcorders can be substitutes for film and 35mm cameras, but the cost of buying these substitutes far exceed the cost of buying conventional 35mm cameras and film.

National There are also many factors at the national level that can determine a firm's success in the host country, including market potential, governmental policies, and economic conditions. China, with 1.2 billion citizens, is the largest consumer market in the world. Economically, China has managed to stay out of the Asian crisis. It experienced a phenomenal Gross Domestic Product (GDP) growth of 8.8 percent in 1997. This growth rate has been consistent over the past two decades. Its photographic industry is still fairly underdeveloped. Kodak's research showed that less than one tenth of Chinese households actually own a camera and each camera only exposes about 4 rolls of film a year. This implies a huge latent demand, making China a very attractive place for investment for film companies.

Chinese leaders want to work with Kodak to bring its photo industry up to world-class standards because it realize the value of invigorating an industry that will contribute to the overall well-being of the nation. China welcomes foreign investments, but it also protects local or state-owned enterprises. There are several policies worth mentioning because these policies can limit Kodak's activities and profitability in China. First, there is the 60 percent duty on imported film that Kodak will have to pay if it fails to meet the domestic content requirement. This could significantly cut into its profit. Because of high duties, a lot of film and photographic paper are smuggled into China through a gray market, with distribution heavily dependent upon Hong Kong based distributors. Kodak has a market advantage because it can make its products locally and not worry about the cost of distribution and duties.

The government bars foreign companies from owning retail stores and manufacturing film locally. However, Kodak has been handpicked by the Chinese government to restructure three failing state-owned enterprises, so it has circumvented this policy and is able to manufacture its products locally.

The Chinese government also granted Lucky Film $240 million in loans and $90 million in grants for it to compete with overseas rivals. This government support for Lucky Film could intensify competition in the domestic film industry, spelling trouble for Kodak and Fuji in the future.

Internal Environment

This section examines Eastman Kodak's financial, technological, organizational and operational abilities and the roles these factors play in its development of sustainable competitive advantages.

Financial Typically, a firm's financial health is comprised of its profitability, liquidity, leverage, and activities. Kodak had net earnings of $5 million at the end of fiscal year 1997, down $1.29 billion from the previous year. The huge drop-off can be attributed to $1.4 billion restructuring costs and a $186 million write-off on in-process research and development. The return on sales went from 8 percent down to zero in 1997, mainly due to low earnings and strong competition from Fuji. The quick ratio, which measures the company's ability to pay off short-term obligations without selling off its inventory, went from 84 percent in 1996 down to 58 percent in 1997. This means that Kodak had less liquidity in 1997. The debt-to-asset ratio also increased from 67 percent in 1996 to 76 percent in 1997, meaning that the company used up more funds to finance its operations. Kodak also used more of its inventory to generate sales in 1997 compared to 1996.

A high inventory turnover ratio is good because the company will have lower inventory carrying costs, but in Kodak's case, high inventory turnover ratio could have a negative impact. Kodak's sales figures in 1997 were considerably lower than in 1996, while the cost of goods sold remained fairly constant. This means that Kodak used up more inventory, but generated less sales. Overall, in terms of profitability, liquidity, leverage and activities, Kodak had a worse year in 1997 than in 1996. This is not the direction that Kodak wants to be headed for the future, of course, but the forecast for 1998 was expected to be less than 1997 due to the strength of the U.S. dollar.

Technological Eastman Kodak has high research and development intensity. Kodak has spent over $500 million in research and development each year to stay on the cutting edge of technology; this figure has more than doubled in the last couple of years. Kodak's breakthrough development of T-grain emulsion technology has taken photography to whole new heights. This technology enables Kodak to make higher-speed film with sharper, more compelling pictures; it also reduces the amount of chemistry needed for processing film.

Recently, Kodak's focus has shifted to digital imaging. Its factories are cranking out an impressive array of digital cameras, scanners, and other digital products. The sales of digital products in 1997 were $1.5 billion, up 25 percent from the previous year. This puts Kodak far ahead of any other digital imaging companies. However, the competition is becoming fierce. Fuji, Epson and Cannon are rapidly producing competing products at lower costs while Kodak is having difficulty maintaining its technological leadership.

Kodak's newest toy, Image Magic, a global network of printing-stations, will be unveiled within the next year. Image Magic allows consumers to manipulate pictures stored on the Internet and print them. Some critics are skeptical about the profitability of Image Magic because they believe that consumers will prefer to use photo-quality printers at home rather than Image Magic at retail stores.

Operational Kodak has recently been in a slump attributable to operational factors. The bloated cost structure, bureaucratic corporate culture, and confusing marketing scheme all have Kodak scrambling for solutions. The first hurdle in Fisher's tenure has been dealing with high overhead expenses, 27.6 percent of sales (compared with the industrial average of 15 percent). Fisher has terminated 15,000 employees, including 200 of Kodak's most senior executives, in order to cut payroll expenses. He also sold off chunks of business, including the chemical and printer businesses, in order to cut costs.

The second hurdle that Fisher faces is the old-fashioned corporate culture involving excessive reports, worthless paperwork, and decision paralysis. In his attempt to change the corporate culture, Fisher has been communicating regularly with top-level management and has instituted pay-for-performance standards.

Finally, Fisher has tackled marketing. Kodak seems to be out of touch with the consumers. Its advertising introduced pricey new products, but failed to explain why the consumers should buy these products. Its exciting digital products lacked advertising. Manufacturing glitches left both retailers and consumers short of products. Fisher has brought in Ogilvy & Mather Worldwide Inc. to handle the majority of Kodak's advertising. He hopes a new marketing scheme will win back Kodak's lost customers.

Corporate-Level Strategy

Geographic Diversification

Kodak puts an emphasis on expanding into key emerging markets around the world. Two main reasons Kodak decided to expand into China are its market size and market potential. China is one of the largest markets in the world, with a population of over 1.2 billion people. It has a high potential for sustained long-term growth; its market is expected to grow at about 15-30 percent annually in the years to come. This will make China the world's largest market in the near future. This is the main reason Kodak wants to expand into China as soon as possible. It has already lost out in many markets to its largest competitor, Fuji Film, due to late entry.

China is the second largest market in the world (following only the United States) for photographic products, amounting to $800 million in sales in 1997. Research by Kodak has also found that there is a high demand in the Chinese market for advanced imaging technology for commercial, medical, and governmental applications.

A third factor affecting Kodak's decision is China's natural resources. Prices of materials for photographic products are not a major concern for Kodak in China. It is not trying to save huge amounts of money on input materials. However, labor resources are crucial. Basing production facilities in China lowers labor costs greatly compared to U.S. production.

Governmental policies are another major issue. Companies based in China have a major advantage over foreign competitors such as Kodak because the Chinese Government does not allow wholly foreign-owned enterprises in certain industries, including the photographic industry. The Chinese government keeps a watchful eye on large foreign companies that could create a monopoly. A 60 percent tariff is imposed on all imports of photographic products, forcing foreign companies to go through gray channels to bring in goods. Gray channels are Hong Kong distributors who bring in foreign goods and then distribute them as domestic goods to the rest of China. Companies that deal through them save massive amounts of money by avoiding high tariffs but must still pay high distribution costs.

Kodak can expand only through limited liability companies such as joint ventures. Kodak recently entered into a large joint venture with three Chinese companies. Kodak intends to invest between $1 and $1.5 billion over the next three to five years in the venture. This money will be used to upgrade technology, improve manufacturing capacity, and expand distribution and marketing capabilities in China. In return, as discussed earlier, Beijing has agreed not to approve any other foreign invested film production ventures for the next four years.

This makes Kodak the first foreign company to work with Chinese authorities to build a world-class industry in cooperation with state-owned enterprises. This type of cooperative enterprise can be quite advantageous to both the host country and the entering firm. A foreign company such as Kodak can benefit from its partners' knowledge of the country's competitive conditions, culture, language, and political and business systems. Because the U.S. is much more advanced technologically, many U.S. joint ventures involve the American company providing technology and products and the local company providing local knowledge. The partner companies will also allow Kodak to minimize costs by giving Kodak access to their existing client bases and suppliers. This is a win-win situation for both the host companies and Kodak. Another advantage is that sharing the costs and risks with local partners cuts down on the high development costs that would be incurred by opening brand new facilities in the host country. Kodak's joint venture in China will still have high costs, however, because of all the technology and machinery that it will provide. Finally, the local partners can provide employees that have the general skills needed to work in this industry. Although Kodak must make the investment to teach employees about new technology, it will avoid the costs of teaching them basic skills.

Product Diversification

Kodak's products are seen as a vertically integrated. It designs, manufactures, and sells many of its own products, such as imaging equipment. But it also uses local businesses to market most of its photographic products, such as cameras and film.

Business-Level Strategy

George Fisher, Kodak's Chairman and CEO, says that Kodak's growth initiatives are based on the fundamental premise, 'Our business is pictures'.

The cornerstone of Kodak's competitive strategy is to reach customers at the peak moment of their interest in Kodak products, that is, the moment they open an envelope with pictures in it. At the low end of the market it competes with many small companies that only produce cameras and film. At the high end, it faces global competitors like Fuji Photo Film and China Lucky Film.

Kodak describes its overall future strategy as a combination of disciplined cost management and top-line growth depending on a strategy of differentiation. These strategies are based on the four building blocks of business: quality, efficiency, responsiveness, and innovation. Kodak is one of the most visible photographic companies in the U.S. due to the high quality of its products and customer services. Kodak is now taking its superior quality to China, where it will continue giving consumers the best products possible.

While committed to maintaining quality, Kodak is also becoming more cost efficient by reducing its infrastructure, refocusing research and development activities, and changing its manufacturing processes. This aggressive restructuring will eliminate about 20 percent of the management structure at Kodak in an effort to streamline and simplify the organization, promoting faster, more accountable, and more aggressive decision making.

Kodak has already proved its dedication to superior customer responsiveness. In its expansion throughout China, it plans to make its services accessible to everyone. Currently there are more than 4650 Kodak express imaging stores in the Greater China Region. It is also expanding its mini-lab assembly operations in Shanghai to help meet the strong domestic demand for film processing equipment.

Finally, a strong dedication to research and development has allowed Kodak to succeed through superior innovations which has kept the company on the cutting edge of photographic imaging technology. One area of innovation is in the rapidly growing digital delivery market. With the help of companies such as Canon, Hewlett Packard, and Microsoft, Kodak intends to link the consumer to Kodak goods and services through Image Magic Print Stations at retail locations around the world. There were already 13,000 of these walk-up image processing stations installed in 1997. This is just one of the innovations that Kodak is working on. New innovations and product improvements are being introduced regularly. By expanding into China, Kodak will be able to develop and produce these innovations at even lower costs, which it can pass on to customers.

International Entry Strategies

Entry Mode Selection

Eastman Kodak Company is no stranger to the Chinese market. Like many other foreign companies, Kodak first entered China's market by exporting domestically produced components and importing products for domestic sales. Although the Chinese government has put many constraints on starting wholly foreign-owned enterprises, Kodak has managed to invest in two of them, Kodak Electronic Products (Shanghai) Company, and Kodak Photographic Equipment (Shanghai) Company. Both produce camera components for export and a small amount of photographic equipment for domestic sale. Kodak has also invested about $12 million in Xinhui KH Optical Company, a contractual joint venture between Xinhui and Guangdong, that produces optical lenses. Kodak's aggressive marketing campaigns and nearly a dozen representative offices around the country have cornered around 3,700 exclusive outlets throughout China. However, as most foreign companies find, exporting and importing can be costly. Even going through the gray channels costs money. Kodak realized that it needed to lower its costs and gain better control of distribution and sales. Its next step was setting up domestic production and distribution facilities in China.

In early 1998, following more than two years of negotiations involving the ministries of Foreign Trade and Economic Cooperation, Chemicals Industry, Light Industry, Machines Industry, and the State Economic and Trade Commission, Kodak announced that it would invest more than $1 billion in China over the next several years, making it one of the largest investments by a U.S. company. The investment will mainly be used to upgrade technology, improve manufacturing, and expand the distribution and marketing capabilities needed to build a strong domestic Chinese photo industry. Kodak strongly believes that the Chinese marketplace will one day be the world's largest photographic market. It has therefore chosen to set up both a joint share company and an umbrella company as vehicles for its investments in China.

Kodak has formed a Kodak-controlled umbrella, or holding, company, Kodak (China) Company Limited, and a new Kodak-controlled joint share, or limited liability, company, Kodak (Wuxi) Company Limited, to produce and market color film, medical and industrial X-ray film, and other products in China and elsewhere in Asia. Based in the city of Shanghai, Kodak (China) Co. purchased the assets of two Chinese domestic photographic enterprises, Shantou Era Photo Materials Industry Corporation, and Xiamen

Fuda Photographic Materials Company Limited, both of which produce color film and paper. A third Chinese enterprise, Wuxi Aermei Film and Chemical Corporation, which is based in Wuxi city and makes medical and industrial X-ray film, transferred its primary assets to Kodak (Wuxi) Co.

The Kodak (China) Co. requires about $385 million in capital and a $1.1 billion investment which will be used for technical upgrading of existing equipment in Xiamen Fuda and Shantou Era. The Kodak (Wuxi) Co. involves about $45 million in capital and a total investment of $80 million to be used in the improvement of existing Wuxi product lines and a new project producing chemicals for film development. In addition to joint share projects, Kodak is also financing the construction of a $650 million, 430,000 square meter production plant in Xiamen. This will be one of Kodak's largest production plants world-wide. It will complement the Xiamen Fuda and Shantou Era operations by producing emulsions, color film, and paper for consumer and professional use. Kodak will also invest more than $400 million to build an industrial park in East China's Fujian Province. The park, located in the Haicang Development Zone of Xiamen City, will become a major production base for Kodak film. To ensure steady growth rates in China, Kodak will also create new distribution networks and marketing activities.

There are several factors that can explain Kodak's entry mode selection. The new companies not only give Kodak access to a huge market, but also show Kodak's commitment to China and willingness to share technology and managerial expertise. The companies will also provide Kodak with more flexibility. Their structure will enable foreign and Chinese investors to participate together in each enterprise while at the same time provide greater operational scope and management flexibility than permitted by either a joint venture or a wholly foreign owned enterprise. They will also enable Kodak to operate an integrated company across tax jurisdictions, with production facilities in two provinces and a headquarters in a third. Kodak feels that the umbrella company will be free to expand its operations anywhere in China by buying up the productive assets of other state owned enterprises or establishing branch offices.

This deal will eliminate most of Kodak's potential competitors in China. With Xiamen Fuda, Shantou Era, and Wuxi as partners, China Lucky Film Corporation (now holding about 7 percent of China's roll-film market) will represent Kodak's only domestic competition. Kodak also hopes that the move will give it an edge over global Japanese competitor Fuji Photo Film which has been distributing its photographic film and paper products in China since 1980 and now claims about 48 percent of the market.

Entry Timing

It is the perfect time for Kodak to set up share companies in China. China's leaders have realized the value of invigorating an industry that contributes to national well being. Both of its new companies are strongly supported by the Chinese government because they are consistent with China's efforts to reform the efficiency of its state owned enterprises. Kodak will make optimum use of Chinese skills and provide much needed capital.

Although Kodak previously established two equipment manufacturing facilities and a joint venture company in China, it was not the first mover. Kodak's major foreign competitor, Fuji Photo Film, had already been distributing its photographic film and paper products throughout China and producing components domestically for export, and state owned enterprises such as China Lucky Film Corporation had been producing and selling its products domestically prior to Kodak's investments. Still, Kodak is considered an early mover, which has both advantages and disadvantages.

Being an early entrant means less competition. As noted, only China Lucky Film Corp. and Fuji Photo Film are serious competitors for Kodak, making it a three-cornered battle. The minimal competition should provide Kodak with more strategic options for expansion.

Kodak's two recent investments has made it the first foreign company to break out of the joint venture mold, which until now has been the most common method of entry into China. In addition, by merging two separate state owned firms in Xiamen and Shantou into a single company, Kodak (China) Co., Kodak has in essence created the first foreign controlled holding company in China. This puts it in the position to gain market power over Fuji Photo Film, which has been cutting into Kodak's U.S. sales. Kodak is in a prime position for expansion and to gain a larger market share, brand advantage, and technological leadership.

In addition, China's current reform policies make it a good time for a foreign company to enter China's marketplace. China's leaders are committed to working with Kodak to improve its photo industry; their cooperation reflects an important step in improved bilateral relations and sets an example for others. This commitment between Kodak and the Chinese government also diminishes the political uncertainties that an early entrant may experience.

One of the biggest costs to Kodak will result from China's inadequate photo industry infrastructure and lack of technology. As an early entrant, Kodak will have to provide much of the capital and technology to develop China's photo industry to meet world standards. Kodak's initial investment of $380 million alone is almost double its 1997 China revenues of $200 million. The equipment it purchased from the three failed state owned plants is useless. Kodak will have to spend another $700 million over the next five years bringing it up to satisfactory levels.

Location Selection

The locations of Kodak's investments will play a major role in its success. Kodak was initially limited to specific regions because of investing in a few state owned enterprises. It finally settled on the cities of Shanghai and Wuxi as its major sites for several reasons. For one, they both fit nicely with Kodak's market objectives. Both cities are well known, have strong economies, and have fairly high growth rates. Shanghai, which already houses many other foreign companies, has a population of roughly 13 million people, accounting for about 43 percent of China's gross domestic product (GDP). Per-capita GDP is about 5,103 RMB, which Kodak hopes will translate into strong purchasing power and demand.

Wuxi is not much different from Shanghai. Although not as large, Wuxi is located in Jiangsu Province, which has a population of about 4.3 million people; 1.06 million reside in the city. Wuxi is one of China's top economic cities. It has one of the best investment climates and most rapid rate of economic development. Its GDP is approximately 80 billion RMB, the sixth highest in China; per-capita GDP is about 18,000 RMB, the highest in Jiangsu Province. Market factors like these make both cities perfect for Kodak's expansion. The joint share investment puts Kodak in the middle of its target market.

Seeking competency also influenced Kodak's decision. Kodak already has two wholly owned production investments in Shanghai. This provides the firm with more familiarity and experience in doing business in Shanghai, which in turn should improve technology and management integration and help it cope with any problems that arise.

Both cities support some of Kodak's strategic objectives. Wuxi is very close to Shanghai that should help Kodak improve its distribution networks. Both regions also speak the same dialect, which should benefit Kodak's marketing activities. In addition, lower labor costs are available in both cities, which fits with Kodak's cost reduction goals.

International Strategies

Partner Selection

It is said that partner selection explains over 70 percent of the success or failure of most joint venture activities. Partner selection is almost certainly the most significant factor in the success of Kodak's joint share investments. Kodak's selection of three failing state owned enterprises, Xiamen Fuda, Shantou Era, and Wuxi Aermei, was based mostly on three factors: compatible goals, commitment, and complementary skills.

Both Kodak and its partners have highly compatible goals. All three failing partners were in need of more capital. They hoped to achieve market power and improve their technology in order to become more competitive and profitable over the long run. Kodak provides enormous amounts of capital and technology which will help bring these companies up to world class standards. In return, Kodak gains access to China's market while taking advantage of the lower costs of domestic production and cheap labor.

All three partners showed commitment to the enterprise, backed by government approval. Officials in Beijing gave Kodak an unprecedented degree of management control as the necessary price for cleaning up China's photo industry.

Kodak also sought complementary skills in its partners to ease technology integration and operations. Both Xiamen Fuda and Shantou Era already owned color film and paper sensitizing plants, and Wuxi Aermei had a black and white film manufacturing plant that produced medical and industrial X-ray film. The fact that these companies were already skilled in similar types of production will be benefit Kodak, even though their equipment was useless.

Overall, Kodak mainly sought strategic factors from its partners, such as marketing competence and industrial experience, rather than financial and organizational factors. Kodak was not necessarily interested in factors such as profitability and asset efficiency. In fact, the only profitable state owned photo industry company is Lucky. The lack of financial strength in the other three state owned enterprises actually proved beneficial for Kodak. Kodak used this fact to gain bargaining power during the joint share negotiations, eventually winning the controlling position in the deal.

Sharing Distribution and Control

During the joint share negotiations, Kodak stressed the importance of having the right company structure. It quickly identified the equity distribution, degree of management control, and corporate flexibility it required to make its billion-dollar commitment work. Kodak now owns 80 percent of the shares in the Kodak (China) Company Limited, with Xiamen Fuda Photographic Materials and Shantou Era Photo Materials owning 10 percent each. Kodak owns 70 percent of the shares in the Kodak (Wuxi) Company Limited.

Kodak's strategic objectives greatly influenced its desire for control. Kodak will be able to lead the management and operation of the companies, as they manufacture, market, distribute, sell, and support Kodak brand products throughout China. Kodak's expected investment commitment also influenced its demand for a majority position. Kodak felt that it should hold a majority of the equity since it essentially offered to buy out three failing state owned enterprises, build them up with cash and the latest technology, and provide employment for more than 2,000 workers.

Kodak appoint David Swift, Chairman and President of Kodak's Greater China Region, to serve as Chairman of both new joint share companies. David Swift previously served as vice president and chief operating officer of the Digital Product Center and has been with Kodak for many years. Having Swift chair both companies is crucial in ensuring Kodak control.

The board of directors for both joint share companies will be stacked by Kodak members. Kodak (China) Co. for example, will have a board of directors consisting of ten members, eight of whom will be appointed by Kodak. With such a large majority, Kodak will have the flexibility and control it needs to make the project a success.

Global Integration and Control

Type of International Strategy

Kodak uses a transnational strategy, a hybrid of global and multidomestic strategies. On the one side, Kodak increases its profitability by reducing costs as a result of exploiting location economies and the experience curve effect. On the other side, Kodak differentiates its product offerings and marketing strategies from country to country in order to accommodate the diverse demands arising from international consumer differences. Kodak gets the benefits of both global and multidomestic strategies and its customers benefit as well.

Type of Global Business Structure

Kodak uses a global product group structure. A product group headquarters coordinates the activities of all foreign and domestic divisions within that product group. The product group managers are responsible for organizing all activities on a global basis. And all of the product group headquarters are under the control of corporate headquarters.

Global Integration

Kodak has recognized diversity as a competitive advantage. Kodak and its employees strive to support a culture that acknowledges cultural differences through action, cultivates unique thinking in teamwork, and values diverse perspectives on common business goals. Kodak's overall corporate diversity objective is to achieve an employee population that reflects the customers Kodak serves and the communities in which it resides. Kodak has been increasing the percentage of women and minorities in its domestic work force over the past few years, as shown in the table below. As a result of these efforts, Kodak was added to the 1997 list of Catalyst Blue Ribbon Board of Fortune 500 Companies with Multiple Women Directors.

Table c6.1 Percentage Increase in Domestic Workforce

	Percent Female			Percent Minority		
	1995	**1996**	**1997**	**1995**	**1996**	**1997**
Total U.S. Employees	27.0%	32.1%	33.9%	13.7%	17.4%	18.6%
Officials and Managers	15.9%	19.6%	21.2%	6.5%	7.3%	7.8%
Professionals	22.3%	23.3%	24.5%	7.9%	8.3%	8.8%
All Others	29.6%	35.7%	37.9%	16.2%	20.7%	22.6%

Kodak also offers diversity and cross-cultural education for managers and employees. Participation in local diversity forums is encouraged. Kodak also has eight employee networks, each dedicated to supporting education and professional advancement in a diverse segment of the population.

Operational Strategies

External Environment

Kodak has joined 23 other manufacturers of semiconductors in a voluntary partnership with the U.S. Environmental Protection Agency to reduce the emissions of perfluorocompounds (PFCs) and hydrofluorocarbons (HFCs). Both PFCs and HFCs typically result from the manufacturing of semiconductors. They are considered potent greenhouse gases capable of trapping solar radiation in the earth's atmosphere.

Kodak has also invested $15 million in 'air scrubbing' technology at one of its key manufacturing buildings, Kodak Park in Rochester. The new technology, called a regenerative thermal oxidizer, can oxidize solvents with up to 99 percent efficiency. Thanks to the oxidizer, the company expects an immediate 86 percent reduction in solvent emissions from this building, exceeding the level of performance required by EPA regulations. Even though film production is expected to double at the building by the year 2000, solvent emissions will still be less than 65 percent of 1997 levels.

An EPA-Kodak pilot project completed in 1997 shows that it is possible to predict a chemical's potential health and environmental effects so early in development that hazards and waste can be avoided and significant dollars saved. In the two-year effort to evaluate the EPA-developed test method, Kodak was able to reformulate five photochemicals under development. In doing so, it has improved its environmental performance significantly and saved the company tens of thousands of dollars in development costs. The project not only determined it was effective, but also that it is transferable, meaning other companies can apply it to chemicals in the early stages of development.

Marketing

Special recognition for Kodak's advertising came from *Adweek*, which named the Kodak Advantix system TV commercials, entitled 'Venice' as one of the Best Spots of 1997. Also recognized for excellence in 1997 was Kodak's ingenious website, www.kodak.com. It received the 'Best World Wide Web Ad' citation in the 6th annual Mar.com Awards, the WebMaster '50/50 Award' for excellence and innovation on the Internet, and the Web Marketing Association's 'Best of Industry' Award in the photography and imaging category.

Finance

In accordance with Kodak's company policy, foreign currency forward contracts are used to hedge certain firm commitments and the currency risk involved in deposit taking and lending activities at Kodak's International Treasury Center. Options and futures are also used to reduce the companies risk in dealing with fluctuating commodity prices. In 1997, Kodak also started to enter into option and futures contracts to minimize its exposure to increases in silver prices.

Human Resource Management

Kodak is engaged in proactive staffing efforts, including diversity recruitment, university associations, student programs, and relationships with national minority organizations. Retention of these people is supported by a comprehensive, company-wide, employee development planning process and other initiatives such as formal and informal mentorship programs.

Employee progress is monitored regularly. Achievement of diversity goals has been incorporated into the Management Performance Commitment Process that determines a portion of management's compensation. Feedback from employees is also constantly reviewed to better understand diversity issues and employee responses to change. One example is the VIEW survey that reaches every Kodak employee at least once a year, asking employees to assess managers according to Kodak values.

At Kodak's Rochester site, the annual cold and flu season increases the number of work absences. In 1994, the Kodak Medical Department began to fight influenza with a free immunization program. In 1996, more than 9,100 employees participated. The cost to administer the program was $70,000; the savings, measured in prevention of lost time, was $1.5 million. In 1997, the number of participants jumped to 11,200, (30 percent of the workforce), the cost was only a little higher ($76,000), with an estimated savings in excess of $2 million.

Conclusion

From 1996 to 1997, Kodak saw significant increases in 35mm film usage around the world. In India there was a 125 percent increase, a 61 percent increase in Russia, and a 17 percent increase in China. Kodak should therefore continue its ventures in emerging markets.

Experts have suggested a few things that will help bring Kodak's focus back. First, it should cross-market between the U.S. and foreign markets in order to protect its market share from Fuji. Second, it needs to continue slashing its bureaucracy while instilling a sense of urgency and mission in its managers. Third, in needs to make simpler products and use advertising more effectively to give customers reasons to choose Kodak. Finally, it should buy a brand-name consumer electronics company to ease its transition into the digital business.

Kodak has diversity incorporated into its participation in external activities. It has developed strong relationships in a variety of communities and with government officials through making corporate contributions and providing small business development. It is recommended that it continue with this corporate diversity strategy as it should continue to bring it a wealth of culturally diverse opportunities.

Case Study 7: Coca-Cola

Executive Summary

Coca-Cola was the creation of pharmacist Dr. John Styth Pemberton more than 100 years ago. Today, Coca-Cola is part of everyday life for millions of Americans. It has become the foundation for one of the largest corporations in the world.

The Coca-Cola Corporation's latest focus is on the Chinese market, where it hopes to make Coca-Cola as common a beverage as tea. It has a tough road ahead of it because it must compete with Chinese soft drink companies such as Jianlibao, which produces a soft drink similar to Coca-Cola. However, Coca-Cola feels that the global appeal of its soft drinks will win it success in China.

Recently, it started a joint venture with the Chinese government to make a variety of juice drinks called Tian Yu Di. This is the first indigenous Chinese brand of beverage developed by the Coca-Cola Company. It is counting on its vast cash flow to enable it to reinvest in order to expand upon its soft drink infrastructure, currently one of the world's strongest distribution systems. Coca-Cola holds an impressive position on the New York Stock Exchange, with its stocks currently listed at $73 per share.

The Coca-Cola company prides itself on superior quality, innovation, input efficiency, and customer responsiveness. It also has an excellent research and development department focused on improving the taste and quality of its soft drinks, along with a department devoted to product packaging research. These are just a few of Coca-Cola's key competitive qualities gives it an edge over local and international competitors.

Company Introduction

History of Coca-Cola

On May 8, 1886, pharmacist Dr. John Styth Pemberton created a fragrant caramel-colored syrup and brought a jug of his creation to Jacob's Pharmacy, Atlanta's largest drugstore. That day, it debuted as a soda fountain drink sold for 5 cents a glass. Frank M. Robinson, Dr. Pemberton's partner and bookkeeper, later suggested the name Coca-Cola for the drink. A few weeks later, Coca-Cola was advertised in the newspaper with the slogan, 'Delicious and Refreshing'. Sales for the new beverage averaged about 9 servings per day for the rest of the year. When Pemberton died two years later, Atlanta druggist and businessman, Asa G. Candler purchased the outstanding shares for Coca-Cola. By 1891, he had acquired complete control of Pemberton's company, with a total investment of $2,300.

In 1892, Candler and three business associates formed the Coca-Cola Company. Its capital stock was $100,000, with an annual advertising budget of $11,401. By 1893, the company paid its first dividend to shareholders; it has paid dividends on its common stocks every year since. The company opened its first syrup manufacturing plant outside of Atlanta in Dallas in 1894. The following year, two other plants opened up in Chicago and Los Angeles.

Candler was an aggressive marketer who promoted the new beverage on items such as calendars, outdoor posters, painted walls, serving trays, soda fountain urns, and clocks. His strategy was to make Coca-Cola available to everyone. The 'Coca-Cola' trademark was first registered in the United States Patent Office in early 1893. Early advertisers tried to discourage consumers from calling the beverage 'Coke', but the nickname was so popular it was eventually registered as a trademark in 1945.

In 1919, Candler sold the Coca-Cola Company for $25 million to Atlanta banker Ernest Woodruff and his investor group. Woodruff's son, Robert, was elected president of the company four years later, to remain in charge for six decades. A big part of his success was a commitment to high standards of product quality. Robert Woodruff re-incorporated the business in Delaware and publicly sold 500,000 shares of common stock for $40 per share.

In 1960, Coca-Cola purchased the Minute Maid Corporation, adding frozen citrus juice concentrates, along with the trademarks Hi-C and Minute Maid, to the company's beverage line. Coca-Cola also acquired Duncan Foods and formed the Coca-Cola Foods Division in 1967, now known as the Minute Maid Company. It also produced and marketed wine in the United States from 1977 to 1983. In 1982, Coca-Cola purchased the Belmont Springs Water Company and also acquired Columbia Pictures Industries, Inc., which joined Tri-Star Pictures in 1987 to form the independent company, Columbia Pictures Industries, Inc. In 1989, Coca-Cola sold the Belmont Springs Water Company, Inc., along with its minority interest in Columbia Pictures Entertainment, Inc. In 1990, it formed the Coca-Cola Refreshment Systems, a new subsidiary that would manage the BreakMate compact soft drink dispenser business in the United States. By 1991, Coca-Cola and Nestle formed a joint venture company intended to manufacture, market, and distribute ready-to-serve tea and coffee beverages under the Nestea and Nescafe trademarks.

The Coca-Cola history has also been marked by changes in its packaging. Bottling Coca-Cola was the first important innovation because it made it possible to distribute the beverage to consumers throughout the United States. Unfortunately, the bottles used by Coca-Cola were basically the same as those used by its competitors, which made it easy for its competitors to sell their products as Coca-Cola. In 1915, Coke held a bottle design competition amongst 30 companies, seeking a bottle that was distinctive both in how it looked and how it felt to hold. The Root Glass Company won the design competition and a year later the bottle was patented. By 1923, Coca-Cola began selling its beverage in six pack cartons. This was a big hit with consumers and became one of the soft drink industry's most powerful merchandising tools.

Mission and Goals

The Coca-Cola company is committed to creating quality products for consumers and value for its shareholders while enhancing its trademarks worldwide. It achieves its mission through an effective distribution system, satisfying customers, allocating resources efficiently, and focusing on global leadership in the beverage industry. It also capitalizes on its strong cash flow whenever possible by reinvesting in the company, paying dividends, and buying back its own stock.

In seeking new opportunities, the company has implemented a value-based management method for developing strategies and evaluating decisions. It has also launched Project Infinity, a seven year, multi-million dollar program aimed at providing its employees with the tools and systems necessary for quick acquisition of knowledge throughout its global network.

Another goal is to give consumers compelling reasons to drink more of its products. It aims to do this by offering special refreshment experiences, as represented by its sponsorship of the Centennial Olympic Games, 1996 World Cup Cricket, and the Africa Cup of Nations football tournament.

In order to increase its procurement capabilities, the company has reorganized its Global Procurement and Trading group and brought in new talent to increase the level of expertise in that function. In order to strengthen its distribution and customer service systems, it has formed two aligned groups within its Marketing and Technical Operations division. One focuses on the execution of sales and merchandising programs, the other on logistics, warehousing, and delicatessen sales.

Coca-Cola invests a great deal in building brand recognition, in part through creative sloganeering, a strategy it has followed since 1886 (see Table c7.1).

Core Products

The corporation's main product is its signature beverage, Coca-Cola. Cola beverages are usually flavored with a blend of orange, lemon, and lime along with vanilla, coca, and kola tastes. Coca-Cola has more of an orange taste than its closest competitor, Pepsi.

The company almost had a major crisis when it changed the Coca-Cola formula in 1985. Its consumers responded with an outpouring of loyalty and affection for the original formula. It was reintroduced a few months later under the name 'Coca-Cola Classic'.

The first soft drink other than Coca-Cola to be marketed by the company was Fanta, introduced in 1960. At first, it was only distributed by European bottlers. Today, Fanta is the fourth best selling soft drink brand worldwide. In 1961, Coca-Cola introduced Sprite, now the fifth best selling soft drink in the world and the forth best selling of the company's beverages. Another major product is Diet Coke, introduced in 1982 and now the number one diet soft drink in the United States. In 1985, Cherry Coke made its debut, achieving a place as one of the top ten favorite soft drinks in the United States by the end of that year. In 1984 the Minute Maid orange soft drink and its diet counterpart were introduced in Canada, then to the United States a few years later. Currently, the Minute Maid soft drink line has more fruit flavors than any other national brand. PowerAde, the company's first sports drink, debuted as a fountain soft drink in 1990 and then in 1993 as a packaged drink. It also offers other beverages in the United States, such as TAB, Mellow Yellow, Fresca, Barq's, Fruitopia, and Mr. Pibb. Finally, the Coca-Cola Company has capitalized on health concerns by offering diet and caffeine-free versions of many of its popular beverages, including Diet Sprite, Diet Cherry Coke, Caffeine Free Diet Coke, and Caffeine Free Coke.

The Coca-Cola Company offers some brands tailored to meet the tastes of national markets. Some of its best selling markets are within its

Middle and Far East Group. Japan is one of the company's top markets, with a record unit case sales growth of 7 percent in 1996. The bottlers in Japan took many important steps to market innovatively while controlling costs. They launched several popular additions to the company's product portfolio, including some new tea products and a milk based drink named Lactia. Another example is its very popular Georgia Coffee line.

China is another strong market for the Coca-Cola Company. The unit case sales growth top 30 percent, led by strong sales of Coca-Cola and Sprite and also supported by the launch of Tian Yu Di ('Heaven and Earth') juice drinks. This is the first indigenous Chinese brand developed by the Coca-Cola Company. Marketing innovation has also been important in China. Soon after the introduction of Coca-Cola to China in the 1920s, it was decided to give the beverage a second name in Chinese characters. After an initial translation failure, however, the company realized that it could not just substitute characters that sounded like Coca-Cola. It turned out that its first attempt, which sounded like Ke-Kou-Ke-La, meant 'bite the wax tadpole' or 'female horse stuffed with wax' (depending on the dialect). Unfortunately, the company did not find this out until after thousands of signs had been printed and posted using this phrase. Eventually, a professor from Shanghai came up with the perfect combination of four simple characters which sound a lot like the English pronunciation of Coca-Cola and translate into the phrase 'Delicious Happy', a far more appropriate slogan for a beverage.

Restructuring Issues

Today, the Coca-Cola company is aggressively expanding by making premium refrigerated fruit beverages available worldwide. This began with the acquisition of the Minute Maid Corporation, which was combined with Duncan Foods in 1967 to become the Minute Maid Company. This was the first company to market frozen concentrated orange juice. It is now one of Coca-Cola's six operating units. Minute Maid provides expertise to the Coca-Cola company in the areas of fruit drinks and beverages as an important part of the company's total beverage portfolio.

An alliance was formed in 1996 with Brazilian-based Sucocritico Cutrale Ltda., the world's largest grower and processor of oranges, to assure a supply of quality orange juice concentrate. By the year 2000, the Minute Maid Company expects its refrigerated products to be available in 50 countries and, ultimately, wherever Coca-Cola is sold.

In the near future, Coca-Cola will be dealing with some major restructuring issues as it has recently changed CEOs. M. Douglass Ivester was the president and Chief Operating Officer of Coca-Cola until his recent promotion to CEO. His biggest challenge will be following in the footsteps of his mentor, Roberto Goizueta. Roberto Goizueta began his career in 1954 as a chemist at the Coca-Cola Company in Havana. In 1961, he fled Cuba and rejoined the company in Florida. By 1974 he was appointed head of Coca-Cola's labs, one of only 2 top chemists allowed to memorize the soda's secret formula. He was an aggressive CEO who propelled Coca-Cola's value from less than $5 billion in 1981 to nearly $150 billion in 1997.

Now, under the direction of Ivester, Coca-Cola is pouring investment into reaching its goal of grasping 50 percent of the United States market by 2001. The plan is to make its products easily accessible by putting a Coca-Cola vending machine or retail point within easy reach of every consumer.

External Environment

Industrial Level

The industry is composed of various soft drink companies, bottling and canning operations, and fountain/postmix wholesalers and retailers. The bottling and canning operations are responsible for buying syrups and concentrates from soft drink manufacturers that are then combined with carbonated water. The finished products are packaged in glass or plastic bottles and aluminum cans, then distributed through different channels such as supermarkets, convenience stores, gas stations, warehouse outlets, and vending machines.

Soft drink manufacturers also sell syrup and concentrates to fountain/postmix wholesalers and retailers, where the soft drinks are served in cups or glasses. Fountain outlets are found wherever consumers make point of sale purchases, in places such as fast food restaurants, stadiums, and convenience stores. At such locations, consumers have their choice of beverage, free of pricing, packaging, and promotional ploys. Purchase decisions are based purely on taste preferences.

National Level

In the United States, Coke has a relative market share of 44 percent, while Pepsi covers 31 percent of the market. Clearly, Coke leads the soft drink market. However, the company faces competition from brands produced by its two major rivals, PepsiCo and Cadbury Schweppes plc.

PepsiCo PepsiCo is currently Coca-Cola's number one competitor in the beverage industry. It is the second largest soft drink maker in the world after Coca-Cola, and has been around nearly as long. Aside from beverages, half of its sales come from its Frito Lay products such as Fritos, Doritos, Lays, and Ruffles. Pepsi, the soft drink, is currently PepsiCo's best selling beverage in the United States. Other brands include Diet Pepsi, Mountain Dew, Slice, Mirinda, and Surge. In addition, PepsiCo owns the rights to distribute 7-UP in international markets. Each of these soft drinks account for more than a billion dollars in annual sales. In 1997, PepsiCo had sales of $20.9 billion and generated a net income from operations of $1.07 billion. The company's brands are almost as popular as Coca-Cola's in both domestic and international markets.

Internationally, Coke still leads the market dramatically with a 48 percent share, compared to Pepsi's 22 percent. Since the two soft drinks taste almost the same, the companies have competed on the basis of price, advertising, and distribution. Rarely are both Pepsi and Coke offered at the same restaurant, so consumers are often forced to accept whichever one is available. They both have strong bottling and distribution networks. PepsiCo and Coca-Cola therefore both rely on brand recognition, clever marketing, and customer loyalty. PepsiCo was the first beverage company to introduce packaging innovations such as the *Big Slam* (a one liter, wide-mouth bottle) and the *Cube* (a 24-pack that easily fits into a refrigerator). The company found these innovations were also cost effective means for transporting its products worldwide.

PepsiCo is currently pursuing emerging international markets by establishing company-owned bottling and distribution operations in France and Eastern Europe. It has also formed alliances with powerful bottlers in Latin America. These strategic moves are being made in response to the company's lagging international market share.

Cadbury Schweppes Cadbury Schweppes is Coca-Cola's second largest competitor and the third largest soft drink maker in the world. The English company, Cadbury, is best known for its candy and sugar products. In

1969 it merged with Schweppes Limited, a company that manufactured carbonated drinks. The two companies consolidated and began expanding overseas, particularly to the United States. Most of Cadbury Schweppes' early involvement in the world soft drink industry was not too successful. In 1986, it bought out Soda Stream Holdings in order to gain more American customers and compete head on with Coke and Pepsi. Cadbury Schweppes holds about 1 percent of the U.S. market at this time.

It carried out a series of acquisitions between 1986 and 1995. For example, the acquisition of Canada Dry and Sunkist brands in 1986 put the company in direct competition with Coke and Pepsi. It then purchased Crush International from Proctor and Gamble in 1989, and acquired the root beer maker, A&W, in 1993. Finally, in 1995, the company made its biggest acquisition ever by buying out Dr. Pepper/7-UP. The acquisition also gave Cadbury Schweppes the rights to distribute 7-UP in the U.S. (while Pepsi still owns the rights to distributing 7-UP in international markets). This acquisition pushed Cadbury Schweppes to emerge as the third largest soft drink company in the world.

Roughly 415 Cadbury Schweppes brand confections and beverages are sold in over 170 countries worldwide. Some of the most popular brand names include: Squirt, A&W, Country Time, Crystal Light, and Mott's Apple. Internationally, its most popular brand is the Dr. Pepper soft drink. In the domestic market, Cadbury Schweppes has a 16 percent market share in the soft drink industry. Total sales of both the beverage and candy business amounted to $34 billion and a net income of $590 million in 1996.

The Cadbury Schweppes bottling system of bottling involves a global network of principal subsidiaries, affiliates, and licensing agreements. The company has a good distribution network, but is not as large as Coca-Cola's or PepsiCo's. Because of this, Cadbury Schweppes' bottling operations are dependent upon its two major rivals in the U.S., where it does not produce any of its beverages. Instead, the rights to produce its products are distributed between Coca-Cola and PepsiCo. About 75 percent of Cadbury Schweppes' Dr.Pepper/7-UP products are distributed through these major companies. Internationally, however, Cadbury Schweppes owns several of its own distribution channels. Cadbury Schweppes plans to strengthen its distribution networks, especially in the U.S., by acquiring more independent bottlers to distribute its products and buying out smaller soft drink companies.

International Level

More soft drink companies are seeking opportunities in international markets because the industry for soft drinks in the U.S. has become saturated. Competition has become intense as a result, but Coca-Cola has taken advantage of this trend. It currently has various plants located all over the world. Its biggest potential market is China, however, since China is the most populous country in Asia.

Currently, Coca-Cola holds 23 percent of China's soft drink market. It faces competition from Pepsi, which has been putting vending machines throughout the major cities and provinces. There are currently 23 Coca-Cola plants in China to Pepsi's 17. Competition from Cadbury Schweppes is unusual, but there are new competitors entering the market, including traditional Asian drink manufacturers (producing bottled teas for example).

Coca-Cola products are consumed by millions all over the world. For example, in 1995 it was recorded that more than 800 million servings of Coca-Cola products had been consumed each day. By 1998, consumption reached a record one billion servings per day. Consumers are loyal to Coke because of its quality and because it has become an American icon. In China, as in most Asian countries and the rest of the world, people drink Coke because it conveys a lifestyle. It is regarded as definitely American and represents Western ideals.

Coca-Cola markets its various brands to diverse groups of people such as families, single people, older people, and children. It also targets people from all walks of life and different ethnicities. In China, however, the company has not yet marketed to any particular segment of the population. Rather, it sees the population as a whole as enjoying Coke and making it the beverage of choice. It also tries to make Coke more accessible in vending machines in hopes of attracting a wide range of consumers.

Internal Analysis

The Coca-Cola Company enjoys many advantages as one of the top companies in the world. Its reputation alone has brought the company much success for over a century. Its success can also be attributed to strengths in technological, operations, organization, and financial aspects of the business, as described in greater detail below.

Technological Strengths

The formulas for Coca-Cola beverages are important trade secrets. Supposedly, only two people in the world currently know the formula for Coke. The syrups and concentrates that Coca-Cola sells to bottling companies have remained a secret for over 100 years.

One of Coca-Cola's main objectives is to create value by building on its trademark, one of the best-known logos worldwide. The brand name is considered a valuable resource that Coca-Cola puts to competitive advantage. The majority of Coke's trademark license agreements are included in the company's bottling agreements, in which the bottlers are required to prepare and package the drinks only as authorized. Because of the success of its brand, Coca-Cola owns many patents and copyrights to protect these trademarks and trade secrets from being purchased or imitated.

Packaging also differentiates Coca-Cola from other soft drinks. Coca-Cola has devoted large amounts of capital resources to packaging research. Important packaging innovations have made its products available to consumers anytime and anywhere. The creation of the contoured bottle gave Coke a unique shape and look. Today's plastic bottles imitate the original bottle shape. Coca-Cola also developed the six-bottle carton, which makes soft drinks more convenient to carry around.

Coca-Cola also has the strength of employee know-how. Because knowledge provides a competitive advantage, the company is focused on enhancing the capabilities of its people. For example, to provide its employees with the best possible information, Coca-Cola has launched Project Infinity, a seven year, multi-million dollar program that will provide tools and systems by which employees can quickly acquire and share knowledge throughout the global market. The purpose of this is to identify and capture opportunities for growth. Another program is the Coca-Cola Learning Consortium (developed in 1996), which is a group dedicated to working with the management of the entire Coca-Cola system to make learning a core capability. Another program focuses on Value Based Management (VBM), which provides tools for understanding what factors create value and what destroy it.

Operational Strengths

Coca-Cola has the advantage of a strong regional and sales network worldwide. Its systems of distribution and bottling are the backbone of its operations and make its number one product, Coke, seem like a local product for consumers around the globe.

Coca-Cola also has strong relationships with its bottlers, to which it offers product quality control, marketing, advertising, engineering, and personnel training. A total of eight anchor bottlers are strategically positioned around the world. The Coca-Cola Company authorizes each bottler to prepare and package products and distribute them in specified territories. The bottler, in turn, is obligated to purchase its entire requirement of concentrates and syrups from the company or other authorized suppliers. Coca-Cola has business relationships with three types of bottlers. Some are independently owned, while in others the company has either a non-controlling or a controlling ownership interest. The independent bottlers produce and distribute about 40 percent of Coca-Cola's unit case volume. About 45 percent of Coke products are handled by bottlers in which the company has a non-controlling interest, the remaining 15 percent by bottlers in which the company has a controlling ownership. There are currently 16 Coca-Cola bottling factories in China, with another 17 recently opened. One locally owned bottler, Swire Coca-Cola, also has rights to manufacture and distribute Coca-Cola products. It produces more than 15 million cases of beverages a year at its plant in Sha Tin.

Coca-Cola has a world class marketing system. Its current marketing strategy involves putting a vending machine or retail point within 'arms length' of every consumer. Coca-Cola tailors its marketing programs to suit the needs of 200 countries. It thus has the ability to conduct a global business while maintaining a multi-local appeal. In the past, Coca-Cola's marketing programs reflected the look of the times. Today, its strategy is to reflect the outlooks of different audiences within each market, while simultaneously underscoring the universal appeal of refreshment. For instance, the company has recently launched 'Smart', the first carbonated soft drink specifically designed by an international company for the Chinese market.

Financial Strengths

Investment Strategies In 1998, Coca-Cola sales amounted to $18.9 billion, with a net income of $4.07 billion. Coca-Cola spends most of this money reinvesting in the company to support its soft drink infrastructure, paying dividends to its stockholders, and buying back its own stock. It builds and upgrades production facilities, extends its worldwide distribution networks, provides employee training, develops and implements integrated marketing programs, and does product and packaging research. In addition, it invests in brand positioning, developing precise consumer communications and seeking consumer feedback.

Sometimes it invests in less developed production and distribution facilities to help them function more like those in developed markets. The company's investments in China, for example, reached about $500 million in 1997.

Coca-Cola's equity investments in certain bottling operations often result in increases in unit case volume, net revenues, and profits at the bottler level, which in turn generate increased gallon shipments for the company's concentrate business. In the end, both the Coca-Cola Company and the bottlers benefit from long term volume growth.

Financial Ratios A time series analysis of Coca-Cola's financial ratios is provided in Table c7.2. The Coca-Cola Company's liquidity ratios were fairly low over 1995 and 1996. This was probably due to huge loans taken in the past which have been used to expand its beverage business. This has also made its leverage ratios increase. Coca-Cola's leverage ratios started out quite high in 1992. It was able to lower this ratio by paying off large amounts of debt in 1994. But the leverage ratio increased again in 1995 as more loans were taken.

Its profitability ratios have steadily increased, as shown by its net profit margin and return on assets, over the past five years. These increases are probably due to global expansion. Its activity ratios show improvement over the same period. The improved inventory ratio demonstrates higher sales in recent years. Coca-Cola was able to increase its fixed asset turnover ratio by using fixed assets more effectively and realizing higher sales on them.

SWOT Analysis

Strengths

Coca-Cola's many strengths, as mentioned earlier, include superior technology, operations, financing, and organization. Its huge amount of capital allows it to invest in stronger distribution and bottling systems and technological innovations. Its strengths also benefit local businesses in the countries in which it operates.

Weaknesses

Coca-Cola's main weakness is in its low-key advertising campaign in the United States. Pepsi is in the lead in terms of creative marketing in the U.S. This could be attributed to the fact that the Coca-Cola company is currently more focused on making its products known to the rest of the world, while resting on its laurels as a leader in the domestic market. However, even in China, Pepsi's effective marketing strategies have been stealing the limelight from Coca-Cola. Now almost half of all vending machines in China sell Pepsi and some traders have stated that Pepsi's advertisements are better. Coca-Cola has recently responded by increasing its investment in marketing, including putting up a neon Coke sign over Beijing's Golden Bridge Building.

Opportunities

Coca-Cola has both the capital and the ability to enter further unexplored markets worldwide and experiment with different products.

Threats

The most obvious threat Coca-Cola faces is competition from other soft drink companies, as discussed in detail above. It not only has to beware its largest competitors, such as Pepsi and Cadbury-Schweppes, but also substitute products from smaller manufacturers such as Safeway Select and Sam's Cola from Wal-Mart.

Another threat is changing trends in consumer tastes. Many people today are turning to coffee-based beverages; consequently, they drink less soft drinks. Consumers have also become more health conscious, which can affect their choice of beverage. This is true not only domestically, but also internationally. Coca-Cola should not overlook the emergence of such trends.

Corporate Level Strategy

The Coca-Cola Company's corporate objective is to increase shareowner value. Since its directors, officers, and employees own approximately 17 percent of the outstanding shares of the company, its corporate objective is clearly aligned with that of its external shareholders. The Coca-Cola

Company believes that increasing shareowner value requires consistent growth in terms of financial results. This is complemented by effective reinvestment in its business.

Diversification

The Coca-Cola Company uses the related diversification strategy for its soft drink business. It thereby hopes to achieve synergy among its various related businesses. Focusing on one business also allows the company to become more efficient. From this, it will gain a competitive advantage in several product markets.

Restructuring

In early 1996, the bottling company Coca-Cola FEMSA (KOF) acquired a territory operated in by SIRSA San Isidro Refrescos in Buenos Aires for a total of US $60 million. During 1995, 13.3 million unit cases had been sold in this territory. This transaction was part of a program to consolidate KOFBA operations. It derived from KOF's appointment as Coca-Cola's anchor bottler for Latin America and included a written commitment offering KOF another territory then served by Refrescos del Norte (RDN), starting mid-1998.

KOF also exercised its option to acquire more of a stake in KOFBA. Its equity now amounts to 75 percent, up from 25 percent. This increase resulted from making a US $121 million capital contribution which was applied to repay US $61 million of KOFBA's short term debt and to finance the acquisition of SIRSA San Isidro Refrescos; and (ii) the purchase of shares of KOFBA from the Coca-Cola Export Corporation (TCCEC) for US $22.1 million. These transactions (together with the refinancing of some of KOF's short term debts) were financed through an 18 month US $165 million bridge loan. As a result, KOF's consolidated indebtedness increased US $79 million.

Business Level Strategy

The Coca-Cola Company has developed a comprehensive business strategy focused on four key objectives: (1) increasing volume; (2) expanding its share of beverage sales worldwide; (3) maximizing long-term cash flow; and (4) improving profits and creating added economic values. The company achieves these objectives by investing in its high-return beverage business and optimizing the cost of capital through appropriate financial policies.

The Coca-Cola Company in China uses a variety of sales techniques including direct sales, presales, telephone sales, handheld computer orders, and EDI (electronic data interchange) to deal with large chain stores. Its Sales Distribution System (SDS) operates in a client/server-based distributive environment which generates a lot of transactions, and thereby a great deal of information which can be analyzed. The SDS needs to flexible enough to handle frequent price adjustments, as wholesale prices are influenced by rapidly changing market conditions.

The Coca- Cola Company has greatly contributed to altering China's soft drink industry. Beverage products used to be unstable in quality and were produced by numerous small, scattered, and inefficient factories. Today, large modern firms produce high-quality products. The Coca-Cola Company's Chinese suppliers have also gained enhanced technology, improved labor productivity, and increased economic returns. The growing profitability of Coca-Cola's Chinese partners has resulted in increased payments to the government. Since Coca-Cola purchases all raw materials in China for production in that country, the company also brings significant benefits to the local economy. Thus, through superior innovation, quality, efficiency, and customer responsiveness, the Coca-Cola Company plays an important role in the success of China's soft drink market.

Finally, Coca-Cola has a strategy of customer responsiveness, as we discovered when emailing our request for its annual reports. A copy was sent to us immediately.

Global Business

The Coca-Cola Company views itself as a global (rather than international) business that happens to be headquartered in Atlanta, Georgia. Through the world's largest and most pervasive distribution system, consumers in nearly 200 countries enjoy its products at a rate of more than 834 million servings a day.

The Coca-Cola Company is divided into six operating units. The Middle and Far East Group covers the highest total population in markets such as Japan, Australia, China, and India. The Greater Europe Group includes Western Europe and the rapid-growth markets of Eastern Europe.

The Latin America Group, which stretches from Tijuana, Mexico in the north to Tierra del Fuego in the south, includes all company operations in Central and South America. The North America Group is comprised of the United States and Canada. The Africa Group is responsible for the countries of Sub-Saharan Africa. Finally, the Minute Maid Company forms the largest marketer of juice and juice-drink products in the world.

Within these territories, the United States, with a 266 million population, has the highest per capita consumption of Coca-Cola with (363 8 oz. servings per year). Mexico is second (332) and Australia comes in third (308). These are all countries where Coca-Cola has been established for a long time. Of the emerging Asian markets, India (with a population of 953 million) has the least per capita consumption of 3. China, the most populous nation with 1.2 billion, has a per capita consumption of only 5. Coca-Cola products are still fairly new to these people. It's products are considered luxuries rather than necessities and indigenous drinks still dominate. In other words, Coke is not yet part of either the Chinese or Indian cultures.

International Business Structure

By contrast with the Coca-Cola Company and its local subsidiaries, many bottling companies are authorized to package and sell its soft drinks within certain territorial boundaries and under conditions that ensure high standards of quality and uniformity. The company takes pride in being a worldwide business that is also local. Bottling and canning plants are, with some exceptions, locally owned and operated by independent business people who are native to the countries in which they are located. Bottlers provide the capital investment for land, buildings, machinery, equipment, trucks, bottles, and cases. Most supplies are bought from local sources, often creating new supply industries and areas of employment within the local economy. Coca-Cola supplies bottlers with syrups, concentrates, and beverage bases, actively engages in management assistance to help ensure the profitable growth of each bottler's business, and offers a broad range of business support services in such areas as product quality control, marketing, advertising, engineering, finance, and personnel training.

International Investment Strategies.

In highly developed markets, such as those of the U.S. and Europe, the Company's primary goal is to make its products the preferred customer choice. It therefore dedicates most of its investment to marketing. In developing and emerging markets, however, its main goal is increased penetration of the market with its products. It commits the bulk of its investments to infrastructure enhancements such as production facilities, distribution networks, sales equipment, and technology. It make these investments by acquiring or forming strategic business alliances with local bottlers and by matching local expertise with global experience.

Currently, 55 percent of the world's population lives in markets where the average person consumes fewer than 10 servings of Coca-Cola beverages per year. Such markets offer high potential growth opportunities. In fact, the emerging markets of China, India, Indonesia, and Russia combined represent approximately 44 percent of the world's population, but the average per capita consumption of Coca-Cola products in these markets is approximately 1 percent of the level in the United States. As a result, Coca-Cola is investing aggressively in ensuring that its products are available, preferred, and a good value. Coca-Cola tailors its marketing strategies to local cultures as well, so that no segment of any population will miss the message that Coca-Cola's products are special and better.

Coca-Cola in China

As noted earlier, Coca-Cola is exerting a significant influence on China's soft drink industry. The Coca-Cola system has been called one of the most important new forces in the growth of the Chinese economy.

One study found that the Coca-Cola system creates six jobs outside its own system for each single job inside it. Each position in a China-based Coca-Cola joint venture can create six indirect employment opportunities. Currently, Coca-Cola directly employs 15,000 people in China but has provided tens of thousands of jobs indirectly to Chinese workers and helped 40,000 to 70,000 retail shops succeed in China.

The Swire Coca-Cola operation in Hong Kong produces more than 15 million cases of beverages a year at the company's bottling plant in Sha Tin. The firm uses a client/server-based distribution system developed for the Hong Kong and China market to help distribute products to some 15,000 customers and process over 3,000 transactions daily. Swire Coca-

Cola depends on its IT system for manufacturing, production, sales, and distribution.

As part of its dedication to civic leadership, Coca-Cola has contributed $1 million to China's Project Hope, which to date has built 50 primary schools and donated books to 100 libraries in underprivileged rural areas in 15 Chinese provinces.

International Level Strategies

Location

Coca-Cola chose to enter China because it was an emerging market with a huge population and high growth. It built one of its first few bottling plants in Shanghai, aiming first to introduce its products to the millions of people living in that city. It felt that Shanghai residents were more exposed to the Western world and would therefore be more open to trying Coke. Coca-Cola's strategy has been to introduce Western drinks in China as cool, refreshing, and a taste of Western lifestyle. The city also had a large middle class with disposable income.

Coca-Cola has increasingly been expanding to rural areas in order to introduce Coke and other products to a more diverse population. There is also less competition for early entrants to these areas, ensuring future market share and brand loyalty. Building new plants in remote towns also has the advantages of cheaper land and labor.

Entry Mode

Coca-Cola's entry mode is mainly through joint ventures. Only local subsidiaries are authorized to package and sell its products. Coca-Cola in China is also local-market oriented.

Entry Timing

Coca-Cola entered China as a first mover in 1927. It later left due to political instability, but its brand name was still remembered when it returned to China in 1979.

The Coca-Cola Company then made an agreement with the Chinese government providing preferential treatment in regards to regulations, operating and industrial policies, joint venture laws, and so on. This agreement expired in 1997. New agreements must be made which satisfy the Coca-Cola company, the government, and the people.

International Marketing

Production Coca-Cola products are produced either in bottles and cans. Canned drinks are served at banquets and in more upscale places in China.

Price Despite fluctuations in the exchange rate and relatively high prices, people prefer foreign colas because of their Western image. For example, Coca-Cola sells for as high as 3 yuan per can while local beverages sell for at most half that price.

Promotion Coca-Cola ads are present everywhere, from television commercials to billboards, radio, newspapers, and magazines. Coke advertisements are designed to suit the local culture, including famous Chinese actors and models (some from Hong Kong, Taiwan, or Singapore) who project a Western attitude. Other types of promotion include lucky-draw contests and game shows sponsored by the Coca-Cola Company.

Recommendations

Our first recommendation for the Coca-Cola Company would be for it to continue its expansion in China in order to meet the demands of Chinese consumers and of point-of-sale retailers. Another recommendation would be to improve marketing efforts, especially within the untapped regions of China. This would allow Coca-Cola to distribute its products not only in major cities, but in the rural areas as well. Our third recommendation is to formulate new soft drinks that appeal specifically to the Chinese market. It should also price more competitively against local rivals. Finally, we recommend retaining the traditional glass bottle because it is more economical and can be distributed more cheaply. In addition, the Coca-Cola bottle is considered a novelty itself and is part of the company's trademark.

Table c7.1 Coca-Cola Slogans Through the Years

1886	Drink Coca-Cola
1904	Delicious And Refreshing
1905	Coca-Cola Revives And Sustains
1906	The Great National Temperance Drink
1917	Three Million A Day
1922	Thirst Knows No Season
1925	Six Million A Day
1927	Around The Corner From Everywhere
1929	The Pause That Refreshes
1932	Ice-Cold Sunshine
1938	The Best Friend Thirst Ever Had
1939	Coca-Cola Goes Along
1942	Wherever You Are, Whatever You Do, Wherever You May Be, When You Think Of Refreshment, Think Of Ice-Cold Coca-Cola
1942	The Only Thing Like Coca-Cola Is Coca-Cola Itself. It's The Real Thing.
1948	Where There's Coke, There's Hospitality
1949	Coca-Cola...Along The Highway To Anywhere
1952	What You Want Is A Coke
1956	Coca-Cola...Making Good Things Taste Better
1957	Sign Of Good Taste
1958	The Cold, Crisp Taste Of Coke
1959	Be Really Refreshed
1963	Things Go Better With Coke
1970	It's The Real Thing
1971	I'd Like To Buy The World A Coke
1975	Look Up America
1976	Coke Adds Life
1979	Have A Coke And A Smile
1982	Coke Is It!
1985	We've Got A Taste For You (Coca-Cola And Coca-Cola classic) America's Real Choice
1986	Catch The Wave (Coca-Cola) Red White and You (Coca-Cola classic)
1989	Can't Beat The Feeling
1990	Can't Beat The Real Thing
1993	Always Coca-Cola

Table c7.2 Time-Series Analysis of Coca-Cola Company

	1996	1995	1994	1993	1992
Profitability					
Gross profit margin	0.64	0.61	0.62	0.63	0.61
Net profit margin	0.19	0.17	0.16	0.16	0.13
Return on assets	0.28	0.28	0.27	0.26	0.25
Return on equity	0.57	0.55	0.49	0.47	0.43
Liquidity					
Current ratio	0.8	0.74			
Quick ratio	0.67	0.59			
Leverage					
Debt to asset ratio	0.28	0.27	0.25	0.26	0.29
Debt to equity ratio	0.73	0.75	0.67	0.68	0.82
Long term debt to equity ratio	0.18	0.21	0.27	0.31	0.29
Activity					
Inventory turnover	7.08	6.21			
Fixed-asset turnover	5.22	4.16	3.97	3.74	3.71
Average collection period	32	34			

Case Study 8: Microsoft

Executive Summary

Since the conception of Microsoft in the garage of owner Bill Gates, the company has been growing at an exponential rate. The company's popularity began with the introduction of the MS-DOS program that provided computer companies with a more user friendly operating system. Microsoft's profit margin increased with the release of Microsoft Windows, a program that facilitated operating systems use by novice personal computer users. With strong financial backing, the company has branched throughout the PC operating systems market. It is now concentrating on the sectors that it does not already dominate, that is, the Internet and corporate computing. Microsoft's strategies at all levels are fused with computer innovation that has enabled it to become the world's dominant supplier of software products. Microsoft monitors principal competitive factors like product features and functions, ease of use, reputation, and price. Microsoft is now venturing into China, the world's fastest emerging market.

Background

Bill Gates and Paul Allen founded Microsoft as a partnership on April 4, 1975. It was incorporated on June 25, 1981. The initial name, 'Micro-soft', soon became registered as the trade name, 'Microsoft'. Within fifteen years of its inception, Microsoft became the world's leading software company.

The company is divided into four groups, including the Platforms Product Group, Applications and Content Group, Sales and Support Group, and Operations Group. Microsoft employs over 15,000 people in the U.S. and roughly 7,000 people internationally. It markets a broad range of products for personal computer use such as development tools, languages, application software, system software, hardware peripherals, books, and multimedia applications. Today, nearly 80-90 percent of the world's PCs use Microsoft's software.

Microsoft's mission has been to create innovative software for the personal computer that empowers and enriches people in the workplace, at school, and at home. Microsoft continues to make software easier to use and more cost effective. It also creates power-pack interactive games for its customers. Moreover, its substantial investment in research and development coupled with responsiveness to customer feedback enable the company to produce advanced technology to meet different customer needs. Microsoft's long-held vision of a computer on every desk and in every home is combined today with a strong commitment to Internet-related technologies that expand the power of the PC to reach users worldwide.

SWOT Analysis

Strengths

Organizational Microsoft's organizational strengths stem from its structure, leadership, and teamwork. The corporation is organized into three basic units, the Internet, Consumer, and Desktop and Business Systems Divisions. Each has its own managing director, allowing each division some autonomy in building itself up.

Although this structure allows for some decentralization, the organization as a whole remains highly centralized, with Chairperson Bill Gates retaining ultimate control. His leadership is another strength, as he has shown exceptional intelligence, vision and energy in running the company. He has also shown great acumen in hiring people who are very skilled technologically or smart about running businesses. The respect that he has earned among Microsoft's talented technical staff is legendary. Respect from employees results in better control and coordination within the company, despite the fact that computer engineers are usually highly independent people.

Gates hires local managers in China to run Microsoft operations. The foreign staff is kept small to prevent dominating the local people or creating an unpleasant image of the company. The Corporate Director for China, Hong Kong, and Taiwan is Bryan Nelson, but the General Manager is Mr. Duh Jia-bin, a local Chinese. Every year Gates visits China in order to talk to customers, government officials, and employees. This type of interpersonal interaction allows Bill Gates to establish *guanxi* connections that in return promote Microsoft's image and lead to greater profitability.

Teamwork is another organizational strength that holds the company together and assists in developing new products. Within the three divisions of Microsoft, small teams are formed that have overlapping functions and tasks. Experts are given managerial power to create products, educate and train others, and develop career paths. Teams follow the rule of 'synch and stabilize', which means synchronizing their work and stabilizing their products in increments as components evolve. Close interaction and analysis builds a network of productive, creative individuals working for the benefit of Microsoft.

Financial Microsoft's financial strengths lies within its cash position and its ability to diversify and invest. The company's total current assets for 1997 were $14,389 million. Its net income and earnings per share reveal an increasing trend in profitability. Microsoft's return on revenue was 25.3 percent for 1996 and 30.4 percent for 1997. The company is also quite liquid, as demonstrated by its current ratio in 1997 of 2.87. Microsoft therefore has almost three times as much current assets as current liabilities. As for leverage, the company's debt-to-asset ratio is .25, indicating that one-fourth of its projects are financed by debts. Microsoft's stable financial strength allows it to have economies of scale in research and development, marketing, and product support.

Microsoft invests heavily not only in its employees but also in many projects and acquisitions. Its strong cash position allowed it to diversify worldwide. In 1996, the software giant bought or invested in 20 companies, nearly doubling the pace of its deal making in 1994. In the past three years, it has spent roughly $1.5 billion on acquisitions and investments.

Microsoft also has the opportunity to expand financially because of tremendous growth in China. In 1997, 3 million PCs were sold in China, and the computer industry's revenue totaled 2.1 billion dollars. Sales in computer products are expected to increase to 8.7 billion dollars by the year 2000.

Technological Microsoft's technological strengths are what makes the corporation a success. Microsoft understands the importance of designing computers for personal use. It recognizes that software, not hardware, presents the greatest opportunities for profit. Its technological advantages are its standard operating systems and applications such as MS-DOS,

Windows, and BASIC. These have given the company a leading edge and competitive control of the computer industry. By creating these programs as standards, Microsoft maintains sales and profits in the short-term. More importantly, it is able to generate new markets based on these standards.

Microsoft established a competitive edge in the Chinese computer market through developing Chinese versions of Windows 95 and Windows NT. Another example of its innovativeness was the formation of the Shanghai Support Center in 1997, aimed at providing assistance for customers in Hong Kong, Taiwan, and Mainland China.

Operational Microsoft's advanced technical ability drives its operational strengths. With high quality software products, Microsoft is able to operate with a strong reputation and image. It has been able to penetrate evolving mass markets and set standards with diverse products. Microsoft improves itself incrementally, slowly replacing old products instead of undergoing complete, immediate overhauls. The company pushes for large volume sales and uses exclusive contracts to simplify its mass marketing strategy.

Microsoft's operations focus on dividing large tasks into smaller ones. It emphasizes the quality of individual commitments. In China, Microsoft's staff of 70 is able to work with hundreds of budding software companies and over 15,000 resellers to sell affordable PCs and mainframes. Its operations are successful because it has adapted its products to the Chinese writing system.

More extensive operations that demonstrate Microsoft's strength are its joint ventures with other U.S. multinational firms and local Chinese firms. Recently, Microsoft joined with Hewlett Packard to develop software solutions that target small and medium size enterprises. Microsoft also contracted its software to Legend, a Chinese computer firm with 26 branches in China. Legend will install PCs with Windows 95 in return for a fee of $12 million a year.

Weaknesses

Organizational One of Microsoft's organizational strengths is also its primary weakness: it is overly centralized. All power rests in the hands of Gates and all important decisions depend solely on his position. This creates the danger of having no competent successor should something happen to Gates. Other repercussions have arisen due to Microsoft's operational strengths and the power it wields. For example, Microsoft is facing the threat of antitrust lawsuits domestically while it continues to compete with other giant computer firms such as IBM, Oracle, and Compaq.

Financial Although the company is presently financially sound, a major weakness that Microsoft faces is the threat of continued growth. Microsoft's cash position has allowed it to expand through investments and acquisitions, but it could lose control if it expands too much. If it continues to absorb other companies, it might end up lacking the ability to coordinate and run all its operations. Another threat to its financial position is the weakening Asian economies, leading to greater uncertainty for Microsoft in that region.

Opportunities

Industrial Opportunities for Microsoft are based on its enterprise software, consumer enterprise electronics, and the Internet. Microsoft's products, including Windows NT, BackOffice, and SQL Server, are starting to be able to handle complex, memory intensive computing tasks that used to require expensive mainframes. Microsoft's NT runs a growing share (55 percent) of corporate nets and network operating systems. Microsoft also shipped abroad 39.8 percent of 3.3 million networking units in 1996.

Windows CE creates another opportunity in consumer electronics for Microsoft. Windows CE is a wallet-sized PC, a tiny device used for keeping phone numbers and schedules, and sending e-mail which is also compatible with Window PCs. New computing devices based on the Windows CE are starting to take off. Windows CE has already been extremely profitable, but Microsoft plans to use it to create new digital appliances, including Web TVs, phones, and even navigation systems for cars.

The Internet is the main focus of Microsoft's future strategies. Microsoft is making a strong push into cyberspace by offering a Web browser and server programs. Starting from scratch two years ago, Microsoft's Internet Explorer now holds 40 percent of the market and is predicted to surpass Netscape as early as mid-1998. Also, Microsoft is now running sixteen different websites it hopes will become moneymakers. For example, Microsoft's CarPoint is already one of the top on-line auto sales sites. CarPoint is expected to generate $100 million for Microsoft by the year 2000.

Other companies, such as Compaq and Digital, also indirectly create opportunities for Microsoft. The merger between Compaq and Digital in early 1998 lowered the costs of manufacturing PCs. This merger is useful to Microsoft not only because Compaq is the biggest seller of Windows PC software, but also because the Compaq/Digital combination will help accelerate Microsoft's push into the heart of corporate computing with the Windows NT and related programs.

The future of Microsoft is quite positive. Many corporations have already standardized their equipment to be compatible with Windows and its desktop applications. They are likely to remain interested in buying software from Microsoft that can help tie their computer systems together.

International Microsoft is already so successful worldwide that it is difficult for the Chinese Government and local companies to resist forming alliances with the company. Gates has become an icon of success, the ultimate entrepreneurial role model for developing countries. China's changing attitude toward foreign investment is also beneficial to Microsoft. The Chinese Government is currently more likely to treat foreign investors as genuine partners and not solely as sources of cash and technology. China's commitment to greater reform is shown by their effort to win entry into the WTO. Also, China wants to be involved in the global information revolution, as demonstrated by its plan to have an information infrastructure in place by the year 2000.

China is a big growing market in terms of its population and consumption. It is the world's fastest growing computer market. Computer sales totaled $7.4 billion in 1995, up 51 percent from the previous year. Six million PC units are expected to be sold by the year 2000. However, since China does not have many operational systems already in place, Microsoft has the chance to gain an even larger share of its overall computer business than it does in existing markets. By offering free software to China's universities and colleges, Microsoft is also creating brand awareness, putting it into a better position for the future.

Threats

National In the U.S., the most serious threat Microsoft faces is the antitrust court battle. Microsoft's productivity suites and PC operating systems dominate over 85 percent of the market. A number of Microsoft's most significant competitors, such as IBM, Sun, Oracle, and Netscape, have jointly protested against Microsoft's various technological developments and marketing strategies that have increased customer demands for Microsoft products. Even winning the suit does not mean Microsoft can rest easy. Once bureaucrats, legislators, and the Justice Department have paid special attention to Microsoft, they may create difficulties for future marketing implementation by Microsoft. Should the Justice Department broaden its suit to include Windows 98 and Windows NT, Microsoft would suffer a great deal.

Although Microsoft claims that its original motive for integrating the browser with Windows was to please its customers, its image could deteriorate drastically if consumer groups boycott its products and operations.

International China's large rural population (75 percent of the total) poses a threat to Microsoft. With such a huge part of the population involved in agriculture, Microsoft may be pursuing an illusion of profitability and expansion that could eventually lead to its downfall. There are also many political uncertainties in China. Microsoft could become confused by trying to distinguish between official policies and preferential treatment for foreign investors. Since there is no clear distinction between the two, it can take a long time to get permits for certain projects. Distribution systems are poor and the lack of infrastructure makes for inefficient transportation. Tariffs are high on high-tech products and there are limitations on imports. Also, Microsoft stands to lose a great deal if the communist-based government were to decide that the evolving capitalist system is too dangerous to deal with, and returns to its earlier socialist ideals.

Available PC technology is another threat. According to the China Research Corporation in Beijing, only about 50 percent of the computers sold in China in 1996 had 8 or more megabytes of RAM, while the Chinese version of Windows 95 requires at least 12 megabytes to run. Therefore, Windows 3.1 will remain the mainstream product in the near future. Needless to say, Microsoft should adjust itself to fit the emerging Chinese market.

China stands to lose its Most-Favored-Nation status (MFNs) because of the friction over human and intellectual property rights issues. If this status is lost, Chinese products would become less competitive and the economy would be in a depression. The resulting unstable economy would be a nightmare for all foreign investors, including Microsoft.

The banking system in China is also far from perfect. The government channels 75 percent of bank credit into state enterprises, most of which are the biggest money-losers in the system. Therefore, it is difficult for the central bank in China to control inflation. An uncontrolled rate of inflation would push up the cost of production, which would create another problem for Microsoft.

Microsoft also faces the threat of software piracy. The majority of the software, as much as 90 percent, being used in Eastern Europe, China and much of Asia actually comes from illegal copies. According to one study, piracy is costing the U.S. software industry $2.3 billion in earnings each year. In conjunction with the Asian economic crisis, it is safe to say that pirated software is going to become even more popular. Since Microsoft is dominant in the software industry and half of its overall revenues come from international sales, pirating software remains a great threat.

Competition Microsoft also must deal with competition from both Chinese computer companies and multinationals such as IBM, Oracle, and Compaq. Gates has already called IBM his biggest competitor. In 1997, IBM generated $78.5 billion, or about $327,000 in revenue per employee. In the same year, Microsoft earned only $13.1 billion, or $58,807 per employee. Clearly Microsoft is the smaller company. Since IBM has its own operating system, this competition has extended into the Chinese market. IBM has already invested in at least six joint ventures with Chinese partners and two information technology centers in Beijing and Guangzhou. Also, IBM has developed a branch office and three factories in China. The company donated $570,000 last year to build a computer-aided software engineering laboratory at Shenzen University.

IBM also focuses on reaching Chinese customers through service centers, often set up near busy railway terminals. In addition, 300 computer engineers around the country provide technological support to customers. This investment in service has been so successful that IBM sales in China have risen by 50 percent annually for the past three years, and are now at more than $500 million.

Oracle is another computer company that threatens Microsoft's position in China. Oracle entered the Chinese market in 1989. By 1996 it gained a large contract for $3.5 million to build China Online. As mentioned before, Microsoft is now focusing on the Internet, but it may become difficult to penetrate the online software market in China because of Oracle's lead.

Local competitors should not be overlooked. According to James W. Jarrett, the head of Intel's China operations, Chinese PCs are quite advanced. Founder is one of the most competitive local companies. It is run by the prestigious Beijing University, which provides the company with some of its top graduates. Since diversifying from Chinese-language software into PCs in late 1995, Founder has zoomed to the No. 8 spot in China. It plans to build 100,000 computer units annually. The second major competitor is the Legend Group, a company with strong distribution and international experience. The Legend Group cut its retail prices for PCs by an average of 20 percent and sold more than 30,000 units in 1997. It may replace IBM as the number one in PC sales in China in the near future. China Great Wall Computer is the third competitor. It has three joint ventures with IBM for PCs and another in videoconferencing with Intel.

The Chinese Government nurtures the local computer industry with low-interest loans and tax breaks and by pressuring foreign software companies to set up joint ventures. Since illegal software is so prevalent in China, the most likely way for Microsoft to make a profit is by licensing its software to local PC manufacturers. As the bargaining power of local manufacturers increases, however, it might become more of a challenge to realize profits from pre-installed software.

Corporate Strategies

Microsoft's corporate-level goal of maximizing stockholder equity is realized through diversifying operations and products. Diversification of operations involves setting up worldwide subsidiaries that improve its market share and profitability. Microsoft operates in Beijing, Shanghai, and Hong Kong. Its investments in these major cities diversify and expand its control over the computer market in China.

Microsoft has a related diversification strategy aimed at spreading out its investments through different locations to minimize risk. This is most visible in its horizontally related diversification scheme that involves acquiring and investing in local and international firms. For example, it acquired WebTV Networks in the U.S. in 1997. Microsoft also signed an agreement with Legend to install Windows 95 on all its PCs. This illustrates that Microsoft follows the related diversification strategy because it

Microsoft also uses strategic alliances as a primary means of diversification. These include licensing, joint ventures, and partnerships. It licenses its Windows operating systems to local Chinese computer firms in exchange for royalty fees. It also has a joint venture with the Beijing government to develop the Chinese Windows 95 program. Its partnership with Hewlett-Packard will develop software solutions for small enterprises in order to target small and medium size businesses in China. This way Microsoft promotes computerization among businesses hindered by outdated technology and poor financial resources. Microsoft also engages in partnerships with original equipment manufacturers (OEMs) such as Compaq, Dell, and Toshiba in order to create a standard for personal computers which ensures a high level of technology for all consumers.

Microsoft has also diversified with corporate restructuring. In early 1996, it reorganized its corporate structure from four divisions to three major platforms (the Internet, consumer and desktop, and business systems). The key Internet unit emphasizes development of Internet applications and content and server products aimed at providing an open platform to the public. Microsoft has transported this organizational structure to its operations in China, as exemplified by opening a customer support center in Shanghai.

By following these diversification strategies through horizontally related expansion, strategic alliances, and restructuring, Microsoft is able to achieve economies of scale while creating maximum value for the firm.

Business Strategies

Microsoft's business-level competitive strategy is focused on differentiation, including product differentiation, market segmentation, and distinctive competency. Its main concern is to create unique products that satisfy customer needs. For example, the products it originally developed in the U.S. are translated into Chinese versions that fit into the Chinese market. Introducing both Chinese and English versions of software products gives Microsoft a competitive advantage over other firms.

Microsoft's customer segmentation is broken down into four units: Enterprise customers (large organizations); Organization customers (small and mid-sized businesses); Education customers (K-12 and higher education); and End users. The majority of end-users in China are individuals in businesses, governmental agencies, and educational institutions. Microsoft is spending $2 million a year training Chinese technicians and programmers to introduce software technology to Chinese people.

Microsoft's distinctive competencies include research and development, mass sales, and marketing. Microsoft's contribution to the growth of the personal computer industry is rooted in the company's development and marketing of its Windows operating systems. Microsoft Windows is the catalyst that has driven the development of a dynamic, intensely competitive, and highly efficient personal computer industry. Microsoft's sales and support units are spread throughout Europe, the Far East, the Middle East, Africa, SE Asia, the South Pacific, India, Brazil, and South America. Through differentiation, Microsoft has established a competitive strategy based on a strong investment strategy covering markets all over the world. Its localization of standardized software in every market reveals its desire for a strong market share.

Efficiency Microsoft also focuses on the four building blocks of superior efficiency, quality, innovation, and customer responsiveness. To achieve superior efficiency, it hires smart people who know computer technology and the software business. It also educates new employees with a learning-by-doing process and mentoring. Microsoft has built worldwide commitment amongst its employees through the leadership of its exceptional chief executive and senior management team. Furthermore, it has built a learning organization based on continuous self-critique, feedback, and sharing amongst different functional units pursuing efficiency.

Microsoft's operating systems provides enormous benefits to software developers and consumers. For example, software developers can freely call upon the operating system servicers for information when developing interactive applications. This allows software developers to be more productive and efficient. At the other end, customers are more likely to choose Windows because there are a wide range of applications that can run on this operating system. Therefore, more software developers are likely to create Windows applications.

Quality and Responsiveness Microsoft creates career paths and ladder levels to retain and reward its technical staff. In China, high quality product training for programmers, systems administrators, and engineers is provided by Microsoft to promote the development of top quality, localized products. It has also established a flexible, incremental approach to product development that periodically incorporates customer suggestions for improving its products. By understanding user perspectives, Microsoft can define and correct problems with products efficiently and effectively at the developmental stage.

Finally, Microsoft provides flexible licensing arrangements, consulting services and support, and training (directly or in partnership with independent solution providers) to help customers create successful business solutions with its products.

Innovation Microsoft has spent $350 million annually since 1992, and will spend $2.6 billion in 1998 alone, on research and development. Microsoft's productive assets depend on ingenuity and the ability to react quickly to competitive developments. Microsoft has three fundamental strategies for ensuring superior innovativeness. The first is rapid development of new software in response to consumer demands. The second is broad distribution of software at attractive prices. The last is close collaboration with other hardware and software companies in order to develop a wide range of compatible products.

International Strategies

The main reason Microsoft entered China is to tap the world's fastest growing computer market. Microsoft believes that China will become one of the most demanding software markets in Asia within the next decade. In 1995, computer sales totaled $7.4 billion, up 51 percent from 1994, and sales of personal computers went up 60 percent to $1.15 million units. By the year 2000, annual sales are expected to reach six million units.

Microsoft first contemplated entering the China market only after adequate intellectual property right (IPR) protections started to be implemented. In 1992, China signed the special 301 IPR protection agreement with the US Trade Representative, indicating its willingness to abide by international copyright standards. China promised it would protect computer programs as literary works when it joined the Berne copyright convention. As central Chinese authorities demonstrated a commitment to combat piracy, invest in advanced technologies, open up toward foreign trade and relations, and make available a high concentration of intellectuals and scholars, Microsoft felt greater optimism for its future in the country.

Entry Modes

Microsoft Corporation was an early mover in the Chinese software market. In 1987, it established an office in Taiwan to oversee business in Taiwan, Hong Kong, and Mainland China. In 1989, it arranged for Hong Kong and Taiwan based software distributors with networks in China to distribute Microsoft products. By 1992, Microsoft made its official entry into China's personal computer market by signing a licensing agreement with a consortium of Chinese PC manufacturers.

The sales of licenses and packaged products are primarily to distributors and resellers. The only way that companies can sell Microsoft products is to obtain a license from the company. This shows that Microsoft is currently using a global strategy to get its products into other markets. Since everything is done through Microsoft headquarters, all products are standardized for both domestic and foreign markets.

Microsoft's first regional support center has been established in Shanghai, serving customers throughout Mainland China, Hong Kong, and Taiwan. The new center offers full technical support services, provided by a team of foreign and locally trained engineers. Service is available 24 hours a day, 7 days a week for customers with premium support contracts.

Microsoft entered the Chinese market through joint ventures that enabled it to increase its established market share and introduce more sophisticated software into the Chinese market. Microsoft's share of each joint venture is 50 percent. Through joint ventures, Microsoft gains access to the knowledge of its local partners as it learns to adapt to new market conditions and environments. It also shares development costs and reduces its risks. The Chinese government favors joint ventures and therefore assists Microsoft in these ventures. The main risks Microsoft runs in engaging in joint ventures is the potential of losing control over its technology, losing the ability to carry out a global coordination strategy, and having foreign partners fail to meet expectations.

Microsoft's local partners include Great Wall Computer, Beijing University Founder, Users Friend Software Co. Ltd. (UFS), Legend, and Beijing Stone. Each local partner captured Microsoft's attention for a different reason. Microsoft chose Users Friend Software Co. Ltd. as its local partner because it is China's largest financial software developer. Microsoft signed an agreement with UFS to develop financial and managerial software. Microsoft and UFS will combine expertise to do everything from technological research to product promotion. Legend is China's leading computer company, with strong experience in early overseas investments. It ships motherboards, the circuit cards that run PCs, to 26 countries. In 1993, Legend became the first Chinese PC maker to open a design center in California. Legend pays Microsoft $12 million annually to load its PCs with the Chinese version of Windows 95.

As the Asian financial crisis unfolded, Gates has made it clear that Microsoft is willing to share its partners' risks. Microsoft has worked aggressively to help its partners stay in business and maintain the availability of affordable products. For example, Microsoft has adjusted payment terms for many small businesses and has found other ways to reduce financial demands on its partner companies, allowing them to remain competitive. Helping legitimate companies remain in business also prevents software pirates from increasing their market share. Gates is committed to making sure that the current financial crisis does not undo the good work Microsoft and the regional governments have done to strengthen intellectual property rights protection.

Local Human Resources Management

Microsoft helps its partners reach professional operating levels by offering management and sales training. In China, it also offers exchange programs in which promising people from key resellers and software developers work for Microsoft for a year or so to pick up skills and experience. Microsoft hires mostly local managers to run operations. These managers, knowledgeable about their home markets, create partnerships with small companies that promote Microsoft products. The company also hires individuals with product expertise and provides them with productivity tools, continuous product education and training, and consistent processes that can deliver quality support for Microsoft products. Currently, Microsoft has more than 75 training centers throughout the country providing information on Microsoft products and computers in general. Microsoft is spending $2 million a year to train Chinese technicians and programmers and putting money into a large number of strategic ties with government ministries, local computer makers, and universities. These efforts are all aimed at helping bring China's software industry into the 21st century.

Product

Microsoft develops, manufactures, licenses, sells, and supports a wide range of software products including operating systems for personal computers, server applications for client/server environments, business and interactive media programs, and Internet platform and development tools. Microsoft also offers online services, sells personal computer books and input devices, and researches and develops advanced technology for future software products. To best serve the needs of users in foreign countries, Microsoft adapts many of its products locally to reflect local languages and conventions. Microsoft products have been adapted to more than 30 languages.

The company's substantial investment in research and development, along with a strong commitment to customer feedback, enables Microsoft to offer technologically advanced products to its customers. The company also provides various product coverage options, ranging from standard no-charge toll telephone support to fee-based services that provide unlimited technical support for all Microsoft products.

Price varies by country because of different exchange rates, but most products are generally cheaper abroad than in the U.S. Prices continue to fall steadily because software products are so easy to manufacture and ship. Microsoft does not have to worry about building and operating factories since it contracts out to other companies to duplicate and package most of its software.

Distribution

To operate effectively in China, Microsoft is developing a strong distribution network. The only way that companies can sell Microsoft products is to obtain a license from the company. These include OEM (original equipment manufacturers) licenses, corporate and organizational licenses, and retail. In almost all cases the products are distributed under Microsoft's trademarks. The sales of licensed and packaged retail products are primarily to distributors and resellers. The company's international operations, both OEM and finished goods, are subject to certain risks common to foreign operations in general, such as governmental regulations, import restrictions, and foreign exchange rate fluctuations. Microsoft hedges a portion of its foreign exchange risk.

Promotion

The company works closely with large advertising and direct marketing firms. Advertising, direct marketing, worldwide packaging, and marketing materials are targeted to various end-user segments. The company utilizes broad consumer media (television, radio, and business publications) and trade publications. Microsoft has programs under which qualifying resellers and OEMs are reimbursed for certain advertising expenditures. The company maintains a broad advertising campaign emphasizing the Microsoft brand and reputation.

Conclusions

Although Microsoft is a powerful business that is currently in firm standing, it may eventually fail due to unforeseen forces. Its extreme centralization and resistance to changes in leadership may deter its advancement, although its technical skills allow it to stay ahead of all its competitors. Microsoft is making great efforts both in the U.S. and in China to decentralize managerial power and sharpen its business and operational strategies to prevent the possibility of other companies becoming major competitors or threats. To achieve its goals, Microsoft invests heavily in numerous computer sectors and constantly strives for levels of quality and innovation that its competitors cannot match. If Microsoft continues its current business practices, it will dominate the world computer industry as it moves into the 21st century.

Microsoft is stable both internally and externally. Its global localization strategy is a success because it caters to customers worldwide. Its investments allow it to diversify in many respects. To continue being successful in China, however, it should be careful to pick partners wisely for all its cooperative projects. Cooperation will allow it to maintain a competitive edge and control over its investments. Secondly, Microsoft should continue to focus on fundamentals. As China becomes even more of a market economy, strong foundations in marketing, distribution, and service will allow the company to reap further profits and growth. The third important piece of advice is to guard its intellectual rights. Although Microsoft has made improvements against the pirating of software, it must continue to uphold this battle. Lastly, Microsoft, like all other companies in China, should focus on minimizing costs. Because China presents a lot of uncertainty due to its communist government and unstable economy, keeping costs low will allow Microsoft to survive over the long run and absorb the benefits in which it has invested.

Case Study 9: Boeing

Executive Summary

Over the past 80 years, Boeing has emerged as the world's largest producer of aeronautical products, including commercial aircraft, military aircraft, helicopters, missiles, rockets, the space shuttle, space station, and satellites. A SWOT analysis shows that its strengths include a strong financial position, good reputation as a leader in the industry, and wide ranging expertise. In China it enjoys excellent relations with the government. A crucial weakness is production inefficiency, however. Opportunities include a growing market abroad, with potential for further expansion into related products and services. Its primary competitor, Airbus, is currently suffering from a negative public image in China, which presents another opportunity for Boeing. It is threatened by the possibilities of loss of government support, new entrants into the market, rising fuel prices, and the Asian economic crisis.

Boeing has enjoyed first mover advantages in the Chinese aircraft market. Of the 400 jetliners in China, 288 were built by Boeing. Boeing also operates pilot training, maintenance, repair, and overhaul facilities and small aircraft components production there. These businesses have been set up through equity joint ventures.

Logistics and the fear of technological leakage have so far prevented Boeing from beginning any large-scale assembly operations in China. We recommend that Boeing change its strategy and start assembling planes in China.

Company Introduction

Corporate History

In 1916, William Boeing and Conrad Westervelt built a seaplane in Seattle. The following year, their company, originally called Pacific Aero Products, changed its name to the Boeing Airplane Company. Boeing grew rapidly during World War I by building training planes for the military.

The war ended and Boeing found another source of revenue in international airmail service. This line of business expanded until Boeing formed a subsidiary called Boeing Air Transport. This business used Boeing built planes (Model 40A) which utilized Frederick Rentschler's new engine design. Boeing and Rentschler merged companies in 1929 and continued to diversify into other aviation related businesses such as Sikorsky Aviation, Stout Air Services, etc.

In 1933, the U.S. Government forced Boeing to separate into two lines of business, aircraft manufacturing and airline operations. The aircraft manufacturing operations became Boeing Airplane. The airline operations became United Airlines. As time went by, Boeing entered other aeronautical businesses such as rockets (it built the Apollo rockets). It also got into the defense business. In 1996, Boeing bought Rockwell's defense and aerospace businesses. Boeing deepened its commitment to the defense business by buying McDonnell-Douglas in 1997. Boeing remains committed to its primary business, commercial aircraft manufacturing, however.

Today, Boeing is the one of the world's largest companies and is America's largest exporter. It has 238,000 employees and $45 billion in annual revenue. It is the U.S.'s only commercial aircraft builder with production facilities in 13 states. Its has a wide range of aeronautical products. Its products include the space shuttle, space station, missiles, rockets, satellites, military jets, passenger jets, helicopters, and so on. If it flies, there is a good chance that Boeing's name is on it.

Boeing's mission is to be a global leader in aerospace by focusing on teamwork and management performance. It is committed to high ethical standards and customer satisfaction throughout its business operations.

Major Businesses and Markets

Fifty-nine percent of Boeings revenues comes from commercial aircraft and 39 percent from military, space, and defense products. Boeing's total 1997 revenue amounted to $45.8 billion. Fifty-three percent of this revenue was generated from the U.S.A, 28 percent from Asia (3 percent from China), and 16 percent from Europe, with Oceania and Africa making up the difference.

Boeing in China

Boeing's involvement with China began over 60 years ago when William Boeing hired Beijing-born but MIT-educated Wang Tsu to be Boeing's first chief engineer. In 1939, PanAm started trans-Pacific flights to Hong Kong on Boeing 314 Clipper planes. U.S. President Richard Nixon arrived in China on Air Force One, a Boeing 707 in 1972. In 1979, Deng Xiaoping toured Boeing's 747 Seattle production line.

Although Boeing does not assemble planes in China, it has plans to establish a major spare parts distribution center in Beijing. This would be one of only three international distribution centers worldwide (London and Singapore are the others).

Boeing has also hosted Chinese manufacturing specialists at its Seattle production facilities, assisted in China's air traffic control management training programs, and trained over 1,000 Chinese pilots in the last three years. It provides its 737 and 757/767 flight simulators to the Civil Aviation Administration of China (CAAC) Flying College at no cost.

It invested $11 million in 9.1 percent ownership of Taikoo Aircraft Engineering Co. (TAECO), an aircraft maintenance, repair, and overhaul (MRO) company. TAECO also converts passenger jets into cargo jets. Boeing's partners include Cathay Pacific, Singapore Airlines, Japan Airlines, Xiamen Aviation Industry Co., and Beijing Kai Lan Technology Development Service Co. (a wholly-owned subsidiary of CAAC). In 1998, Boeing entered into a joint venture with Aviation Industries of China (AVIC) and Hexcel Corp. to produce aircraft parts. Boeing has agreed to buy the JV's output for 20 years. Finally, out of 400 jetliners operating in China in 1997, Boeing had built 288.

External Environment

Economic

Perhaps the most significant of the external forces facing Boeing is the Asian economic crisis. In the past few months, Asian countries have experienced severe currency devaluation and a stock market crash that has stemmed the inflow of foreign investment and considerably dimmed the outlook for the entire region. As a result many Asian countries may be forced to cancel their aircraft orders. Philippine Airlines has already canceled its order for four 747's and the prospect of more cancellations seems to be imminent. Boeing, which has dramatically increased its work force and production capacity in recent months to meet rising demand, may suddenly be forced to absorb huge losses if more contracts are canceled. This could also provide its main competitor, Airbus, with an opportunity to win some of these contracts after the Asian economies stabilize. Furthermore, if the economic crisis persists in Asia, the rest of the world may find itself in a global recession. Should this occur, the global market for aircraft, which has been rising, may be materially affected.

Political

While the Asian economic crisis does have a significant impact on the future of Boeing, it is by no means the only external force that Boeing has had to contend with recently. Government agencies can have dramatic effects on global corporations like Boeing. In particular, Boeing has had to deal with investigations by the FAA (Federal Aviation Administration) into its production processes following the unexplained crash of a Singapore SilkAir 737 jet. The FAA looked into Boeing's quality control procedures and in 1997 issued a statement declaring Boeing's paperwork 'out of control'. The FAA found, among other minor imperfections, loose or missing screws on finished planes. While the results of the FAA investigation are still pending, it is evident that any negative review or shutting down of production for an extended period of time would severely affect the continuation of Boeing as the world's dominant aircraft manufacturer and supplier.

With the absorption of McDonnell Douglas, there was great concern in the United States over what was perceived to be Boeing's growing monopoly over commercial aircraft manufacturing. Europeans who unequivocally condemned the merger echoed this discomfort. When the merger was cleared by the American courts, the Europeans immediately registered a complaint and sought another investigation. Ultimately the merger was approved but only under tight restrictions. It stands to reason that any move Boeing now chooses to make will meet with much scrutiny.

The relationship between the United States and Chinese governments have what can only be described as a marriage of convenience or a love-hate relationship. China enjoys MFN (Most Favored Nation) trade status with the United States and yet the U.S. is actively blocking its entry into international organizations like the WTO, ostensibly because of its stance on human rights. The reasons for this apparent contradiction of attitudes lie in a war of conflicting ideals. From a purely pragmatic standpoint, the United States cannot afford to alienate China, if only because U.S. corporations would raise their voices in protest. As domestic industries mature, U.S. corporations are actively seeking new markets for investment. As the most populous country in the world, China is a tempting target. Thus, with pressures from many influential people, the U.S. government is almost forced to adopt a conciliatory stance in its relations with China. However, the United States, as the lone remaining world superpower, has an image to uphold. Here is where the conflict arises. As the self-appointed moral and economic conscience of the world, the United States cannot be seen to condone or have dealings with countries that commit 'immoral' acts.

China, on the other hand, recognizes the opportunities for gain that come from a close association with the U.S. With technological and infrastructural investment coming from the U.S., China sees itself as a potential economic and political superpower. While there are many countries that are similarly eager to enter China, access to U.S. power, influence, and technology would give China instant credibility and consideration on a global scale. Yet it too has an image to uphold. China wants to be seen as neither obsequious nor incompetent. Therefore, it will strive mightily to at least portray a veneer of independence and competence. Thus, a tenuous balance is struck between these two nations. With warring purposes and ideals, it would seem that future relations between the two nations will continue to be strained and marked by periods of animosity and strife. This should always be a constant concern for Boeing and other U.S. companies operating in China who will undoubtedly be used as pawns in this political game.

Social Considerations

Another thing Boeing will have to deal with is 'guanxi'. In English, the concept can roughly be translated as goodwill, in a business sense. A company must establish good connections with other companies in China, but most importantly the firm must establish good relations with government officials. Good guanxi can ensures smooth operations and even preferential treatment, but bad guanxi with the government can spell disaster for a firm.

The government plays a significant role in the world of Chinese business. Most of the firms in the market were or still are under direct governmental control. This ensures governmental protection of those industries and a significant barrier to foreign firms. The government can restrict the shipment of materials a firm needs or pair the firm with a weak partner in a joint venture. A firm must be on the government's good side if it wants to succeed in China.

Domestic labor unions and corporate watchdog groups are the most likely sources of objections to the use of foreign labor. When a company like Boeing moves production facilities abroad, there are many potential negative ramifications. There will be the typical negative reaction from domestic labor unions who resist attempts by large corporations to move production facilities abroad, regardless of fiscal pragmatism. Similarly, activist groups may try to uncover cases of exploitative labor practices.

In addition to domestic resistance, Boeing may encounter local resistance to its efforts to expand. While it may seem economically illogical, there still exists a significant portion of the populace that resents foreign intrusion and expansion into their country. Just as U.S. citizens objected to Japanese attempts to set up automobile plants in the U.S., Boeing may encounter resistance from the local Chinese populace.

The concept of lifetime employment has been prevalent in China. This practice has kept less qualified employees in many positions. This condition is starting to change with the privatization of many companies, but it can still tie a firm's hands.

Technological Considerations

China wants to construct a viable aircraft manufacturing industry. However, it possesses neither the technical know-how nor the manufacturing infrastructure to make such a venture profitable. Boeing has a wealth of knowledge and is exceedingly capable of building aircraft. Much of its competitive advantages rest in this knowledge. If the world became privy to the design and production attributes of Boeing's products, some of Boeing's advantages would be lost forever. Therefore, Boeing jealously guards its knowledge. It also wants access to the potentially lucrative Chinese market, however. China's intentions are not a secret; the usual price for market access is technology or knowledge transfer. Boeing must question how much it is willing to sacrifice in order to gain access to China. In this case, Boeing seems willing to concede knowledge of the construction of 100 seat aircraft while retaining proprietary knowledge about jumbo jets. China is more than willing to accept this trade, but desire for future technological transfer could escalate requirements. Should China be successful in gaining the requisite knowledge to build 100 seat aircraft, it will undoubtedly want to learn more. Therefore, the price of admission to the market may ultimately include the plans for the jumbo jet. The only hope is that by the time China assimilates its newly acquired knowledge this information will be obsolete.

Advances in computer assisted design and automated production processes are especially evident in the automobile industry. However, in the aircraft manufacturing industry, a lot of the assemblage and design is done by hand, with little more than hand tools and dated software. Boeing is especially susceptible to advances in production technology. Its production processes are exceedingly inefficient and do not make use of available technologies.

Many companies are actively seeking to internationalize their R&D functions. The reasons for this push generally fall into three categories: 1) transfer products and processes from central headquarters to the international sales and production operations with the intent of creating units to develop new and improved products expressly for the local foreign market; 2) invest abroad to take advantage of cost differences between countries, locating R&D functions where the cheapest resources are available; and 3) access to technology. Given these three kinds of reasons, should Boeing transfer some of its R&D facilities to China? Superficially, the answer is no. Aerospace research and development require access to some of the most sophisticated and expensive facilities in the world. Given the fact that most of these facilities are located in the U.S., there would seem to be no reason to internationalize Boeing's R&D functions. However, looking into the future, one may see a need for expansion. Given China's desire to establish a viable aerospace industry, it could provide an amenable, supportive environment for foreign investment in this area.

Five Forces Analysis: Commercial Aircraft Manufacturing

1. New Entrants Overall, assessment of the potential for new entrants into the aircraft industry is favorable to incumbents.

i) Economies of Scale (High): It stands to reason that in a complex, high tech industry such as commercial aircraft manufacturing, large economies of scale ought to exist. However, while these incumbent advantages do exist, it should be noted that Boeing, the leading player in the industry, has not been able to fully capitalize on what should be an enormous advantage of scale. This is due, in large part, to its antiquated and inefficient production processes.

ii) Product Differentiation (Hard): While commercial aircraft can be moderately differentiated according to cabin configuration and seating capacity, these differences are not marketable. Furthermore, since both of the major manufacturers make aircraft in each available class (Small <30 tons, Medium 30-50 tons, and Large >50 tons) any new entrant to the market will have to find different ways to carve out a niche in this market. Boeing has attempted to provide maintenance and services for its products, but this has had little discernible effect towards differentiating its product offerings.

iii) Switching Costs (Moderately Low): With the growing perception of commercial aircraft as commodities, buyers are free to look for the best price in the market. However, there still exists the possibility of time cost. An airline that gives its order from one provider to the other may be prioritized differently, especially if the order is fairly small.

iv) Capital Requirements (Very High): The Capital investment necessary to produce even relatively small capacity (100 seat) commercial aircraft is very likely to run in the hundreds of millions of dollars in plant and machinery costs alone. Furthermore, the investment required for maintaining appropriate levels of inventory and supplies will also raise start-up capital investment by millions of dollars.

v) Access to Distribution (Moderate): For existing firms in the industry, distribution channels are fairly well established. Airlines from around the world travel to either Boeing or Airbus' corporate headquarters to place orders and usually strive to expedite the delivery of the aircraft.

vi) Absolute Cost Advantages (Does Not Exist): There are many temporary cost advantages, but none are sustainable.

vii) Governmental Policy (Some Barriers Erected): While there are no global quality standards for aircraft, barriers exist on the national level. Any participants in this industry, especially new entrants, will have to meet the strict safety and industry quality standards that are maintained and regulated by individual government agencies. For example, in the United States the FAA plays an active investigative role in all domestic aircraft manufacturing. However, it may be the case that some countries have no such barriers; a fledgling aircraft manufacturer could gain a share in these markets.

viii) Expected Retaliation (Yes): At present there exists a global duopoly. The two incumbent firms will most likely do their best to limit the number of new entrants into what is potentially a very lucrative industry.

2. *Rivalry* Overall, rivalry is moderately favorable to incumbent firms.

i) Rate of Industrial Growth (High): After a slump in the early 1990s, the world's airlines have rebounded and are now seeking to expand their fleets. China alone has ordered 50 planes for over $3 billion. It is forecast that worldwide air travel will continue to increase about 4.9 percent per year for the next 20 years. As a result, incumbent firms in the industry are seeking to expand production capacity to meet this rising demand.

ii) Capacity (Severe Under Capacity): It has been estimated that over the next 20 years, the total market for new commercial jets will exceed $1.1 trillion. This translates into a need for about 16,160 new jets. At the industry's present levels of production (roughly 600 jets per year) there will be an expected shortfall of about 4,160 planes. If orders from Asian airlines are reduced due to the region's present economic crisis, the shortfall, while still evident, may not be as dramatic.

iii) Products Perceived as Commodities (Yes): There is an increasing perception amongst buyers that there is little appreciable difference among competing aircraft. This perception does have some foundation. Technological innovations and the evolution of aircraft technology are few and far between. Airplanes are now becoming standardized products with little to differentiate them except price. Furthermore, as the industry continues to streamline its production processes, customer specifications and design options will likewise become more limited, thereby furthering the commoditization of the product.

iv) Fixed Costs (Moderately Low): The majority of production costs are generally associated with materials, inventory, and labor, all of which contribute to variable costs. Boeing's production processes are labor intensive. This implies that as demand increases, costs will increase accordingly.

v) Balance of Firm Size in Industry (Very Unbalanced): The recent merger between Boeing and McDonnell Douglas and the consolidation of Airbus Industries in Europe have unbalanced the entire industry. It has become a global duopoly where nearly all available commercial aircraft orders are split between two firms.

vi) Structure and Origin of Firms (Different): The two major players in the industry are somewhat different in origin. Boeing is an American firm widely recognized as a giant in the industry. It is characterized by a top down corporate structure. Airbus is a loosely knit consortium of European companies characterized by a sprawling bureaucracy and infighting stemming from conflicting national interests.

vii) Firms Committed to the Product (Few): There are basically only two companies that produce commercial aircraft on any appreciable scale.

viii) Exit Barriers (Fairly High): Perhaps the biggest barrier to exit would be the relinquishing of a position in the global duopoly and hence the opportunity to capitalize on a growing and lucrative market. On a more tangible level, any company that chooses to leave the industry faces the prospect of not fully recouping all its capital investments. Furthermore, it would seem likely that the global market would be unwilling to let a single aircraft manufacturer hold a monopoly.

3. Substitutions This force is favorable to incumbent firms. Given the fact that the primary buyers for commercial aircraft are commercial airlines, it stands to reason that the list of available substitutes is very limited. For example, ground transport or ships are not viable substitutes for commercial airlines. Since commercial airlines require aircraft, the only available options would be buying second hand aircraft or cargo transport or leasing aircraft from other sources.

i) Price Performance of Substitutes (Fairly Low): One would suspect that the prices of these substitutes are probably much lower than that of new aircraft. While this is true, there can be other trade offs and costs attached to these options including higher insurance rates and conversion and maintenance costs, especially if the planes are older, worn, or ill-suited for their intended usage.

ii) Switching Costs (Fairly High): Switching to either cargo transport or second hand aircraft would most likely lead to the company being characterized as low-quality. Switching costs could be immeasurably high in terms of corporate image.

iii) Buyer Propensity to Substitute (Fairly Low): Again, this would probably be dependent on the goals and position of the prospective buyer. If an airline wants to be a no frills, low cost competitor, then it may decide that used or older aircraft will suit its needs (e.g., Mahalo Air). The propensity to substitute would be high. Airlines that wish to compete on a far more ambitious scale, however, cannot consider these alternatives viable. Leasing has more potential, but is limited by the lack of lessors to meet demand and cannot be considered a reliable substitute.

4. Buyer Power This force is neutral to unfavorable.

i) Size of Buyer Purchases (Large): Buyers tend to buy new commercial aircraft mainly for one of two purposes: to expand or start a fleet or to replace older or disabled aircraft. At present, the bulk of existing orders for aircraft falls into the first category. Airlines in foreign countries are expanding or acquiring new fleets of aircraft in order to meet demand. Their orders tend to be very large. China is no exception, since most of its airlines are at the beginning stages of development. It will have to buy a significant amount of planes in order to adequately service the area.

ii) Buyer Switching Costs (Low): Airlines are now in a better position to wrangle good deals from the participants in the industry due to the increasing dependence of manufacturers on commercial aircraft sales and the size and scope of their orders. Since China's market is highly sought after, both Boeing and Airbus are willing to make concessions if only to gain a foothold there.

iii) Seller Switching Costs (Fairly High): The only available market for commercial aircraft are airlines or governments. If the seller wishes to pursue individuals or corporations it will soon find that the market is not nearly as lucrative.

iv) Products Perceived as Commodities (Yes): As stated before, there is an increasing perception among buyers that there is little appreciable difference among competing aircraft. While product image and perceived quality does tend to play some role in differentiation among competitors, China is more concerned with obtaining technology from any company willing to provide it.

v) Threat of Backward Integration (Low): Since the capital requirement necessary to produce commercial aircraft is exceedingly high, few commercial airlines have the means to accomplish backward integration. Even airlines backed by capital provided by governments may not consider the requisite investment of time and resources warranted by the potential cost benefits.

vi) Product's Impact on Quality of Buyer's Products/Services (High): Obviously, the aircraft is the most integral part of any airline's core business. Without aircraft, an airline is not an airline.

5. Supplier Power This force is assessed as moderately favorable to incumbents.

i) Number of Suppliers (Many): There are only a few suppliers for some of the more high-tech or specialized parts of aircraft manufacture, but by and large a lot of the raw materials used airplane construction are provided by a wide range of suppliers.

ii) Buyers are Fragmented (No): Since there are only two available buyers of consequence, there is little fragmentation.

iii) Buyers' Importance to the Suppliers Business (Moderately Low): Suppliers providing specialized parts will depend on the aircraft industry for the bulk of their annual sales. All other suppliers do not have this dependence on the industry.

iv) Product's Importance to Buyer's Success (Largely Unimportant) and Buyer Switching Costs (Relatively Low): Aircraft are made up of many separate parts, some of which are vitally necessary, while others are extraneous and have little impact on buyer success. For the most part, switching costs are also negligible.

v) Threat of Forward Integration (Low): Since the capital requirements necessary to produce commercial aircraft are exceedingly high, few parts suppliers would be able to accomplish forward integration. Furthermore, it would make little sense for these parts makers to intrude upon an industry that requires so much technical expertise in many disparate areas.

Internal Environment Analysis

SWOT Analysis

After nearly a hundred years in the aircraft manufacturing business, the Boeing Company has weathered a multitude of challenges from any number of competitors to emerge as the dominant player in a global duopoly. With its 1997 acquisition of McDonnell Douglas, its last significant domestic competitor, it would seem that Boeing needs only to sit back and reap the benefits of its position. However, while Boeing's position as the market share leader is enviable, its position may still be considered tenuous. Boeing is a company with many inherent strengths and a few correctable weaknesses. The question is how it will use its strengths to deal with opportunities and threats that arise.

Strengths Boeing has had a long, close association with the Chinese government ever since it exported ten 707's to the Civil Aviation Administration in China (CAAC) in 1972. This association is characterized by an extensive network of working relationships that has resulted in manufacturing joint ventures and a 72 percent market share for Boeing. Strong, or at least positive, relations with the government are essential for success in China.

Aside from being one of the world's best known corporations, Boeing is also one of the wealthiest. It has billions of dollars in cash reserves. While this in and of itself is not a marketable advantage, it is, nonetheless, a considerable strength. By having these large stores of cash available, Boeing is well equipped to capitalize on opportunities that its competitors are unable to act upon due to insufficient resources. In particular, Boeing's cash and financial standing have not only allowed it to buy out domestic competition but also to expand horizontally. Furthermore, Boeing is able to sustain short-term losses during periods of fundamental and necessary change. In particular, Boeing is wealthy enough to make considerable long-term investments in China's infrastructure before reaping an acceptable return.

Boeing is one of the most recognized names in American industry. Its favorable reputation for quality makes its products highly desirable. Boeing's image is an enormous strength, especially when competing for bids against lesser known or new competitors. This is especially true in emerging markets new to the airline industry. When building their fleets, most airlines would rather invest in quality and recognized brands. China is no exception; all other things being equal, Chinese airlines prefer Boeing planes.

Boeing possesses a full complement of aircraft. It makes both one-aisle low capacity planes and wide-body intercontinental jumbo jets along with a whole host of intermediate sizes. Boeing can therefore supply airlines with planes tailored to their needs. This is particularly advantageous for Boeing in dealing with China. Since Boeing is capable of producing both high-capacity, long-range aircraft and regional 'puddle-jumpers', it can sacrifice some proprietary manufacturing knowledge in exchange for purchasing commitments for the rest of its aircraft. It would take decades before

China could assimilate the sum total of all the production expertise that Boeing possesses. In the meantime, Boeing is a supplier of both production knowledge and aircraft.

As a direct result of its recent acquisition of Rockwell International and the merger with McDonnell Douglas, Boeing has secured a market leadership position. Boeing sets the terms and operating conditions for the aircraft manufacturing industry. Since most planes are made by Boeing, its flight deck platform and configurations are de facto global standards.

Weaknesses Boeing's major weakness is inefficient production processes. These inefficiencies can be traced back to a few key elements. First, the processes are labor intensive and low-tech. Instead of automation and assembly line efficiency, the production process consists mainly of small teams of workers using hand tools. This increases per unit costs and the time it takes to produce aircraft. Furthermore, errors in assembly are more likely to occur than in automated processes.

Second, its airplanes are overly customized. With demand on the rise along with growing price consciousness, catering to consumer needs is unnecessary and even harmful especially if the corporation accrues high production costs for even small alterations. When changes require hundreds of pages of drawings, thousands of hours of engineering time, and millions of dollars of resources, it is time to rethink the corporate philosophy.

Efficiency is further hampered by non-standardized and incompatible computer software among Boeing's various departments. While the implementation of computers and technology is usually seen as a means towards efficiency, in Boeing's case this has not been true. It has schematics and information stored on about 400 different databases. As a result, information is not easily transported across departments. Until complete standardization occurs, this factor will continue to hamper operational efficiency especially with respect to inventory control.

Finally, it has inefficient supply and procurement channels. Parts cannot be ordered until customers choose which particular configuration they want. Production may be halted since some necessary parts are not kept in inventory.

These production problems are the root causes of many other weaknesses including higher costs of production, underperformance in sales and profit, inability to meet production demands, and inability to capitalize on potential opportunities.

Another weakness is a confusing and complicated organizational structure. As a direct result of recent mergers and acquisitions, the reporting structure at Boeing is not yet clear. While this is probably a temporary condition, it nonetheless exacerbates internal production problems. This leads to difficulties in making effective decisions and slows implementation of the production restructuring plans. This is especially problematic for a company hoping to expand its overseas production capability. If Boeing wishes to continue its expansion into China, it must first streamline and shore up its internal organization before it can even hope to successfully integrate its offshore manufacturing capabilities. Boeing is seeking to alleviate these problems, but the process has been slow.

Another weakness is Boeing's corporate image as a primarily American company, which is not entirely desirable in China. This image is likely to persist so long as the majority of its production and development processes remain in the United States. This is a weakness that cannot be easily addressed without significant investment and effort. Therefore, Boeing will be vulnerable to any wave of anti-foreign feelings on the part of either the Chinese government or the general populace.

Opportunities Boeing has some opportunities in the increased demand for products in China coupled with the global boom in the commercial airlines industry. After a slump in the early 1990s, the world's airlines have rebounded and are now expanding their fleets. China alone has ordered 50 planes for over $3 billion. With only two aircraft manufacturers around the world, the options are limited. Of the two competitors, Boeing is by far the best known and more respected. Furthermore, by holding over 2/3 of the global market in aircraft with 100 or more seats, Boeing could reap enormous profits if it steps up production to meet increasing demand.

Boeing's primary competitor, Airbus, suffers from a negative public image and has shown a lack of good faith with regards to its agreements in China. It has attempted to withdraw from its contract with AVIC to build 100 seat aircraft in China. Like Boeing, Airbus also suffers from large production inefficiencies and a corporate structure not conducive to changing environmental conditions. While Airbus can successfully compete with Boeing on price, it must undergo significant internal changes in order to sustain its competitive position. Whichever corporation is successful in restructuring its internal processes first will gain a decided advantage over the other.

Another opportunity is the potential for expansion into related products and services triggered by its expansion into the defense industry via the acquisition of Rockwell. It now has the opportunity to manufacture communications satellites and spacecraft. Given the prevailing trend towards price sensitivity and deferral of new plane purchases, Boeing would also be served by establishing maintenance services, especially for airlines in emerging markets. China would provide Boeing an excellent opportunity to dominate both plane manufacturing and aircraft support services.

With Airbus' 100 seat aircraft project in limbo and Boeing's recent acquisition of the MD-95 (also a 100 seat airplane), Boeing is presented with a golden opportunity to capitalize on the projected increase in regional air traffic in Southeast Asia and China. It has a product that will be in great demand since Airbus will no longer produce the 100 seat aircraft in China. The potential sales of the Boeing 717 are exceedingly high. Furthermore, since the 717 is actually a McDonnell Douglas product, Boeing could share production knowledge of the 717 without compromising some of its unique technology.

Boeing has been setting up pilot training facilities in China. For a relatively small capital investment in flight simulators and instructors, it is training future pilots. By educating and acclimating these pilots to a particular flight deck, it is seeking to establish a Boeing standard for China. This would be an immeasurable advantage since the pilots themselves would exert pressure on airlines to purchase Boeing planes over Airbus, which has a markedly different flight deck.

Threats Boeing's inability to capitalize on the growing demand for commercial airplanes could buoy sales for its chief competitor and enhance Airbus' prestige and competitive position. Since Airbus has government backing, it is capable of driving prices below what the market would ordinarily dictate, thereby cutting potential profits. These tactics could lead some of the more price conscious airlines to choose Airbus over Boeing, especially if Boeing is incapable of producing aircraft in a reasonable time frame. In particular, the increase in China's demand for aircraft may prompt the entry of new and perhaps more efficient competition . Should this occur, this will undoubtedly compromise Boeing's future profitability and position as market leader.

It is no secret that China eventually wants to be able to produce its own aircraft and is actively seeking to embark on joint ventures with aircraft manufacturers in order to secure both technology and technological knowledge. The possibility that China could one day become a competitor is real, although the time when this could happen is still far distant. Nevertheless, it remains a threat.

Another threat would be a prolonged economic downturn in Asia coupled with a trend toward reduced prices. With the domestic market somewhat stable, Boeing must look to other markets around the world in order to maintain profitability. Boeing has invested heavily in increasing its production capacity and corporate presence in Asia. Thus, the present economic crisis in Asia represents a key threat to Boeing's profitability. With increased dependence on markets abroad, Boeing is exposed to unfavorable economic and political situations. Furthermore, a prolonged downturn in Asian economies will likely hamper China's economic health. This in turn could mean that the time horizon for profitability for the region will increase. Buyers are also likely to demand even lower prices on aircraft.

With the scaling back of defense budgets and governmental expenditures in general, the once steady stream of lucrative military contracts are becoming rarer and less profitable. Without reliable government contracts, aircraft manufacturers are becoming dependent on sales of commercial aircraft. This has given commercial airlines a subsequent increase in bargaining power exacerbated by the increasing perception among buyers that there is little appreciable difference among competing aircraft.

Another potential threat is instability in the Middle East leading to oil price increases. As oil prices increase, airline profits go down. As profits go down, airlines are less likely to purchase new planes to replace old ones or expand their fleets. Since Boeing only sells newly made planes, it could experience a drop in orders and revenues. While Chinese purchases of Boeing planes may be subsidized by the government to some degree, it is nonetheless susceptible to increasing oil prices.

After lobbying for the rights to produce a 100 seat commercial aircraft with AVIC (Aviation Industries of China), Boeing was rejected in favor of Airbus. This came as a surprise to both industry experts and Boeing executives. The reason for China's rejection of Boeing stemmed not from any particular objection to Boeing itself, but rather from China's political relationship with the United States. The U.S. was actively seeking human rights concessions from China at the time, so China retaliated by rejecting Boeing. Boeing's future is therefore unfairly tied to U.S. - China relations.

Financial Analysis The revenues and expenses accrued from Boeing's overseas subsidiaries and joint ventures cannot be easily separated from its aggregate financial statements. The revenues from Boeing China Inc. are subsumed into the whole. Since Boeing China Inc. is not self-sufficient or independent, a separate analysis of its financial standing would most likely distort the reality of the Boeing's financial situation. It therefore makes sense to discuss Boeing's total financial standing in order to assess its prospects for further expansion and investment into China.

The commercial aircraft industry, as of 1997, is a global duopoly in which one of the companies is not fully public, so there are no industrial base ratios with which to compare Boeing. While it may be argued that financial ratios taken by themselves are of little worth without industrial standards against which to judge them, there are still many generalizations that one may make from trends and discrete numbers.

Analysis of Boeing's financial ratios serves to accentuate existing internal and external problems. In particular, inventory, production and pricing problems are highlighted. However, it should be noted that these financial results only reflect the current situation. As newer markets, as in China, become increasingly important, Boeing must remake itself to capitalize on its inherent strengths. Boeing has the opportunity to build an infrastructure in China that may ultimately alleviate some of its production and inventory problems. Given its history of achieving sales commensurate with total assets, such an investment would aid its financial position.

Net Sales and Gross Profit In order to properly assess the implications of net sales and gross profit, it is necessary to consider each curve in reference to the other. Ideally, the slope of the gross profit curve should mirror or be greater than that of the sales curve. However, while Boeing's sales have increased significantly since 1993, its gross profit (Sales-COGS) has remained flat and even taken a slight downturn. When increases in sales are not met with similar increases in gross profit it implies that products are unable to command prices in proportion to production costs. It would seem that in many cases Boeing is not capable of instituting a fixed profit margin. It is probably letting its competition dictate pricing. This trend is likely to continue in China unless Boeing takes some steps towards differentiating its project from Airbus in the minds of the Chinese government. Given the fact that China is still a relatively new market, Boeing does have an opportunity to change the trend. Should Boeing accomplish this goal, then as the percentage of sales from the region increases in the following years, there should be a dramatic increase in the slope of the gross profit curve. Until that time, the downturn in the gross profit curve is cause for concern.

Cash and Inventory These balance sheet items speak directly to the heart of Boeing's financial strengths and weaknesses. The value of Boeing's carrying inventory steadily increased for four years until 1996, when it flattened out. While the increase in inventory costs may be indicative of increased sales, when it is juxtaposed with the cash line, one sees that total cash took a significant downturn. Boeing's cash stores (and other current assets) are what allow it to meet short-term obligations. Ideally, one should carry less inventory and increase cash. This would allow Boeing greater flexibility and freedom to meet any prolonged economic slump. This is especially relevant for Boeing in China, where it will take many years and a lot of cash before its investments turn a profit. To help improve its position, Boeing ought to instill a just-in-time manufacturing philosophy in order to minimize the value of its carrying inventory.

Profitability The net profit margin refers to after-tax profits per dollar of sales. Boeing's net profit margin has been in a downward trend for five years. In 1997, Boeing posted a net loss; there were no profits to speak of. While this is most likely a temporary situation brought about on by the assumption of pre-tax charges, the trend may be cause for concern. It reflects the growing price sensitivity in the industry and aggressive pricing by the competition. Should this trend continue, the future profitability of the firm will depend on reducing operating costs.

Liquidity The current ratio reflects the firm's ability to meet its short term obligations. Ideally, a firm ought to have at least a current ratio of 1. A firm with a current ratio of at least 2 is considered liquid. For the past five years, Boeing has had a current ratio fluctuating between 1.36 to 1.78. This implies that it is in a fairly decent position to meet its short-term financial obligations. Liquidity must also be assessed with respect to current inventories, however.

The quick ratio gauges a firm's ability to meet its short term obligations without having to rely on sale of its inventory. A firm that has a quick ratio greater than 1 has enough cash reserves to meet its current obligations without having to sell inventory. Boeing's quick ratio has fluctuated between .58 and .88. This means that Boeing must rely on the inventory sales to meet its needs. It is therefore especially susceptible to order cancellations or any significant downturn in demand. Should there be a buying freeze on new planes and order cancellations, Boeing will have to obtain some form of financing to meet its current liabilities.

Leverage The debt-total assets ratio measures the percentage of total funds that are provided by creditors. A ratio of .5 implies that a firm is 50 percent debt financed. Boeing's debt-total assets ratio has not exceeded .18 for the past five years. This suggests that Boeing is more apt to choose equity financing as opposed to debt financing. Boeing may have an explicit limit for tolerance of debt.

Debt-equity refers to the percentage of financing provided by creditors as opposed to that provided by owners. If the debt-equity ratio is less than 1 then the majority of the financing provided is from equity and vice-versa. Since Boeing's debt-equity ratio has ranged from .26 to .51, the majority of its financing has come from equity. There was a significant increase from 1994 to 1996 in the ratio, however. During this time, a lot of R&D and development of the 777 airplane occurred and, in order to finance this, Boeing turned to both debt and equity financing by making approximately 650,000 more shares of stock available for sale to the public and assuming billions of dollars in new loans.

Activity The inventory turnover ratio measures whether or not a firm holds excessive inventory in stock. The greater the ratio, the less inventory the firm tends to hold. Boeing has experienced a significant rise in held inventory since 1993. This tends to suggest that airlines may be deferring or breaking buying agreements with the company. While an increase from 1996 to 1997 does imply that Boeing is selling planes at a quicker rate, the ratio is still significantly less than it was in 1993. It should be noted that there is a backlog in orders and excessive demand, yet Boeing is still selling planes at a slower rate. This is due to its non-standardized production processes in which each plane is customized to the buyer specifications. The increase in inventory turnover reflected in 1996 to 1997 may be somewhat indicative of Boeing's attempts to standardize its product offerings.

Total assets turnover tells whether or not a firm is generating a sufficient volume of sales for the size of its investment. The total assets turnover ratio in this case is fairly stable, hovering around 1. This suggests that Boeing's annual sales are roughly equivalent to its total assets. While a ratio significantly larger than 1 is preferable, there is probably little cause for concern.

Operational Activities

Purchased Supplies and Inbound Logistics Since airplanes are comprised of many disparate and specialized components, Boeing must deal with a great number of suppliers. When Boeing seeks to establish production processes abroad, many parts must still be imported because there are very few available suppliers who can make the necessary specialized parts. This inherent lack of suppliers, coupled with Boeing's inefficient production processes and antiquated inventory control system, has accrued high inventory maintenance and warehouse carrying costs. Production backlogs and work stoppages are commonplace, as work crews wait for delivery of components, while piles of unused and unnecessary inventory litter the production room floor. Obviously, if Boeing expects to compete in any market abroad, it should not transfer its present production problems. Boeing's ventures into China are especially problematic, since it must go through domestic distributors and local parts manufacturers before it is allowed to import parts from abroad. While there are not that many available local parts suppliers, there still remains the logistical problems involved with obtaining parts from a multitude of different sources.

Outbound Logistics Since most planes are simply flown to their intended destination, any problem or cost advantage that one company has over the other has more to do with internal deficiencies than delivery methods. Having said that, since Boeing has numerous internal problems, especially with its production and paperwork, Airbus is likely to process orders more efficiently and therefore not hold onto inventory for any extended period of time.

Some aircraft parts are manufactured in China and other areas abroad. For example, fuselage portions, which are of a significant size, must then be shipped to Boeing's primary assembly areas. This complicates outbound logistics.

Sales and Marketing Boeing has already established a widespread name recognition and a reputation for quality. It has so firmly ingrained itself into the corporate psyche that it does not really need any extensive advertisement. Except for a few small and less well-known products,

Boeing's name and image are sufficient selling points. It also has a full complement of aircraft types. Thus, it is suited to meet the particular needs of a wide range of markets. This is especially important to many large airlines around the world. Airline deregulation has lifted some of the aircraft buying restrictions that airlines previously had to follow. Now, airlines are free to purchase any size of aircraft to meet their needs. Thus, Boeing can provide one-stop shopping for many airlines. This is also how Boeing markets itself in China, with an additional proviso. Marketing and sales pitches usually also include some kind of assurance of investment. In other words, China seeks manufacturing agreements as part of sales agreements and vice versa. Therefore, Boeing's sales and marketing operations in China are more partner and purchase agreements than supplier - customer transactions.

Service Perhaps the biggest problem with Boeing's service is its inability to meet product delivery deadlines. There is a backlog of orders worldwide. This inability can be directly traced back to Boeing's production inefficiency that forces Boeing to pick and choose which orders to fulfill first. These tend to be the larger orders so some of the smaller airlines get pushed to the wayside. While Boeing is presently seeking to improve its production cycle time, it has left many dissatisfied customers in its wake. At present, it is trying to improve its aircraft maintenance and servicing business. This could gain it a competitive advantage.

In China, servicing problems could be addressed by increasing manufacturing capabilities. Many problems can be traced back to lack of local responsiveness. Since Boeing, relatively speaking, does not have a large part of its resources invested in China, its responsiveness is fairly low. Thus, by increasing investment, Boeing will be forced to become more responsive and hence its service activities will tend to improve.

Technological Environment and System Development

Boeing, by virtue of its proximity to the JPL (Jet Propulsion Lab) and some of the best engineering schools in the world, has ready access to current research and technology. Furthermore, Boeing has devoted a considerable portion of its yearly revenue to R&D and consistently makes use of state of the art technology and computerized systems (although it has failed to integrate these systems). In addition to its own money, Boeing also receives a large sum from government agencies such as NASA as research grants. This helps Boeing recruit quality research scientists. It should be noted, however, that while Boeing has a clear edge on R&D, technological innovations and breakthroughs have become much rarer than in the past. As a result, its return on R&D investment will most likely fall in the future, so Boeing will have to reconsider its resource allocations.

Organizational Environment

While Boeing's bureaucratic problems may not be as extensive or debilitating as those of Airbus, it nonetheless has problems with its management structure. Boeing has always been a company of significant size; managing and maintaining the different departments is an unwieldy task. Recent acquisitions and mergers have made this task much more difficult. Furthermore, an archaic accounting system, the FAA investigation, a cross-platform computer nightmare, and a lack of corporate vision have all contributed to the problem.

Human Resources Management

Boeing's compensation and benefits package is generous. Boeing is also a relatively decent workplace. There have been no major reports of labor unrest or union troubles. Boeing will have to lay off a large number of temporary hires as it streamlines its production processes. This suggests that Boeing may not be willing to make deep commitments to its work force when fiscal realities are adverse.

Global Corporate Strategies

Entry Mode Selection

China's economy is unique offering varying entry modes to foreign firms. Boeing's entry into the Chinese aerospace industry has been characterized by an extensive network of working relationships and has gradually evolved from exporting to EJVs.

For most firms just entering the global market, exporting is favored because it allows them to avoid the costs of establishing manufacturing operations in the host country while achieving experience curve effects and location economies. Boeing first began exporting to China in 1972 when

China's flagship carrier, the Civil Aviation Administration of China (CAAC), ordered ten 707s. Boeing continues to export its aircraft to China's airlines, and currently owns a 72 percent share of them. This means that 288 of the current 400 jetliners operating in China are actually owned by Boeing.

During the late 1970s, Boeing increased its involvement with China through what is characterized as industrial cooperation. It established two BOT operations for the production of major parts and assemblies. The Xian Aircraft Company is responsible for the co-production of 737 vertical fins, horizontal stabilizers, forward access doors, and 747 trailing edge ribs while the Shenyang Aircraft Company oversees production of 757 cargo doors and 737 tail sections. Overall, over 2900 planes currently flying worldwide include major parts and assemblies built in China.

During the 1990s, Boeing has participated in several joint ventures. It has invested $11 million into the Taikoo Aircraft Engineering Company (TAECO), a joint venture with Cathay Pacific, Singapore Airlines, Japan Airlines, Xiamen Aviation Industry Co., and Beijing Kai Lan Technology Development Service Co. (a wholly owned subsidiary of AVIC). More recently, Boeing has entered into an equity joint venture with the government controlled AVIC and the Hexcel Corporation for the production of composite parts for commercial planes.

Finally, Boeing has entered China's market through developmental programs. At the request of China, Boeing has provided assistance in developing China's air transportation infrastructure. With an emphasis on management skills training, improving safety, and increasing capacity, Boeing has: built a spare parts center in Beijing; hosted Chinese manufacturing specialists to further industrial cooperation; provided customized training for accident investigation, piloting, and maintenance; assisted in air traffic control management training programs; helped airlines establish safety departments and programs; provided Boeing-owned simulators to China's CAAC Flying College free of charge; trained more than 2000 pilots and mechanics; and established the Boeing Asia headquarters in China.

As Boeing's relationship with China continues to progress, Boeing eventually hopes to establish a wholly owned subsidiary to manufacture aircraft. Currently, the Chinese government is opposed to such involvement by Boeing because it would like to gain access to Boeing's technologies and manufacturing methods instead.

Entry Timing

Boeing's history of cooperative relationship with China reflects its long term strategy aimed at dominating the rising Chinese market. Its past relations have not only helped it develop an extensive operations network, but have also given it first mover advantages. Its risk taking approach has provided it with the advantages of preemptive marketing power and an initial lack of competition. In addition, as the first mover into China, Boeing was able to work closely with the CAAC and the Chinese government in establishing personal guanxi relations, which are critical for doing business in China.

Industry/Project Selection

The airline industry in general has been faced with a growing number of problems. It has been in a recession caused by weak demand, scarce finances amongst airlines, falling values for second hand aircraft, and rapid and often unpredictable changes in aviation policies. At the same time, international air travel has been experiencing rapid expansion and heavily increased air congestion over major routes and gateways. For most international airlines, this problem translates into a need to develop secondary international route networks as a means of relieving congestion and reaching new destinations.

In recent years, Boeing's strategic approach has changed dramatically. Whereas it once focused 90 percent of its efforts on the commercial sector, it now puts in 60 percent commercially and 40 percent into the defense and space sectors. Defense development is driven mostly by geopolitical rather than economic forces. Space has also brought a growth element with the explosion in commercial satellites and launch capabilities driving the business. Demand in the commercial sector is based on business cycles. Combating the troughs often meant not only finding new markets, but being more creative and entering other parts of the aerospace business such as flight training and safety. In China, Boeing's options are limited strictly to the commercial sector. Pursuing other areas does not offer the same benefits of market share growth and long term profits which the development of commercial airlines did elsewhere and is also politically risky.

Location Selection

The airline industry has focused on the Asian region in expanding international air networks. Newly rising Asian countries are in a period of rapid growth with a high demand for air travel. Future airline growth will be led by travel to, from, and within Asia. Boeing forecast that by the year 2010, Asia would account for over 40 percent of the total world air traffic.

More specifically, Boeing saw China as a potential market with growing needs for both international and regional flights. With other transportation options limited, air travel is by far the fastest and most convenient way to go, especially for people living in the heavily populated and industrialized southeastern regions of China. The air transportation market in China has been growing at an annual rate of about 19 percent. Boeing forecast that China alone would purchase 20 percent of all new aircraft produced and spend at least $40 billion on commercial jets over the next 20 years. In addition, China has dominated the air finance market in Asia, making it a highly prized customer. Its financial requirements have been estimated between $3-7 billion annually. Such attractive conditions presented Boeing with an opportunity to enter an Asian country with rising industrial needs to play a critical role in shaping its airline industry around Boeing products and involvement. The main difficulties it faced were China's lack of technological leadership and support industries.

Locations Within China Boeing's investment into the Chinese aerospace market currently stretches along the north and southeastern portion of the China. Not only are these areas densely populated, they provide the added location benefits of proximity to countries such as Taiwan, Japan, and developing Southeast Asia. The primary regions Boeing now operates in are Tianjin, Xiamen, and Beijing.

The lure of Tianjin rests mainly on favorable policies toward foreign investment. The local government in Tianjin is given a great deal of autonomy in dealing with foreign companies and investors enjoy various tax breaks. As the home of 9.3 million people, it is the largest city in Northern China, rich in its human resources capital, and an ideal site for infrastructure development to support the aircraft industry. The BHA Aero Composite Parts Company is building a new composites plant in the Tanggu Marine High-Technology Development Zone of Tianjin. This area is also the site of an aircraft maintenance certificate course offered by the Civil Aviation Institute of China and established by Boeing and the CAAC.

Xiamen, a coastal city in the Fujian province, is the site of Boeing's joint venture operations with Taeco. In addition to the aircraft maintenance facility, Taeco also boasts extensive staff accommodations, a four-story training center, and an aviation program in conjunction with Xiamen University. Much of Taeco's success is due to the province's status as a Special Economic Zone (SEZ). The Chinese view this coastal zone as one which could facilitate the import of raw materials and finished products necessary for exporting processing and assembly operations. Politically, the province is well connected with Chinese living in other parts of the world (including Taiwan) and the government hopes the area will be attractive to investment and trade linkages. Fujian's SEZ status has thus yielded several general investment incentives. Companies can benefit directly from commodity (reductions or exemptions in import/export tax duties on goods) or factor (tax holidays, investment allowances, subsidies) protection. Investors can also take advantage of indirect incentives such as simplified investment applications, guarantees of capital flows and profit remittances, and legal protection of industrial rights, in addition to lower corporate taxes than in other parts of China. Both Boeing and the Chinese government have high hopes that Boeing's investment in this region will eventually promote Xiamen's status to that of 'Aviation City', a high-tech aerospace industrial complex.

Finally, Beijing is a city of economic and industrial importance to China's aviation industry. Rich in its technological, human, economic, and industrial capabilities, as well as an established nexus in the international flight routes, Beijing is ideal as the center of Boeing's activities. Boeing's regional headquarters was established here in 1994. Boeing operates one of the world's largest spare aircraft parts centers at the Beijing Capitol Airport. Comparable to Boeing facilities in London and Singapore, the center is able to ship any of 35,000 parts in just 2 hours. In addition to Boeing parts, the center stocks parts from 25 other suppliers, provides support for component repair and overhaul, and provides logistics training for airlines. The company's support team also includes on-site technical experts that are able to deliver customized, hands-on training and operations support to each of Boeing's customer airlines in China.

International Cooperative Strategies

Partner Selection

Taeco is a joint venture valued at $63 million. It is managed by the majority shareholder, Hong Kong Aircraft Engineering Co. Ltd., and specializes in Boeing 747, 737, and 757 maintenance, repair, and overhaul services. The venture had been operational for a year and half before Boeing joined Singapore Airlines, Cathay Pacific and Japan Airlines as an equity shareholder. Boeing's buy-in represented a first for the company in China. It was an effort to broaden its business into other aspects of commercial aviation such as airframe maintenance and pilot training. Taeco was selected because of its specialization on Boeing aircraft. With Boeing's involvement, the venture will now be able to expand its range of services. In addition, all of the shareholders have ordered a combined total of 537 Boeing jets. Boeing's involvement thus expands its presence and network in the Chinese marketplace, giving it the advantage of exporting its planes to airlines there while providing skilled maintenance and modifications.

Boeing's second joint venture, the BHA Aero Composite Parts Company, was finally established recently after two years of negotiations. The partners in this operation are Boeing, Hexcel Corp., and the local Aviation Industries of China (AVIC). Its goal is to produce composite parts for secondary structures and interior applications for commercial aircraft. Boeing's subsidiary, Boeing Commercial, is directly involved in the manufacturing of aircraft, space missiles and parts, helicopters, and electronic components including computer and software products. Its capabilities are highly compatible with those of Hexcel, a company of about 4600 employees which acts as an international manufacturer and marketer of lightweight, high performance, composite materials, parts and structures for the aerospace, defense, recreational, and general industrial markets.

Government Involvement

Aerospace operations undertaken in China are heavily impacted by two governmental bodies: the Civil Aviation Administration of China (CAAC) and the Aviation Industries of China (AVIC). Together, they oversee all ventures or developments in the aerospace industry while providing crucial input based on their marketing analyses. Unlike foreign investments in other countries, where contact is established between two independent parties, all aerospace related investments and programs are negotiated through AVIC or the CAAC. Partners for joint ventures are usually selected based on the industry's strategic goals and assessment of the 4 Cs (compatibility, capacity, complementarity, and commitment). It is not unusual for either of these organizations to invest in operations directly or indirectly through their own subsidiaries.

The CAAC, once China's flagship carrier, decentralized its control over China's air transportation system in 1984, forming six major regional carriers. Nonetheless, the CAAC is China's aviation regulator. In the past, Boeing has worked with the CAAC to develop the airline infrastructure, including the Civil Aviation Flying College, China's premier pilot training academy. Boeing has also established an aircraft maintenance certificate course at the Civil Aviation Institute of China (CAIC), and supported CAAC's efforts to improve China's aviation system, accident prevention training, safety data collection and analysis, certification training, and air traffic management.

AVIC is responsible for the development of aerospace strategy and industrial/technical/ economic policies and regulations, including medium and long-term planning. It is also involved in contracting and implementing major systems engineering, coordination, R&D, production, and logistics support for major aerospace products. AVIC assists in overseeing airline operations and selecting foreign partners who possess desired capabilities and compatibility. Boeing's cooperation with both agencies are key to its past, present, and future success in China.

Sharing Distribution

Boeing's entrance into the Taeco joint venture was achieved at the price of US$11 million, a buy-in which gave it a 9.09 percent share. This stake resulted from a combination of new shares and vendor shares from existing shareholders. The majority shareholder, Haeco, now owns 41.82 percent. Cathay Pacific, Singapore Airlines, and Japan Airlines each hold a 9.09 percent share, similar to Boeing. Xiamen Aviation Industry Co. owns 13.64 percent while the Beijing Kai Lan Technology Development Service, a wholly owned subsidiary of the aviation regulatory body CAAC, holds an 8.18 percent stake.

Boeing's other joint venture, the BHA Aero Composite Parts Co. represents a more typical joint venture in China. Established as an equity joint venture, all three partners have an equal equity share. Boeing has agreed to purchase the joint venture's production output (composite parts for secondary structures and interior applications for commercial aircraft) for a minimum of 20 years.

International Strategy

Strategic Orientation and Global Control

Boeing took an analytical approach to entering and investing in China. While its strategy incorporated risk taking and adapting to market demand, its main goal was to seek out a combination of market effectiveness and cost efficiency. The relationship between China (more specifically the CAAC and AVIC) could be best characterized as one of mutual benefit.

Boeing benefited from the ownership advantages of capital, technology, information, management, organizational skills, and economies of scale. It presented internal core competencies that were in high demand, since China wanted to gain Boeing's innovative capabilities, management, and technology. By operating in China, Boeing also realized location advantages. Its guanxi with the CAAC and AVIC authorities allowed it to tap into a growing market early on and gain a huge share of the commercial airline market. Boeing has also been able to protect its manufacturing and technological rights through internalization.

In helping develop China's airline infrastructure and participating in several joint ventures, Boeing has also realized the benefits of a value chain. Its primary activities in China first focused on exporting planes to meet growing air transport needs. It then capitalized on its close relationship with the Chinese government by moving into secondary activities. Unlike the competition, Boeing contributed to pilot training, air safety, and maintenance which helped familiarize pilots and other air traffic workers with Boeing planes. Certified Chinese pilots then trained others to fly Boeing aircraft. This gave Boeing an advantage since the airlines prefer to buy aircraft with which their employees are comfortable. Boeing also capitalized on its investment in joint ventures. Taeco, for example, provided maintenance and modifications specifically suited to Boeing planes, further improving the value chain.

Type of International Strategy

Boeing's aircraft export resulted mainly from pressure to reduce costs. Tapping into the global market in this segment created the potential for Boeing to increase its profits through increased demand while realizing cost efficiencies such as economies of scale. Boeing also offered a wide array of jetliners of varying size, capacity, and capabilities, although with little room for product specialization per country or region. With local responsiveness at a minimum, Boeing was able to pursue a global strategy in its export operations.

While exporting required little attention to local considerations, the rise of competition and the relative immaturity of China's aerospace industries required more involvement from Boeing in its joint ventures and infrastructure development. The joint ventures focused on component parts production and Boeing aircraft modification, activities which required a moderate degree of responsiveness to the local market. This was increased by the high degree of dynamism and complexity of the local environment and the necessity to work with the CAAC and AVIC. Pressure to respond and adapt locally led to the development of flight training and safety programs. Such an investment in local human resources pushes China to become synchronized with the rest of the global aerospace industry.

At the same time, Boeing needed to maintain a certain degree of global integration in that the parts manufactured and the planes maintained and modified in China had to be compatible with aviation industry standards and other Boeing planes operating worldwide. Boeing's effective management was also greatly admired in China. Boeing thus possessed organizational strengths and competencies which allowed it to maintain global control over its operations, resulting in a hybrid transnational strategy.

Conclusion

Of all the foreign companies that operate within China's borders, Boeing would have to be in the most advantageous position. With its long history of a close relationship with China and its position as global market leader in commercial aircraft manufacturing, Boeing stands poised for unlimited economic benefits. It has already enjoyed first mover advantages. There is now an entire generation of Chinese pilots who can only fly Boeing planes and would need to be retrained at great expense if they were to fly Airbus planes. Providing the infrastructure and complementary products and services for its primary product, aircraft, has worked well for Boeing.

Despite its favorable standing and bright future, however, there is cause for concern. Boeing has made so many commitments to airlines that it cannot meet aircraft delivery schedules. It already has production problems exacerbated by agreeing to fill even more aircraft orders rather than let Airbus get an edge in the market. Meanwhile, Boeing continues to assemble planes only in the U.S. for logistical reasons. An assembly facility in China would be a big commitment because it requires building all major airplane parts near the facility itself because they are too large to transport.

Despite the cost and risks of proprietary technology leakage, we recommend expanding production in China in order to meet worldwide demand. China already wants an aircraft manufacturer to assemble 100-seat planes within the country. Boeing could provide the technical expertise necessary for this assembly while supplying the parts that China cannot produce on its own. Boeing would take the risk that China will learn how to build its own planes and no longer need Boeing's help, but this could happen anyway. Boeing would benefit by expanding its capacity, working with a partner who is motivated to learn how to build planes, and enhancing its relationship with China which will help when China's need for jumbo jets increases. As Boeing sets up manufacturing plants in China, it will also decrease its dependency on suppliers from abroad and speed up procurement channels, resulting in backward integration.

Meanwhile, Boeing should insulate itself against the threat of worsening U.S.-China relations by being vocal in its support of Chinese economic goals and political objectives (such as joining the WTO). It should also demonstrate its commitment to strengthening relations with China by shifting production of the MD-95 (Boeing 717) to existing McDonnell Douglas production facilities in China. At the same time, Boeing should negotiate long-term contracts with Chinese airlines and the government in order to protect itself against competition.

While layoffs and mass firings may be a part of modern corporate life in the United States, the Chinese may not take kindly to layoffs during times of economic hardship. Boeing ought to avoid mass temporary hiring and later firing, if it wants to maintain good relations in China and avoid labor unrest. At the same time, Boeing should offer wage benefits that compare favorably to competing wages in China, while establishing working relationships with local communities and making some concessions to decrease resentment towards foreign intrusion. Establishing further educational facilities will also improve its human resources management and relations.

Boeing ought to consider diversifying into maintenance and repair services to assure itself of getting business regardless of prevailing economic conditions and improve its relations with foreign customers.

It should set up regional parts distribution and assembly centers at key locations around the world to minimize outbound logistics problems and capitalize on potential cost advantages.

Boeing should seek to capitalize on automated production processes to decrease its susceptibility to labor unrest and charges of labor exploitation.

Boeing should also begin to implement the same evolutionary process that has been successful so far in China in other large countries, such as India, that have an increasing need for aviation services.

Boeing should rethink its allocation of R&D expenditures. To date, Boeing has primarily concerned itself with product quality and innovation. However, at the present time, these considerations are of moderate or limited worth. Instead, Boeing ought to concentrate R&D efforts on cost reduction and production improvements.

Overall, caution and circumspection are called for. Boeing cannot afford to be careless or myopic when it stands poised to gain immeasurable benefit from a continued association with China. It should aim at long-term goals of over twenty years, at least. The future of Boeing's success no longer resides in the maturing market of the United States, but rather in the promised potential of emerging world markets like China.

Case Study 10: KFC

Executive Summary

Kentucky Fried Chicken (KFC) is presently the largest fried and rotisserie chicken restaurant company in the world. KFC is represented in over 76 countries and offers more than 300 products. KFC is a subsidiary of PepsiCo, and is one of three restaurants in PepsiCo's 'restaurant' industry segment. The other two restaurants are Pizza Hut and Taco Bell. PepsiCo also has two other segments, 'beverages' and 'snack foods'.

KFC is one of the many pioneering Western companies that have entered the uncertain but potentially lucrative Chinese market. In fact, KFC was one of the first Western-style restaurant brands in Mainland China. Extensive strategic research by KFC, prior to its initial investment, promised huge profits. The decision has paid off. Currently, KFC has over 140 restaurants in Mainland China.

KFC's success in China is due to superior products and distribution technology coupled with a systematic global strategy. Its strict managerial practices led to its initial success. Location selection has also been extremely important in determining the success of individual restaurants.

It has had its share of problems, including cultural differences during employee training, lack of qualified Chinese-speaking managers, lack of utilities and infrastructure facilities, and delayed construction of some KFC restaurants.

KFC will have to be more flexible during its future expansion if it wants to continue its success in China. At the same time, it must be willing to expand into even remote locations if it wants to remain a leader in China's fast food market.

Company Introduction

In 1939, Mr. Harland Sanders started with just one store and a chicken recipe containing 11 secret herbs and spices. He was offered his first franchise in 1952 in Canada. In 1964, at a time when the fast food industry was rapidly growing, he sold KFC for $2 million to John Brown and Jack Massey. By 1969, KFC was on the stock exchange.

Between 1971 and 1986, major ownership changes occurred. First, Heublein Inc. bought KFC for $275 million. Then in 1982 KFC became a subsidiary of R. J. Reynolds. In 1986, it was converted to a subsidiary of PepsiCo for $840 million. Over the past 12 years, it has revamped its management and marketing style completely.

With KFC once again going strong at home in the United States, it has set its sights on foreign countries. In 1987, it opened its first Western-style fast food restaurant in China. By 1994, it opened its 9,000th restaurant worldwide in Shanghai. It has announced that it will spend an additional $200 million to set up 200 more locations in China.

KFC realizes that its franchises are vital assets and that quality is important. It recognizes that its number one leaders are its regional managers, who must be able to respond swiftly to customer needs. Each restaurant is operated as though it were unique. Recognition is given to employees demonstrating necessary capabilities, showing that the company cares about its employees. KFC believes that in order to be a leader, you must act like a leader. A lot of weight is placed on satisfying customers. This is achieved though teamwork, positive energy in the workplace, coaching and support, recognizing achievement, and encouraging ideas. KFC also believes in being accountable so that customers can trust the company.

From the beginning, Sanders stressed the importance of customer satisfaction along with quality and service. However, during the early boom years it lost that idea, resulting in its acquisition by various companies and several phases of management restructuring. Now it seems to be getting back on the right track.

KFC's strategic goals are to tap the large Asian market potential as a first mover, expand further into China, supply the demand for KFC fast food, build *guanxi* relations in China along with a strong identity, and maintain control of management.

External and Internal Environment Analysis – SWOT

External Environment

Opportunities Throughout the Far East Asian region, there is an enormous potential for American style fast food. China, the world's most populous country, presents an enticing market. In the 1980s and early 1990s, China's real GDP averaged a growth rate of about 8 percent. Between 1990 and 1993, real growth in per capita income averaged 9 percent at the national level, 12 percent in cities, and 4 percent in rural areas. During the same period, the annual increase in food and beverage retail sales averaged 19 percent. Even after adjusting for inflation, the average was 12 percent. Since the government heavily subsidizes necessities such as housing, health-care, and transportation, many consumers can afford to purchase luxury goods, even with a per-capita income average of only $1,700 to $2,000. Currently, however, there is only one United States brand restaurant located in China for every five million people.

The Chinese government has welcomed investment by Western investors. The poultry industry is one of the top priorities of China's agricultural modernization plans. It is therefore given a lot of support by the government, which presents an opportunity for restaurants such as KFC that rely on chicken products.

Threats Expanding into China occasions a great deal of uncertainty. Opportunities and risks vary widely from city to city and the criteria for evaluating suitable locations remains unspecified. The unstable economic situation throughout Asia may also affect China over the long run.

The complex legal system, problems with sourcing and distribution, an inadequate infrastructure, and lack of local management expertise all present threats. Even basic utilities, such as water, gas, electricity, and telephone services, may be difficult to obtain in certain locations in China. Even in Beijing, applications for service can get misplaced or services be unavailable for no apparent reason.

Investors must deal with the concerns of government officials that China present a positive image to the outside world. Chinese laws and regulations also prohibit certain activities desired by KFC. For example, when KFC first opened in China, wholly owned subsidiaries were prohibited. On the other hand, in bicultural joint ventures such as between Chinese and Americans, there is a threat of conflict due to differences in culture, customs, and beliefs.

In China, franchisers need to be aware of the possible concerns associated with the enforceability of contracts and the near certainty that its franchisees will, at least in part and for a time, be instrumental in the plans of central, provincial, or municipal governments.

The Chinese have had limited exposure to quality products; they have long, albeit reluctantly, been forced to accept substandard goods. This may work against KFC's QSC (quality, service, and cleanliness) policy. The recent outbreak of Hong Kong's bird flu has also had a dramatic impact on chicken sales at markets and restaurants. One province even banned chicken imports. Despite doctors' assurances that cooked chicken is safe, restaurants specializing in chicken dishes also said business was down.

Meanwhile, competition is increasing from other fast food enterprises. McDonald's wants to open 200 mores stores in China. Burger King, Wendy's, and Pizza Hut are also already in the market, and T.G.I.F., Des Plaines, Bresler's, and Domino's Pizza are all looking at opening up restaurants in China. Japanese, Korean, Taiwanese, Australian, Indonesian, and the Filipino fast food companies and franchises also have development plans for China. For example, Japan's Mos Burger reportedly plans to open 3,000 units by 2010. The longer KFC delays in its expansion, the greater the threat of conceding the market to competitors.

Five Competitive Forces i) Buyer Bargaining Power - Low: The bargaining power of the buyer is low because of the size of the market is so large that individual buyers have little impact on competition. The number of buyers creates a huge opportunity for KFC to expand.

ii) Supplier Bargaining Power - Moderate: The bargaining power of the supplier is KFC's chicken is provided by local suppliers. In order to expand in China, KFC needs to maintain a stable supply of chicken. KFC has tried to minimize shortages by using multiple local suppliers.

iii) New Entrants - Moderate: In the immediate future, new entrants are unlikely to greatly impact KFC due to the lengthy amount of time usually required to set up operations in China. However, in the long run there is a great threat of competition from new entrants.

iv) Substitutes - Low: The competitive pressure from substitutes is low. Chicken is a more popular meal than hamburgers in most Asian countries. Also, KFC offers noodles on its menu unlike pizza or hamburger restaurants. KFC has the opportunity to offer an American style experience that is different from most other food establishments.

v) Existing Rivals - Moderate: There are already many small local vendors, but they serve different needs than the large food chains. Large foreign competitors such as McDonald's also have a strong presence in China, but the size of the market allows room for existing competitors to operate without significantly affecting KFC. In the long run, KFC will start to feel their impact, however, as competitors expand operations.

Internal Environment

Strengths The acquisition of KFC by PepsiCo provides KFC with heavy financial backing for further growth. The 1996 annual report and financial review for KFC were part of the report put out by its parent company, PepsiCo. Income statements, balance sheets and cash flow statements for all subsidiaries were consolidated, however the annual report did provide some financial information for the various industrial segments within PepsiCo. The growth rate in net sales from 1991 to 1996 for PepsiCo's restaurant industry segment for international operations is almost three times larger than its United States operations. The growth rate in operating profit from 1991 to 1996 for international operations is almost double that in the U.S. This shows that the restaurant industry in the international market does possess an enormous potential and that PepsiCo has been taking advantage of these opportunities.

KFC is now the world's largest chicken restaurant company with extensive experience in international operations including outlets in Japan, Singapore, Hong Kong, Australia, the United Kingdom, and South Africa. Its average sales per store throughout Asia is $1.2 million compared with $750,000 in the United States.

KFC was the first western restaurant to open in Mainland China. Today, many KFC sites in China average 10,000 to 12,000 transactions per week, compared to only 2,000 per week in the U.S. This success can be partly attributed to Tony Wang, who has had a long and productive history at KFC and a proven track record for successful negotiations with the Chinese government. He laid the foundation for KFC to enter China.

The opening of the first KFC restaurant in Beijing in 1987 was covered by local newspapers and the national press and was watched with great interest by millions of Chinese. This outlet was expanded in 1992 from 500 to 700 seats and now serves 2 million customers a year, KFC's highest single per unit output of chicken meals in the world. Today, with 140 locations, KFC has the most Western-style fast food restaurants in China, followed by McDonald's, Japan's Mos Burger, and local western style fast food chains such as California Fried Chicken, Ronghua Fried Chicken, and Hong Kong's Café de Coral. KFC has adapted its advertising campaign to suit local preferences, including a Cantonese version of the 'We Do Chicken Right' advertisements. Its Chinese customers consider the food an affordable treat presented in a nice atmosphere. KFC's control mechanisms are designed to ensure standard levels of quality, service, and cleanliness (QSC) at all of the restaurant's chain stores. This fits the positive image in Asia of American fast food restaurants as famous, air-conditioned, and hygienic. Despite its trendy American image, however, KFC provides a food product that is not too strange for Asians. Chicken is already familiar in China and much cheaper and more widely available than beef. An increase in health conscious consumers also raises the consumption of chicken.

Working for a foreign joint venture is an attractive opportunity for many Chinese because foreign partners often pay considerably above local wage levels. KFC devised an additional incentive scheme to encourage worker productivity. Incentive pay played a major role in improving employee attitudes toward KFC's QSC policy. Customized training videotapes were developed by KFC to educate Chinese employees about fast food.

Weaknesses There is not much KFC can offer China in terms of technology, since KFC is more of a service provider dealing with food products. This is a weakness, since the government provides much more support for enterprises bringing new technology to China.

Expansion costs for each new restaurant is high. A large amount of money is required to find and negotiate with partners, sign leases, and gain operating permits. KFC has also had trouble getting a constant supply of quality chickens from the local supplier, Animal Production. It has also had to rely on local partners for assistance in obtaining utility services, but often finds it difficult to press for timely and adequate service.

KFC faces the most problems in human resources management. In China, family contacts are often used to land highly sought-after jobs, but KFC insists on treating all applicants equally. No referrals are accepted under any circumstances. All training expenses are then borne by KFC. Employees seemed to have little understanding of the principles of quality, service, and cleanliness demanded by KFC. They felt that sales would not suffer and morale would improve with a slackening of company standards. Even though incentive pay has played an important part in improving employee productivity, employees still require constant supervision which places a lot of strain on local management.

There are only a limited number of Chinese-speaking KFC managers, many of whom are already in Hong Kong and Singapore. Entering the Chinese market thus demands precious managerial resources, while control is more difficult to maintain in international operations. At the same time, there have already been conflicts between KFC-appointed managers and local employees. The latter have a tendency to turn to KFC's Chinese partners for support in dealing with KFC-appointed managers.

KFC's management practices, which are regarded as essential to the operation's profitability, have lead to disputes with Chinese partners. The strictness of KFC's QSC standards has already angered local partners who believe that lower standards would be acceptable to customers and more profitable. Local partners also have different perspectives on their roles than does KFC. They believe they understand Chinese customers much better than KFC does and should participate in improving operations, but so far they have felt left out of the decision making process.

Global Strategy

Kentucky Fried Chicken was fascinated by China, a nation characterized as one of mystery and intrigue, as well as virgin economic territory. No other American fast food company had entered the country, but this also meant KFC had to be cautious. Tony Wang, formerly vice-president of KFC in Southeast Asia, felt that KFC had a definite competitive edge, however, because developing the poultry industry is a top priority in China's agricultural policies.

KFC's global strategy has been driven by both internationalization and internalization concerns. As part of its internationalization campaign, China is important because it allows for further development in Asia and provides strategic operational alliances among suppliers. It gave KFC first mover advantages and provides a huge potential market for KFC's products.

In regards to internalization, KFC did not forget the problems it faced in the 1970s in Hong Kong, Japan, South Africa, and Australia. Resistance to corporate control resulted in many shops developing their own menus, store designs, and marketing methods. Suddenly, KFC lost its identity. Market share declined and KFC incurred heavy losses. Eventually, it were forced to close all its stores in Hong Kong. The OLI framework suggests, however, that service specific industries who expand internationally tend to become less homogeneous, and must adapt to market conditions. This dictates more of a multidomestic strategy. However, these macro theories have not worked for KFC when it has tried to operate in radically different environments. As a result, KFC's strategy is still closer to a global strategy than a multidomestic one, at least in China.

KFC envisions operational synergies establishing supply centers to support its restaurant operations. Should this be successful, it would help KFC expand and aid in building key relationships with Chinese partners and the government.

Global Corporate Strategy

Regional Selection

At the time KFC began to consider expanding to China, it was owned by RJ Reynolds. RJR managers fully backed expansion to China as a means by which they could penetrate the increasing cigarette market. Setting up an American style fast food operation in China was an enormous task, however. It was clear that strategy was critical. RJR managers were culturally out of touch with China, so they hired Wang to take over the project. He was not only Chinese and spoke Mandarin, but had a proven track record concerning negotiations with the Chinese government. But he also understood KFC's corporate culture, having been educated in the United States and having spent his initial career working for KFC in Louisville, Kentucky.

Wang's initial findings about the feasibility of entering China were negative. He was convinced that major changes in the attitudes of Chinese employees would be required for operations under the KFC banner. Moreover, because employment is guaranteed in Chinese society, hard working employees would be hard to find. This meant that time-consuming training programs would be necessary, adding to the already heavy start-up costs. Wang was also concerned about the money needed to find partners. However, it was also clear that being a first mover would have many benefits. Wang finally decided the potential benefits were worth the risks. He felt that since it would take a number of years before actual operations would begin, and further delay would open the door to competitors, it would be best to start negotiating entry to the Chinese market as soon as possible.

Mode of Entry

KFC entered the Chinese market following a hybrid incremental strategy in which it has taken sequential, slow, and logical steps. First, it set up key partnerships with local organizations, including export avenues and supply vendors, for a single restaurant. After testing the water and gaining experience, it began to expand. Although KFC does not fit a true sequential entry model, it is clear that it has incorporated parts of the concept.

The Tricon company acts as an umbrella company for Pepsi-Co. (including Pizza Hut, Taco Bell, and KFC) worldwide. Local partnerships in franchise-like relations are typical of KFC's operations in many parts of the world. A 10-year lease for the first KFC site in China was negotiated with local partners, Animal Production and the Beijing Tourist Bureau. The agreement for the equity joint venture position stipulated that KFC held 60 percent equity and would provide the general manager, train and hire the staff, and set operational standards. The Beijing Tourist Bureau held a 27 percent equity position and Animal Production, 13 percent. As KFC expanded beyond the first Beijing location and gained experience, contacts, and momentum, its partnerships began behave more like ordinary franchises.

To view KFC's network in China as a simple franchise arrangement would fall short of reality, however, for it is more complicated than that. Supplies are critical to fast food restaurants, so KFC has developed an extensive supply network along with its own secondary business as a supplier to lesser restaurateurs. New entrants face stiff competition as they try to master the local distribution network. They may end up providing KFC with a greater secondary market as a supplier. This arrangement allows KFC to grab a larger share of the market's revenue than it could exclusively through restaurant sites.

KFC operates several partnerships with poultry producers in China. The amount of poultry consumed at its 190 locations is remarkable, making imports and related tariffs prohibitively expensive. Therefore, setting up partnerships with local suppliers like Animal Production has been critical to KFC's success. It still has to import potatoes for french fries, however, due to poor growing conditions in most of China for that food product. Developing relations with officials at key ports of entry has also been key to maintaining good import flow.

The evolutionary investment approach allows a company like KFC to hedge against risky environments like China. Although KFC started with a majority joint venture (JV) rather than a minority JV or product import/export, it was still more evolutionary than revolutionary. It eventually moved into more franchise-like operations as expansion continued. Currently, KFC has a mix of JV-franchises and a few wholly-owned subsidiaries.

Timing of Entry

KFC entered China through Beijing in 1987, having successfully run other locations in Asian countries like Malaysia, Indonesia, and Japan. Early success in the Southeast Asia market gave it confidence in its ability to balance corporate control with the demands for local responsiveness. Its hybrid-franchise network has allowed the company to maintain this complicated balance of control and local effectiveness.

Entering as the first western fast food restaurant posed many risks. China was not as open as it is today, social unrest was more prevalent, and there were many unknown factors. In taking on these risks, it established a critically important strategic position with the consumers and government officials. Establishing local suppliers and adapting its products, menu, and operations allowed the company to become successful as its learning curve improved. As a fast food pioneer, KFC gained brand recognition while establishing important contacts. In a challenging environment, the first mover decision paid off.

KFC can now capitalize on this position by: 1) increased marketing inertia; 2) expanding to new markets; 3) using its established supply and distribution channels as a contractual supply-network for new entrants. Latecomers will have to focus more on niche opportunities as first movers like KFC have already established an important position. This is currently happening in China as competitors entering niches such as Mexican food products. KFC and other first starters have created significant barriers, however.

Location Selection

KFC has a presence in every major Chinese market, including Beijing, Shanghai, Guangzhou, Liaoning, Jiangsu, Zhejiang, Sichuan, Fujian, and Guangdong. KFC generally selects locations near major ports or metropolitan centers and builds out from there. This allows the company to first create a strategic network of government and port authority contacts, materials suppliers, and distribution resources before going to riskier locations. For example, after starting in Beijing, KFC focused on populated coastal areas and then moved into more remote areas.

KFC chose Beijing as its flagship location for several reasons. First, Beijing is China's second most populous city, with over 11 million people. Second, KFC would be exposed to many Chinese citizens traveling to the city for business. Beijing also has a well-developed infrastructure, including a subway, highways, and international airport. It is close to ports and suppliers of poultry and has a large pool of educated workers. Politically, KFC saw Beijing as riskier than other locations, but the infrastructure and affluent population swayed KFC to start there.

In choosing other locations, KFC considers several factors. It wants sites that will be nearby poultry suppliers and have transport facilities for bringing the supplies to the restaurant. The market size and other characteristics should be compatible to KFC's goals and products and the location should enjoy favorable governmental policies. Low labor costs and a favorable labor supply are also important. For example, KFC had many applicants from which to choose in filling positions in Beijing. They were able to choose from the best possible candidate pool compared to almost any other potential Chinese location.

The interior regions of China remain largely untapped. Moving inward, KFC should use currently established networks and systematically, incrementally move to nearby markets that will support its strategic goals.

Industry/Project Selection

Choosing the industry is not difficult since KFC specializes in making a special chicken recipe along with a variety of supplemental menu items.

KFC has successfully integrated backwards to take greater control of its supply chain. KFC China has vertically integrated by building a valuable distribution network involving local suppliers and partners, internal distributors, port authority officials, and various local government administrators. This network has been one of the key elements to KFC's success in China. Most KFC product [chickens] is raised within China; this has helped build favorable relations with government officials as KFC pays hard currency for supplies. Vertical integration with local production allowed KFC to gain a competitive advantage as a first mover and then in setting a positive track record which has led to greater leniency from the Chinese government regarding imports of raw materials such as potatoes.

KFC should continue to focus on its core area of competency. Chicken is a favorite meal in China's fast food industry and significant growth opportunities still exist, especially in more northern regions. Expansion of the vertically-integrated supply network will allow KFC competitive expansion advantages while providing a possible source of secondary incremental revenue, as discussed above.

Partner Selection

Franchising is the entry mode of choice in many markets where political risks and cultural unfamiliarity encourage the strategic use of locals. The downside of too heavy a reliance on this system is the possible erosion of system integrity. That is why KFC started with a different kind of partnership in China. Choosing Chinese partners such as Animal Production and the Beijing Tourist Bureau allowed KFC to hedge political risks while securing an important supply of poultry. KFC had key U.S. educated, Chinese nationals on its payroll while negotiating the initial majority JV in Beijing. This local knowledge greatly improved KFC's position in the negotiation, and sped the whole process.

As KFC gained more experience and presence in China, expansion started to outpace its ability to contract with the same level of quality partners at each new location. Expansion led KFC to lean toward starting minority JVs and franchises, although it maintains majority JVs and wholly-owned subsidiaries at each key location.

International Strategy

KFC has taken risks in entering China early in search of market share. Since much of its sales have been in soft currency, it is clear that the company is taking a prospector approach. As touched on earlier, KFC has progressed from a more controlling majority JV focus to minority JVs and franchises for new stores in China. KFC's China operations really offer a diverse mixture. Perhaps it is this mixture which has allowed the company to successfully balance control and local responsiveness. Achieving this balance is always challenging for multi-domestic and global operations. KFC maintains process control by hiring and placing key personnel. It also controls key resources like the KFC trademark and recipe. It also, as explained earlier, holds a majority equity position in key market areas or gains complete control with wholly owned subsidiaries. Location diversification has allowed KFC to sacrifice control during location expansion to less strategic areas.

This mix of both corporate and local control is best described as hybrid-global. The company pursued a global product strategy during the early years in China. Later, it adapted its product more to local markets, shifting its global product strategy to a more locally-responsive hybrid. Its management and quality control in its restaurant locations is global-transnational, while its distribution, supply, and product adaptation to the local market are better described as transnational-multi-domestic. Since the transnational strategy is a common denominator, KFC is more transnational than global.

Conclusion

Kentucky Fried Chicken has been successful in meeting its initial corporate strategic goals for entering China. It was the first American fast food company to penetrate the highly protective Chinese market and currently leads all other Western fast food restaurants in China.

KFC's continued success in China depends on remaining flexible during future expansion. China is not a homogeneous country culturally, nor is it a coherent system in which development in one region works in others. Progress in the south may not produce progress in the northwest. KFC must identify these differences if it is going to adjust and implement its strategic corporate goals throughout China.

It is important to build on the many successes KFC has had in China. Ironically, its inflexibility in regards to strict managerial practices and quality control led to its initial success. It enabled KFC to maintain its identity and become recognized by its customers for hygienic surroundings and safe, quality food. This has been vital to its operations in China. Maintaining its identity strengthened its corporate presence in the country, making it harder for followers to duplicate its product and service.

KFC may also want to consider the possibility of adding new product lines into its expansion plans in China. Continued growth of its supply network will also allow it to grab a larger share of revenue than it could exclusively through current locations. KFC should continue expanding throughout both China and Asia in general. It will need to continue making quantitative analyses in choosing new locations. There are many more locations in China that are untouched and still provide significant opportunities for sales growth. This expansion will allow KFC to stay ahead of the competition and remain one of the leaders of China's fast food industry.

Index

About the Author

Dr. Luo (Ph.D, Temple University 1995) is an associate professor of international management at the College of Business Administration, University of Hawaii. As a Dennis Ching Teaching Excellence Award and CBA Teaching Excellence Award recipient, he teaches strategic management, multinational management, global business, and Chinese management at the undergraduate and MBA levels. His research interests are in the area of international expansion, global strategy, and Chinese management. As a Regents' Medal for Excellence in Research at UH, Dr. Luo has published over forty research articles and five original books since 1995. Before coming to the United States in 1992, Dr. Luo served as a provincial official in China in charge of international business for six years.

For Product Safety Concerns and Information please contact our EU representative GPSR@taylorandfrancis.com Taylor & Francis Verlag GmbH, Kaufingerstraße 24, 80331 München, Germany

Batch number: 10725991

Printed by Printforce, the Netherlands